BACKLUND

FROM ALL-AMERICAN BOY TO PROFESSIONAL WRESTLING'S WORLD CHAMPION

—◆—

BOB BACKLUND AND
ROB MILLER

Foreword by "Rowdy" Roddy Piper

SPORTS
PUBLISHING

To Corki, for standing by me all these years.

To Vincent J. McMahon, for giving me the chance of a lifetime.

———◆———

Sports Publishing books may be purchased in bulk at special discounts for sales promotion, corporate gifts, fund-raising, or educational purposes. Special editions can also be created to specifications. For details, contact the Special Sales Department, Sports Publishing, 307 West 36th Street, 11th Floor, New York, NY 10018 or sportspubbooks@skyhorsepublishing.com.

Sports Publishing® is a registered trademark of Skyhorse Publishing, Inc.®, a Delaware corporation.

Visit our website at www.sportspubbooks.com.

10 9 8 7 6 5 4 3 2 1

Library of Congress Cataloging-in-Publication Data is available on file.

Cover design by Tom Lau
Cover photos courtesy of the author

Paperback ISBN: 978-1-68358-444-5
Ebook ISBN: 978-1-61321-696-5

Printed in the United States of America

Table of Contents

FOREWORD BY "ROWDY" RODDY PIPER

I was barely twenty years old.

Bob Backlund was the world champion from New York. He had come in to the Olympic Auditorium in Los Angeles, where he always drew a lot of money. On this night, however, he had just arrived from Tokyo, where he had just completed a tour with Antonio Inoki's New Japan promotion the night before. Promoter Mike LaBell had asked Vince McMahon Sr. if his champion could stop over in Los Angeles on his way back from Japan and defend the World Wide Wrestling Federation's Heavyweight Championship at the Olympic against his America's Champion.

Vince Sr. agreed.

I was the America's Champion.

The hype for this match had been terrific, and the building was completely sold out. In fact, I think because of fire code issues they had to turn people away from the box office that night.

At the appointed time for the main event, we climbed into the ring, went through the pre-match introductions, and then started tussling back and forth and back and forth. The time limit was sixty minutes, and Bobby took me with him for fifty-nine minutes that night. I know I got some frequent flyer miles from that match.

Bobby and I had never met before in the ring anywhere, in any promotion, so it was a real testament to his skill in the ring that he could come in there cold, against a guy he had never been in the ring with before, having just gotten off a long and grueling Japanese tour and a long plane flight from Tokyo to Los Angeles, and to then go fifty-nine minutes with me and make *me* look good. And you know, for Bobby to be going around like that, not just around the WWWF territory at the time with the same few guys, but to Japan and wrestle guys who don't speak English, and to Toronto, or Florida, or St. Louis, or to the West Coast where we were—and to wrestle guys he had not worked with before—that's not easy to do. And unlike a lot of champions before and after him, Bobby would not come into a territory and give you a cheap fifteen minutes where he did a few signature moves, took most of the match, and then got the hell out of there. To the contrary—Bobby would give you whatever the *fans* wanted—and if that meant he was out there for forty-five minutes or an hour, then that's the way it was. And he'd make you look like a million bucks doing it.

The night I got to wrestle him, and I remember the night like it was just the other day because it was that memorable a night for me, I learned a lot. To be able to keep the people on the edge of their seats for fifty-nine minutes, now that's saying something. And you know given Bobby's style—there weren't a lot of rest holds or running away and stalling outside the ring and killing time. You were working hard all the time, chain wrestling from high spot to high spot. We were throwing arm drags and dropkicks and leapfrogs and monkey flips and body slams and hip tosses and vertical suplexes. Bobby was so pure in there and so quick and could string moves together so quickly and with such precision—trust me when I tell you—you had to be on your toes to keep up with Bobby Backlund.

And the people were screaming. They were digging it!

To be honest, that night in the ring with Bobby was probably one of my better pieces of work from an artistic and technical point of view that I ever had—because later on, as the business started to change, that old-school honest style became dwarfed and eventually totally eclipsed by show business and standard set pieces night after night after night. But that night, wrestling Bob Backlund at the Olympic taught me not just how to get over with the people, but to stay over with the people. And Bobby did that, seemingly with ease.

The night that I got to go wrestle Bobby Backlund was, for me, a showcase for promoters all around the country. It advanced me in my career, because LaBell raved about it, and the promoters understood, okay, this kid Piper can go. You know, a lot of wonderful things happened for me after that. For Bobby to be that generous with me, stopping over on his way back from Japan and giving me as much of the match as he did, that left me on top of the world. I was more over with the fans after that match—even though he pinned me—than I had been before he came. And it takes a lot of psychology, a great wrestler, and a great storyteller to do that. It was such an honor for me, especially then as such a young kid, to have had that opportunity to learn from him and to have had that kind of experience with him in a one-off match that he totally could have mailed in.

Sometime after that match, he sent me a wheel—you know, the Bob Backlund workout wheel that you've seen him use on television. I tease my son, Colt Toombs, who is an MMA fighter, because to this day, he still uses that wheel that Bobby gave me thirty years ago. I used to tell Colt stories about Bobby and our joke was always that the wheel Bobby gave me could have been used as the front wheel of an airplane. It was built so solidly that it was impossible to wear out. And you know what? That is kind of a metaphor for Bob Backlund.

When I was asked to do something for this book, Bob approached me in such a polite and humble way, that I had to remind him that the honor was mine. The honor in being able to give something back to this man is mine.

Back in the day when Bob Backlund was the world champion, there were many talented guys that had been brought up in the old territory system. Back then, you would stand on the shoulders of the guys that had come before you, and who taught you how to wrestle, and how to understand ring psychology and crowd psychology and pacing. The competition in those days was heavy, man. And Bob Backlund managed to cut through all of that, and to work his way up, the honest way, to become the world champion, and then to stay there for almost six years. Six years was like a lifetime in our sport.

And even in our "sport," where the outcomes may have been prede-termined, the competition for who got to occupy that spot was as fierce as it was in any sport or any profession. You know, with pro wrestling, people tend to think that it is a "team" sport—that you rely on everyone, but indeed it's not. To become truly successful, you have to be able to cut the line. Everyone wants to kind of try and do business and get along, but everybody also wants to be on top. So the question is: how do you get to the top?

That's not so easy to do.

But Bob Backlund did it.

And the bigger question is, once you're there, how do you find a way to stay there for all of those years, stay healthy, and still get along and be able to work with people?

That's even harder to do.

But Bob Backlund did that too.

For almost six years, he was the world champion of the most lucrative territory in the wrestling business, filling the biggest buildings night after night after night. To get to that kind of a place, you need all the legs of the table: the technical part, the psychology part, the showbiz part, and the ability to talk people into the seats by making them want to suspend disbelief and buy what you are selling them. They have to believe in you. And believe me when I tell you, the fans believed in Bobby Backlund.

But how do you get to the top of the business, manage to stay there, and then also manage to have a legacy where practically everyone in the industry, to a man, thinks highly of you? Well that's the hardest thing of all, and Bobby Backlund did that too.

For a world champion to take some twenty-year-old regional cham-pion fifty-nine minutes and make him look like a million bucks and leave him a stronger force in the territory than before the match . . . well that is the epitome of what a world champion is supposed to do. Bob Backlund came to Los Angeles that night and did his job masterfully. He personi-fied everything that the world's heavyweight champion should be—in the way he lived, in his diet and work ethic, in the way he carried himself as a man, in the way he interacted with the people and the promoters, and in the way he acted in the dressing room. And that's why everybody in the business has so much respect for him.

Backlund was a shy guy, but he was also the first person to break the ice and come up to people he didn't know and shake hands and say hello. If you wanted suggestions on training or health, he was there to help you. Yet at the same time, despite being such a nice person, he could hold his own anywhere. No one was going to take anything from Bobby Backlund inside the ring or outside the ring that he didn't want taken. He had all the elements that a real-deal champion should have. If I had to compare Bobby with somebody, I'd compare him to Lou Thesz. Lou Thesz was as real as they come—and so too was Bob Backlund.

A lot of people don't know that Bob Backlund was the guy who set my career on its path, but in that one hour in Los Angeles all those many years ago, he did just that. And I have never forgotten it.

Bob Backlund was a true gentleman and a champion in every sense of the word. He was the epitome of what a champion should be. He was, and is, a credit to our business. More of all, though, you know, Bobby Backlund has a heart of gold.

Just a heart of gold.

—"Rowdy" Roddy Piper

INTRODUCTION

Every child needs a hero.

Growing up in a middle-class neighborhood in suburban Manchester, New Hampshire, in the late 1970s, my friends all idolized someone whose poster could be found taped up over their beds. For my athletic friends, these heroes were the Boston sports legends of the time: Orr and Bird; Grogan and Yastrzemski. For others, who tempered the awkwardness of those years by taking up an instrument and starring in a neighborhood garage band, it was Daltrey and Townshend, or Jim Morrison, or Mick Jagger, or Geddy, Alex, and Neil.

My hero, though, was someone totally different.

I first discovered him while flipping channels after swim practice on one nondescript, drizzly Saturday morning late in the autumn of 1980. There, at age nine, somewhere on the dial between the *Bugs Bunny/Road Runner Hour* and *Candlepins for Cash*, I got my first introduction to the "sport" in which he had the starring role.

Initially confused by what this spectacle was all about, I watched as this guy used a dazzling array of athletic moves to deftly pin the shoulders of a much bigger and scarier-looking opponent to the mat for a count of three, delighting the people who had jammed into the dingy fairgrounds arena to cheer him on. A guy who had the lean, strong body and chiseled but kind young face that plainly came not from a bottle or a syringe as they often do now, but from years of dedication and hard work in the gym and on the mat.

With the battle behind him, I watched as this man approached the microphone held by a very young Vince McMahon Jr., and calmly described his plan for beating someone named Sergeant Slaughter.

This Slaughter, he said, was a Marine Drill Instructor who would do anything to win the championship belt. Furthermore, Slaughter was the master of an unbreakable submission hold, known as the "Cobra Clutch," which, when applied, would render its victim unconscious . . . But with hard work and dedication, and with all of us behind him, said the man being interviewed, he would do everything in his power to avoid the Cobra Clutch, and find a way to win and keep the championship belt for all the fans that deserved a proper role model . . . a champion they could be proud of. He hoped we'd all show up to watch the battle at the Boston Garden *that night* and cheer him on to victory.

I was totally hooked.

At the time, I was a serious young athlete—a swimmer competing on the same team with people who would go on to win gold medals at the Olympics and the Goodwill Games. I believed in training hard, playing fair, and "saying my prayers and eating my vitamins," long before Hulk Hogan would go on to popularize that phrase. My new hero spoke to me because he was all about those things, albeit on a much bigger stage.

He was known as the "All-American Boy" because of his clean-cut, youthful good looks, humility, and plainspoken manner. As I would soon learn, he was also drawing overflow crowds into the East Coast's largest hockey arenas and civic centers. From Bangor to Baltimore, Madison Square Garden to the Tokyo Dome, crowds of men, women, and children, young and old, were coming out in droves to cheer him on to victory.

Somehow, this straight-shooting guy was finding a way to hang in there for twenty or thirty minutes nearly every night with challenger after challenger, one more imposing, nefarious, and downright scary than the next. There were Russian strongmen and Samurai warriors; Wild Samoans and tough-talking cowboys; street fighters, masked men, and giants. Through it all, each night, this All-American Boy would dazzle the crowds with elaborate displays of wrestling holds, bursts of quickness, and jaw-dropping feats of strength. He would also withstand unspeakable beatings until he found the moment when he could capitalize on his opponent's one passing mistake. Then, with a single dazzling move, he'd pin his opponent's shoulders to the mat for the fatal three-count that would allow him, once again, to retain his title.

In these matches against these formidable foes, he was forever the underdog—and I identified with him, because I suppose I saw myself that way too.

In 1980, I was a nine-year-old boy growing up in the anonymity of middle-class suburbia, and my hero was Bob Backlund—the Heavyweight Champion of the World Wrestling Federation.

For the next several years, I didn't miss a week of wrestling on television, as I closely followed the career and exploits of my new hero. Wherever I went in competition, Bob Backlund came with me. As I sat quietly in the locker rooms of aquatic centers around New England, mentally preparing for my big races, I would think about Bob doing the same in the bowels of a nearby arena before a title defense. Whenever an older kid tried to bully me on the playground or in the neighborhood, I would think about Bob standing up to any one of the scary, bigger guys ("heels" in wrestling parlance) he was forced to wrestle in defense of his world championship. With that in mind, no playground bully ever seemed to be quite as tough.

When I first tuned in to all of this as a happy-go-lucky nine-year-old, I didn't know that the outcomes of these professional wrestling matches were prearranged, and the fact is, it wouldn't have mattered much if I had known. Nor does that fact matter much in the telling of Bob Backlund's story, because the meaning of Backlund's life isn't as much about the outcomes of his wrestling matches as it is about the man and his journey and the defining choices he made along the way. Choices that left an indelible mark on him, on all of those he touched with his remarkable acts of generosity and kindness, and on the entire wrestling industry.

Of course, the stories Bob Backlund was "telling" in the ring mattered mightily to the fiscal bottom line of the World Wrestling Federation, to the livelihoods of his opponents in the ring with whom he split a percentage of the gates each night, and as such, to his own viability as the champion. For in professional wrestling, the world championship match was always the main event of the evening, and because of that, the champion was heavily relied upon to draw the house. Knowing this, Vince McMahon Sr., the majority owner and Chairman of the Capitol Wrestling Corporation or what was then known as the World Wide Wrestling Federation, had searched the world for an iconic "All-American Boy" to replace the wildly successful but aging Italian superman and "Living Legend" Bruno Sammartino as his champion—and McMahon had gambled big on the relatively unknown Backlund to be that man.

There were smoky backroom machinations that led to McMahon finding Backlund, and inside politics that nearly derailed McMahon's carefully scripted plan. There were colorful opponents that Backlund faced as he criss-crossed the globe in defense of his world championship belt looking to deviate from the promoters' booking strategies and "go into business for themselves." There were unsavory promoters that Backlund was forced to deal with in all corners of the world, road stories from the infamous pro wrestling fraternity, temptations visited upon him, and a remarkable degree of worldwide fame and recognition that made it nearly impossible for him to go anywhere without being mobbed by fans. All of these stories are a huge part of Backlund's life story. But of equal importance were the positive messages of personal courage, confidence, and hope that Bob Backlund was delivering, by his own example, to me and to hundreds of thousands of young kids my age across the country and around the world.

———◆———

I managed to coax my father to take me to a couple of the seasonal wrestling cards held locally every six weeks during the summer at the John

F. Kennedy Memorial Coliseum in my home town of Manchester, New Hampshire. The decrepit 2,500-seat half-moon community hockey rink served as the venue. There, we sat ringside, cheering my hero Bob Backlund on to victory and successful title defenses against the likes of George "The Animal" Steele, "Golden Boy" Adrian Adonis, and "The Russian Bear" Ivan Koloff.

As we grew older, my friends and I anxiously awaited the turn of the season and the announcement of the spring's first wrestling card, which would inevitably turn into a bicycle-driven pilgrimage to Fred's Tackle Shop on the Saturday morning when tickets went on sale. Fred had fewer teeth than he had fingers (and he was missing several of both), but his odd-smelling Army-Navy surplus supply shop, crammed to the gills with survival supplies, was the exclusive presale location for wrestling tickets in those days. Fred was always waiting with a jagged smile for us to fork over the twelve dollars that each of us had carefully saved up from our paper routes or allowances in order to secure a cherished ringside seat to the matches.

———

Eventually, though, as it does for all sports heroes, Bob Backlund's championship reign and his time in the spotlight came to an end. On the day after Christmas in 1983, back in Madison Square Garden where it had all begun, the "All-American Boy" entered the Garden ring with a "neck injury" suffered in a just-televised attack at the hands of his hated archrival, The Iron Sheik of Tehran. Backlund's injury had just been broadcast to the millions of viewers of the WWF's television programming that very morning. The Sheik had challenged Backlund to attempt to swing his Persian clubs over his head—a feat which, the Sheik claimed, no American was tough enough to pull off. Backlund, of course, answered the call in defense of his country to the delight of the fans who chanted "USA! USA!" in unison and urged Backlund to put the Sheik in his place. Backlund succeeded in swinging the clubs, only to have the Sheik attack him while he was performing the exercise, causing one of the legitimately 50-pound wooden clubs to (not legitimately) fall on the back of Backlund's neck.

With that as the setup, the badly "injured" Backlund valiantly battled the Sheik in the main event that night at the Garden, but was eventually trapped in the Sheik's dreaded "camel clutch"—an unbreakable submission hold wherein the Sheik sat on Backlund's back and pulled upward on his chin, bending his neck and back nearly into a right angle. Backlund refused to submit and relinquish the title, and instead hung there limply, on the edge of consciousness, with the TV announcers screaming into their microphones that Backlund had to submit or risk permanent injury.

Then, suddenly and without warning, a white towel came flying into the ring—thrown reluctantly by Backlund's longtime manager, "Golden Boy" Arnold Skaaland, signaling Backlund's submission and relinquishment of the championship to The Iron Sheik. "I had to save Bobby's career," Skaaland later maintained in the televised post-match interviews. "He would never have given up. Sheik woulda had to kill him."

Bob Backlund's reign as champion was over. After nearly six years, the "All-American Boy" had lost the world championship to an Iranian madman on the night after Christmas. The wrestling world and, indeed, "all of America" was left in a state of shock and turmoil.

One month later, Hulk Hogan substituted for an "injured" Backlund, pinned the Sheik at Madison Square Garden, and "Hulkamania" was born. This swept into being a new era of sports entertainment complete with a "rock and wrestling connection," MTV, Cyndi Lauper, dancing girls and Wrestlemania, where TV-star Mr. T donned the tights as Hogan's partner. Pursuant to Vince McMahon Jr.'s master plan, rasslin' had gone mainstream.

Amid all of this new glitz and glamour, the people just seemed to forget about their plainspoken hero, Bob Backlund. And that, of course, is when the true measure of a man is taken.

When the lights go out and the crowds have moved on, too many heroes fall.

But not mine.

With Hogan catching fire nationwide, Vince Jr. offered Backlund a lucrative contract to stay with the company provided that Backlund would turn his back on the fans, dye his hair, become a "jealous heel," and spend the rest of his days attempting to vanquish Hulkamania.

Backlund, however, knew that the "All-American Boy" he had portrayed in the ring for so many years was less a character in the McMahons' passion play than it was his authentic self. He also knew that the credibility and influence that he built up in the real world in the previous six years was far more important to him than money. During those six years, Bob Backlund the professional wrestling character and Bob Backlund the man had become one and the same. To "turn heel" and destroy that character, as Vince Jr. was asking him to do, would be to repudiate the very essence of the person he had become in real life. And once done, there would be no going back.

Faced with this choice, Bob Backlund opted to walk away. Backlund returned home to Glastonbury, Connecticut, to raise his young daughter with the wife who had been his college sweetheart.

From there, Backlund watched as professional wrestling exploded into a billion-dollar worldwide industry. But with that new cross-cultural exposure and evolution into a pop culture phenomenon, the once passable "sport" evolved into farce, and the ever-increasing physical demands on its characters led to rampant steroid and drug abuse and premature deaths too numerous to count.

For most of the next decade, during pro wrestling's pop culture heyday, Bob Backlund absented himself from the international stage. And in those intervening years, while Bob Backlund was home raising his family, my interest in professional wrestling likewise faded. I moved on to other things, and admittedly, I lost track of the man who had once been my childhood hero.

* * *

Fast-forward to the spring of 1993—my junior year of college. One night, upon hearing that the WWF was in town, a group of my roommates and friends made plans to head over to the New Haven Veterans Memorial Coliseum to see the show. As I had discovered, even at a rarified place like Yale, there were professional wrestling fans among the ranks. Professors of American Studies, psychology, and sociology studied it as a cultural phenomenon. My friends, roommates, and fellow students—doctors, lawyers, entrepreneurs, and political leaders-to-be—readily admitted a previous (and in some cases, ongoing) fascination with "the sport."

Word of our planned adventure got out, and by the time the evening rolled around, our posse was a dozen strong. I had no idea what the matches were that night, or even who was scheduled to appear, but was just happy to recapture a moment from my earlier childhood: to feel the excitement of that first glimpse of the three-roped wrestling ring standing empty in the middle of the arena, with the smell of stale popcorn and cheap beer in the air. A haze of cigarette smoke hung low over the crowd as we walked into the arena, and there was a buzz in the air as the 12,000-seat New Haven Coliseum filled to capacity.

It was good to be back.

Later that evening, the "Heartbreak Kid" Shawn Michaels, then the federation's Intercontinental Champion, came to the ring for a title defense. The challenger, who came running out of the locker room in his old red, white, and blue American Flag ring jacket, to an oddly tepid response from the crowd, was none other than my childhood hero.

Bob Backlund was back!

Bob and Shawn put on a true wrestling clinic for the fans—a twenty-some-minute match (rare for the "cartoon era" of wrestling) which Bob won after Shawn Michaels could not answer the ten-count and was counted out of the ring. This, of course, allowed hometown hero Backlund to win the match, but allowed Michaels to hang on to the championship—which could still only change hands via a pin or submission—just like in the old days.

As the crew dismantled the ring after the matches, I recognized Tony Garea, a babyface from the past now serving as a road agent for the company, standing by the exit. I walked over and struck up a conversation, and mentioned to Tony how Bob's match with Shawn had been a wonderful reminder of the old days—and wondered aloud whether Bob would be able to "get over" with the people and recapture that old magic again.

"The fans don't appreciate the same things anymore," Garea lamented.

Turns out, he was right. In 1993's postmodern, dawn of the Internet world, Bob Backlund's wholesome, play by the rules, All-American hero persona wasn't selling anymore. In many cases, the crowds were now cheering for the immoral heels to beat the good guys. Vince McMahon Sr. was gone, and so too his reliable old model of good always triumphing over evil in the end. In fact, in the WWF of 1993, good and evil were, in many cases, no longer even distinguishable.

That night, however, I began what was to become an eighteen-year odyssey to recapture the magic of my childhood. Seeing Bob Backlund again made me want to relive the matches and interviews that had so entranced me when I was young. To hear the dramatic ring announcements from the old carny Joe McHugh, young upstart Gary Michael Cappetta, or Madison Square Garden's Howard Finkel. To listen again to Vince McMahon Jr. and Gorilla Monsoon's compelling play-by-play on the live wrestling cards then-broadcast through the miracle of early cable television on HBO, Madison Square Garden Cablevision, the PRISM Network in Philadelphia, and, later, on the USA Network.

In the years since then, and with the help of many others, I reached back across time and pieced together one of the most complete video-taped collections of Bob Backlund's matches. Watching those live wrestling cards and their supporting TV shows again, it is remarkable how well the stories stand up, both the "angles" drawn up by the "bookers," and the stories told by Bob and his opponents in the ring.

I followed Bob's return to wrestling with renewed interest, but noted with sadness as Tony Garea's comment that night in New Haven proved correct. Try though he did, my then-forty-two-year-old hero couldn't sell his story of hard work, clean living, and perseverance to the kids growing up in Generation X. Instead, this generation of wrestling fans cheered a group of "heels" like Michaels that broke the rules, defied authority, objectified women, and referred to themselves, appropriately, as "Degeneration X." Backlund's George Foreman–like resurgence upon the wrestling scene he had once captivated for more than six years was, in this new era, sadly failing to catch fire.

By then, however, Backlund's daughter Carrie and his legions of young fans had grown up into adulthood, and Backlund had been privately pondering how he could get his message across to this new generation of wrestling fans. One night, on cable television's leading show, the WWF's Monday Night RAW television program, it all came together. I watched in amazement as Backlund "snapped," locked his deadly Chickenwing Crossface submission hold on his towel-throwing former manager Arnold Skaaland, and began to rant and rave about the moral depravity of the modern wrestling fan. I watched with a smile of appreciation in subsequent weeks as my old childhood hero "got heat" with this new generation of fans by becoming an "out-of-touch," eccentric, and highly volatile force, donning a red bow tie and suspenders reminiscent of your former high school principal, and lecturing everyone about their vices and failings.

As Bob put it, "I just decided to be bad by being good."

I must admit that I was never a fan either of Hulkamania, or of the crazed, bow-tie-wearing, lunatic heel "Mr. Backlund" character that Bob invented and assumed in the 1990s. For me, as a fan, the magic spell that pro wrestling had cast on me was broken that night in December 1983 when Arnold Skaaland threw the towel ending Bob's reign as the champion.

My childhood hero was, and always will be, the soft-talking, clean cut, sportsmanlike Bob Backlund—the underdog World Champion entering the ring with his loyal manager Arnold Skaaland and vanquishing challenger after challenger. That is the Bob Backlund that I will always choose to remember. And in Bob's heart, that is the authentic Bob Backlund that he hopes we will never forget.

But to his peers on the inside of the business, the "Mr. Backlund" character that Bob created is revered to this day as one of the most remarkable strokes of creative genius the industry has ever seen. It was, of course, at its essence, a social commentary on the changed and blurry mores of the fans and society at the time.

Vince Jr. had wanted to turn Bob Backlund into a jealous heel back in 1984 and have him try to stop the spread of Hulkamania. Although Backlund could have made millions doing so, Backlund turned Vince Jr. down because he had a young daughter who wouldn't have understood why her friends suddenly hated her father, and because, he believed, the legion of children who idolized him wouldn't have been able to understand and process why their hero suddenly turned his back on them, became "evil," and started cheating, breaking rules, and acting without principle. Cynics will say that Backlund cost himself a fortune by becoming a "mark" for his own character. Others, this author among them, would say that Backlund understood that his wrestling persona had grown to transcend the world of professional wrestling—and his place as a role model for young people became bigger and more important to him than his role in the World Wrestling Federation.

So Backlund had waited, bided his time, and stayed in peak physical condition until his daughter was older and his young fans had grown up. Then, in his forties, Backlund re-emerged, defied all odds by returning to a wrestling world that hadn't seen him for nearly a decade, and became the most hated heel in the sport by becoming its conscience.

It was a story that took the wrestling world by storm and once again, "put butts in the seats" all over the world—culminating in Backlund's world title victory over then-champion Bret "The Hitman" Hart at the 1994 Survivor Series. Backlund's second title run would prove to be brief—but it introduced him to a whole new generation of fans, and a whole new generation of professional wrestlers who grew to admire him, for his remarkable physical conditioning, his knowledge of the business, and for his ability to read a crowd and induce passion—the three old-school hallmarks of what a professional wrestler was supposed to be.

———•◦•———

Fast-forward again to 2009. I am now back in New Hampshire as a partner in a prominent, old-line New England law firm where I have once again discovered unlikely wrestling cohorts—old wrestling fans who will gladly put down their pens to reminisce about seeing Bruno and Backlund and Andre and Pedro at the old Boston Garden. I am now a dad to two young boys, and married to a woman who views all of this "wrestling stuff" with a sort-of bemused fascination—wondering how her otherwise serious-minded litigator husband could possibly be drawn into this fantasy world of men in tights playing out a battle of good versus evil.

"It is a soap opera for men," I try to explain to her—"a microcosm of the world's problems and ills played out in a wrestling match." I have to smile when I realize how ridiculous this sounds when you say it out loud.

In reality, though, it is really much more than even that.

For me, and I suspect for a great many others out there, remembering the glory years of the "All-American Boy" Bob Backlund evokes memories of a far simpler time, before computers, and the Internet, and smartphones—and before the world got itself in such a hurry. A time before "playdates," and before every minute of every day of a child's life was scheduled. A time when kids would still gather in the streets and neighborhoods on lazy summer days to play stickball or kick the can, collect and trade baseball cards, play Atari in each others' basements, and then congregate on a neighbor's front porch to discuss how Bob Backlund was going to get past the new challenge of "King Kong" Mosca, "The Magnificent" Muraco, or whatever seemingly insurmountable new heel had been groomed on Vince Sr.'s "Storyboard" for a run at the underdog "All-American Boy" and his championship belt.

For me, and for many others like me, Bob Backlund was, like *Star Wars*, Atari. and MTV, an iconic emblem of a place in time that we now look back on with more than a little nostalgia. Surely I am not the only one who drives past the dilapidated half-moon ice rink in town with my kids in tow and, looking back over my shoulder, sees myself as a still-idealistic child, chattering in a group of friends outside the arena's back door on a muggy summer night, waiting for that first glimpse of the ring set up in the center of the building. Waiting and wondering how Bob Backlund would even *survive* his match this time against the 315-pound insane cowboy Stan "The Lariat" Hansen, never mind find a way to actually pin him.

You see, for me at least, remembering Bob Backlund is like remembering our childhood—recalling old friends, and coming of age, and a simpler life that seemed much more black and white than the myriad shades of gray we now know life to be. Bob Backlund was someone to cheer for. A true to life hero. Someone who was unambiguously good, and just, and right. Always the underdog, and yet, somehow, someway, ultimately, always the winner.

There was just something right and comforting and reassuring about that.

And of course, that was precisely the way Vince McMahon Sr. wanted it: his vision of what the story of the All-American Boy should be. That is exactly the way he drew it up in his "Storyboard"—and that is what he searched the world to find, and what he ultimately found in Bob Backlund—the boy he hand-picked to play the role. And Bob Backlund was, of course, the last great story in Vince McMahon Sr.'s long and wildly successful life of storytelling—the hero he created for us at a time in history at the height of the Cold War when America, and particularly America's kids, needed one most.

⬥

And so, it was against this backdrop that one day, in the fall of 2009, I found myself up very late one night re-watching the wonderful baseball movie *Field of Dreams*. Near the end, there are two moments in that film that always bring me to tears. The first is the moment when Moonlight Graham pauses for a moment on the baseline before making the choice to step across it in order to save Ray Kinsella's daughter from choking, knowing full well that the choice would mean that he could never go back to being a ballplayer. And the second is the moment where the haunting line "if you build it, he will come" finally pays off, and Ray gets to have the catch with his father that he never got to have as a kid.

Of course, the entire movie is really about bringing a hero back to life by telling his story. Watching *Field of Dreams* that night got me thinking, once again, about Bob Backlund. I wondered where he was, and if he was getting old, and whether he was living somewhere in obscurity, in a place where no one remembered him. My own father had recently passed on, and as I watched that night, I found myself in the middle of something of a midlife crisis, longing to find my childhood hero, and to relive some of those old times again.

So I did what everyone does today. I Googled him.

I learned that Bob Backlund had staged a respectable but unsuccessful run for Congress in 2000 as a Republican in Connecticut, that he was running a heating oil company (Backlund Energy) in Glastonbury, that he was still married to his college sweetheart, and that his daughter had grown up to be a marine biologist. I saw that he looked very much as I remembered him, perhaps with a few more laugh lines and crow's feet—but still in fantastic physical condition. Most importantly, as I Googled further, I learned that no one had ever written a book about the story of his remarkable life.

And that was the moment when the strands of a new dream started to come together.

It started with a simple letter—written from the heart of an old fan who was missing his dad and wanting to recapture a bit of his childhood. In that letter, I explained to Bob what an impact he'd had on my life, what an inspiration he had been to me, and to so many of my friends, and I asked him if he'd be interested in telling his story. I dropped the letter in the mailbox, smiled, shook my head at the goofiness of it all, and never expected to hear anything back. It was cathartic, though, and that, I told myself, would have to be enough.

About three weeks later, I took a call on my cell phone, appropriately, as I was driving home from the gym.

"Mr. Miller, this is Bob Backlund calling," the caller said. I pulled the car over into the breakdown lane to avoid running off the road.

He'd been waiting twenty-five years for a letter like the one I sent him, he said . . . but it had never come. Although many different sportswriters had approached him to do a book—none of them seemed to really "get" who he was or what his life had really been about. My letter, he said, had reached into his heart, justified the difficult choices he had made, and confirmed for him that he had done the right thing. We had a great first talk, and agreed to meet up in a few days at the Glastonbury Town Library to discuss the project.

That meeting was supposed to last an hour. We ended up talking all day.

When I first met Bob, he gave me a big hug, thanked me for finding him and affirming the life choices he had made, and hoped aloud that the man he actually was and the life he had actually led would live up to the expectations of someone who had once called him his hero.

It wouldn't take very long to determine the answer to that question.

⬥

It is true that every child needs a hero. But sometimes, adults need them too.

At the time I met Bob Backlund again, what I needed most was a return to basics and fundamentals—someone with standing in my life to look me in the eye, and remind me about choices and responsibilities and the importance of making good decisions. The message Bob Backlund delivered to me in 2009 wasn't much different from the message he delivered to me in 1982, but the second time around, it proved to be far more meaningful. And it is humbling indeed to know that I arrived in Bob's life at a time when he, too, needed something: one of his oldest fans to emerge from the mists of time to remind him of the reason why he had made the choices he did, and that those choices were, indeed, the right ones.

Writing this book has been a dream come true for me in many ways. It has allowed me to relive my childhood one more time. It has allowed me to meet and get to know great people like Bruno Sammartino and Harley Race and Terry Funk and Roddy Piper, and to talk to them about their experiences as pro wrestlers and in life. It has been a chance to learn about the history and inner-workings of the always-fascinating pro wrestling industry.

But best of all, it has been a chance to say thank you to my childhood hero. Thank you for making the choices you did. Thank you for staying true to your principles. Thank you for not selling out when nearly everyone else did. And thank you for being a role model so worthy of the many years of work that have led to this day.

—Robert H. Miller
Hopkinton, New Hampshire
June 2015

1

The Die Is Cast

"Render more and better service than you are paid for, and sooner or later, you will receive compound interest from your investment."

—Napoleon Hill, "Go the Extra Mile"

———◆———

"Bobby, can I speak with you for a moment?"

Vincent James McMahon Sr., founder and chairman of the World Wide Wrestling Federation, was always impeccably dressed in a suit and tie. His silvering hair was perfectly coiffed, and although he smiled easily, his piercing eyes conveyed the message of serious business.

He was a master of human psychology and an astute observer of people, frequently lurking unobtrusively in the shadows, riffling a stack of quarters in his hand, his eyes always trained on people's faces and his ear listening intently to the crowd's reactions. Although by this time, he flew up from his home in Florida only for the monthly show at Madison Square Garden and for the two days of television tapings that occurred every three weeks, he was constantly on the phone with his deputies. Not much got past Vince McMahon Sr.'s meticulous attention to detail.

He was the most powerful and successful professional wrestling promoter in the United States, controlling the country's most populous region, its largest arenas, and its biggest television markets. The World Wide Wrestling Federation was the most lucrative wrestling promotion in the country, and Vince McMahon Sr. was the man whose business savvy and creative genius had made it that way. He was rarely seen on camera, but he commanded significant respect from his business partners, his fellow promoters around the country with whom he collaborated, and of course, from the stable of professional wrestlers who worked for him.

Vince McMahon Sr. was also a man of purpose and of very few words. When he asked to speak with you, it always meant something.

"Come with me, Bobby."

It was April 1977, and we were standing in the cramped and dirty locker room of the old Philadelphia Arena on the corner of 45th and Market Street in West Philadelphia. That was where the World Wide Wrestling Federation held its television tapings every third Tuesday before they were moved to the Allentown Fairgrounds and the Hamburg Fieldhouse in the name of cheaper rent and better lighting.

I had been flown up to Philadelphia from Atlanta, where I was working for Jim Barnett and Georgia Championship Wrestling. A few weeks earlier, Barnett had called me into his office to tell me that Vince McMahon had his eye on me and wanted to give me a "tryout" at the next set of WWWF television tapings. Vince Sr. and Jim Barnett often shared talent, so Barnett had encouraged me to accept Vince's invitation.

I wrestled three tag-team matches and a singles match at that first set of TV tapings, and things had gone well. Before I left to go back to Atlanta, Vince Sr. shook my hand and invited me back for the next set of tapings in three weeks.

At the time, those television tapings were the lifeblood of the World Wide Wrestling Federation, and the way that Vince Sr. got his storylines across to the fans. There were two television shows, called Championship Wrestling and All-Star Wrestling, which were essentially hour-long ads for the live wrestling events they supported. Each show featured five or six "squash" matches where the territory's newest villains, known as "heels," would be introduced and hyped to the fans in quick three-or four-minute matches against local guys known as "jobbers" they would "squash" with little or no trouble. Each heel would typically have a terrifying final move, called a "finishing hold," that he would showcase in these matches, and which the announcers would hype to the moon. The territory's established heroes, known as "babyfaces," would also appear in televised matches against these jobbers, and would also be made to look quick, dynamic, and unstoppable.

The hottest heels and babyfaces would then appear separately, in pre-taped interview segments with Vince McMahon Jr., where they would hype the matches they were going to be having against each other in the upcoming weeks, in the arenas and civic centers and high school gyms around the territory. Wrestlers and their managers would arrive at the television tapings around nine in the morning and spend all day cutting these promos for the upcoming three-week itinerary of matches up and down the East Coast from Bangor, Maine, to Washington, D.C. The federation's entire roster would be there, reading, eating and drinking, or playing cards, waiting for their turn to cut promos.

Tapes of these one-hour television shows would then be "bicycled" to the various television stations up and down the East Coast, with each local television station getting the geographically specific voice-over announcements and interview segments for the upcoming matches in their local area, which had all been pre-booked and listed in Vince McMahon's master calendar and storyboard. A quick glance ahead in that calendar would tell you who you were wrestling, where, and on what day—while a quick reference back would tell you what had happened in that town in the prior month, so you could make reference to it in your interview and personalize it for the fans who would be watching the interview. That would make it feel like the match was just happening exclusively in their town. The WWWF had perfected this system of hyping their house show matches better than any other promotion—and that definitely contributed to the federation's considerable success.

On my return trip to the second set of tapings, I wrestled a series of matches to be aired sequentially on the WWWF's weekend television programs during the subsequent three weeks. This was done to give the viewers the illusion that I was actually wrestling in the territory and building up credentials and a winning streak even though I was still wrestling full-time for Jim Barnett down in Georgia Championship Wrestling and hadn't actually set foot in a single WWWF building outside Philadelphia. In the days before the Internet, social media, and the nearly instant way that news travels now—it was easy to perpetuate an illusion like this.

I had just finished wrestling "Pretty Boy" Larry Sharpe—one of Vince Sr.'s most skilled in-ring guys, and a guy who Vince frequently used to "test" the talents of new, would-be stars. Larry, who went on to run a successful wrestling school near his hometown of Paulsboro, New Jersey, was a great worker and could anticipate and respond well to whatever moves and maneuvers you tried to put on him, and "sell" those moves convincingly. That would allow Vince Sr. to examine how well you could put an offensive series of moves together, and how good your timing was. Larry also had a wide repertoire of offensive moves at his disposal, which he could string together with ease, and which would make you demonstrate how convincingly you could sell an opponent's offense. This, likewise, would allow Vince Sr. to evaluate how realistic your in-ring work appeared to the fans.

Many wrestlers failed to make the cut in these "tryouts" because they either hadn't mastered how to build a match with a series of offensive moves, or because they couldn't effectively and convincingly "sell" their opponent's offensive moves. When that happened, these "tryout" matches would go "dark"—and never actually appear on the television broadcast.

As I toweled off after my last match, Vince. Sr. touched my elbow and led me quietly into the men's room. The men's room in any arena's locker room always served as Vince Sr.'s mobile office. It was the location he chose for every important conversation I ever had with him because it was the one place in an arena where you could reliably get a bit of privacy. Even at Madison Square Garden, as I would later learn, this is where Vince preferred to conduct his private business—away from the ears of the boys in the locker room, the probing eyes and ears of the newspapermen, photographers, and magazine writers who would prowl the back halls of the larger arenas looking to "expose" the business, and out of earshot of anyone else who might be listening.

I followed him into the men's room, as requested. He turned and locked the door, and then turning back to me, looked me square in the eye and then dropped the bombshell.

"Bobby, I've decided to put the belt on you."

His words hung in the air. I wasn't even sure I had heard them correctly.

Given that I had only wrestled six matches in front of him and had not yet set foot inside a WWWF arena, I was astonished, and struggled to find words. I opened my mouth to try and respond, but no words came.

"Next February at the Garden," he said.

My mind was racing. Bruno Sammartino still had the WWWF championship, and the look on my face must have communicated my uncertainty of how this was all going to take place.

"Billy Graham is going to beat Sammartino in Baltimore next month and run with the belt for a while. You'll get it from him at the Garden next February."

I had just been entrusted with one of the most closely guarded secrets in wrestling—knowledge of not one, but two pending world title changes. Vince's hottest heel, "Superstar" Billy Graham, was poised to stun the wrestling world by defeating Vince's aging Italian superhero, "The Living Legend" Bruno Sammartino, for the championship on April 30, 1977, at the Baltimore Civic Center. Sammartino had, for many years, been box office gold. But Bruno, then forty-one years old, had held the title for two reigns totaling eleven years, and had informed Vince Sr. that he wanted some relief from the grind of traveling the territory and around the world month after month defending the title.

Graham was going to be allowed to run with the title for several months—enough time to give some of the territory's top babyfaces the rub of some world title matches and a chance at some main-event money going around the territory. Vince had already told Graham that he would only be serving as an interim champion and would only hold the belt for as long as it took Vince to find and establish his next babyface champion.

Apparently, that had just happened.

"I've been looking all over for an All-American Boy," Vince explained. "Someone who can play the role of the underdog, but take care of himself in the ring, and protect the title. Everyone you've been working with says you're the guy, and I think they're right."

"Thank you so much," I managed. "I don't even know what to say."

"Don't worry about anything," Vince said. "You just keep wrestling for Barnett and come up to do television for me every three weeks. We'll be building you up over the next several months, and exposing you to the fans slowly. We'll let you know when the timing is right to come up and start working the house shows.[1] Okay?"

With that, he shook my hand, looked me in the eye, and smiled.

"Congratulations. This is going to be great."

With that, he whirled on his heel, turned the lock on the bathroom door, and was gone. This entire life-altering conversation lasted less than two minutes. There were no contracts. Money was never discussed. Just a look in the eye, a firm handshake, and a smile, and the deal was done.

Vince McMahon Sr.'s word was his bond—and that was just fine with me.

I would later learn that there was much more to this story.

---

1 The "house shows" were the regularly monthly schedule of matches in the big-city arenas, smaller city civic centers, and small-town gymnasiums around the WWWF territory from Maine to D.C. that was the federation's bread and butter.

2

Where It All Began

"Who remembers the people whose weak wills kept them mired in mediocrity?"

—Napoleon Hill, "Self-Discipline"

——◆——

To really understand me, to understand why Vince McMahon Sr. chose me to be the "All-American Boy" he was searching the world for, and to understand why I made many of the decisions I did in professional wrestling and in life, you really have to start way back at the beginning. For me, that beginning lies back in the heartland of this great country, in a place where life was, and for the most part still is, pretty simple and straightforward.

Although a lot of wrestlers' hometowns were kayfabed[2] to fit the characters they played in the ring, my in-ring character and my real persona were pretty much one and the same. I really was born in a little town called Princeton, Minnesota—a small farming community of about 2,500 people located about 45 miles north of Minneapolis. I grew up on a small farm, in a rustic little clapboard farmhouse. My mom cooked meals at the school, worked around the farm, and otherwise spent her time raising us. She had flaming red hair and a positive attitude no matter what was happening around her. I definitely got my outlook on life from my mom. She was the glue that kept our family together.

I have two siblings. My older brother Norval is four years older than I am, and my younger sister Mary is four years younger. Neither was very

---

2 In professional wrestling, *kayfabe* is the portrayal of facts or events as true or real and not of a fictional or staged nature.

athletic. Norval was a prettyboy who loved spending time with the ladies and always had to have a fast car. I think he used those things to escape the reality of our lives. He worked in construction most of his life. Mary was a nurse at a local hospital. Both still live in Princeton.

My parents were first-generation Swedish immigrants who were used to working hard for every dollar and saving everything that they possibly could—but the truth of it is we pretty much lived day-to-day. There were no luxuries in our lives as we grew up in the '50s and '60s. We didn't have a television, and we only had one old car, and we ate whatever we could grow off the land or raise in our barn.

Until I was two years old, I rarely left my crib and didn't get the opportunity to socialize with other toddlers. I was left to just lay there, which, I was later told, may have affected the structure of my spine, giving me my unusual upright posture. Because I just laid there, I never raised my head up, and because your head is the heaviest part of your body, this prevented my spine from forming a proper "S" shape.

We had outdoor plumbing, and I can remember, even as a small child, going outside to pump the water from the well and hauling it into the house in buckets. You'd always want to make sure you went to the bathroom before it got dark out because it was a long, cold walk to the outhouse. During the long Minnesota winters when I was grow-ing up, my brother and sister and I would huddle around the fireplace with our mother at night and listen to *Gunsmoke* on the radio. It was really cold in the house, which wasn't very well insulated and was heated entirely by wood. At night, we slept under piles of heavy covers trying to stay warm.

As I was growing into a boy, my father's three brothers would often come over to the house, and they would all start drinking. Eventually, one of them would say, "there is something wrong with him," referring to me. I would often overhear them talking, which made me feel really bad about myself, and I would retreat to the basement to get away from them. I felt worthless and unloved and very much alone.

I got my first pair of shoes from Ernie—the man at the dump. They were cowboy boots, and one of them had a hole in it that I patched with a piece of cardboard, which didn't help much. In the winter, the snow would get into my boot so my foot would be cold and wet all day at school, but it was all I had.

My dad worked at a concrete fabrication plant that made bridge beams, and also did some farming and worked on various construction crews. He was a good man when he wasn't drinking—but that wasn't very often.

We never knew when the "monster" was going to come home. Dad had a violent temper, and that was very hard for my mom. Dad wasn't a good drinker, and when he came home in that condition, anything could happen. There were far too many nights growing up where we would wake up in the middle of the night to hear my mother screaming, and things crashing in the house. When our father was finished with our mother, I would hear his heavy, shuffling footfalls on the squeaky stairs of our house as he trudged up to the second floor where my bedroom was. Some nights, he was so drunk that he would fall on the stairs and tumble heavily back down to the bottom and lie groaning there for awhile until he managed to pick himself back up and try again. When I heard him coming, I would always pull the covers over my head and try to hide. On the nights when he made it to the top of the stairs, he would come into my bedroom, stinking of alcohol, and sit on the edge of my bed mumbling to himself or talking gibberish while I hid there under the covers shaking.

I couldn't ever have people over, because I never knew when my dad might come home in that violent condition. In all the years I was growing up, I only had a person stay over one time—and that night was so horrible, he never wanted to come back again. The next day at school, he told everyone what he had seen and heard at my house, which made me want to crawl into the deepest hole and be away from everyone making fun of me and my family. After that, I was too embarrassed to have anyone over and no one would come over anyway. One time, when Norval was seventeen or eighteen, my father was beating my mother so severely that Norval had to jump into the fight to save her. That was the night that years and years of anger came out of Norval, and he beat my father so severely that the next day, my father had bruises all over his face.

We suffered in silence for years, trying to block out the horror of what was happening in our home.

People have often wondered why I was so shy and reserved, kept to myself so much, and had trouble being confident, or looking into the camera. The fact is that when you grow up in an environment like the one I grew up in, you are constantly hiding from the world, not wanting anyone to know the truth about what is going on in your life. I went to school hoping it would be a better and a safer environment than I had at home, but school was just as bad for me, but for a different reason. In school I was very scared because I couldn't answer the questions the teachers were asking me. I was a very poor reader and I couldn't remember anything, so I was always looking down at my feet, trying to hide, hoping that the teachers would call on someone else, and praying that I could just get through another day without being noticed. I got held back in third grade, which made things even worse, because I was no longer even with the same group of kids. All of this just reinforced my feelings of being a complete and utter failure.

When I was seven years old, I started playing tee-ball in the local town league as a way of getting out of the house. To get to tee-ball practice, I would ride an old rusty bicycle I found at the dump about 4 miles to town over the soft, sandy farm roads. The roads were so soft that the tires of that bike would sink down into the sand so I had to stand up almost the entire time just to keep the bike moving. I'd have to stop and rest a couple of times on the way, so I was always exhausted and late by the time I got to practice. The coach was an impatient and unkind man, and he would yell at me for being late and tell me to go play right field—but I didn't know where right field was, so he would yell some more and embarrass me about that. Every time he yelled at me, it reminded me of the monster I was living with at home, which made me even more anxious. I was a very uncoordinated child. During my first tee-ball game, I struck out twice despite the fact that the ball was sitting motionless on a tee right in front of me—and everybody laughed at me.

After tee-ball practice, I would stop on the way home and visit my grandmother at the old-age home in Princeton. She was totally blind by the time I was born, so she never actually saw me physically, but she used to love having me sit with her, and hold her hand, and tell her about my games. I was often reluctant to go see her, because I was so embarrassed that I never had anything positive to tell her. She loved baseball, and I wished so much that I could tell her about getting a hit or making a good play so she would be proud of me. But I never made plays like that, and I didn't want to lie to my grandmother. I would then ride my bike back home through the sand again, and by the time I got home, I was so tired, I would often fall asleep. One time I fell asleep in the barn next to my bike, and when my father found me, he whipped me for sleeping before I brought the wood in for the night.

My mother did what she could to protect me. One day she tried to save me the ride on my bike by dropping me off at practice. The problem was, our car was so old it made a lot of noise and was falling apart, and when the kids at practice saw us, they all made fun of our car and of how poor we were. Things just felt so hopeless to me.

I started wrestling when I was in fourth grade (ten years old) for Coach Bill Shultz. Technically, I was supposed to spend half of the physical education period playing basketball, and half of it wrestling, but I was so uncoordinated and inept at basketball that he allowed me to spend the entire period on the mats. I really wasn't any better at wrestling and got whipped by the other boys in the wrestling drills, but something about wrestling felt different to me.

When I got to sixth grade, we moved to the high school and I started to fall in with the wrong crowd. I was hanging around with people a lot older than I was, primarily kids I met working on the farms. Those kids were a big influence on my behavior, and I started skipping school, drinking beer, getting into a lot of fights, and staying out all night—but any of those things was better than going home.

Fighting became a badge of honor for me. I had so many negative things going on in my life that simply getting some positive attention from someone else, even if it was just someone patting me on the back after I got badly bloodied in a fight felt good to me. Home was a disaster. School was a disaster. My social life was a disaster, but this group of "friends" was giving me a place to go other than home. I finally felt like I had found some people I could trust. My life on the edge continued like that for nearly two years until one fateful night when everything changed for me.

It happened at a place called the Kitten Club, in a little town called Longsiding, Minnesota. You had to be twenty-one to get in, but they didn't card me, because the owners were really just interested in whether you had money to buy beer. There was a motorcycle gang from Minneapolis there looking for a fight. I was with a group of my older "friends" who agreed to fight the gang and asked me if I was willing to help them, and of course, I readily agreed. The would-be combatants spilled out of the club onto Highway 169, stopping traffic in both directions. As I went out into the middle of the highway and got ready to brawl, I glanced behind me and froze.

I was the only one out there.

None of my "friends" had actually come out on to the highway to back me up. Turning back to the reality in front of me, I looked at the gang of bikers with their chains and tire irons and didn't know what to do. I stood there, trying not to show that I was paralyzed by fear and praying that someone would come out to help me . . . but no one did.

After some tense moments, the lead gang member just gestured at me to go. I think they actually respected the fact that I was willing to go out there by myself to fight them. But that was the moment that I finally realized that these "friends" of mine weren't really going to stand by me, and weren't the kind of friends I wanted to have.

I was very fortunate that learning that lesson didn't get me killed.

I walked the 7 miles home from the Kitten Club that night. During those three hours, as I walked in the dark on the side of the road, I struggled to figure out how to know whether somebody was really your friend or not.

After that night, I trusted no one for a very long time.

The beginning of the eighth grade produced the first of several major turning points in my life. I had been given a football physical exam form but hadn't yet gone to see the doctor. I was going to give it back to my football coach, Mike Scavinack, who was also my science teacher. I went to see him after school to tell him that I was not going out for the football team because I wanted to spend my time wrestling. That was a lie. The truth was that I wasn't committed to putting in the kind of time and effort necessary to be successful in sports, or in anything else.

When I left Mr. Scavinack's room that day, though I still had the physical exam form in my hand. To this day, I'm not sure what he said to me to convince me to go get my physical and channel my energy into football—but that's exactly what happened. I took the physical, tried out for football, and made the team—and that probably ended up saving my life.

If I had quit football that day, I would have dropped out of school and become a statistic. On a number of occasions, I had been an eyelash away from making that choice. I owe a lot to Mike Scavinack. I hadn't really shown him anything to justify him spending the time with me trying to convince me to play football, but he was a teacher—and he had that special something in his heart that made him want to try.

I was struggling mightily as a student and was humiliated by my inability to perform in the classroom. I would look at the words in the books but not retain anything. I was only a little better at math but had a really hard time following the lessons. I couldn't keep up with the other kids in the classroom. Some kids got As, and seemed to be able to get those grades pretty easily. My teachers let me skate by with Cs, even though I wasn't learning anything, so that I could continue to qualify to participate in athletics. I also joined the wrestling and track teams so I had a sport to concentrate on in every season and someplace to go other than home.

I was committed to not missing a day of wrestling, track, or football practice. No matter how badly things went on the field, on the track, or in the gym, it was always better than facing the reality waiting for me back at home.

He Was Dedicated

Bob Backlund was a quiet, likeable kid. His natural ability was about average as a youth, but the degree of dedication he developed separated him from all the others.

—Jermone Peterson, Bob Backlund's football, wrestling, and track coach from eighth to tenth grade

Despite my efforts to use athletics to get my life on the right track, things didn't start happening for me right away. We were too poor to afford to buy any exercise equipment, but around this time I made a barbell out of a pipe and two five-gallon pails filled with cement. When I tried to lift it, though, I was too weak to even move it.

During my sophomore year in football, I was a 170-pound offensive end of little distinction. I also had a mediocre year on a good wrestling team. Wrestling at 154 pounds, I was eliminated from the district tournament in the first round, and winning seemed like an impossibility for me.

No matter what I was doing, it seemed like I was being met with failure at every turn.

After the district tournament was over, I went to regionals just to watch the matches and cheer on my teammates who had qualified. When that was over, I went to the state tournament that was held that year at the Williams Arena at the University of Minnesota. There I closely watched a guy named Kirk Anderson, a sophomore like me who was wrestling one class above me at 165 pounds, make it to the finals and win. For a sophomore to win the state tournament at that weight class was virtually unheard of. I thought a lot about what it had taken for him to accomplish that, and about the hard work and commitment he must have been putting in to allow him to accomplish that at such a young age.

Kirk Anderson's improbable victory became imprinted in my mind. Watching his march to the championship made me realize that I wanted to do that too. I had found a role model; someone who I could really look up to.

Meanwhile, at the same time, a new football coach Ron Stolski had just come to Princeton High. He was a big believer in weight training, and he got me really interested in weightlifting and training in general. My sophomore teammate Ross Johnson and I went to Minneapolis with Coach Stolski and looked at four or five different gyms to determine what kind of equipment they had, and to research the most beneficial programs for high school football players. It was exciting to be asked to travel with Coach Stolski and Ross, just the three of us. It was a great bonding experience, which I had never had before in my life.

When we got back, Coach Stolski started holding weight-training sessions at the school at 6:30 a.m. every Monday, Wednesday, and Friday. My mom was a cook at the school, so I would catch a ride with her at 6 a.m. to lift weights until the first bell. Ross and I never missed a day, and then when school let out for the summer, I found myself again having to improvise at home.

I asked Coach Stolski for an old football helmet, and attached a 25-pound barbell plate to the top of it with a bolt and a nut and went for long runs with that helmet on to strengthen my neck. That summer, after doing so much weight training at school, I was also finally able to lift my homemade barbell—which provided me with my first positive reward for my efforts and made me realize that what I was doing was actually working.

Junior year, I had a better season in football. I still didn't excel, but I played every down of every game. When wrestling season started, I was already in good shape, but I dieted down to 175 pounds from about 190, worked hard with my coaches, and concentrated on technique and improving my balance and quickness. I went unbeaten through the regular season and became a crowd favorite because of my enthusiastic approach to every match. I had become so strong that I was able to throw my opponents around the mat with ease.

Before the Princeton Invitational that year, the coaches met to draw up the brackets. The coach from St. Francis was talking up my role model from the previous year, Kirk Anderson, who was the reigning state champ in the 165-pound weight class—now one weight class *below* me. Anderson's coach was doing a lot of chirping that there was no one in the Princeton tournament who could give Anderson any competition. So my coach, Dan Brockton said "well, I have this Backlund kid at 175, and he's undefeated so far, I bet he can give Anderson a run for his money." So Anderson's coach moved him up a weight class, and the coaches put us in opposite brackets so that, barring an upset, we would meet in the finals.

Well, as the fates would have it, Kirk Anderson and I *did*, in fact, meet in the finals. Anderson was the defending state champ in the 165-pound weight class, and I was the undefeated challenger at 175, where we were both now wrestling. There wasn't a lot to cheer about in Princeton in those days, so the match was pretty built up in the area newspapers. The match was held at my school, and the gymnasium was packed full of people. When I stepped out onto the mat at the beginning of the match, my mind was strangely clear. I didn't doubt for one moment that I could beat Kirk Anderson. The crowd was cheering and chanting my name.

It was the first time in my life that anyone had ever cheered for me.

Princeton kids were from the wrong side of the tracks, so to speak. A lot of the spectators at our athletic competitions didn't like to see the kids from Princeton do well in athletics. They wanted to see some cleancut, handsome businessman's son do well, as opposed to the derelict sons of some country farmers. But that's why it was good that wrestling was an individual sport. You could prove yourself on your own merits, and not have to worry about publicity, or politics, or the whims of the referees. It was just you, down on the mat, all by yourself—and if you pinned your opponent, there was no room for politics or subjectivity.

I liked that.

The match didn't really live up to all the hype, as I whipped Anderson 7–2 on points. He couldn't do much at all with me. Given how much I had idolized Anderson the year before, beating him that decisively in that match gave me my first tangible reinforcement that hard work pays off. I was also able to answer the question I had asked the year before about how Anderson had been able to accomplish so much at such a young age. The answer was simple—you just had to work harder than everyone else!

Until that point in my life, almost every lesson I had learned had been a negative one. But this was the tipping point for me, and I was starting to get some recognition for the right reasons! As soon as I realized that, I felt ready to take on the world, and I understood that there was a way out for me if I could simply go out there every day and outwork everyone else.

I won the rest of my matches that season, went on to win the districts and the regionals in my weight class, and then went on to the state tournament at St. Cloud State University—about 30 miles from Princeton.

A "Clod from the Sticks"

A bunch of the coaches were sitting together and started talking about this 175-pounder from Princeton. They didn't know his name. A coach from one of the more elite programs said, "he's just a muscle-bound clod from the sticks—don't worry about him," and just dismissed him out of hand. That kid was Bob Backlund. In one of the early matches in the tournament, a high-seeded kid charged at Bob like a bull to start their match. Big mistake. Bob thrust his arms forward, mainly in defense, and tossed the kid backward to the edge of the mat. Bob handled him easily. The kid was totally psyched out by that one move.

—Coach Dan Brockton, Bob's junior year
high school wrestling coach

When the tournament seedings came out, it was apparent that if everything played out the way that it was expected to, I would be wrestling a guy named Randy Brekke from Faribault, Minnesota, in the finals. I had already wrestled and defeated two guys during the regular season who had beaten Randy Brekke, so everyone was telling me that I had it made. I had never been the tournament "favorite" before, and I had never experienced that kind of publicity and attention.

I started to believe the hype.

Before all my other matches, I had always gone through the same warm-up routine—but this time, I didn't take much time to get ready. I was too busy thinking about being crowned state champion in a few minutes' time. When I went out onto the mat to wrestle, I didn't stop to shake my coach's hand on the way out, which I had also always done.

I went to the middle of the mat for the introductions and looked Brekke in the eye.

All season long, I had been very aggressive. I had almost always gotten a takedown in the first minute of action. But Brekke caught me by surprise, took *me* down, and almost pinned *me* in the opening moments of the match. Before I knew what had happened, he had built up a five-point lead on me. I tried to make up the points, but even though I had done conditioning work all season long, I felt lethargic, and eventually, that lethargy turned to desperation. I was not yet ready to take on the world because I had not yet learned the critical importance that mental preparation has in sports.

Randy Brekke beat me on points and walked away with the state championship. The truth is, Randy Brekke had taken the match seriously, prepared himself properly, and gave the match and the moment the respect it deserved. I had not—and as a consequence I handed Randy Brekke the Minnesota state championship. Maybe he would have beaten me anyway—but the point is, I didn't even show up that day, because I had drifted from the principles and behaviors that had put me in the position to win it in the first place.

A lot of my family and friends had come out to cheer me on, and I walked off the mat with my head down for the first time that season. I took a shower, and then came out still with my head down. When I saw my parents standing there, the tears came, and they just started flowing—not because I got beat, but because I knew I hadn't given it my best. I had allowed myself to get cocky, and had just learned a tough lesson for it.

That felt much, much worse than simply losing.

I turned away from my supporters and walked out of the building. Nothing seemed important to me anymore. I walked around thinking about myself and what a fool I had been to listen to and believe all of the talk about my being "the best." I remember going to school the Monday following that loss in the state finals and not being able to remember my locker combination. That loss took everything out of me. It took a long, long time for the pain of that loss to fade from my memory.

That was also the second major turning point in my early life.

The loss to Randy Brekke at the state championships was the most memorable and important wrestling match of my entire wrestling career. It was also the match that taught me to never take *anything* for granted— one of the most painful and important lessons that I ever had to learn.

I would never make that mistake again in any amateur match I ever had in my career. From that day on, I took my matches one at a time, never looking ahead to the future or assuming anything from looking at my opponent's win-loss record. I was no longer interested in hearing my opponent's name, where he was from, who he had beaten, or who had beaten him. After that humiliating loss to Brekke, I understood that each time, no matter where I was or who I was wrestling, that I had to simply go out there and give every ounce that I had to give, to never, ever give up, and to never take anything for granted.

Never again would I beat myself.

Looking back over my life now, I'm actually happy that I lost that match to Randy Brekke—because that loss caused me to make a lot of lasting changes in the way I approached athletic competition, and life in general. If I had still beaten him after such lackadaisical preparation on my part, I might have gotten complacent. Instead, that loss gave me a new respect for the importance of preparation and hard work—an ethic that would carry over into my work entertaining fans in the professional ranks as well.

More than a few times, years later, when we were wrestling in a small town high school gym in front of five hundred people on a one-off Tuesday night, some of the guys I'd be in the ring with would want to take it easy and just go through the motions. Any time I was tempted to do that, I thought of Randy Brekke—and it made me remember that the fans in that small town on that Tuesday night had worked just as hard for the money to pay for their ticket to see me wrestle as the people in Madison Square Garden had paid for theirs—and that every fan in every building deserved to see the very best that I had to give them.

— ◆ —

Going into senior year, I had been elected captain of both the football and wrestling teams, and I was really looking forward to my final year of high school. Ross Johnson and I continued as training partners that summer.

Ross and I were very different people. He was a straight-A student and a very religious guy. He didn't do wild things, and led a very restrained life. But through our training, we got to be as close as brothers.

We trained hard, and had big dreams.

And I had finally found a friend I could count on and was beginning to trust.

There came a point in our training that summer, though, where I was getting a lot stronger, but Ross was getting weaker. We couldn't figure out why. We checked his diet and his sleep patterns. He was eating well, and we were doing practically the identical workouts. It was very discouraging for him.

Just before football season started, we found out that Ross Johnson had leukemia.

I had to take Ross' position as fullback that year. It was a hard year, as Ross couldn't play football anymore and we all watched helplessly as he got weaker and weaker. Ross battled to the end, insisting on working out with us in the weight room and trying to train with the team and work himself back to health. He came to all of our games to cheer us on.

In the end, though, Ross Johnson lost his battle with leukemia. He died that year at the age of eighteen.

Ross and I had talked about a lot of things while we were training— about life, and our goals for our lives. Ross had a clear picture of where he wanted to go. He was full of dreams and big ideas—of going off to college, getting married, playing professional football, and having lots of children. By contrast, I didn't really have any idea about what I wanted from my life. I had expected so little of myself for so long, that I had never even really thought about it. But Ross Johnson pushed me to see further, dream bigger, and understand that deep inside yourself, it was okay to set lofty personal goals. A lot of the dreams that I have fulfilled in my life are dreams that Ross Johnson first showed me were okay to dream.

Senior year, I was recruited by a few schools after football season, but I was monomaniacal in my focus to right a wrong during wrestling season. Fueled by the still painful memories of what had happened in the finals of the State Championships the season before, I went 26–0 and won the 1968 Minnesota state wrestling championship at 175 pounds. It wasn't as exciting as it had been my junior year when it was all fresh and new. Senior year, I was much more cautious. I was totally focused on winning and took no chances. It was certainly exciting to win the state title though. My combined record as a junior and senior was 51–1.

The only blemish on my record was the loss to Randy Brekke.

The Strongest Ever

Bob's ability to push himself is what made him different. Often, after the regular practice was over and everyone had gone home, he would stay and work. Sometimes he'd ask me to stay with him and just continue to drive himself. He'd come to my house when the gym was locked up on a holiday or something, and ask me to open it up so he could work out. As for wrestling, Bob was the attraction. The crowds just went for him. I've heard many, many people say that he was the strongest high school wrestler that they'd ever seen. I can still remember one match in a tournament when another team just conceded a loss to Bob in their match at 175. They put in this kid who was probably 20 pounds lighter, and throughout the match, this kid kept screaming and yelling like he was being murdered out there. I asked Bob afterward how hard he was squeezing this kid, and Bob smiled at me and said, "I didn't want to hurt him, coach. I could have squeezed a lot harder!"

—Dan Brockton

I had been recruited by quite a few colleges. The University of Minnesota was pushing the hardest, but I made clear to them that

I wanted to both play football and wrestle—and their coaches had told me that I couldn't do both. That didn't interest me, so I turned them down. North Dakota State's wrestling coach Bucky Maughan, a decorated wrestler who had won a state high school title in Pennsylvania and an NCAA national championship at Morehead State, was pushing pretty hard too; but he was a new coach up there and was just getting established. I liked Coach Maughan a lot, and I was hoping that he would be able to make things work out for me. In the end, though, he was too new there to exert much influence—so with my dreams of playing both football and wrestling scuttled at least for the time being, I ended up packing my bags and heading to junior college in Iowa.

That is what amateur wrestling did for me. Wrestling took me from the brink, gave me a sense of purpose and confidence, taught me critically important life lessons, and most importantly gave me a future. That is why I have always encouraged kids to become involved in amateur wrestling and why, after I became established, I started the Bob Backlund Kids' Wrestling Tournaments. Amateur wrestling saved my life—and I wanted to be sure that other kids would have the same opportunities.

Incredible Transformation

Bob and my wife are both from Princeton. In 1965, when I was visiting Princeton, my wife's younger brother Gary was a member of the Princeton High wrestling team. I had just graduated, so I went over to the high school practice to help out my brother-in-law and to get in a workout. The coach asked me if I wanted to work out with this kid named Backlund. He was a sophomore then, and was about 5' 10" and maybe 155 pounds. I weighed around 145 then, so I said, "Sure!" He didn't know much about wrestling then, and he tried to muscle me, so I had no problem throwing him around pretty easily. I left the practice not really even remembering the kid's name.

The next Christmas, which was Bob's junior year, I was back in Princeton and again attended a practice to work with Gary. I remember asking the coach about this big muscular kid who was lifting weights in the corner of the gym. And he told me, "That's Bob Backlund—the kid you wrestled last year." I couldn't believe it was even the same guy. He had made an incredible transformation over the year since I had seen him. There would be no wrestling with him this year!

I went over and talked with him, though. He was extremely shy, and I had to work really hard to pump even a few words out of him. That year, though, I remembered his name, and made a note to myself to see how he did in the state tournament. As you know, he took second in states that year, and the following year, when I again returned to Princeton, I made it a point to talk to him in practice. He had developed even more by then (his senior year) and he had these large charts that he made to record the weight and number of reps that he did in each lift. I knew right then that he was a wrestler I'd like to have in our program at North Dakota State. And that year, he went on to become Minnesota State Champion.

In 1968, the NDSU wrestling program was just getting off the ground, and scholarship money was practically non-existent. I talked and talked with our football coaches to try and interest them in Bob, but for some reason, they didn't think that a young wrestling coach who had never played football was their leading talent scout. So they didn't offer Bob a scholarship, and we couldn't—so Bob ended up starting off at Waldorf.

—**Bucky Maughan, head wrestling coach, NDSU**

3

The NCAAs

"Definiteness of purpose is the starting point of all achieve-ment. Study every person you can think of who has achieved lasting success and you will find that each . . . had a plan for reaching that goal, and each devoted the greatest part of his or her thoughts and efforts to that end."

—Napoleon Hill, "Develop a Definiteness of Purpose"

———◆———

With no four-year college prepared to allow me to pursue both football *and* wrestling, I decided to enroll at Waldorf Junior College in Forest City, Iowa—a small Lutheran school about 200 miles from Princeton. Waldorf had very good football and wrestling programs, and had agreed to allow me to pursue both. There were only about six hundred students, and it was very quiet socially, but it kept you on your toes academically. At the time, it was also one of the only junior colleges that had dorms.

I drove down to Waldorf in my '57 Olds and got there a bit early for preseason football. I met a lot of people from all over the country because Waldorf, being a Lutheran school, drew a lot of students from outside the region. It was a very different atmosphere from Princeton—a town where everyone pretty much knew everyone from birth to death. At Waldorf, I didn't know a single person.

I earned a starting position on the football team, and played offensive guard and defensive end for Coach Dick Bosdorf, and was on the field for every play on both sides of the ball for every one of our eight games that year. That is also where I earned my nickname "Tiny" because I was pretty muscular when I arrived at Waldorf.

> **Totally Committed**
> Even though I've placed ten players in the NFL in the past twelve years, Tiny is the player who stands out the most in my mind. He wasn't the best football player I've ever coached, but he was my most totally committed athlete. Everyone looked up to him. He is a totally self-made person, and others tried to follow him because of the example he set.
> —Dick Bosdorf, Waldorf Head Football Coach

I also wrestled in my first year at Waldorf for Ron Nelermoe. Coach Nelermoe was very strong and pretty hard to handle. Usually coaches don't get on the mat with their wrestlers and actually wrestle them—but there really wasn't anyone else on the team who could push me, so it fell to him to do so. To his credit—he did!

I lost one match that first year, by one point to a kid from Iowa named Joe Hatchett. That was my first loss in almost three years, and I was so upset because of it that I didn't come out of my room for three days. Eventually, they had to send a couple of football players to come drag me out.

Back then, the national junior college wrestling tournament was almost as strong as the NCAA tournament was. There was some very, very good wrestling done at the junior college level by kids who were really excellent wrestlers, but may not have had the grades or the money to go to a four-year college. By way of example, Chris Taylor, who wrestled in junior college in Michigan, couldn't win the national junior college tournament. He finished third one year, and second the next year—and then went on to Iowa State, which was kind of the powerhouse of Division I wrestling at the time, where he was a teammate of the legendary Dan Gable. At Iowa State, Chris won the NCAA Division I tournament twice, and then went on to win the bronze medal at the Munich Olympic Games.

He Had Heart

Even though I only coached Bob for one year before I moved on to Concordia, I remember him well. Bob placed third in the JC Nationals that year, losing to the eventual JC champion, and then coming back to win the losers' bracket. He was the best all-around athlete I have ever seen. He was a workhorse, and he had heart, willpower, drive, dedication, strength, speed . . . well, he had everything. But that wasn't God-given. He earned it.

—Ron Nelermoe, Bob's wrestling coach at Waldorf

In the fall of my second year, everything was different. I tried to be the first one on the field and the last one into the lunch line. I wanted to show them that I was totally dedicated to sports.

Always Worked Harder Than Anyone Else

Oh, he was dedicated all right. I met Bob when we were both freshmen at Waldorf College. It was a new environment for all of us, and it was interesting watching all of the ballplayers size each other up as we arrived. One of us, in particular, stuck out. Backlund. He wasn't that tall, but man, was he put together. And quiet. The guy didn't say two words for about the first three weeks of practice. But I knew that if he ran into somebody with that body of his, he was really going to be a show. I think one of the things that really stands out about Backlund was the way he was able to reach down within himself when he really wanted something. He had intestinal fortitude like none of us had ever seen. We'd practice football for two hours a night, get done, and then he'd go to this little side room off the locker room and pump iron and then be the last one into supper—often making it just before the dining hall closed. One day, he asked me and another guy to spot for him and there was this bar on the weight bench that had more weight on it than I'd seen anywhere. It was 405 pounds. I spotted him one rep with that, and his muscles and veins were standing out so tight and the sounds that were coming out of him were sounds that can only come from deep within your soul. That's how Bob was. He always worked harder than anyone else.

In our freshman year, it was a tradition that all of the freshmen got thrown into the showers by the sophomores. You had two ways to go. You could either go peacefully and let them walk you in and drench you, or you could put up a tussle. But no one escaped getting drenched. I put up a pretty good tussle, but about six or seven of them finally subdued me and got me in there. Well, then, I saw that they were headed for Backlund's dorm room, so I decided to hang around and watch the show. When they got to Backlund's door, he opened the door standing there in blue cutoff shorts and no shirt, with his arms folded in front of him. The posse of sophomores informed him that he was going into the shower, and he politely informed them that he wasn't in the mood to take a shower. They looked him up and down for a few seconds, and then just went to the next door down.

— **Paul Felix, Bob's friend at Waldorf**

We went 9–0 that season and Waldorf was ranked ninth nationally. I was named a first team All-American defensive end.

A Standing Ovation

At the Waldorf Athletic Awards Banquet that season, Bob was presented the Honor Athlete Award. I'd been at Waldorf eighteen years, and that was the only time I have ever seen a standing ovation for a student. Bob was just so dedicated and respected.

— **Dick Bosdorf**

During my sophomore wrestling season, we had a new coach— Neil Boyd. Before that season started, we went over to Luther College in Luther, Iowa, for a scrimmage against their JV team. I was in the locker room getting dressed and watching a guy who was strutting around in there acting pretty full of himself. He looked familiar but I couldn't place him. Eventually, he came up to me and introduced himself.

It was Randy Brekke.

He had changed quite a bit. Instead of the hardworking humble guy he was when we were juniors in high school, now, he was cocky. I had no idea what weight class he was in, but I was really hoping he was wrestling at 190, because from the moment he introduced himself to me, I was totally focused on getting him onto the mat that afternoon and righting an old wrong.

Unfortunately, it was not to be. Brekke was still wrestling at 177, while I had moved up to 190. If I could have physically done it, I would have jumped into the sauna and sweated off those 13 pounds right then and there just for the chance to take him down. I kept telling Ron Pierce, our 177 pounder, how Brekke had beaten me as a junior and what to expect from him. I think I was more excited for Ron's match than I was for my own.

When Pierce's match started, it was clear that Brekke had gone backward rather than forward. Ron went out there and whipped Brekke easily. He was ahead 8–2 on points when he pinned him!

It was obvious to me that day that I had gotten more out of losing that state championship match to Randy Brekke in St. Cloud than he had gotten out of winning it. He had become cocky and less dedicated. I had become hungrier and sharper and more focused—and notwithstanding the very public defeat, had continued to progress forward. Seeing Brekke there at that scrimmage was reinforcement for me of what had already been a very important lesson.

Wrestling season went well that year, and once again, ended with me in the finals of the Junior College Nationals—this time at 190 pounds against Joe Hatchett, who gave me the toughest match I ever had in my wrestling career. We could both bench over 400 pounds, and we both had to cut weight to get to 190. Both of us had breezed through the tournament into the finals. There was serious intensity on the mat that day as we prepared to square off. We were like two bulls out there. It was a total defensive struggle, and neither of us would give an inch. Ultimately, he beat me 2–1 on points.

He Was An Inspiration

I was there in the stands for that epic showdown. You could just feel the energy and intensity when they squared off. And you know, usually, when you wrestle such an incredible match in a national final, even if you lose 2–1 on points, you'd feel good about yourself. I vividly remember Backlund after that match as we headed back to our dorms. I just said, "Nice try, Tiny," and he responded with a barely audible "yeah" and then went back into his room and stayed there by himself for a day or two. You could just see the wheels turning in his head, thinking of what he had to do to get by Joe Hatchett and claim the NJCAA championship. I had sort of known this all along, but I knew from watching the way he reacted that day that Backlund was going to end up at the top of the heap of whatever he decided to do. He just wanted to be the best, and he was willing to reach deep down inside and get whatever he needed to get to achieve those goals. He was an inspiration to me and to the other athletes around him. To see him working that hard made all of us reach down and get a little more too.

—Paul Felix

After wrestling season ended, I wanted to transfer to North Dakota State University in time for the spring football season so that the coaches could get to know me there, but, unfortunately, we were in the middle of a semester and NDSU was on the quarter system, so the credits couldn't transfer to permit me to do it.

Dinner Can Wait

Two years later, I was a little more established, and I convinced the football coaches who had dismissed me previously that we should go after Bob Backlund. I was going to Princeton that Christmas so the plan was for me to talk to him about attending NDSU. They also asked me to visit with a running back at the high school that they had their eye on. I invited both athletes and their parents out to eat, and we were to meet at a place called "The Farm"—which was the nicest eating place in Princeton. The running back and his parents showed up but Backlund and his parents were late. The running back knew that Backlund was out running. It seemed that everyone in Princeton knew of Bob's habit of running endless miles wearing a football helmet with a large weight strapped to the top of it so he could strengthen his neck while he ran. The Backlunds finally showed up and his parents apologized for being late and, in fact, explained that Bob had been out running, that they never knew when he would finish, and that to him, his workouts came before anything, even a recruiting dinner! We convinced Bob to attend NDSU as a football player and a wrestler.

—Bucky Maughan

As I feared, when I transferred to NDSU, the head football coach, Ron Erhardt, who would later go on to coach the NFL's New England Patriots, didn't even know who I was. He just knew that I was a defensive end, my 440 time, and that I was a JC All-American and a pretty good wrestler. Coach Maughan had clearly wanted me a lot more for wrestling than Coach Erhardt did for football. I could sense that almost immediately.

I didn't have a lot of money, and I certainly wasn't the best dresser. I used to just wear an old wool sweater and overalls everywhere because that's basically all I had. I know that annoyed Coach Erhardt, especially the one time I went on his local football television program dressed like that. I think I embarrassed him—but I couldn't afford anything else. Whatever money I made in the summers went toward food and gas, and it went fast.

Coach Erhardt's record at NDSU, however, was an impressive 46–3–1 over the previous five seasons, which had allowed him to recruit strongly—and the football at NDSU was really good. Erhardt, however, was a tough, remote, and unfeeling guy. It was very hard to break in there starting in the fall. I didn't get onto the starting squad until Paul Bothof, the team's starting defensive tackle, was killed in a hunting accident during the season. Obviously, that was a terrible tragedy, and the last way you'd want to make any team, but I resolved to make the best of it and to honor Paul's memory through my play on the field.

Around that time, I also kept seeing this young woman around campus. Up to that point in my life, I hadn't really had much time for girls, so whenever a girl came up to talk to me, I blushed a lot and didn't really know what to do or how to act. I found out the woman's name was Corki, and that she was a swimming instructor on campus.

One day, after practice, I met her in the fieldhouse where she was helping to set up for a wrestling meet. She took a look at me and said, "You know what, you're in pretty good shape, you should try out for the wrestling team." Someone clued her in as to who I was, and it made for a nice moment—and she was the one who was blushing! My friend Keith Maring eventually got fed up with my shyness around Corki and just told her that I wanted to ask her out. Fortunately, she said "yes!"

We had a successful season, and ended up beating Montana 31–16 in the 1970 Camelia Bowl. I had twenty-two tackles and recovered two fumbles in that game. It was a real thrill to travel to California as a team, and to play on television in front of a national audience. Toward the end of that first season, though, I started to figure out what Coach Erhardt was really like. He used up a lot of his players, and put the school's win-loss record ahead of a lot of players' physical well-being. He was very competitive and wanted to win at any cost, and he made a lot of choices to rush players back from injury and get them out on the field in what might have been in the best interest of the team, but not necessarily in the best long-term interest of the individual players.

I think Erhardt's goal was to get a professional coaching job in the NFL, and he was making the choices he needed to make to accomplish that for himself. Rather than having a good relationship with his players, and trying to develop their talent, it felt like he was using them to run a factory. Erhardt was also the athletic director at NDSU, and I think he used that position to his advantage and to the advantage of the football team. I know that Coach Erhardt had a reputation in the NFL for being a nice guy and pretty popular with his players, but he and I never connected on any level.

After our Camelia Bowl victory, I joined up with Coach Maugham's wrestling team. I had missed a lot of the wrestling season because of our late Bowl game appearance, and at my first workout with the team, I weighed in at 230 pounds. I faced the prospect of having to lose 40 pounds through a combination of diet and exercise to make weight at 190.

I did it in eight days.

I ran in place almost endlessly, and lost 10–15 pounds per practice wrestling in layers of sweats. I'd drink water, but ate no food, so I'd gain by fluid replacement at night, but lost it all and more during the next day's practice. On the last day of that crash diet, I was within 4 pounds of 190 and went to the wrestling room, turned the heat all the way up, and ran in place for two hours. I would jog for ten seconds, then run fast for twenty seconds, over and over. Given what I was trying to do, it was better to run in place than to jog around because when you run in place, no cool air hits you, so your body temperature stays higher.

I was so dehydrated, I couldn't sweat. I got within a half-pound of 190 and then took a shower and started to walk back to my dorm. I had to lay down in the snow because I was so weak. One of the football coaches came upon me lying there and helped me back to the fieldhouse, where I just laid there spitting, trying to get rid of that last half pound.

That was the day of our match with Morehead State. The weigh-in was at noon, and I was committed to making weight and being able to wrestle. I made it, but the process of shedding 40 pounds in eight days had left me so weak, that I was useless to the team. Needless to say, even though I am telling this story to explain how I transitioned from being a 230-pound defensive end to a 190-pound wrestler in eight days, I would strongly discourage anyone reading this from ever trying to replicate what I did. It was a very unhealthy and dangerous thing to do, and it could have had deadly consequences.

I wobbled my way out onto the mat that day against Morehead State, and although I gave it my best shot, I had no strength or stamina and was a sitting duck for my opponent at 190. Nevertheless—it felt good to be back out there, and was a relief to be working with Coach Maughan after enduring a season under Coach Erhardt. After taking that loss, I went 8–0–1 in the dual meets the rest of the way that season, and made it to the North Central Conference Tournament Final. In that final, I was coasting along with a 6–0 lead when I got caught in a cradle and pinned by Randy Omvig of Northern Iowa. The hometown Iowa fans were thrilled by Randy's win. Disappointed, I looked ahead to the NCAA Division II tournament, which started a week later in Fargo.

That year, as the national tournament came around, I hadn't compiled a qualifying record because I couldn't wrestle while we prepared for our Bowl Game appearance in football. In the tournament, only the top ten wrestlers in each weight class were seeded. Because of my short record, I wasn't seeded. Although Coach Maughan had lobbied the tournament directors to seed me based on my win-loss percentage and my unusual circumstances, the tournament officials took the position that I simply hadn't wrestled enough matches earn a seed. Based on the way they build the brackets at the national tournament, the top-seeded guys wrestle the unseeded guys first, and the middle seeds face each other—much in the same way that they do it at March Madness. As an unseeded entrant, I would have to wrestle all the top-seeded guys first.

On the first day of that NCAA Division II National Wrestling tournament, which we hosted at NDSU, I probably had the best single day in wrestling that I've ever had. I won *all* my matches, and mowed down a bunch of unsuspecting top seeds in the process. Because I was unseeded, a lot of the top seeds took me for granted and underestimated me. There were a bunch of pretty unhappy coaches fuming at the tournament directors that day!

On the second day of the tournament, I faced Randy Omvig from Northern Iowa in the semifinals in a rematch of our North Central Conference tournament final where he had snuck a cradle on me for a pin. This time, there would be no such luck for Randy, and I thrashed him and punched my "unseeded" ticket to the finals. There, I would meet the tournament's number-one seed, Gary Maiolfi, from Cal Poly, in the championship match.

Electrifying

The NDSU fieldhouse was standing room only, and place was buzzing with energy. After sparring around on their feet for much of the first period, Bob ended up in a whizzer (double overhook) counter applied by Maiolfi, the Cal Poly Wrestler. Bob bearhugged Maiolfi to counter the whizzer and the two just stood there like two titans in a deadlock for what seemed like forever. Backlund just stood there and squeezed and squeezed while the entire place was on its feet. Finally, Maiolfi was just completely spent, and collapsed to the mat. Backlund had completely squeezed the life out of his opponent with the bearhug, and used it to become national champion. The response he got from the crowd when Maiolfi went down was the most electrifying thing I have ever heard at a collegiate wrestling match.

—**Bucky Maughan**

Throughout that tournament, I had used a single-leg takedown as my go-to hold, so that's what Maiolfi was expecting and guarding against. Once I made it to the finals, though, I decided to change up my game plan and try to surprise my opponent with something different. I had used the bearhug in a few of my matches back in high school, but Maiolfi hadn't seen me use it before. It worked like a charm. Winning the 1971 NCAA Division II National Championship in front of my home fans in Fargo was a dream come true for me—as it represented the end of a very long, hard road. The fact that I had to come from the bottom to win it from an unseeded position was symbolic of that road—and made it just that much sweeter.

Meanwhile, Corki and I had been dating awhile and things were going well between us, so I asked her to come home with me to Princeton to meet my parents. I told her that we had a swimming pool, and that we could make a nice little vacation out of it. She thought she really had something in me, a collegiate NCAA wrestling champion from Princeton with a swimming pool at home! I didn't understand her misperception until we got to St. Cloud, and there was a sign for Princeton, Minnesota, and she realized that we weren't actually going to New Jersey.

Anyway, we got to my parents' farm, and of course, she asked where the pool was, thinking that we had our own pool! I, of course, meant that there was an outdoor pool in town that we could hang out at—that Princeton had a nice public pool. I didn't even comprehend that there were families wealthy enough to have their own private pools.

We had a really nice time, though!

———※———

By the time we were seniors, Corki and I knew that we were going to get married, but we both wanted to have some money in our pockets before we did. We also decided not to have a wedding because we wanted to save the money for something better later on in life. Some people want to have a big wedding. We thought it would be better to have a house to live in!

Although football went well my senior year (we went a combined 16–2–1 in the two years I played at NDSU), and despite the fact that I was now an NCAA national wrestling champion, I still hadn't connected in any way with Coach Erhardt, even after I was named a Division II All-American. When football season ended, I was once again near the 230-pound mark for football, and I just couldn't bear the thought of having to go through the turmoil to drop weight back to 190 again. I was carrying twenty-four credits, trying to finish school, and I was worried that I wasn't going to be able to do all of it well.

I met with Bucky, and we decided that I would come with the team on its Christmas tour of Pennsylvania, but that instead of dropping weight, I would wrestle as a heavyweight. I won all four matches on the tour, but I just wasn't in the same kind of physical shape at 230 that I had been in when I wrestled at 190. I knew that when I had to compete against a top heavyweight, I would be in trouble.

During my senior year, I went 8–3 in dual meets, finished third in the conference tournament, and fifth in the NCAA tournament in the heavyweight division.

A Legends at NDSU

During his senior year, Bob decided not to try to cut to 190, because he was convinced that he was going to get a tryout in the NFL following his being named an All-American. I could understand that.

During his senior year, Backlund had become a legend in the NDSU athletic department. On their way to football practice, Erhardt had every player stop at this crude isometric bar that had been cemented into the ground and perform a series of isometric lifts. The thing was two four-by-four posts with an iron bar crossing about two feet off the ground. Most of the players approached the bar, just grunted, got red in the face and went on their way. Bob, who never faked a grunt, went up to the thing, grabbed hold of it, and pulled the entire apparatus right out of the ground! Needless to say, the team had a new hero after that.

Backlund and the isometric posts is a story that comes up whenever people around here talk about feats of strength. This just added to the Backlund Legend at NDSU. The bearhug collapsing his opponent at the National Championships, the running in place to lose 40 pounds in eight days to make weight, and the story of the isometric posts are all still told whenever the old wrestlers get together. Bob has been inducted into the NDSU Athletic Hall of Fame, and we have pictures of Bob both in my office and in the ticket office wearing the WWWF Championship belt. He is always a big topic of conversation whenever he comes to town. When Bob comes to Fargo, we usually get together and go to the Elks Club where a lot of the Bison boosters and fans like to hang out. He is always the talk of the club, and spends most of the night signing photos.

—Bucky Maughan

As you will see as you read on, there have been a number of seemingly unexplainable coincidences that have happened in my life—most of them for the good. The first of those coincidences happened in the spring of 1972 at the YMCA in Fargo. I used to work out there sometimes—it was an old YMCA with a weight room in the middle and a balcony circling around the weight room with a running track on it. On that particular day, I was doing bench presses and I noticed that there was a professional wrestler in the weight room with me doing curls.

That man was none other than "Superstar" Billy Graham.

I had grown up watching the American Wrestling Association's (AWA) brand of professional wrestling on television in Princeton, and I had seen Billy Graham before. I recognized him immediately. As anyone who knows Billy will tell you—his huge physique and long bleached blonde hair made him pretty much instantly recognizable!

The AWA was holding a card that night at the Fargo Civic Center, and Billy had come to the YMCA to get a workout in. I shook his hand, and told him that I was wrestling and playing football at North Dakota State and that I had grown up watching the AWA. He asked me if I had considered becoming a pro wrestler when I graduated from college. I told him that I hadn't considered it because at that time, I was hoping to end up in the NFL. He looked at my physique and told me that I should consider it. We talked for a few more minutes about the business, and then shook hands again and went our separate ways to finish our respective workouts.

It was a brief, chance meeting. Most would call it a fluke. But the truth is, as ironic as it is, it was "Superstar" Billy Graham who put the first real thought of becoming a professional wrestler into my head.

And as most of you probably know, the fates would have it that Billy and I would meet again.

4

Breaking In

"Find out what you want most in life, and go after it."

—Napoleon Hill, "Build a Positive Mental Attitude"

———————

I spent the spring quarter of my senior year student-teaching in North Dakota at Fargo South High School, under Jerry Larson, the high school wrestling coach. I was still hoping to get drafted to play pro football in the NFL.

That spring, however, I learned that Coach Erhardt had been telling the pro scouts that I "wasn't interested" in playing professional football. I have no earthly idea why he would have been telling people that, because playing professional football in the NFL had been my goal the entire time I was at NDSU. By the time I found out what Erhardt was telling the scouts, however, it was too late to do anything about it.

It is hard for me to have any respect for that man. I know that Erhardt ended up as a head coach with the New England Patriots and offensive coordinator with the New York Jets, but I just didn't have any respect for the way he conducted himself, the way he treated his players at NDSU, or the way he unilaterally downplayed my NFL prospects. To this day, I don't know for sure what our issue was, but I suspect that it might have had something to with the fact that I was recruited to NDSU by Coach Maughan, and not by him. I always worked hard for Coach Erhardt, but it is very clear that he and I were just not on the same page. It's funny how life tends to work these things out, though. Who knows what would have happened if Erhardt had pushed me to the pro scouts, and I had caught on with an NFL team?

After college, I ended up in Mundelein, Illinois, playing semi-pro football at the Chicago Bears training camp. I made so little money playing for that team that I had to hand out brochures for a company door-to-door just to make enough money to live. I was paid per piece for doing that, so I just incorporated it into my workout routine and ran my entire delivery route, so I made it work for me. I made enough money to cover rent, to have a place to work out, and to buy enough food to get by. I was living in a boarding house with ten other guys doing the same thing I was doing, so I had a three-foot by ten-foot space on the wood floor just big enough to roll out a sleeping bag, and that was about it.

It was a pretty depressing scene and it would have been very easy to get demoralized and just give up.

But I didn't.

In the face of that totally discouraging situation, I stayed positive and worked out harder and harder every day to keep myself in absolutely peak physical condition while I waited for my chance to come. I knew that I didn't have control of *when* that chance would come—but I did have control of what kind of shape I would be in if and when it did.

Deep down, though, I knew that I didn't have much chance of getting into the NFL from a semi-pro team, because the NFL was getting a steady stream of talent from the college ranks every year, and anyone they plucked from a semi-pro team never seemed to stick. Those were the guys who always seemed to be in the first round of cuts during training camp and ended up getting stuck on the practice squads. The writing was on the wall for me. I recognized that my chances of actually making it to the NFL were pretty slim.

There were players on that team that had been there ten years waiting for their chance to make the pros. I decided I wasn't going to wait around for a chance at my dream—I was going to go after it! Little did I know that one of life's little coincidences was about to strike again.

When the season was over, I went back to NDSU and finished the credits I needed to graduate, and in the spring, I moved to Anoka,

Minnesota, outside Minneapolis and lived with a guy named Elroy Carpenter, who had been a friend of mine in high school. I was taping sheetrock during the day, and working out every day at the 7th Street gym in Minneapolis when my chance finally did come.

There was a man at the 7th Street gym who would always watch me work out. I knew he was somehow involved with professional wrestling because he was working in the gym with a lot of the guys, like Mad Dog Vachon, Billy Red Lyons, and Red Bastien, who I had grown up watching in the AWA. The man turned out to be pro wrestling trainer Eddie Sharkey.

One day, Sharkey just came up to me during my workout and introduced himself. As Graham had before, Sharkey asked me if I had ever considered getting into professional wrestling. He knew that I had excelled in high school and college wrestling, and mentioned that, with that background and my build, I should give it a try.

It seemed like the fates were steering me toward an outcome. Twice in one year, I was being invited to join the pro wrestling fraternity. This time, I wasn't going to let the chance pass me by. So I said "yes" to Eddie Sharkey.

And that's how it all began for me.

I became a student of Eddie's, who charged me a flat fee of $500 to train me. He had a professional-style ring in the 7th Street gym, which was just lying on 2x6s on the floor—it was not on a platform—so we couldn't learn how to get thrown out of the ring. We trained for three days a week in the evenings after work, learning holds and maneuvers, how to hit the ropes, and how to "chain wrestle"—putting together the strings of moves that you would use in a professional wrestling match.

Obviously, there were major differences between wrestling in the amateur ranks and professional wrestling. In the amateurs, the goal is to pin your opponent's shoulders to the mat for one second, or to win the match on points by dominating your opponent on the mat, taking him down, and controlling the action. Joint locks and any other kinds of submission moves were forbidden. Of course, amateur wrestling is also a legitimate athletic competition. In professional wrestling, the goal is to pin your opponent's shoulders to the mat for a three-count, or to make him concede the match by submission. You could also win the match if your opponent was counted out of the ring, or disqualified, or if the match was stopped because your opponent was bleeding too severely to continue. Professional wrestling, while certainly still very athletic, was entertainment. While a working knowledge of amateur wrestling certainly helped in professional wrestling by providing you with a catalogue of moves you could call upon to tell a story in the ring, or to protect yourself if you needed to, it was also important to remember that professional wrestling required a give and take in the ring that necessitated *allowing* your opponent to get the upper hand on you in a match. To me, that was one of the hardest adjustments!

Eddie trained me for about seven months. We worked on "ring presence," submission holds, and professional pinning combinations that had more visual flourishes than the amateur ones did. He taught me how to throw a dropkick. Most importantly, though, he taught me how to execute high spots without hurting my opponent, and how take "bumps" without getting hurt myself.

Taking a bump, whether it is a hiptoss, a bodyslam, a suplex, or a piledriver, is all about making sure that your body and your opponent's body are in the right position to land at the end of the move. As the person taking the bump, it is about learning to land as flat as you can, and dispersing the impact over as large an area of your body as possible. Think of it like going across thin ice on skis. You can make it across a sheet of thin ice on skis, where you would fall through on foot, because you are dispersing your weight over a larger area. It is the same principle in wrestling. If you take a bump with your entire body, rather than landing on, say, a shoulder or your hip, you can properly disperse the impact and avoid injury. You want everything to hit the mat at the same time—and your opponent is supposed to protect you by executing any move so that your body is in the proper position to make that happen.

As the person calling and then executing the "high spot," you have the responsibility to ensure that the move is understood, and that the timing is right so your opponent can react properly to what you are doing. Professional wrestling is often compared to a "dance," and that is really pretty accurate. You are constantly responding to what your opponent is doing. Every move needs a countermove to support it. Miss even one, and someone can get badly hurt.

It doesn't really matter that a move is predetermined if you have a 280-pound man up above your head upside down in a vertical suplex. If you move him too close to the ropes or the turnbuckles, if your timing is off, or if your move is not predictable, you might as well be doing it for real. And of course, while you are busy protecting yourself and your opponent—you need to make it look like it's real and that you are, in fact, trying to hurt him, so that the fans' suspension of disbelief isn't dispelled.

It was a lot to take in. One day, though, Eddie pulled me aside and told me that I was ready to make a go of it. He told me where to go to get some professional photographs taken, and then gave me a list of names, addresses, and phone numbers of regional wrestling promoters all around the country. He told me to send a photo to each of those promoters and then follow up with a phone call about two weeks after that and to tell them that Eddie Sharkey sent me.

He wished me good luck.

And that was that.

I sent those photographs all over the country—to Stu Hart in Calgary, and Jim Barnett in Georgia, and Paul Bosch in Houston and Eddie Graham in Florida, and Fritz Von Erich in Texas and Roy Shire in San Francisco and Mike LaBell in Los Angeles. I kept working taping sheetrock for minimum wage, training at the 7th Street gym at night, and waiting for the responses that never came.

Finally, Eddie told me to just start calling the promoters. Once I started doing that, I realized how hard it was to actually get a wrestling promoter on the telephone! It seemed that they were always too busy. Or not in the office. Or at least saying that they were not in the office! That's if they even had an office! Others said they were full, or to try back in a few months.

I remember feeding coins into a payphone waiting and waiting (and waiting!) for Stu Hart from the Calgary promotion to get on the phone. When he finally got to the phone, he talked so slowly that the phone cut out because I had run out of money. I never did call him back—and thus managed to avoid getting stretched in the infamous Hart dungeon—the basement of the Harts' family home in Calgary which was set up wall-to-wall with wrestling mats, and where Stu Hart was famous for working over his students while teaching them the craft.

A couple of days later, when I had money in my pocket again, I called Leroy McGuirk's office in Tulsa, Oklahoma. McGuirk was the head of the Tri-States promotion that, ironically, actually covered parts of four states: Oklahoma, Louisiana, Missouri, and Texas. McGuirk was also a former NCAA champion himself, having won the Division I title at 155 pounds wrestling out of Oklahoma A&M (now known as Oklahoma State) as a junior in 1931. At the time he won that title, he was blind in one eye, which made the feat even more amazing.

By the time I called on him, though, Leroy was totally blind, having lost the sight in his other eye in a horrific automobile accident. He obviously couldn't see my pictures personally, but he had some office person there review my credentials with him, and he learned that I was also an NCAA champion. He liked that about me, and we talked on the phone about amateur wrestling a little bit, and after chatting for a while, he offered me a tryout. He gave me a house show date in Baton Rouge, Louisiana, in two weeks' time, and told me he would meet me there.

I was on my way.

5

From the Sheraton to the Trunk
(Tri-States, 1973)

"Turn all unpleasant circumstances into opportunities for positive action. Make this an automatic habit, and your success will multiply."

—Napoleon Hill, "Build a Positive Mental Attitude"

———◆———

The Sunday after receiving the invitation to try out with Leroy McGuirk, I packed everything I owned into the back of my very used 1968 green Chevrolet Impala that I had bought earlier that summer for $200. In retrospect, I probably should have invested in a better car given how much driving I was about to be doing—and because that Impala would end up being much more than just a car to me in those early years.

When the car was packed, my mother stood in front of our little homestead in Princeton, gave me a big hug, told me she loved me, and told me to do my best. The naysayers, though, were out in force. People told me that I was wasting my time, and that I would never make it in pro wrestling. They said, "We'll see you back here in a month hanging sheetrock." Fortunately, I didn't listen to them, and I made myself a little promise to prove them all wrong. And with that, I struck off from Princeton, Minnesota, a twenty-one-year-old, bound for Baton Rouge, Louisiana, and determined to make it as a professional wrestler.

At the time I left Minnesota, I had $20 in my pocket, and by the time I got down there, I had spent it all on gas and food. Fortunately, I was about to have my first professional wrestling match, and I knew that the match was going to be held at a pretty decent-sized arena, so I made a hotel reservation for myself at the Sheraton Baton Rouge, because I had picked up, through bits and pieces of conversation in various places, that a lot of professional athletes stayed at Sheratons.

My first match ever was against Ron Starr—who was pretty green himself back then, but who would go on to have a long career in the NWA and the WWC down in Puerto Rico. During my days training with Eddie, we were always in a ring in a gym with no fans watching—so having an arena full of people waiting as I left the locker room and went to the ring was a very different feeling.

Although I had wrestled in front of large crowds before, it was always as an amateur. Had this been an amateur match, I would have been fine, but it wasn't, and so I wasn't. My head was spinning as I tried to remember all the things Eddie had taught me about knowing my place, not stealing too much thunder from the guys on the top of the card, and how to listen to the crowd and get them on your side. I was young, naïve, very nervous, and wanting very much to make a good first impression. As I got to the ring, I climbed up the steps and tried to vault myself over the top rope and into the ring, but the ropes were looser than I expected, and I ended up spinning around and falling into the ring. I could hear the crowd laughing at me, which obviously wasn't the reaction I was looking for.

I don't remember much about the match—I was told to job for Starr, and that's pretty much what I did. He called all of the spots, and I just worked on following his lead and selling for him. He didn't give me much offense, and I didn't really expect to get much. I was just trying to make the timing look good, and to make sure that neither of us got hurt.

When the match was over, I rolled out of the ring on the wrong side of the arena, and got completely disoriented trying to find my way back to the dressing room. One thing you probably haven't thought about is how similar the four sides of an arena look when you've been wrestling for ten minutes and have sweat and the lights in your eyes. These weren't places like Madison Square Garden with one central aisle that you walked down, and lots of people working crowd control to steer you to where you needed to go. This arena had four walkways through the crowd, one on each side of the ring, and I had no idea which one of them led back to the dressing room. So I just tried to sell it like I'd had my bell rung—but in reality, I was actually lost and growing increasingly nervous about it. I'm sure everyone in the back was probably thinking "rookie!" But I had gotten through my first match unscathed, and I did eventually find the way back.

I took a shower, and checked out with the promoter running the building that night. He told me that I had done a good enough job to earn some additional bookings—and brought out a book that had a calendar in it with the list of dates for the rest of the month. The matches were listed there—and I was told to find my name on each night's card, and to write down which towns I needed to be in and on what days. I could also see my opponent for each night, although that didn't mean much to me since I didn't know anyone in the territory. My next date was not until five days later in Shreveport—but after that, it looked like I was going to be working pretty regularly.

I was excited to have survived the tryout, and I could barely contain my enthusiasm. I signed a requisition, and got an envelope with my first payday in it! I stuffed it into my pocket and didn't open it until I was back in the front seat of my car.

I pulled out the envelope and thought about what I was going to do with the money. First, of course, I was going to have to pay for my lodging at the Sheraton. I thought about treating myself to a good steak dinner to celebrate making it as a pro. And then, I thought about sending some home to my parents to help out with my younger sister Mary.

I opened the envelope and found . . .

Five bucks.

One five-dollar bill.

That was it.

I had grown up watching the AWA and given the size of the crowds the AWA was drawing at the time, I had always assumed that wrestlers made a good living. Obviously, I had assumed too much. As I sat there in the parking lot, I was trying to figure out how to ration the five dollars in order to put enough gas in the Impala to drive to Shreveport, buy food, and find a place to stay for the next four nights.

And then I went to a payphone at the nearest gas station and cancelled my reservation at the Sheraton!

With no money to get a room at even the cheapest motel in the area, I found myself 1,000 miles away from home, and effectively homeless. I bought a couple of cans of tuna and a can opener, and that became dinner. I drove around, and eventually found a church parking lot, pulled in, and with nowhere else to go, I curled up and went to sleep in the trunk of my car.

All my earthly possessions were there in that car with me. Fortunately, I could lock the trunk from the inside, which was a good thing. That first night down there, I didn't get much sleep. In the Louisiana summer, even the nights were stifling. The air in the car was oppressive and heavy. It was hard to breathe, and I was worried about getting enough air. I was also worried about getting robbed, because all night, there was a gang of pretty rough guys standing near my car talking. One time, they even sat on my car. I could hear their voices clearly, and felt the car sink down when they sat on it. They clearly didn't realize that there was someone sleeping inside it!

The next day, I went to the YMCA to work out and started to have some real doubts about what I was doing. I was twenty-one, very far from home, didn't know *anyone*, and was sleeping in the trunk of my car. It was hard not to feel a little desperate. As crazy as it sounds, though, I was better off than a lot of the people I saw down there on the streets at night.

I gathered my wits and decided that my next order of business was finding a way to defend myself if someone tried to break into my car.

I couldn't afford a gun, but I did manage to procure an old wooden baseball bat for some extra protection.

My second night in Baton Rouge wasn't much better. The same gang was hanging around the area, so I moved the car to a different church parking lot, but just found a different gang! It was hard to get any rest. I kept wondering whether someone might try to break the windows during the night, and whether I was going to end up in a fight with a gang trying to steal the few things I had. I slept fitfully, clutching my bat and struggling for air. I thought a lot about home, about Corki and my parents.

I wasn't ready to quit, but I didn't want to stay.

I was getting used to sleeping in the trunk, but my body was getting run down. I couldn't believe I had worked this hard, and that this was the return that life was giving me. In retrospect, those first few weeks were rock bottom for me. No one could write to me because I had no permanent address, and I couldn't even afford the few coins to call home, because I needed every dime I could muster for food. I was lonely—and the wrestling fraternity provided no help, because I didn't know anyone in the territory.

As I have done so many times in my life when things looked bleak, I turned to exercise to keep my spirits up. I went to the local gym every day, and I trained as hard as I could, and washed up in their bathroom. Working out put my mind at rest and gave me a release.

As it turned out, wrestling in the Tri-States territory was pretty tough. The trips between the towns were long, and the crowds were rough. One night we'd be in New Orleans, the next night in Tulsa, Oklahoma, 700 miles away, and then back to Shreveport, Louisiana, for the TV tapings, and then off to Houma, Louisiana, which was about 30 miles from New Orleans, where we had just been. Because Leroy was blind, he relied on others for the information that promoters use to make decisions about who to push. There was a real diffusion of responsibility. It wasn't always clear who you were answering to, and internal locker room politics were running rampant.

Jake Smith, who was known as "Grizzly" both because of his appearance and his disposition (and who was the father of Jake "The Snake" Roberts), was the booker. More than anywhere else I wrestled, the Tri-States territory bore the closest resemblance to professional wrestling's origins in the traveling carnivals. Everywhere we went, it seemed like there were fans who wanted to challenge the wrestlers. So in many of the towns we visited, before the matches began, Grizzly would bring four or five of us out of the locker room and out into the ring. There, he had also lined up four or five "marks" (fans who were not smart to the business) who wanted to try their hand against one of us.

Grizzly usually arranged it so that the other three or four guys in the ring looked a lot meaner than I did, so the marks almost always picked me. This, of course, was all part of Grizzly's plan, because he knew that I could handle myself easily against these mostly drunk guys trying to show off for their girlfriends.

Night after night, I would wrestle these marks, one after the next, before the matches started. Because I was a clean-cut babyface, I wasn't intimidating to them, and so they weren't expecting to get manhandled—but that's what Grizzly expected me to do—manhandle them. None of those arenas were air-conditioned, so on most nights, the arenas were oppressively hot before the fans crowded into them. Once the bleachers and the seats were full, the temperature rose by at least 15 degrees and the air smelled like a combination of body odor, sewage, and stale beer. On some nights, it was hard not to throw up—except that I didn't have much in my stomach anyway!

Against the bigger marks, I would usually just break them down to the mat and ride them, making them carry my body weight in the oppressive heat until they blew up, gasping for air, too tired to continue. I would pin some of them with headlocks, put them in full nelsons, or the Chickenwing Crossface, or an arm bar, or a hammerlock and apply just enough pressure to make them give up. At that time in my career, I wasn't as schooled in hooking and shooting as I was later on in my career when I needed those skills to protect the world title—but I relied on my strength, amateur wrestling knowledge, and a few tricks I picked up along the way to take care of business. Slowly, these little "exhibitions" earned me the respect of my peers and the office guys.

To me, though, wrestling these marks was like playing around—a chance to break a sweat and get in a little extra workout. One night in Lafayette, I wrestled nine people in a row out of the crowd before the matches began. I loved it! For some of the other pros who didn't have a background in amateur wrestling, though, these bouts sometimes got pretty scary, and they'd have to break a nose or gouge an eye, or use a rear naked choke to subdue a bigger mark. Failure in one of these scenarios was simply not an option. If you were a professional wrestler and got man-handled by a drunk mark who came out of the crowd in jeans and cowboy boots, it would hurt the legitimacy of the business in the eyes of the fans, and your career, at least in that territory, would be over.

For the entire time I worked the Tri-States territory, I ate tuna fish out of a can, drank as much water as I could get at the gym or the public library, and lived in my car. As I slowly earned the respect of my peers, I was occasionally able to hitch a ride with some of the other wrestlers, or to split the cost of gas with them if I was driving, which enabled me to save a little money. I trained hard, worked hard in the ring to learn the craft, watched almost every match every night to see how different wrestlers handled the crowds and built emotion in their matches, and slowly but surely, I earned the respect of the promoters working under Leroy.

Most nights, I was "jerking the curtain" (wrestling in the opening match) working as "enhancement talent"—selling other people's moves to make them look good, thereby "enhancing" their own heat. In the beginning, everyone I stepped into the ring with was calling the matches, and the direction from the promoters was for them to squash me without giving me any comeback, rally, or any meaningful part of the match. I was effectively a crash-test dummy for everyone I stepped into the ring with. Given my amateur background, it was a humbling experience, but the fact that the office trusted me enough to wrestle the "marks" from the crowd provided me with a glimmer of hope.

I stayed positive and remembered Eddie Sharkey's instruction that wrestling in the territories was professional wrestling's real training camp. I was out there to learn the craft—and the small civic arenas and gyms in these small southern backwater towns were the classrooms of our profession. The opportunity to climb into the ring every night with a different opponent who wrestled a different style—those opportunities were the laboratories by which the art of our profession was taught and passed down from one generation of workers to the next. With that mindset, I worked hard every night to "sell" my opponents' moves realistically, and to learn to take the bumps from a wide range of offensive maneuvers safely but convincingly. I was polite, respectful, never complained, and always willing to do whatever was asked of me. But for every moment of that time, I was also closely observing what people were doing, and soaking up knowledge like a sponge.

In retrospect, those few, laborious months in Tri-State were very important to me. I ended up having a pretty meteoric rise in the wrestling business, so being forced to spend that time at the beginning of my career, jerking the curtain, enhancing other people, and laying down for just about everyone I wrestled (many of whom couldn't have gotten a point on me on their best day in an amateur match) kept me humble. I learned the business the way one *should* learn it—by starting from the bottom and working my way up.

As time went on and I paid my dues, I began to be booked into fifteen-minute draws at some of the house shows. I was given the chance to call some spots, show a few moves, and try to win over the crowds. Eventually, I even got a couple of wins.

Then, one day, Terry Funk came in to work a main event in one of the towns in the Tri-States territory. For some reason, he paid attention to me, and we got into a conversation in the dressing room. He knew I was a rookie and asked how I was doing. I told him that I was learning a lot, but I quietly admitted to him that I was getting pretty run down from living in my car. I didn't know it at the time, but Terry and his brother Dory (who was known as "Junior") were running the Amarillo territory. Before our conversation was finished, Terry gave me his phone number and told me to call him when I was ready to make a move. It was the first meaningful contact I made in the wrestling business—and, as will become clear as you read on, it turned out to be a really important one.

A couple of weeks later, Grizzly came into the dressing room and told us that Terry Funk wanted a couple of us to do jobs for him on TV in Amarillo.

I was one of the guys selected.

Anxious to explore something different, I made the long, hot drive from Shreveport to Amarillo. That set in motion a long chain of events that, one to the next, would ultimately take me all the way to the world championship.

It was the end of the beginning.

6

Getting Funked Up (Amarillo, 1974)

"No one has ever attained outstanding success in anything without . . . having been reinforced through contact with others that allowed them to grow and expand."

—Napoleon Hill, "Establish a Mastermind Alliance"

———•◆•———

The Funks ran their television tapings in a small studio in Amarillo, Texas. When we arrived, the original plan was for me to work in a television "squash" match with one of the territory's biggest stars—"Captain Redneck" Dick Murdoch—and for my fellow job guy, Jerry Usher, to do the same for Terry Funk. But when we got there, as I was getting changed in the dressing room, Terry walked in, remembered me from that night in the Tri-States territory, took one look at my physique, and totally changed the plan.

Now I was going to be working with Terry on television. But instead of squashing me, Terry explained, he was going to give me my first "push" in the business. Terry explained that he was going take me in the ring, play a little cat and mouse, and toy around with me like he was *going* to squash me, but then swerve the fans by giving me a big comeback, letting me rally against him, show a flurry of moves, catch a couple of near falls, and then go toe-to-toe with him and take him all the way to a ten-minute television time limit draw.

It is important to note here that, at the time this happened, Terry Funk had already established himself as one of the top wrestlers in the world and was the Western States Heavyweight Champion—the Amarillo territory's top honor. About a year later, Terry would go on to capture the

NWA World Heavyweight Championship from Jack Brisco in Miami—so to get an opportunity like this in the ring with Terry was a *very* big deal. Other than the one conversation I had with him back in Louisiana, I didn't know Terry at all, so needless to say, I was both shocked and incredibly grateful that he was offering me a push like this.

The match itself was a huge success—due entirely to Terry's brilliant booking idea. Fortunately, since television from the Tri-States area did not reach Amarillo, the Amarillo fans hadn't seen me job for the entire Tri-States roster, so I was a total unknown to them. All they saw when I came into the ring in the studio that day was a fresh-faced, young rookie with a good physique.

This time, when I came out to the ring, I completed my vault over the top rope and played to the fans a little bit, jumping around and smiling and shaking a fist, trying to draw their empathy. The crowd's response was predictably understated. They didn't know what to make of me—whether I was just another jobber who was going to get squashed by Terry, or whether I might be something different. They were waiting for Terry and me to tell them a story that would lead them to whatever emotional reaction they might have.

Terry called the match in such a way that the energy from the crowd built slowly but steadily. Initially, he dominated me to make the fans think they were watching just another squash. Then, he gave me a couple of moves here and there to tease a comeback, but then crushed it. Then he built it up again, higher this time, and then smothered it again before it could completely ignite. By the time I mounted my big unexpected comeback and Terry actually let the reigns loose and let me run, the crowd was cheering wildly for this unknown young rookie, sensing that they were watching something new and exciting.

The fans were eating out of our hands.

When Terry couldn't put me away before the ten-minute time limit expired, and the bell rang signaling the end of the match, they were on their feet and jumping up and down screaming and cheering.

Terry Funk made me that day.

Why? Because Terry Funk was the master of crowd psychology. He had an idea that he thought would work, laid it out meticulously by teasing the fans and building it slowly and carefully until it burst into flame. I had played my part well—providing the credible look and the properly executed moves, selling what I should, and then rallying in order to make the story believable in the eyes of the fans.

But this little example shows the incredible power and potential of good and creative booking.

That ten minutes in the ring with Terry taught me one of the most important and enduring lessons that I ever learned in the wrestling business: that the business survives by the constant ebb and flow of the tide—whether in a single match, in a feud or series of matches, in the booking strategy for an entire territory, or in a career. You had to be willing to give in order to get, and when that was done properly, both wrestlers and, in reality, an entire territory would become more successful because of it.

Of course, Terry's actions, while incredibly generous toward me, weren't purely magnanimous. By giving me this comeback against him on television, he was also birthing his territory a credible new babyface. By showing the fans that I could go toe-to-toe with him, he was effectively telling the fans: "Hey, get behind this kid. He's the real deal, and you should buy a ticket to see him if he wrestles in your town, because he has the skills to beat anyone on any given day." And that unpredictability, of course—the hope that the underdog might pull the upset and win—is what puts butts in seats—and drives the success of our business.

After seeing how the fans in the studio reacted to our time-limit draw on television, Terry Funk invited me to stay in Amarillo and work the territory. So I went back to Tri-States, gave my notice, finished my dates for Leroy, and then drove to Amarillo to begin a new phase of my career.

Having lived frugally enough to save up a little bit of money, and after being assured by Terry that the payoffs in the Amarillo territory would be good enough, not just to get me out of my car trunk, but to actually put a real roof over my head, I took a room at the Holiday Inn in Amarillo for $6 a night. The hotel was right across the street from a country western bar called "The Joker" — a rough place where all the boys went after the matches.

This change of scene, however, presented me with a new problem. Unless you were looking to get your ass kicked, you couldn't go into The Joker without a pair of cowboy boots on.

I didn't have any cowboy boots. All I had was a well-worn cheap pair of sneakers.

I was literally living day-to-day, and although I had finally been able to stop sleeping with a bat in the trunk of my car, I didn't even have enough money to buy a secondhand pair of boots at the local thrift store.

Dick Murdoch heard about my situation and welcomed me to the territory by presenting me with a brand new pair of cowboy boots. Murdoch was a big deal in Amarillo — at the time, he was working a big angle with a guy named Jim Dillon, who would later go on to become better known, in the '80s and '90s, as James J. Dillon — the leader of the "Four Horsemen" in the NWA. I have never forgotten that simple act of kindness that allowed me to feel like one of the boys for the first time.

Amarillo was a really hot developmental territory in the NWA in the '70s. The Funks lived there, and Murdoch and Dillon were both based in Amarillo, and as such, all of those guys had homes or apartments there. The young guys, myself included, thought that was the coolest thing — to actually have your own bed and your own furniture in a territory where you were wrestling. That concept would remain foreign to me for several more years — but I was grateful just to be out of the trunk of my car.

Back at this time in the early '70s, almost no one in the wrestling business had a written contract, or any kind of guaranteed tenure in a territory. The only thing you could really rely on was that if you got invited to work a territory, you'd be there for at least two weeks. This was because a territory typically needed at least two weeks to wind up any storylines and arrange for comings and goings in the bookings, and in the television interviews, newsletters, or newspaper ads hyping the local house shows. When Terry asked me to work Amarillo, I really had no idea how long I'd be staying.

As had been in the case in Tri-States, each week at the TV taping, I would just be given a list of dates that I'd be wrestling and the names of the towns and the buildings I'd be wrestling in. As soon as the TV taping was over, the wrestlers would pile into cars and head off to ride the circuit for the week. That's the way the business was—it ran pretty much week to week, and hand to mouth.

My first date on the road was a match in Lubbock against a guy named "Mr. Wrestling." When I arrived in the dressing room and saw the booking sheet, I was shocked to learn that I was going to be "going over" Mr. Wrestling by pinfall! Mr. Wrestling was a big name back then, and I was a very green rookie who had just arrived in the territory, so winning a match like this was a big deal. But Terry liked the way I looked, liked the way the people had responded to me during our TV match, and wanted to keep the momentum behind me. Terry had visions of how he wanted to use me in the territory, and jobbing me out my first day out on the road, even to someone as well-respected as Mr. Wrestling, wouldn't have allowed the momentum to keep building behind me. Terry never told me anything about what his plan *was* for me, of course. He just told me that he just wanted me to act like a wrestler in the ring, and to keep doing what I had done in the ring that day in the studio in Amarillo against him.

The shocked fans in Lubbock responded to my pinfall victory over Mr. Wrestling with even more enthusiasm than they had shown in the television studio. Now, we really had something!

Although the Amarillo territory was also known for some wild and woolly brawls, feuds, and Texas Death matches, the Funks never forgot that first and foremost, the name on the marquee was wrestling—and while the punching and kicking and brawling definitely had a place in the sport—the best stories were told in the ring through the pacing and psychology of chain wrestling. I think that was one of the primary reasons the Funks were so successful in developing talent in Amarillo, why so many guys wanted to have the chance to work down there, and why the fans supported the territory so solidly for such a long time.

Remembering those days, I am very grateful to the Funks for helping to set me on my way. Dory Funk Senior had passed away a couple of months before I got there, so Terry and Junior had become the bosses, and Murdoch, who was the territory's other major draw, was highly respected among the boys and frequently solicited for booking ideas. I was just a young, naïve kid. As I did in Tri-States, I trained hard with the weights every day, did a lot of running, worked really hard to keep myself in great shape, and made every move in every match against every opponent look as good as I could possibly make it.

I also listened closely to every bit of advice I got from Terry and Dory and Dick. All three of them were masters at knowing the personality of each town on the circuit, and reading each town's crowd from week to week. They would frequently know what the fans wanted in a given week just from the vibe or the buzz in the building before bell time. Other times, they would gauge the crowd's reaction to the early matches, listening to the people, understanding what they wanted, and delivering it to them in the main events.

I knew the people were taking to my fast-paced amateur moves, so I just went out there night after night, trying to execute those moves crisply and with lightning speed, all the while listening to their reactions and trying to learn what else they wanted to see from me. The proper mindset, as explained to me by Terry and Junior, was to listen to the crowd each night after your flurries and high spots, and figure out how to best entertain them. And every night, and every town, and every crowd was a little different—depending on who was there, what was in the news, how the weather was, and, of course, on who your opponent was. Some nights, the crowds liked the straight amateur chain wrestling. Some nights, they wanted the high-flying stuff. And some nights, they just wanted the emotional release that only a full-out brawl could provide.

One of the other things that Terry and Junior and Dick began to teach me during my time in Amarillo was about the pacing, not just of your own match, but of the entire card. The idea was for each match to sequentially build the energy in the building until the crowd was at a fever pitch for the main event—and then, of course, to leave something unresolved for next time so that the fans would buy tickets to the next week's show be primed to.

If you were working the opening match, your job was to warm up the crowd—give them a pretty basic wrestling match, with a few nice moves mixed in—but being careful not to rob the later matches on the card of any of their energy. By way of example, you never wanted to use the finishing move of someone higher up on the card in the middle of your match because doing so would rob that move of its mystique. Although I frequently used the piledriver in my matches, I would never use that move if I was wrestling in one of the early matches on a card because that is too much of a high spot for an early match placement. Early matches were for headlocks, hiptosses, and chain wrestling. The highest you would want to get in an early match was, perhaps, to throw a dropkick or to do a crisscross into the ropes. The idea was for everyone on the card, each match, one to the next, to work together to build the energy, and for each successive match to draw a hotter crowd response than the one before it.

In some towns and territories, where there were intermissions, the promoters would put a hot match—sometimes even the hottest match of the night—right before intermission. Properly executed by its participants, that match would blow the roof off the place, and then send the people into intermission in a frenzy, where they would immediately flood the box office windows to buy tickets for the next week's show, and then work off some of that energy at the concession stands buying beer, food, photographs, and whatever other paraphernalia the promoters were selling. Then, when the card resumed, the first match after intermission would start again to build the energy toward a final blowoff match at the end of the card—which would often (but not always) see the babyface win in order to send the fans home happy. Or, of course, the match would end with a cliffhanger in order to being the fans back to see a rematch, or the match in some other form.

Knowing the "business side of the business," as opposed to simply being a good technical wrestler, was, of course, critical to becoming a seasoned professional who could understand his role night to night and execute that role appropriately to ensure the success of the entire card. You can't really teach the business side of the business in training camp. That was something you had to pick up from the masters, night by night, in the Elks Halls and high school gyms, and ice rinks along the way. Coming out of Tri-States, I didn't really have any feel for that—but it is definitely something that was emphasized in Amarillo—and something that Terry, Junior, and Dick took the time to make sure I understood.

Amarillo was also the place where I learned to speak "Carny." I was driving from Amarillo to Albuquerque one day with Ken Farber, one of the Amarillo territory's referees, when he turned to me and asked if I knew how to speak "Kizzarney." Needless to say, I had no idea what he was talking about—so he explained to me what Carny was and how and when to use it.

Carny was a secret mode of encoded speech that professional wrestlers (and originally the workers at the old traveling carnivals from which the term originates) used to communicate in the ring, with the referee, and in public when we didn't want anyone else to understand what we were saying. It's really pretty easy, but unless you know what you're looking for and what the "code" actually is, you can be looking right at someone speaking in Carny and not have the first clue what he is saying.

The way it works is that you introduce a nonsense syllable or syllables—usually "izz" or "e-azz" but it can be any syllable agreed upon by the carnies—between the first letter and the rest of the word, or between the first syllable and the rest of the word. So, for example, if we were in the ring, and I wanted to communicate to you that "it's time to go home," I would say, "Teazzime to geazzo heazzome." Carny was used in the ring if the referee needed to communicate something to the wrestlers, or if wrestlers needed to communicate to each other within earshot of the fans. But we also talked Carny in bars, nightclubs, airports—anywhere we wanted to communicate privately with each other when there were marks around.

Another thing I did not fully appreciate back then was understanding how much politicking was going on behind the scenes, with guys trying to ingratiate themselves with the bookers in order to get better angles, or better spots on the cards. Some of the boys in the dressing room were always working the promoters or the booker for angles, spots, and titles, or were constantly grousing about the way they were being used. Early on, I made the decision not to get involved in any of that, to understand my role on a particular card, whatever it was, and then to simply go out and execute my match to the best of my ability. Maybe it was naïve, but I trusted that if I got over with the people and did my job for the card as a whole—that the rest would take care of itself.

As the days stretched into weeks in the Amarillo territory, the Funks continued to put me over, and I started to build a relationship with the fans on the circuit, who were now waiting to greet me at the arena doors, gathering in my corner of the ring for pre-match autographs, and cheering for me with increased energy. I had also been accepted by the boys in the dressing room, and was getting included in the carpools between towns to save money, and asked to go out and have a few beers after the matches. It felt good to be part of the group down there. I felt more at home in Amarillo than I did in any other territory in my career.

During my time in Amarillo, I called Corki three times a week from a payphone somewhere out on the circuit. She was still back in West Fargo, North Dakota, where, right out of college, she had secured her dream job as a teacher and gymnastics coach. She would always ask me how things were going, and I would tell her that I was having fun and doing well, and learning a lot. Corki wasn't smart to the business back then—she didn't really understand what it was all about, and her father understood it even less. But on one of those calls, she announced that she missed me too much for us to stay apart any longer, and so she was quitting her job and coming down to Amarillo to join me. She attached a U-Haul trailer to her Volkswagen Beetle, filled it with all of her earthly belongings, and then pointed the car south and made the long drive to Amarillo to be with me.

Corki and I have been together ever since.

In the Amarillo territory, the big territorial belt was the Western States Heavyweight Championship. Unless the NWA World Heavyweight Champion or the International Heavyweight Champion was on a swing through the territory, the Western States Heavyweight Championship match was usually the main event at the top of the card, and the contests and feuds, or both, that developed around that belt were primarily used to draw the houses out on the circuit. When I got to the Amarillo territory in the spring of 1974, Terry was the Western States Heavyweight Champion, which made all the sense in the world to me, because Terry knew what he had to do to draw a house, how to develop angles, and how to keep the people coming back.

One afternoon, after I'd been wrestling in the territory for about three weeks, we pulled into Abilene, Texas, which was our weekly Friday night stop. Abilene was run by a promoter who was very close to the Funks. I had been scheduled to wrestle Terry there for the Western States Heavyweight Championship, and in the dressing room a few hours before the matches, Terry pulled me aside.

"You know, Bobby—these fans are really taking to you," he said. "I just talked it over with Junior, and we think that in order to keep that going and to get this to the next level, we're going to put you over tonight and get the championship on you for awhile."

I was shocked.

Less than a month before, I had been laying down for every guy on the roster in Tri-States, and sleeping in the trunk of my car with a baseball bat. Now, I was about to pin Terry Funk and become the lead guy in the Amarillo territory.

The tide was coming in.

The Funks had some really good performers in Amarillo at the time, and it made me feel pretty good about myself that they had chosen me for a run with the strap, especially so soon. I also think they were doing their friend in Abilene a favor by having the title change in his town—because whenever a title changed in a town, it would bump the gates there for a good while afterward.

As hard as it may be to believe, at the time, Terry Funk was a very popular babyface champion in the Amarillo territory. The fans had not seen him pinned very often, and he wasn't about to let just anyone walk into his territory and pin him. But that night in Abilene, Terry finally came clean. He explained to me that both he and Junior saw something special in me, and they thought that I would really connect with the area fans by scoring an underdog, upset pinfall victory over him and taking the championship.

And so it was decided.

Terry and I had a very clean *wrestling* match that night. There wasn't any punching or kicking or eye gouging—because neither one of us wanted to turn the other heel, which can easily happen in a babyface match if either one of the wrestlers is perceived to be adopting heel tactics to get the advantage. So we just did some good old-fashioned back and forth chain wrestling, letting the cheers of the crowd be our guide. Eventually, we had the people at a high point, and Terry gave the signal that it was time to "go home" with the finish he had dreamed up for this, which was, in essence, a prolonged false finish followed by a surprise ending.

I had Terry up for the atomic kneedrop, which I had recently adopted as my finishing hold and which others in the territory had been selling to the moon for me on our previous runs around the territory. Terry, though, was holding onto the ropes in an attempt to block the execution of the move. The fans were on the edges of their seats, cheering and yelling and dying to see what was going to happen next. We held the move there long enough to get the crowd to a frenzied peak, and then, just at the right moment, I abandoned the effort and just dropped Terry into a hard side suplex and quickly covered him for the pin next to the ropes.

The referee counted one, two, three, and it was over.

The crowd was stunned. They were screaming and cheering and jumping up and down in the stands.

The fans in Abilene could not believe what they had just seen. If I was sitting in the stands, I would have been shocked too. I had only been in the territory for three weeks, and I had just beaten Terry Funk to become the Western States Heavyweight Champion — my first championship as a professional.

The crowd was roaring. The upset was selling.

Terry had given me a lot of offense in the match, and basically made me look like a million bucks. Again, this was part of the ebb and flow of a feud and a territory. Terry and Junior had decided that they were going to push me. I got the early draw against Terry on television to establish credibility, then took that momentum out onto the road and beat a lot of good competition around the circuit, leading up to this title match in Abilene. By letting me catch that upset fall on him for the belt, Terry elevated my status with the fans to the next level. Did it rob Terry of any of his status? Not really. It was a hard-fought, highly entertaining match with a quick and somewhat fluky, yet decisive, finish. Enough to get my credibility to the next level, while also leaving Terry with more than enough credibility to come back and challenge for the belt in rematches around the circuit and ensure future business for the territory.

The title win also had the not-at-all-insignificant economic benefit of moving me to the main-event position on virtually every card that didn't feature either the NWA World Heavyweight Champion, who was only in the territory a few times a year, or a title defense by the International Heavyweight Champion, who came through every couple of months. I began to earn the first really meaningful money since I left Minnesota.

Looking back with the perspective of time, even though I would hold the Western States title for only a short time, this was the moment that signaled the end of my time as an inexperienced rookie in the world of professional wrestling, and propelled me forward as a serious wrestler in the eyes of the fans, and someone who was now being relied upon to draw houses for the promotion.

Amarillo was a great place to learn how to tell a story during a match—starting with nothing and creating love and hatred, finding a peak, and then delivering a finish that left the people wanting more. Terry and Junior, like their father Dory Funk Sr. before them, emphasized that part of the art. That part of the learning experience, coupled with the fact that both Dory Sr. and Junior had held the NWA World Heavyweight Championship, made Amarillo a great territory for developing talent.

Terry and Junior also enjoyed a very good rapport with the promoters in most of the other NWA territories, which made talent exchanges into and out of Amarillo a regular occurrence. There was always tremendous talent down there, and while I was there, I got to wrestle and learn from a lot of great wrestlers of varying styles, including both Terry and Junior, Stan Hansen, Tommy "Jumbo" Tsuruta, Pat O'Connor, the great Mexican wrestler Ricky Romero, J. J. Dillon, and Kurt Von Steiger.

The Funks were also very big in Japan, and at the time I arrived in the territory, they had developed a new professional relationship with Japanese promoter Shohei "Giant" Baba and his promotion, All-Japan pro wrestling. Through this arrangement, the Funks would book Amarillo guys to work over in Japan, and Baba would send one or two of his hot young rookies over to train with the Funks and learn the American style.

In 1974, Tommy "Jumbo" Tsuruta, who would later go on to become the AWA World Heavyweight Champion, came into the territory. Tsuruta was on the Japanese Olympic wrestling team at the 1972 Olympic Games in Munich. Given that Tommy and I were both trained in amateur wrestling, the two of us spent a lot of time training on the mats and working on things together while he was in Amarillo.

When Tommy returned to Japan, he told Baba about me and insisted that I should be invited to come over and wrestle a tour in Japan. At the time, Japan was known to be a tough place for a young American wrestler to "get over." It would often take years of tours and jobbing to the Japanese stars before an American wrestler would be put over. Because of Tommy's kind reference, however, I didn't have to go out and prove myself for years in the ring in Japan. Even though he was a rookie, because he had made the Japanese Olympic team, Tommy had instant credibility with Baba, and Baba had a lot of respect for him.

The International Heavyweight Championship was created and used by Baba and the Funks as a bridge during their talent trade. When the International Champion was in the territory and on the card, he was on top. At the time I was there, Ciclon "Cyclone" Negro was the International Champion. I had several matches with him for the International Heavyweight Championship, and really enjoyed working with him. He was a big man who knew how to wrestle and could really move. He had wrestled all over the world, particularly in Australia and New Zealand, and because of that, he had learned different styles and ways of calling matches from the people he had worked with over there. He was an artist in the ring.

Outside the ring, I was a little leery of Cyclone because he was kind of a tough guy who seemed to attract more than his share of trouble . . . but inside the ring, he was always very professional. He knew that in most of the places he went as the champion, his match was the main event— and because of that, he was always oriented toward making sure that the people got their money's worth out of his match. Cyclone is not nearly as well known in the United States as some of the other top guys of our era, but I'd put his skills right up there. He was a good hand who didn't mind traveling the world, could work heel or face, and worked well with all styles, shapes, and sizes. I think that's why Baba and the Funks chose to put him on top.

Cyclone worked frequently in Japan, but that belt also provided a lot of booking flexibility in the United States. As the "international" champion, he could (and did) travel to different territories as part of talent exchanges, and defend the title in other NWA territories where his in-ring skills immediately established his credibility, even to a crowd that had never seen him before. He also became an immediately credible challenger to the NWA World Heavyweight Champion, and provided some additional booking interest by offering the possibility of a champion-versus-champion tilt.

The Funks also maintained a very cordial relationship with St. Louis promoter Sam Muchnick, so they were able to trade talent with Sam quite a bit to keep new faces coming in and keep the booking fresh and interesting.

It was also during those early days in Amarillo that I started what would become my career-long tradition of using my free time to visit with kids in the local hospitals, or finding local youth wrestling teams in the towns we visited, meeting their coaches, and helping to train the kids. The drives from town to town in the Amarillo territory weren't that bad, so I usually had a good part of each day free to spend as I wanted. A lot of the guys liked to get to the towns early and either play cards, work out, or spend time socializing with the ladies.

Having been given such a big break down in Amarillo, and having been so surprisingly and warmly embraced by the fans down there, I was on top of the world and wanting to find a way to give something back. As you now know, I spent a lot of my early years living on the edge. My life could have gone either way except for the fact that I had a couple of teachers and coaches who had cared enough to save me from myself. With this first taste of professional success and kids now waiting to shake my hand or get my autograph, I recognized that I might now be in the position to do the same thing for others.

I resolved that I wanted to try and use my story to inspire other kids to stay in school, find their passion, and stay out of trouble.

I just started doing these things because it made sense to me. No promoter ever talked to me about these things, but apparently, I was the only athlete down there who was doing these things regularly. People were responding so positively, which only made me want to do more of it. For me, I think that realization represented my passage into adulthood. I was a professional wrestler now, and I was on my own. I no longer had my parents or a teacher or a coach looking over my shoulder and telling me what I should be doing. There was no one making sure that I was following a proper diet, not drinking too much beer at night, getting my daily workouts in, or staying true to my core principles. Now, the only person that I had to answer to was myself.

In early May 1974, Eddie Graham came to Amarillo. Eddie was the boss of the Florida-based NWA promotion Florida Championship Wrestling. He and the Funks had a very close relationship, routinely trading talent and good-natured ribbings. At this point in their long history of going back and forth, I think the Funks had most recently ended up keeping some of Eddie's best young talent a little too long, and Eddie was looking to exert some revenge.

At the time Eddie visited, I was the Western States Heavyweight Champion, and Eddie walked into the dressing room with me and yelled out, "Hey Bobby, you're coming back to Florida with me!" He did that to serve notice to Terry and Junior that he intended to get even with them. Little did I know that later that year, the rib would end up coming true!

I got to carry the Western States championship for about ten weeks, and during that time, had some terrific matches with people like J. J. Dillon, Junior, Tommy Tsuruta, Chris Taylor, and Pat O'Connor. I also teamed with Dick Murdoch and Junior at various times. Those were exciting days, and things really got rolling along.

Stan Hansen was also in Amarillo coming up through the ranks at the same time that I was. Stan was a couple of years ahead of me in terms of overall experience and eventually, because of the Funks' relationship with Baba, he became a really big star in Japan. Stan went to college in Texas and he was from nearby Borger, originally—although I don't think he trained as much with the Funks as I did. There was always a little bit of tension between Stan and me about that because he literally grew up in that territory, and yet I came in there and got the push. That deep-seeded animosity would eventually boil over in 1981 when Stan came to the WWF for a series of matches with me at Madison Square Garden over the WWF title.

Karl Von Steiger was another monster heel in the territory at the time. Karl played a goose-stepping Nazi, and he was very good at it. He wasn't just all punching and kicking though—he was big and imposing and knew how to wrestle. The memories of World War II were still fresh enough down in Texas back then that the people utterly despised him. He was a good person for me to work with, because it was easy for me, as the young American rookie, to get the people's total sympathy and for Karl to bring the full fury of the people's heat down on himself. That recipe proved to be box office gold.

Going through that process with Karl was a very valuable learning experience for me, as it gave me my first real exposure to wrestling's well-worn concept of the ethnic heel, and how to play off of that as a babyface. I had had a good run, but now the Funks were setting up for the next big thing—a new feud between Karl, as the hated German heel, and Dick Murdoch as the outlaw Texas cowboy and soon-to-be American hero.

Once more, the ebb and flow of wrestling was calling for a change, and this time, it was my turn to make it happen for someone else. The plan was to have Karl cheat, but to beat me pretty convincingly for the championship—and then to mock me as an American who couldn't beat him. I dropped the Western States title to Karl on May 22, 1974, in Lubbock, selling like crazy in the process. The next night, I had a rematch with Von Steiger in Amarillo, and once again, sold like crazy for Karl—so that the fans would see him as a seemingly unbeatable villain. I then stepped out of the way as Dick Murdoch adopted the role of the unlikely babyface promising to liberate the Amarillo territory from Nazi tyranny.

One week later, with everything properly set up, Murdoch beat the tar out of Von Steiger in Amarillo, reclaimed the Western States Heavyweight Championship for the people, and the tide rolled in again.

The observant long-time fan will note the remarkable similarity between this setup and the storyline we used nearly twenty years later at Madison Square Garden when another hated ethnic heel, Khosrow Vaziri (The Iron Sheik), ended my nearly six-year run with the WWF championship, only to have another American hero, Hulk Hogan, step in the following month and vanquish the hated Iranian to win the title back for the USA. Once a successful storyline—always a successful storyline . . .

As I have already mentioned, Dick Murdoch treated me like a son during my time in the Amarillo territory. Aside from buying me my first pair of cowboy boots, Dick also let me ride with him from one town to another. He had a pickup truck with a gun rack on the back and a big pitbull he used to ride around with. He was also really into country western music—especially Tammy Wynette.

Back in those days, though, there was something about Dick's life outside the wrestling world that was tugging at him. Dick clearly missed his family when he was out on the road, and he was on the road a lot back then. When I was riding with him, he never wanted to talk about his family or anything other than the wrestling business and country music. The only thing he would say to me, over and over again, was that it was critical to keep your family life separate from the business. I think it was one of those unspoken "learn from my mistakes" moments, delivered from the wise veteran to the idealistic rookie with the young girlfriend.

I took Dick's advice to heart, which is why, during my forty years in professional wrestling, Corki and I always kept our family far away from the wrestling business. In fact, in all of those years, Corki saw me wrestle only a handful of times. I also tried to shield Corki from associating at all with just about anyone in the business—and to be honest, she wasn't hard to convince about that!

A lot of the women who were married to or associated with wrestlers were actually living off the wrestling and the wrestlers—most of them didn't have their own lives, interests, or careers. Corki was the total opposite—she was a very independent and educated woman, and as soon as she got down to Amarillo, she set about on finding a job and building her own life for herself.

It should also come as no surprise that there are things behind the scenes in the wrestling business that are not conducive to the stability of a wrestler's family—and the wrestlers' wives and girlfriends were always talking about that. A lot of them were very gossipy, sharing road stories while simultaneously worrying about what their own husbands or boyfriends were doing. In every town we stopped in, there were groups of young women hanging around outside the dressing rooms looking to meet wrestlers. Many of these women would literally throw themselves at you as you were arriving at or leaving the arenas. It was just one of the realities of the business.

There was also always a place in each town where the women would congregate after the matches—usually the bar at the motel where we would stay overnight. They knew when we would be there because the schedule was pretty regular and they'd be there on the same schedule if that was something you wanted to be involved in. I was completely committed to my relationship with Corki, so that scene was not anything I ever got tangled up in. That was just another reason, though, why we thought it best for Corki to keep her distance from the business.

I did enjoy going out and raising heck with the boys after the matches. I liked to drink beer, and I could drink with the best of 'em. We played all kinds of games in the bars in those towns, played pool and darts, and just had a great time.

━══◆══━

Tommy Tsuruta's kind words to Baba earned me an invitation for the first of what would end up to be many opportunities to wrestle in Japan. My first trip was a long three-week tour from July 9–24, 1974, as part of the Amarillo/All-Japan talent exchange. We went over there in the heat of the Texas summer because the buildings in the Amarillo territory were not air-conditioned and it got so sweltering in those venues in July that it was hard to draw a good house no matter how good the card was.

That first trip to Japan was hard for me. It was my first time being overseas, and the thought of being in a foreign country for three weeks was both exciting and scary. I didn't have much money to allow me to explore the country, and I didn't really even have a proper suitcase to travel for that many days.

When I arrived in Tokyo, I was anxious to set up a routine, so I asked one of the guys where the gym was that the wrestlers used. He directed me to the place, and when I got to the building, the name, Hatch's Gym, seemed awfully familiar to me. I asked around, and suddenly realized why. As improbable as it sounds, Clark Hatch, the gym's owner, was, in fact, from my little hometown of Princeton, Minnesota!

The Hatch family was involved in construction, and I knew Clark's brother well from my childhood days in Princeton working on his crew. Clark had gone over to Japan during the war and stayed there when it ended and opened a gym. Needless to say, I logged a lot of time there over the years. Hatch's Gym became my "home away from home" whenever I was in Japan.

The first thing I had to learn on that initial foray into the Japanese rings was just how differently Japanese fans reacted to a professional wrestling match. In Louisiana, Texas, and New Mexico, which had been the geographic limit of my experience in professional wrestling to that point, I had grown accustomed to the southern fans being very boisterous and animated at the matches. American fans typically cheered wildly for the babyfaces and screamed and threw things at the heels. They were very emotional, wore their hearts on their sleeves, and always let you know what they were thinking. Back in the early to mid-1970s in Japan, however, when you would go to the ring, the fans in the arena would barely cheer at all—they just sat and watched. People over there were taught, from a young age, not to show emotion. As a wrestler, that cultural difference made it very hard to gauge the crowd's response to anything, so we used a style almost like shoot wrestling and tried to read faces and figure out how the fans were reacting.

As a young American wrestler going to Japan back then, it was also very important to do something to get the fans' and the promoters' attention. On my first visit, Baba asked me to wrestle Tommy Tsuruta in an amateur match in a little workout room over there. I think they wanted to see how I would fare against Tsuruta, who was Baba's up-and-coming young Japanese star.

Tommy was tall, but he didn't have a lot of strength—and at that time, I was at the peak of my power. I liked Tommy a lot, but I destroyed him on the mat. I felt kind of guilty about that, since Tommy's good word to Baba is what got me to Japan in the first place, but business was business, and I wasn't about to let Tommy beat me in a legitimate amateur match. Fortunately, he was good-natured about it.

I think that entire episode was a way for Baba to determine what kind of position they were going to put me in. The Japanese promoters really respected guys who knew what they were doing in the ring, and word of my victory over Tsuruta in that little amateur match got around the Japanese wrestling community very quickly. After that first tour, I never really had a problem either getting booked in Japan, or being treated well while I was over there.

On that first tour, however, I jobbed to everyone. I wrestled Tommy Tsuruta a bunch of times and put him over. I wrestled the Destroyer (Dick Beyer), who was legendary in Japan, and I also wrestled Danny Hodge at a carnival/circus kind of thing where we did a demonstration of amateur wrestling. Danny had been a silver medalist in the Melbourne Olympics (1956) and was one of the most competitive people I've ever met. We played a lot of cards over in Japan and Danny was ruthless—he wanted to win at everything. I also got to spend some time in the ring with the boss—Shohei "Giant" Baba—the man who ran the All-Japan promotion.

Baba was a very gentle man, but in the ring he could be hard to work with because of his size and because his repertoire of maneuvers was limited. There were only so many things you could do in the ring with a man who stood six feet ten inches tall and weighed 320 pounds. Baba also didn't like being taken off his feet too much, which compounded the difficulty in working with him.

I also got to spend some time on that first tour tag teaming with Mil Mascaras. Working with Mascaras taught me another one of professional wrestling's important lessons—how to protect your image in the ring and make sure you get enough of the action. Mascaras was already a big star, including a movie star, in his native Mexico—and I think all of that went to his head a little bit. In the ring, Mascaras always wanted to shine, and consequently, he sometimes forgot about the obligatory ebb and flow of action that was necessary to create an emotionally entertaining match.

Most of the people I worked with over the course of my career had the right intentions—namely to put on a good and entertaining match for the people each night, and not simply to protect their own character and make themselves look invincible. Mascaras, though, was different.

He really didn't like to sell much for his opponents in the ring, and I think that hurt the overall quality of his matches. Mil was a tremendous athlete, and had a fantastic look with his colorful capes and masks and wrestling pants. He also had a dazzling array of high-flying moves like dropkicks and bodyblocks and flying body presses and flying head scissors. The irony was that if the man had sold more in the ring for his opponents, to the point of looking vulnerable to defeat, his inevitable rallies and comebacks with those sensational moves would have been that much more spectacular. But because he sold so little, his matches tended to be shorter, and the dramatic arc of his matches was pretty flat.

When I was in the ring with Mascaras in a tag-team match, I literally had to fight to make sure I could get a little time in to make a few moves. You just knew that Mascaras was going to try to take the spotlight and not sell very much, so I usually tried to do the short-arm scissor and a couple of other memorable high spots that I knew the fans would remember.

Japanese fans were very interested in watching matches that were skillful, with people trying to get in and out of holds and you could almost see them squirming in their seats and moving while you moved. If they liked what you did in the ring, they would clap for you at the end—but they wouldn't show you much emotion during the match. That slowly evolved as people over there adopted the American style. In Japan, in those early years, they used to wrestle with the lights on in the arena, so everyone sat quietly. In America, by contrast, wrestling happened in a darkened arena with lights on over the ring—which made it easier for people to express their emotions without being self-conscious about it. Later, the Japanese adopted the American style of putting lights over the ring and darkening the arena so people started expressing their emotions more freely. Over time, wrestling in Japan became more like it is in America—but it took quite a while to get there.

Even though it was exciting for me to be over there, time in Japan seemed to pass quite slowly. Corki didn't go with me that time and I really missed her. We stayed at a big hotel in Tokyo, and took a bus to the buildings in the other cities where the matches occurred on the tour. I was a creature of habit by then, and I wasn't used to the food, which became a bit of an issue for me.

When I was on the road in Amarillo, I would eat two or three large meals a day. I was training hard with heavy weights, so I had to consume a lot of food. If Corki made a chicken, she would take her portion, and I would eat the rest of the chicken. Out on the road, I'd wake up in the morning and immediately look for a place to work out, and after the gym, I'd be looking to stock up on protein. I had cans of tuna fish with me at all times, and the most important tool I had in the car with me was a can opener. I also drank a lot of milk—maybe a half a gallon at a time—for the protein and the calcium. I also carried hard-boiled eggs on the road with me for the same reason. In the afternoon, we'd drive to the town where we'd be wrestling that night and immediately head for the place where we could get a big slab of prime rib.

In Japan, however, no one ate like that. The Japanese people were eating sushi and soba noodles and things like that, and that threw my diet for a loop, because I really wasn't used to it. I ate every kind of fish they had over there. I didn't mind fish, but I think that is part of the reason that people started bringing protein powder with them on tours of Japan. Milk wasn't really very big over there either because there wasn't a lot of space to graze cows—so those were two staples missing from my diet.

I also missed being out there on the road by myself in my own car, being able to make my own choices about when I would come and go, when I would eat, and when I would work out and arrive at the arena. In Japan, we were always on a bus, and that forced you into the community on the bus, which I didn't necessarily want to be a part of. For some people in the wrestling business, the camaraderie in the dressing room or on the bus was the entire reason they were in the business.

Not for me.

I stayed in the Amarillo territory into the fall of 1974. It was a time of incredible personal growth for me—and I picked up a lot of very important knowledge and lessons down there that would help me throughout my days in the wrestling business. The Funks were big on letting a young wrestler evolve into a character with time rather than pulling an idea off the rack and just telling you what character they wanted you to portray. They also focused on getting you to excel at a few particular maneuvers unique to you, and then, once you had that foundation, building on that repertoire of maneuvers, a couple at a time, so that you would always had something in reserve. We developed a repertoire of "go to" moves, and then pushed ourselves to work outward from there, learning and perfecting more moves to add to our repertoire. We learned how to work a shoot-style chain wrestling match, as well as a back-alley brawl, so that we would always have something reliable to draw on to entertain the fans. Terry and Junior hammered into us the importance of having a backup plan in case what you were doing in the ring on a particular night wasn't selling with the fans in the building.

Another thing the Funks taught me was how important it was, as a young wrestler, to find a place out of sight of the fans where you could watch the matches that the veteran guys at the top of the card were having. The point, of course, was to learn how the veterans put a match together, engaged with the fans—particularly on nights when their initial approach to the match wasn't grabbing the crowd—and how they adapted their approach to give the fans what they wanted. The fact is, there are only so many scenarios that can happen in the interaction between the wrestlers in the ring, and the crowd watching the match. By mastering those different scenarios and becoming facile at moving between them when the fans demanded it, you could be confident in your ability to adapt to what they wanted and to avoid delivering a stinker that caused them to boo you or chant "boring!"

Getting the *"boring!"* chant was the kiss of death for a wrestler and the surest sign of laziness or a lack of adaptability. Even in a curtain-jerker, there were *always* ways to give a raucous crowd what they wanted without stealing the thunder of the guys further up the card. All of this focus on the fundamentals of crowd psychology was the reason why, from the bottom up, so many of the guys who trained in Amarillo went on to have very successful careers in the wrestling business.

Going into the ring for close to an hour with guys like Terry and Junior and Dick Murdoch—who were very talented guys in terms of telling a story in the ring and making it interesting for the people—was like going to school and getting an education in the wrestling business and making a little bit of money at the same time. Some nights, we made only $30 or $40—but other nights we made $100 or more, and wrestling six nights a week, we were able to make a respectable living. My days in the Amarillo territory were a wonderful experience that gave me many of the tools that were critical to my success as I moved on in my career—and, of course, I will be forever indebted to Terry Funk for seeing something in me, rescuing me from the obscurity of the Tri-States territory, and giving me my first break in the business.

One night at the TV tapings in Amarillo, Eddie Graham, the majority owner of Florida Championship Wrestling, was back in town. Graham and his minority owner, Jim Barnett, who owned Georgia Championship Wrestling, and the Funks had a longstanding tradition of swapping talent. That night, Terry came to me and told me that I would be going to Florida "for a couple of weeks" to work for Graham and Barnett.

It was a strange feeling to be leaving Amarillo, even for just a short break. Corki and I had fallen into a nice routine, and even though we were still living in the Holiday Inn, the place had started to feel like home to us. Corki took a leave of absence from her job working as a gymnastics instructor at Nards Gymnastics Club, and came to Florida with me. Fully anticipating that we'd be back, but not wanting to keep paying nightly rent at the Holiday Inn when we weren't there, we left many of our personal things that we had brought down with us from Minnesota in the custody of one of my biggest fans in Amarillo.

We would never return.

Fitting the Mold

Bobby Backlund came in here and immediately, from the very start, you could tell he was different. Sure, he was in phenomenal physical condition and he knew how to wrestle, but he also wanted to do things the right way. We never smartened up anyone in the Amarillo area unless we felt like they would be an asset to the business. We didn't push people that we didn't think were good people. We were always looking for good guys who could take care of themselves, and take care of an area, and take care of a belt if someone came up and tried to double-cross them. And Bobby fit that mold. We just loved him. We thought the world of him and we did whatever we could do to further him along in the business. There were definitely certain things that we taught to Bobby and did for Bobby that we didn't do for everyone. Hell, we would have loved to have kept Bobby in the Amarillo area for a lot longer—but it wasn't in his best interest to stay. He had learned what he was going to learn from us about the business, and it was time for him to spread his wings. I remember him leaving Amarillo with Corki and headed for Florida, and I knew that Bobby was going to go places.

—Terry Funk

7

When Two Weeks Last Forever
(Florida, 1974)

"There are many travelers on the road to happiness.
You will need their cooperation, and they will need yours."

—Napoleon Hill, "Inspire Teamwork"

———————

Before heading to Florida, Corki and I drove back home to Minnesota for a few days of vacation and to visit our parents. At Terry Funk's suggestion, while I was at home in Minnesota, I called Verne Gagne and told him I would be around for a few days, so he kindly arranged for me to work a couple of dates just to stay sharp and keep a few dollars in my pocket. During that brief trip, I got to have a match in Fargo where I went to college, and a match in St. Paul. I also stopped in to see Eddie Sharkey, work out with some of his new recruits, and share some of what I had learned during my first year out on the road.

After that brief respite, Corki and I drove to Tampa, Florida. The plan was for us to spend "a couple of weeks" there working with some of the Florida guys. At Eddie Graham's suggestion, we rented a little apartment on Armenia Street very close to the Sportatorium. It was a one-room efficiency with a little pool in the middle of the complex surrounded by the apartment buildings. The apartment was basically like a hotel room except that the rent was by the week rather than by the night. Because we had left our table back in Amarillo, we grabbed an old electrical spool off the side of the road to use as our kitchen table!

Corki and I got married by a justice of the peace in Tampa on October 31, 1974. It just felt like the right time to take the plunge!

Most days, I rode a bike from our apartment complex to the Tampa armory or to Harry Smith's gym to work out. Eddie Graham, his son Mike, and Jim Barnett all had their offices upstairs at the Sportatorium in Tampa which, despite its grandiose name, was really just a small building that held a ring and enough room for about one hundred people in the audience for the TV tapings. Despite its small size, though, the Sportatorium looked good on TV.

As had been the case in both Baton Rouge and in Amarillo, every so often, someone would come down to the Sportatorium looking to break into the wrestling business. Unless the person had been referred by a trusted professional wrestling trainer, however, Eddie always treated these individuals with suspicion.

He would always start them out with a workout with me.

Typically, I'd take them outside into the Florida heat and humidity and work out with them for an hour doing four or five hundred squats, pushups, sit ups, burpees, and jumping jacks. I would just work them out until they vomited, collapsed, or quit. Most people wouldn't survive that first workout with me, or if they did, they would never come back. While this may all sound like a form of inhuman hazing, it was a necessary part of the business—and I was kinder and gentler than most of the hookers and shooters who ran the proving grounds in the various territories. All I did was work people out until they dropped. Some of the other guardians of the business actually made it their business to seriously hurt these people.

You have to remember that this was back in the mid-1970s, when the mystique and uncertainty about the predetermined nature of professional wrestling was still a closely guarded secret. Because of that, people were always trying to "expose the business" by trying to infiltrate our ranks, learn the secrets, and then sell the truth of what we were doing and how we were doing it to the outside world. The only way to keep that from happening was to impose this "proving ground" between the outside world and those of us on the inside.

There was one guy in particular who I remember coming to the office wanting to try out. He asked me whether I would work out with him, but I was backed up with other obligations and I couldn't start with him for a week. He insisted, though, so Harley Race came down from the office and talked to him. Harley also tried to get this guy to wait a week until I could work out with him, because after taking a look at him, Harley knew that I would be able to turn him away from the business by just doing a workout with him that he couldn't possibly survive. But the guy wasn't willing to wait even a week—which made both Harley and me smell a rat.

Harley told the guy to change into his gear, made him sign a release, took him into the ring, and promptly hit him with a forearm smash in the mouth so hard that he broke most of the guy's front teeth. The guy's mouth was a bloody mess, and we later learned that he ended up having major reconstructive surgery on his face. We never saw the guy again.

That was how we protected the business.

After my first couple of weeks in Florida, I assumed Terry or Junior would call and say it was time to come back to Texas, but I never heard from either one of them. Of course, this was in the era before cell phones and car phones. With most of us living in weekly housing arrangements in motels, we didn't have home phones either, so it wasn't the easiest thing to get in touch with someone. Most of the time, messages were left for us at the wrestling office of the promotion where we were working, or we used payphones to communicate with friends and family.

I just went where the promoters told me to go—and things got rolling for me in Florida, so we just stayed. Like Amarillo, the Florida territory under Eddie Graham was a hotbed of great training and lots of young wrestling talent looking to take advantage of that opportunity.

Tony Charles, an English wrestler, was staying in the same complex we were staying in. Tony was a good technical wrestler and worked out very hard—and he helped me further my progress with the technical side of professional wrestling by working on some new maneuvers with me, and teaching me English-style mat and chain wrestling. Les Thornton, another English wrestler who Eddie Graham liked a lot, was also there at the time. Les was a hooker who knew how to hurt people. He and I used to work out together, and Les taught me a lot of things about joint locks, nerve holds, and ways to take control in the ring if your opponent suddenly decided not to cooperate—skills that a world champion would need.

I was still very green, and very much a work in progress when I arrived in Florida. I had the "look" that the promoters liked because I was in great shape and had good stamina, but I didn't really have an established "character" or "persona" yet. In Tri-States, I was primarily a punching bag for the territory's established heels. In Amarillo, the Funks had refined my raw skills and gave me a chance to try out the underdog hero role and let me ride that all the way to a short run with their territorial belt. But as had been the case when I moved from Tri-States to Amarillo, because Amarillo TV was not shown in Florida, the Florida fans had never seen me before. So I had to start over, toiling at the bottom to middle of the cards, working to draw the interest and passion of the crowds each night, and eventually, hopefully, work my way back into being a fan favorite again.

Most pro wrestling "characters" back then evolved and developed over time. That's what Eddie was doing with me. He was putting me into the ring with a wide variety of opponents, both heels and faces, letting me develop and get experience, and letting the people decide what I was going to become.

Florida, despite being a single-state territory, was rough to travel. We drove an average of 3,000 miles a week criss-crossing the state from venue to venue. On a typical week, we would start at the Sportatorium in Tampa on Wednesday morning doing TV and recording promo interviews, and we'd stay there until we finished. Then we would pile into the cars and drive 300 miles one way from Tampa to either the Miami Beach Convention Hall or the Jai Alai building. Miami was always on Wednesday nights. Eddie Graham had a private plane he used to make that trip, so sometimes I'd get the chance to fly with him to Miami. He had a pilot, and about six or so guys could fit in the plane. A lot of times, it was Mike and Eddie and Steve Keirn and Dusty and me. If the NWA World Champion or some other big name like Andre or Baba was in Tampa the night before and would be going with us to Miami, that person would get to ride in the plane, and either Steve or I would have to vacate our seats. If it was Andre, *both* Steve and I would have to vacate our seats!

After the matches in Miami Beach on Wednesday night, we would shower up and then turn the car around and drive north up the coast 400 miles to Jacksonville for the matches on Thursday night. After Jacksonville, we'd have to turn the car back south and make the 300-mile drive back down south to Fort Lauderdale for matches on Friday night, and then cross the state westward for 250 miles to St. Petersburg, Sarasota, or Punta Gorda for the Saturday night cards.

Sunday was a day off in Florida, so we'd all head back to Tampa and spend time with our families.

Then, on Monday, we'd cross the state again from Tampa to either Orlando or West Palm Beach and then turn around and head back to Tampa or Fort Myers for matches on Tuesday night.

I was averaging $50 to $100 per night wrestling in Florida. The payoffs were all based on how big the building was, how many people were there and where you were on the card, but the biggest thing I remember, other than how much talent there was to learn from, was just how much driving there was!

My time in Florida was another chance to gain experience—another stepping stone in terms of developing into the kind of performer I wanted to become. There were a lot of different guys that I faced down there, from many different backgrounds different and the characters were all different so, every night, I'd go to the ring and pick up something new. Each person had different ideas about how to develop a match and tell a story to the crowd. For anyone serious about getting better at their craft, it was impossible not to soak up knowledge like a sponge.

The other thing I learned in the Florida territory is that if you showed up reliably and worked hard every night no matter where on the card or how they were using you, the promoters would respect you, want to get to know you better, and want to use you in increasingly meaningful spots on the cards. It didn't happen overnight, of course, but I definitely sensed a professional respect that developed over time.

In the NWA, all the promoters knew each other and were all at least loosely tied together by the alliance. Although some were closer to each other than others, the promoters all met at annual meetings and often talked to one another during the year—so word of a young wrestler's hard work and reliability was passed along from the head of one territory to another—which gave you a chance to travel to the different territories, get work, and continue to learn and develop.

I was never a good schmoozer. Unlike many of the boys, I never cozied up to promoters or the top talent in a particular territory to propose ideas or to try and "game" my way to the top. I just did what came naturally to me—but I do attribute my consistent success in the territories, and ultimately, in the business as a whole to two main things: first, the things I did outside the ring, like going to hospitals and schools, and helping kids, which, as it turned out, the promoters liked because it brought positive attention to the business; and, second, going out every night I stepped into the ring to try to tell a good story, protect my opponent, make my opponent look good, and give the fans an entertaining match to remember me by, no matter where I was, what the booking was, or how many people were in the crowd.

As I have mentioned before, Eddie Graham relied on Hiro Matsuda, Harley, and me to stretch the newcomers. Matsuda could do hundreds of squats in one set, and although he had not been an amateur wrestler, he had been trained by Karl Gotch—perhaps the greatest legitimate shooter who ever lived. Matsuda, thus, had evolved into one of professional wrestling's most notorious "policemen."

Perhaps a bit of explanation would be helpful here.

A highly trained amateur wrestler is knows how to use leverage to take you down and control your body. An amateur wrestler, however, would not necessarily be able to quickly hurt someone or to totally subdue a much larger rogue wrestler in the ring, because in amateur wrestling, you are coached specifically *not* to apply chokes or holds that work against nerves or joints.

A shooter, however, is someone who is not only trained in the amateur arts, but who also knows how to work against the joints and nerves — and can quickly "hook" you by manipulating a body part against a joint or a nerve and put you in an excruciating submission hold in the blink of an eye. "Hooking," in other words, is just a part of being a shooter. You can't be a shooter without being a hooker.

Legitimate professional-wrestling shoot matches ended back in the 1920s. Before that, there *were* real professional wrestling bouts around the country. Wrestlers would promote themselves, with each man putting up purse money for a match. Those matches typically had one-hour time limits, and were scheduled for the best two out of three falls, where a fall could be won either by a three-second pin, or by a submission. Only choking, eye-gouging, biting, and strikes to the groin were barred. If someone did not win two out of three falls within the one-hour time limit, the bout would be declared a draw.

When the legitimacy went out of the sport at the end of the 1920s, and professional wrestling matches started being staged with predetermined endings, the art of shoot wrestling went underground. In modern professional wrestling, it more or less started and ended with Karl Gotch, who was perhaps the only truly legitimate shoot wrestler of our generation. The rest of us — guys like Danny Hodge, Matsuda, Harley Race, Jack Brisco, the Funks, Les Thornton, and Khosrow Vaziri, had been trained in shoot wrestling, and could call upon those skills when necessary. Those were the guys who the old-school promoters would use to protect the business. They were also often the guys looked upon to carry the world titles.

Both Danny Hodge and Les Thornton taught me hooking skills at the beginning of my career. Once you have these skills, it is scary how easily you can subdue someone if you need to—and these are critical skills to know if you are going to be entrusted with the responsibility of carrying a belt outside your territory.

———⇒•⇐———

In the Florida territory, the biggest venue we wrestled in was the Bayfront Center in St. Petersburg. The place held somewhere between 10,000 and 12,000 people for wrestling, and unlike the other buildings in the territory, we wrestled there only about once every month or six weeks, so they generally loaded up the card to make sure we would fill the building.

On June 14, 1975, I wrestled there in front of the biggest crowd I had ever experienced up to that point (outside of Japan). The main event featured Jack Brisco defending the NWA World Heavyweight Championship against "Mr. Wrestling" Tim Woods. On that night, in addition to the world title match, Hiro Matsuda defeated Ken "Dutch" Mantell to reclaim the NWA Junior Heavyweight Championship; the "Minnesota Wrecking Crew" Ole and Gene Anderson battled to a no-contest with Rocky Johnson and Tiger Conway Jr. over the NWA World Tag-Team Championship; Killer Karl Krupp bested Pepper Gomez to win the Southern Heavyweight championship; I unsuccessfully challenged Bob Roop for the Florida Heavyweight Championship; and Gentleman Jim Dillon drew with Mike Graham in the Florida television championship match. All of that happened on the same card—which *also* included a match between Dory Funk Jr. and Harley Race.

Talk about a supercard!

On that card, there were a lot of matches vying for the fans' attention. You would (and could) assume that Jack and Tim would blow the roof off the building in the main event, so the trick was to find something in your match that would be different and interesting and could capture the hearts of the fans. Bob Roop and I ended up having a great, largely amateur match that night, which, based on where our match fell on the card, provided a nice change from some of the brawling that went on before and after us. It was very exciting for me just to be able to get into the ring in that kind of electrically charged atmosphere with so much talent on the card, and that many people jammed into a building to watch. As it turned out, it would be the first of many such nights in my career—but that was the first one on American soil—so it really sticks out in my mind.

By that point, I had developed a good relationship with Eddie Graham, and it gave me an opportunity to get to know Jim Barnett. Eddie Graham, his son Mike Graham, and Jim Barnett were my "bosses"—the three guys who ran the Florida promotion. Jim Barnett was the principal owner of Georgia Championship Wrestling, but he also held a minority interest in Florida Championship Wrestling and was a pretty common presence down in the Florida office when I was there.

One day at the Sportatorium office, Barnett pulled me aside and explained that he and Eddie had talked, and that the two of them thought that it was time for me to head up the road to Georgia to wrestle for him in Georgia Championship Wrestling.

And with that, my first tenure in Florida came to an end.

The First Battle of Atlanta (Georgia, 1975)

*"Live in a style that suits your physical and spiritual require-
ments, and don't waste time keeping up with the Joneses."*

—Napoleon Hill, "Build a Positive Mental Attitude"

———◆———

When we first arrived in Atlanta, Corki and I were prepared to go apartment hunting again, but Jim Barnett told us that he had already found us
a clean and safe place to live in College Park. None of the other territorial
promoters had ever done that for us before—so we thought that was really
nice, and I took it as a good sign that he intended to treat me well.

That was a good read.

My first match in the Georgia territory was against a young Jerry
Lawler at the City Auditorium in Atlanta. That old place was one of my
favorite arenas in the entire country to wrestle because the emotion in
that building was off the charts. The building, which was built as a theater,
had balconies that hung right out over the ring, which put the people
right on top of you. The acoustics were terrific—so when the crowd there
got lathered up, the building would shake. When I got to the Audi that
night and found out I was wrestling Jerry Lawler on my first night in the
territory, I just assumed I would be putting him over—but it turned out
that Barnett had decided to open me with a pop by putting *me* over in my
Atlanta debut.

It was a pretty awesome win to start me off, and the people responded.

The Atlanta territory was much different from Florida because the
longest drive was about 150 miles. Most days, that meant that we were

able to be home all day, work out at our leisure, have lunch with our families, and then take off and head for the town where we were wrestling sometime in the afternoon. The circuit ran from Augusta to Macon to Atlanta to Columbus to Griffin, with occasional spot shows in Savannah and other small towns. I made somewhere between $150 and $300 dollars a night wrestling in the Georgia territory, and sometimes, especially in Atlanta, we'd make more than that. Georgia was an especially profitable territory to wrestle in because we didn't burn a lot of gas, and everyone went home every night and didn't have the expense of paying for motel rooms out on the road. Given how close the towns were to one another, the guys who jerked the curtain were often home in bed by the time the main event hit the ring!

The Georgia territory was really popping at the time—and we were drawing great crowds in virtually every town we visited. There was a lot of great talent in the territory when I got there, but I was very fortunate to have had the advantage of working in front of Jim Barnett quite a bit down in Florida, so by the time I got to Georgia, he knew me well. Jim had designs on making me into a top of the card singles wrestler in Georgia, and before I knew it, I was main-eventing with some of the people you could only dream about getting a match with.

On August 29, 1975, for example, I had my first-ever world title match, against then-champion Jack Brisco for the National Wrestling Alliance World Heavyweight championship. To set up that match, Barnett had booked me into a ten-minute time-limit draw with Brisco on television, during which Jack had given me a number of near-falls and really made me look like I could beat him. It was my first really close look at what a world champion was *supposed* to do with his challengers.

I had a lot of respect for Jack Brisco—he had wrestled at Oklahoma and was also an NCAA national champion. He was very fit, looked like a wrestling champion, and was also a shooter. I was excited to get in the ring with him in the main event on such a big stage. The Omni was completely sold out—I think there were around 13,000 people in the building. Up to that point in my career, that was certainly the biggest match I had been in, and other than in Japan, it was the largest crowd I had ever wrestled in front of. I remember being very nervous climbing into the ring that night, and Jack could sense that. Being the consummate pro that he was, though, he called some simple moves to get me through my early match jitters when I know I was a little stiff and tight. Although Jack won the match with a quick inside cradle, he really let me hang in there, get a lot of offense in, and catch a number of near-falls on him, and by doing that, he definitely put the "shine" on me and left me stronger, in the eyes of the fans, than I had been before the bout.

I did my favorite move on Jack that night—where he caught me in a short-arm scissors, and I just deadlifted his entire weight off the mat, up into the air, up onto my shoulder, and then placed him on the top turnbuckle. The crowd popped tremendously for that move because they recognized the kind of strength it took to pull it off. Unlike most other moves in professional wrestling, there is no way that your opponent can help you with that one. You just have to concentrate the energy and cheers of the crowd into an adrenaline rush, and then use brute force—and there were not a lot of guys in the business who had the core strength to execute that move in the ring. I know it impressed Jack that night. Even though I lost the match, I had definitely gained stature in the eyes of the people. That is what having a great match with a great champion can do for you.

The level of respect that I had for Jack Brisco after that match could not have gotten any higher—because of the way he conducted himself in the ring, how generous he had been in our match, and, of course, for what he had done in amateur wrestling in Oklahoma and his success in the NCAA tournament.

Three hours later, however, my view of Jack Brisco would be forever changed.

After the Omni card, Dusty Rhodes and Jack and Gerry Brisco asked me if I wanted to go for a ride with them in Jack's Thunderbird. I gratefully accepted the offer. In Atlanta, there is a bypass that goes around the city, and we were flying on that bypass with Jack behind the wheel. I was sitting in the back seat with Gerry Brisco having a beer when all of a sudden, I smelled a strange smell. Although I had never smoked marijuana before, the smell was unmistakable. I used the electric switch to put my window down but someone put the window back up. I tried to put the window back down but the window was locked.

"Jack, I can't get my window open, would you please unlock the window?" I asked.

Jack and Dusty just laughed in the front seat and wouldn't unlock my window. These were the top guys in the territory, and it certainly wouldn't have been a bad thing to fit in with them, because they could certainly have helped me to get ahead. But I knew that what they were doing was wrong, and I knew that I didn't want to be there.

A couple more minutes went by, and the car was filling up with pot smoke.

"Jack—please stop the car and let me out," I asked.

But Jack didn't stop the car.

I looked to Gerry Brisco who was sitting with me in the back seat. But Gerry just shrugged.

We pulled into a club and Jack and Dusty got out. I didn't know where I was, but I got out of the car, looked around to get my bearings, and just started walking. I didn't care so much that those guys were smoking marijuana—that was their own choice and their decision—but I certainly didn't want to be riding in a car with someone who was smoking dope while driving.

Making your way in this world is all about the decisions you make for your own life, and I didn't want those guys taking that right away from me. I didn't want to be a captive in that environment, I didn't want my body getting polluted with that stuff, and I certainly didn't want to run the risk of being in a speeding car with an impaired driver. So I made the choice that I thought was best for me, and walked home. It took me nearly all night, but I didn't care. I knew I was making the right choice for me.

What happened that night certainly diminished my respect for Jack. He was the NWA World Heavyweight Champion, and was supposed to be a role model both for the fans and for young wrestlers like me. In that way, he certainly let me down. But it was a good learning experience for me to encounter that kind of behavior at the very highest levels of our sport, and among the people I most respected. I guess that's why I ultimately became kind of a lone ranger in the wrestling business. I wanted to control my own environment and to be responsible for my own decisions.

I never rode with those guys again, and I was never asked.

After that title match with Jack, I faced Gerry Brisco around the circuit in a series of babyface matches, most of which went to the time limit. We put on a chain wrestling clinic that the fans really seemed to enjoy. It was always dicey to do those babyface matches, because there was always the potential that the crowd would side with one of us over the other and push one of us to become the heel. If the crowd had taken one of us in that direction, we would have gone with it—but fortunately, it never actually happened. The crowds kept us both babyfaces and just cheered us both pretty much everywhere we went—so ultimately, Jim Barnett decided to go with what the people wanted and turned us into a babyface tag team!

Once that happened, Gerry and I traveled around the territory working together, and soon received a title shot at the Georgia Tag-Team Championship which, at that time, was held by Dick Slater and Bob Orton Jr. (later Cowboy Bob "Ace" Orton in the WWF), managed by Gary Hart. Both Slater and Orton could really work, and we had a number of very entertaining tag-team title matches with them around the territory. Gerry and I eventually beat them and enjoyed a brief run with the belts in the fall of 1975.

In Georgia, the heels and babyfaces were kept separate all the time, so I only got to mingle publicly with about half of the roster—which was really too bad, because there was such an abundance of good young talent in the Georgia territory at that time. Night after night, I found myself in the ring with incredibly talented guys, and wrestling in the upper half of the cards, so it was all about making it look good and listening to the crowds, figuring out what they wanted, and learning as much as I could from guys I would never have imagined being in the ring with.

I have always been grateful to Jim Barnett for giving me those opportunities.

During my first stay in Georgia, I continued to develop a pretty close friendship with Les Thornton. Les and I would go to the gym and play a game with a deck of cards where we would take turns turning over a card and do however many squats the card required. Aces or Jokers were thirty, face cards were ten, and everything else was face value. We had a lot of fun with that—and it was a way of keeping our workouts interesting.

During that time in my career, I was lifting heavy weights, benching, and doing a lot of deadlifts to help me execute the short-arm scissors. I never did a lot of running because of all the pounding on my hips and knees. Squats were good for wrestling, though, because you are up and down so much. Les also continued to teach me more and more shooting skills.

At the end of the fall of 1975, Jim Barnett called me into his office and told me that Sam Muchnick had called and asked to get some bookings with me in St. Louis. I knew from the chatter I had heard in the other territories that being invited to wrestle for Sam Muchnick in St. Louis was a very high honor, so I was excited to get the opportunity. Barnett explained to me how different the St. Louis territory was from the other wrestling territories in the NWA, in that it was essentially a one-city, one-day territory where you only wrestled twice a month. You'd fly in, tape the Wrestling at the Chase TV program, which they used to set up all of the angles, wrestle at the Kiel Auditorium, and then fly back and continue to work in whatever territory you had come from.

I wanted to go back home again to Minnesota to visit my parents, so I asked Jim if there was a way to work all of that out. Jim set up a tryout for me in St. Louis in December 1975, explaining to me that if it went well, Mr. Muchnick would probably ask to use me more often. Jim gave me about a month off to spend some time at home, explaining that he wanted me back in Georgia the first week in February 1976 for an additional three-month babyface run. After that, he explained that I would head back to Florida Championship Wrestling to do another run with Eddie Graham. So as Corki and I drove out of Georgia for our long-awaited trip home, I had a scheduled tryout with the NWA's premiere booking office, and about six months of additional work in Georgia and Florida lined up ahead of me. Things were really starting to build a head of steam.

It made for a happy drive, and a pretty good holiday season!

9

I'll Be Home for Christmas (AWA, 1975)

"Time is relentless in preserving the seed of an equivalent benefit that hides within a defeat."

—Napoleon Hill, "Learn from Adversity and Defeat"

━━◆━━

When I returned home to Minnesota, I again called Verne Gagne to see if I could get booked in the AWA territory while I was at home just to stay in ring-shape and to keep up my timing. Verne used me during those days mostly as enhancement talent to get his stars over. To be fair, though, we both knew I wasn't going to stay in the AWA for long, so there was no reason he would have put me over.

Verne was a bit of a control freak, and unlike a lot of the other regional promoters, he actually went to many of the towns on the AWA circuit, so he got to see me wrestle personally quite a lot. Every night, I would get to the building, go into the dressing room, and figure out where my match was on the card, and see who I would be putting over. To some, this might seem like a step backward given where I had already been, and how I had been treated in the other territories where I had wrestled. But I didn't see it that way. To me, it was simply an opportunity to stay in shape, keep up my timing, make a good impression on another influential promoter in my home region of the country, and keep a few dollars in my pocket. Moreover, since the AWA was not broadcast into Florida or Georgia, there was no danger of any harm to the reputation Eddie Graham and Jim Barnett were building for me.

As I had learned from both the Funks and from Eddie and Jim, when you are asked to put someone over, part of being a success in the business is knowing how to do that the right way. Done properly, it is possible to both make your opponent look strong in going over (which is what the promoters are asking you to do), but also draw the interest and emotion of the fans so that they rally behind you, even in defeat, and even night after night. As I had been taught, you cannot necessarily control the whims of a promoter, or the results and finishes that promoter calls for. What you *can* control as a professional, however, is *how* you execute that promoter's directives. A skillful performer can lose a match on any given night but still win the enduring support of the people.

In the AWA, most of the guys I wrestled were well-known heels, so they wanted to be hated and encourage the people to rise against them. The more successful they were at doing that, the more "heat" they would have with the fans. The more heat a heel had with the fans, the better the bookings they would subsequently get, and the more money they would make.

Conversely, I was trying to get over with the fans as a babyface, so I got to play the underdog a lot and make a lot of furious comebacks that would fall just short—but which would still energize the people and have them on their feet thinking that I might be on the verge of pulling off the upset. When I would fail at this, often because the heel would cheat or do something behind the referee's back, the people would hate the heel more, which is exactly what the heels wanted. And my comeback, even though it would fall just short, would have fans believing in me—which connected us emotionally to each other—which is what I was trying to accomplish. A win-win situation was achievable in these situations, and as long as I didn't allow the heels to take all of the action and just squash me, we could both come out with what we needed. Fortunately, because of my amateur background and because of the experience that I had already had, Verne was giving me enough time in the ring to do this—and most of my opponents realized that they stood to gain more from our matches if we were able to take the energy up higher than it would have gotten if they just used me as a crash test dummy.

Interestingly, even though the AWA was so geographically expansive, we didn't wrestle every night. At that time, the AWA had its proven towns, and didn't wander much from that itinerary. There was a lot of travel. In the AWA, we weren't just crossing one or two states, sometimes we were crossing several states, and if we drove, we weren't returning home on the same day. You could be in Denver one night, Winnipeg, Manitoba, the next night, and then Green Bay and Milwaukee, Wisconsin, two nights after that. I'm from Minnesota, so the cold and the dark doesn't bother me very much—and I actually love to drive—but there was more travel in the AWA territory than in any of the other territories that I had been in so far, and winter driving in that neck of the woods can be pretty difficult with the ice and blowing snow. It was certainly a radical change from Amarillo, Florida, and Georgia.

Because of how spread out the territory was, Verne had a plane that fit about six people (and a pilot), and he chose who got to fly with him. Because I was putting Verne's talent over without complaint and having a lot of pretty compelling matches in the AWA, I was sometimes given the honor of flying with Verne on some of the longer routes. Other times, though, when there was more senior talent in the territory, there wasn't room for me in the plane, and I'd have to drive.

In the AWA, given how far the driving routes were, in order to make ends meet, it was very important to be able to split the costs of travel by riding with others. If I was the "wheel" (the driver), it was important for me to make sure my seats were filled with people contributing to the costs of gas and paying a little extra for the privilege of not having to pay attention to the roads.

It was during this first brief stint in the AWA that I first crossed paths with Khosrow Vaziri—the man who would later go on to be known as The Great Hussein Arab and The Iron Sheik. Khos had recently emigrated to the United States from his native Iran after competing for Iran in Greco-Roman wrestling at the 1968 Olympic Games in Mexico City. He had also legitimately served as a bodyguard for the Shah's family. After the 1968 Olympics, Khos's childhood idol—a former gold medal Iranian wrestler—turned up dead in a hotel room. His death was ruled a suicide, but Khos believes to this day that the man was murdered by the government for political reasons and he was fearful that the same thing could happen to him. So Khos came to the United States on a student visa, won a gold medal in the AAU championships in wrestling, and after that, came to Minneapolis and became an assistant coach to the 1972 United States Greco-Roman wrestling team with Alan Rice.

I always loved wrestling Khos because we could do a lot of interesting amateur moves in the ring and mix them in with the pro moves. We could almost anticipate each other, and we had a very easy time putting on entertaining matches in the ring for the fans. Verne liked it, because he was a big fan of amateur wrestling, so Verne allowed Khos and me to do a bunch of twenty-and thirty-minute draws featuring a lot of chain wrestling and mat work early in the cards that would warm up the crowds for the brawls that came later.

At that time, Khos was very powerful, very disciplined about his diet and his training, and was a very honorable man. Over the years, it has been hard to watch what happened to him, and what the choices that he made did to his career, and his life and his family. It almost makes me want to cry because I had so much respect for Khos, everything that he went through for real in Iran, and how he came to the United States and helped our young wrestlers so willingly with his talent and his energy and his ideas.

I also worked quite a bit with Bobby Duncam in the AWA, which was quite a contrast from working with Khos. Duncam had been an offensive lineman for the St. Louis Cardinals, and I liked him very much. He wasn't in the greatest of shape when he was wrestling, but he always worked very hard in the ring and played the role of a rough and tough cowboy very well. That gave us the opportunity to tell a straight hero/villain story, and to sell me as the underdog trying to rally to beat the much bigger and rougher heel. I stayed pretty much to my style, trying to use holds and speed, and by the time our matches were over, Duncam was always gassed—but we worked hard to put on good matches. Duncam was very over as a heel with the AWA fans, so I was asked to put him over every night, but the booked finish was usually some last-minute dirty trick that put the heat on him but allowed me to keep the fans on my side.

I know that Bobby appreciated our matches and the fact that I was willing to sell for him and put him over. Those matches were actually very important for us, because it gave us a base to work off of when Duncam later came to the WWF in 1979 for a series of title matches with me when I was champion. Of course, by then, the roles had reversed, and Bobby was being asked to put me over. This is yet another example of how the tides in wrestling ebb and flow, and why it was so important to play your role well, whatever was being asked of you. The wrestling fraternity was not *that* big, and people in the business had long memories. If you were willing to put someone else over and make them look good when asked— they would be much more likely to return the favor for you down the road.

The most memorable match of my brief time in the AWA, though, was my first match with Harley Race in Omaha, Nebraska, right before I left the AWA to head back to Georgia. Harley was a *really* big star in the AWA back then, and I can remember watching him on television. He started wrestling as a teenager in the carnivals taking on all comers—and he was a tough guy both in the ring and out of the ring. Harley had several years on me in the business, and was much more experienced than I was. I was very excited to get in the ring with him and to see what we could do together. When you climb into the ring with an experienced hand like Harley Race, you don't have to worry about much. What I was focused on that night was what I could learn from how he called the match and got the people—and that is definitely what I was focused on. As a thank-you for my good work for him, Verne let us battle to a time-limit draw, and before time expired, we had the crowd roaring with a couple of pretty-good false finishes. I know I represented myself pretty well in the ring that night with Harley.

That match in Omaha with Harley Race provided three important teachable moments that would reoccur throughout my career in wrestling. First, in the wrestling business of the 1970s, a random one-off match in some forgotten town somewhere that really connected with a crowd and caught the eye of a promoter had the potential to significantly accelerate your career. Second, any chance you got to climb into the ring with an influential wrestler and to have a great match could also change your fortune, because the more-experienced guys often talked to the promoters about the promising new guys. Finally, and most importantly, given those first two things, it was critically important to always be in great shape, look your very best, and be in position to put forth your best effort every night—because you just never knew when an opportunity might come. All you knew is that when it did come, you'd better be ready to take advantage of it.

When I called Verne Gagne and asked him whether I could get a little work while I was back in Minnesota, I knew I wasn't going to be spending much time in the AWA. A lot of people in the wrestling business would have loafed through those matches for some easy paydays. Many people would have resented being asked to put guys over night after night, especially if they had already tasted success and carried championships in other territories like I had.

I didn't approach it that way.

My mantra always was, the harder I worked at my craft, and the more I attended to the goal of giving every opponent and every crowd in every town the very best I had to give—the better things would go for me. That was certainly the lesson of my time in the AWA. Verne Gagne was initially jobbing me out to his established stars. But when he saw what I looked like in the ring, and the effort I was giving him, he was impressed. As he watched that night after night, he gave me better and better opportunities to entertain the fans. First, it was just the occasional reward of being able to fly with him rather than make a long drive. Next, it was the chance to wrestle to draws with people like Khos rather than simply putting everyone over. But most importantly, as a thank-you on my way out, Verne gave me a chance to get into that ring in Omaha and have a long match-ending in a draw with Harley Race. At the time, Harley Race was a big star, and had been the reigning Missouri Heavyweight Champion for nearly a year. I, of course, was about to go to the Missouri territory to wrestle for Sam Mushnick. And Verne knew that.

That "chance" night in Omaha would prove to be extremely influential to my career.

By the time we returned to Georgia, I had bought a Corvette, so Corki and I were riding in that and towing Corki's Volkswagen Bug behind us. Approaching a little town in Tennessee where we had decided to stop for the night, the Bug somehow came uncoupled from the Corvette and went rolling down the road past us.

I watched the Bug go by and turned to Corki and said, "Hey, that little bug that just went by us looks just like your car!"

She took one look at it and said, "Bob, that is my car!"

Corki got out of the Corvette and sprinted down the road after her Bug. It was a hilarious scene. Fortunately, Corki's Bug rolled harmlessly to a stop in an empty lot without crashing into anything or hurting anyone.

We were lucky . . . but that was the end of our tandem-travel.

After that, Corki insisted on driving her own car.

10

A Star Is Rising: Florida and Georgia (1976)

"Going the extra mile makes you indispensable to others . . .
do for them what no one else does."

—Napoleon Hill, "Go the Extra Mile"

If you've read this far, you can see that I am doing my best to tell my story chronologically. I chose to do that on purpose, first, so that you can experience the story the way that I experienced it—as it actually happened—and second, because the successes that I experienced in my life built one on the next as I went from Louisiana to Amarillo to Florida to Georgia to the AWA and then on to St. Louis, as you will read shortly.

At this point in the story, however, the effort to stay chronological becomes difficult, and as such, the telling becomes a bit more confusing. Suffice it to say that the Bicentennial year 1976 was the year of my most significant professional development. During 1976, I worked in three of the most important and influential territories in the National Wrestling Alliance—Georgia Championship Wrestling, Florida Championship Wrestling, and the St. Louis Wrestling Club. It certainly made for an interesting life.

When I got back to Georgia Championship Wrestling in February of 1976, Jim Barnett didn't have a defined plan for me because he knew that my principal push during that time would occur in St. Louis. So Jim moved me around, giving me some good scientific babyface matches against the Brits Tony Charles and Les Thornton, some tag-team work with Rick Martel, and my first couple of matches against a young Greg

Valentine. Jim planned to give me about a three-month run in Georgia and then to send me back down to work with Eddie Graham in Florida again. This gave me a chance to work with more people of different styles, to continue to work on my timing, and in particular, to get more of a feel for working in tag-team matches, which I really hadn't had that much experience with up until that point in my career.

My babyface matches in Georgia typically ended up being clean matches with handshakes at the beginning and the end, and they usually went off early in the cards, to get the fans warmed up. The fans never pushed me toward the heel role in any of those matches, and Jim Barnett never wanted me to experiment with being a tweener. Barnett simply wanted me to build more experience as a pure babyface, and I was grateful for the opportunity.

I had my one and only match against Abdullah the Butcher down in Georgia. Wrestling Abdullah was a little bit like wrestling George "The Animal" Steele. Although I liked both of those guys personally, I didn't enjoy being in the ring with them as much as I did wrestling other guys, because I liked to wrestle at least a little bit of every match in the amateur style, and that just wasn't going to happen in the ring with Abdullah. Abdullah's gimmick was to use every foreign object he could find around ringside and hide in his wrestling pants to carve you up with—so, by default, the storyline when wrestling him was to try to avoid getting clobbered by whatever weapon he had, try to convince the referee that he had it, and then, when that didn't work, to get your hands on every equalizer you could find in order to defend yourself.

There were no wrestling holds called in a match against Abdullah. He was the Butcher, and the fans came to see the bloodbath and carnage he provided, so if he didn't butcher you and leave you with a crimson mask, he didn't give the fans what they came to see from him. His was a very unique character, and he was very, very over, particularly in Japan where he was as big a star as there was in the business.

Abdullah was very established in Atlanta, so he was the boss and got to call the match. I was definitely leery of him when I learned I would be wrestling him, but as it turned out, I didn't need to be. I thought he might be heavy on me, but he wasn't at all. He was very good to me in the ring and he didn't carve me up with a fork like he did so many other guys, but his character was limited, so there was only so much he could do. Abdullah was very wide at the shoulders and frankly, he was wide all the way down—but he was a good person.

I also wrestled Randy Savage while I was down in Georgia. Back then, Randy was just coming off a pretty good run in minor league baseball in the St. Louis Cardinals and Cincinnati Reds organizations, and his personality was just perfect for the wrestling business. Savage was very charismatic, good with the people, and a great athlete—and we had some great matches together. As I learned from many of my mentors, your wrestling persona is much more credible when it develops and evolves naturally in the business over time. Randy's did just that. You could see the origins of the "Macho Man" character down in Atlanta—but he didn't become the fully evolved heel character for another eight years or so. He let it evolve naturally, and that's why his was such a new and refreshing and great character when he first arrived on the scene in the WWF in 1985.

Our second stint in Georgia went by quickly. I got a nice little respite for about six weeks before I started having to fly to St. Louis for the Kiel and TVs, and had a pretty easy schedule until the beginning of May, when I headed back down to Florida to work with Eddie.

In May 1976, I had my first dates back in Florida Championship Wrestling working for Eddie Graham. When I got back down there, Eddie didn't really tell me anything about how long I was going to be there, or how I was going to be used, so I just settled into a routine again.

We moved into an apartment on Buffalo Avenue in Tampa. I liked it there because it was very hot and humid and easy to get a good sweat going during a workout—which was something that I always loved to do. Corki liked the Florida territory too because the heat and humidity is also her kind of weather. She quickly got a job teaching gymnastics at a club down there, and settled into her own life away from the lights and the chaos of wrestling.

Most of Eddie Graham's top guys in the Florida territory had been in the business a long time, and because Florida was one of the premiere territories in the NWA, it definitely took longer to earn your stripes down there than it did in some of the other territories. Eddie didn't just put you into main events right away. But he kept me busy, put me on the cards every night, and gave me a variety of opponents to work with. I really couldn't have asked for more.

By the time I returned to Florida in 1976, I'd actually only been in the professional wrestling business for two years. Many of the guys who broke into the business around the same time I did were still serving as enhancement talent or jerking the curtain in smaller regional promotions. I had been very fortunate to have been fast-tracked by the Funks in Amarillo, and because of how much influence Dory and Terry had in the business at the time, I was set on a whole different course with Eddie in Florida and Jim Barnett in Atlanta.

The Southern Heavyweight Championship was the premiere title in the Florida territory, and was defended in both the Florida and Georgia territories. "The American Dream" Dusty Rhodes was really over with the fans in Florida and by that time, had pushed his blue collar image as the "son of a plumber" to the point of becoming an almost larger-than-life character. As Dusty became increasingly loved by the fans, however, he also flexed his muscles more with the office, and Eddie lost some of his leverage as a direct consequence of Dusty's stardom. Dusty would often suggest certain angles or finishes to his matches—which, of course, was a totally foreign concept to me. It also didn't ingratiate Dusty much with

Eddie or many of the other boys who saw him as something of a relentless self-promoter.

From what I experienced, I think most people inside and outside the wrestling business either loved Dusty or hated him. There didn't seem to be much of a middle ground given how strong Dusty's personality was. I was one of the people who liked him. Like mine, the character that Dusty played was one that closely resembled who he was in real life, but was also one that he evolved into—it wasn't a character that someone just handed him off the shelf when he first broke into the business. You don't just wake up one morning and decide that you are going to be "The American Dream" and show up to the arena that night and pull that off. "The American Dream" was another one of professional wrestling's most successful and carefully evolved characters—one that Dusty built over his many years in the business.

Dusty lived his character and he was *very* good at what he did. He connected deeply with the Florida and Georgia fan base, and he was definitely one of the better interviews in the business (once you figured out how to understand what it was that he was saying through his heavy lisp and exaggerated Texas drawl). There were a lot of people who thought he was cocky and pushed himself on the bookers and promoters too much—but the fact is that Dusty captured the hearts and minds of the Florida fan base like nobody else ever did, and both Dusty and the promoters knew it. He was somebody who could put the butts in the seats down there better than anyone else, and because of that, he was a one-of-a kind performer.

During my two stays in Florida, and even in the years after when we saw each other in Japan and in the WWF, I always got along well with Dusty. We weren't close friends, but we talked quite a bit about the business and we drank quite a bit of beer together. Nobody was bigger than Dusty in Florida or Georgia.

Nobody.

Jack Brisco lost the NWA World Heavyweight Championship to Terry Funk on December 10, 1975, in Miami and came off the road after two and a half years traveling as the world champion. After that exhausting schedule, Jack wanted to settle down into a territory and relax for a while. Since he was living in the Tampa area at the time, and had already successfully carried the Florida Heavyweight Championship four times, Eddie Graham wanted to put that title back on Jack. So after taking some time off, Jack won the Florida Heavyweight Championship from Pak Song on April 17, 1976, at the Bayfront Center in St. Petersburg, Florida. As the Florida Heavyweight Champion, Jack was responsible for headlining and main-eventing the cities and towns on the Florida circuit—occasionally supported by an appearance by the Southern Heavyweight Champion or the NWA World Heavyweight Champion. It made all the sense in the world for Eddie to use someone like Jack, who had just been the NWA World Champion, to carry the promotion.

Jack lost the Florida title about a month later, on May 25, 1976, in Tampa to Bob Orton Jr. Needless to say, a victory like that over someone who had just been the NWA World Champion signaled a big push—and Orton was definitely getting a big push from Eddie down there at the time. Orton, of course, would go on to fame later on in the WWF as "Cowboy" Bob Orton and then as Roddy Piper's henchman "Ace." He had been trained by Eddie and Hiro Matsuda and was a terrific wrestler who could really work in the ring.

The Ortons were based in the Florida Championship Wrestling promotion, and Bob Jr. had been wrestling there for almost five years when he got his push with the Florida belt. So it was definitely his time. After a couple of months running with the belt, Orton feuded with Dusty Rhodes and eventually lost the Florida title to Dusty on July 27, 1976, in Tampa. Dusty then held the Florida title until November 1976, when he was beaten by "Superstar" Billy Graham, who was being groomed to take the WWWF World Heavyweight Championship from Bruno Sammartino.

Graham held the belt until vacating it in March 1977, right before beginning his run as the WWWF champion.

I mention this brief lineage of the Florida title during the time I was there to give you an idea of the kind of A-list talent that Eddie Graham had assembled at Florida Championship Wrestling. It was a great atmosphere to wrestle in, and a great time to be coming up and learning from some of these greats in the business. I wasn't discouraged at all to be working the lower mid-card on many of those nights, because I really hadn't paid my dues like a lot of these guys had. Frankly, I'd been fortunate that my hard work had allowed me to get to the top of the cards in Amarillo and Georgia as quickly as I did!

I also did a lot of tag-team wrestling in Florida, teaming up with guys like Mike Graham (Eddie's son), Gerry Brisco, and Steve Keirn. We wrestled guys like the Ortons (Bob Sr. and Bob Jr.) who were the Florida Tag-Team Champions, the Assassin and the Missouri Mauler, Orton Sr. and Bob Roop, and the Hollywood Blondes.

Obviously, when you wrestled as a tag team, it was important to like your tag-team partner and to be compatible with him outside the ring, because once you were involved in a tag team, it meant that you and your partner were traveling together, and working together almost every night. Fortunately for me, I liked Mike and Gerry and Steve a lot, and we had a lot of fun working together.

Tag-team wrestling was another common booking trick used to keep somebody busy without hurting them. There is a big difference between wrestling in a singles match, and wrestling in a tag team or a six-man tag-team match. In a singles match, you have only one other person to communicate with and work with in order to tell a compelling story in the ring. In a tag-team match, though, that communication triples—as you have to communicate well with your partner, and with both of the guys you are wrestling against.

The goal of tag-team wrestling is to create a match people are going to enjoy—one that will be favorable to everyone in the ring. Done well, a tag-team match can be very entertaining. There is a lot of action, and a well-orchestrated tag-team match can be very interesting and very popular with the fans. The key to a good tag-team match, though, is to keep the focus on what is going on *in the ring* unless it is everyone's intention to have something that is going on outside the ring help the development of the match inside. For example, it would be totally proper and appropriate for a babyface partner standing on the ring apron to rally the crowd to help inspire his partner in the ring taking punishment to come make the tag. On the heel side, it was totally appropriate for the heels to interact with their manager outside the ring, to get or hide foreign objects from their manager, or to interfere from the outside in the match while the referee's back was turned.

It is a major no-no, however, for the person outside the ring to be jawing with the fans, "grandstanding," or doing things to draw attention away from the guys inside the ring. Grandstanding by doing any of these things to draw attention to yourself rather that to keep the attention on the storyline of the match was a fast way to irritate both your partner and your opponents. For a successful tag-team match, everyone had to be working together toward a common story and the betterment of the match as a whole. When individual egos got the best of people and individual wrestlers were in it for themselves or their own character, though, the match suffered.

It was Eddie Graham's idea to put Steve Keirn and me together for a run with the Florida tag-team titles, because Steve and I both liked to work the quick, amateur style, and Eddie thought that would be exciting for the fans to see. We won the Florida Tag-Team Titles from Bob Roop and Bob Orton Sr. at the Sportatorium in Tampa on June 29, 1976, and defended the belts around the Florida territory against a host of challengers that summer including the Ortons, the Briscos, and the Assassin and the Missouri Mauler. It was a pleasure to be in the ring with all of those guys because they all knew how to wrestle and how to entertain people — which gave us a lot of options in our matches.

We dropped the titles at the end of the summer on September 7, 1976, to the Hollywood Blondes, Buddy Roberts and Jerry Brown. Roberts, of course, would go on from there to work as Fabulous Freebird Buddy Roberts (along with Terry Gordy and Michael Hayes) for Fritz Von Erich in World Class Championship Wrestling.

During this time in Florida, I worked most intensely on my ability to listen to a crowd and understand what they were asking you for. Every night, in every city or town, the crowd would be different in mood and makeup. The art of "reading the fans" is something that takes a while to acquire, but once you can do it, no matter where you are or what a crowd is like, you can always let them take the match where they want it to go. Giving the fans what they want to see, within reason, is the name of the game. It is what keeps them coming back to the box office to buy tickets.

By way of example, if I was wrestling in a lower-midcard babyface match in Orlando, and the fans that night were not interested in seeing mat wrestling or chain wrestling and were letting us know it, then my opponent and I would have to switch it up and adjust. Maybe we would mix in more speed work, like moves off the ropes, hip tosses, arm drags, dropkicks and head-scissors, or more high flying moves to get the people going. If that didn't work, maybe one of us would take offense to someone throwing a forearm, or not breaking cleanly out of the ropes, and have the match devolve into fisticuffs. It usually didn't take much to get the fans going and to find something that they liked. But you have to be listening to know what the people want.

It was also very important to know what happened in the matches before you so you didn't repeat things that the fans have already seen. The bookers tried to take care of this, at least to some degree, by making sure that all of the booked finishes on a given night were differently paced, that all of the matches on a particular card ended with a different finisher, and that they didn't have three disqualification finishes on the same card. Everything from the beginning of the match to the finish was ad-libbed by the guys in the ring, so it was incumbent on the wrestlers to make sure that they weren't duplicating high spots that had already been done earlier in the card—or robbing a later match of its high spots or its booked finish. If the main event was slated to end with a piledriver that resulted in a pin, you didn't want to show one to the fans earlier in the evening that ended with someone kicking out.

Every building had a place where you could go to watch the matches where people wouldn't see you, and I always made a habit of doing this. Taking this approach gave me insight into what a particular crowd was like and what it was looking to see that night, provided me with examples of how other wrestlers, especially the top ones, paced their matches, pulled off angles, and handled particular finishes, which I could use in my future matches. It also helped me know what the fans had already seen so I could give them something different. A lot of guys just played cards or socialized in the dressing rooms before and after their matches. I was really serious about the business and about improving my craft—so I took full advantage of the opportunity to learn every night from some of the top guys in the business who were working in Florida at the time. I learned a lot from doing that, and seeing how guys responded to different situations—which gave me a wealth of ideas to pull from when I found myself in the same situation on another night.

The other thing that watching all those matches gave me was a real appreciation for the art of planning and building a card. The booker would always try to pace the evening in the same way that two wrestlers would try to pace a match. A well-planned card would start with a mellow match, maybe two babyfaces who would trade headlocks, do a reverse or two, maybe have one guy throw a dropkick or use the ropes, and have someone win with an entertaining or upbeat move to get the people in the right frame of mind. The job for the guys in the opening match was to help people who had just come from doing something else in their lives get oriented to the idea that they were watching professional wrestling. The opening match was pretty critical in that regard, so you wouldn't want it to be a match where people are just sitting around doing boring rest holds, but also you wouldn't want it to be a match where there is a lot of punching, kicking, or high spots, because if you did that, you'd be robbing from what the guys later in the card would do to take the people's energy up to the next level.

The second match on a card might be the first heel-babyface match, where the action gets upped a little bit. In the second match, you'd look to draw the crowd's emotion in a little more, and give them the sense that they were watching someone "good" that they were supposed to like and support compete against someone "bad" that they were supposed to dislike, and who would not hesitate to break the rules or cheat to win. Then you'd go from there, depending on how many matches were on the card. On a big card, the third match would be the first serious contest between a babyface and a heel where the outcome might have been seriously in doubt.

When I was the world champion in the WWWF, if I was going to be coming back to town the following month (like at MSG or the Philadelphia Spectrum, where I wrestled every month if I was in the United States) my match was usually scheduled as the fourth or fifth match on the card, right before intermission. Vince McMahon Sr. set up his cards that way so that the outcome of my title match would be known before intermission so that the "buzz" about the match could build, to permit them to announce my opponent in the main event on the next card before the end of the night, and to not have to wait to start hyping the next match on the following weekend's television taping.

Wrestling fourth or fifth on a given night may not have been the ideal spot for me, but it unquestionably helped sell a lot of tickets. If you have a captive audience of 20,000 potential ticket buyers all amped up with emotion because of something they just saw, why would you not take advantage of that? Vince Sr. had big 15,000- to 20,000-seat hockey arenas to fill on many nights in a given month, so it was incumbent on him to take full advantage of whatever marketing advantages he could key into. In many of those towns, including New York and Philadelphia, tickets for the next card were put on sale through Ticketron or Teletron (remember those?) and through the arena box office either the same night, or the morning after the card. If we did our job, the following morning, there would be a line of people waiting to get the best possible seats for the next month's card when the box office opened. In many of the territories, however, where the buildings were smaller, the last match on the card would be the blowoff on the theory that you'd want to send the fans out on an emotional high, and simply use your television tapings to hype the next card.

As I mentioned before, during the time I was on my second runs in Georgia and Florida, I was also wrestling for promoter Sam Muchnick in the St. Louis Wrestling Club. That is where my story goes next.

11

The Audition (St. Louis, 1976)

"Forget the old saying, 'Don't put all your eggs in one basket.'
You have to put all your eggs in one basket and concentrate your
attention on protecting that basket and getting it to market!"

—Napoleon Hill, "Control Your Attention"

<hr/>

To those fans that know me primarily or completely from my days as the WWF World Champion, the story of my days with the St. Louis Wrestling Club may come as a pretty big surprise to you. The fact is, St. Louis was the crossroads of my career—the place where my die was cast and the cosmic tumblers settled into place and directed me to New York and to my life as the World Wrestling Federation's Heavyweight Champion. But for a single voice in the NWA board of directors, the course of wrestling history in both the NWA and the WWF might have been changed forever.

The St. Louis Wrestling Club was *the* most influential territory in the National Wrestling Alliance. St. Louis's place at the pinnacle of the NWA's loose confederation of territories was secured because of the reputation and influence of its promoter, Sam Muchnick. Muchnick, along with Tony Stecher and Wally Karbo of the Minneapolis Boxing and Wrestling Club (which would later go on to break away and become the AWA), Orville Brown of Kansas City, Pinky George of Des Moines, and Max Clayton of Omaha, had founded the National Wrestling Alliance in 1948. By the time I got to St. Louis in late 1975, the Alliance, of course, had grown much larger, and Muchnick, who had served as its president for nearly a quarter-century, was the only remaining original member of the Alliance who was still promoting.

Because of his incredible history in founding the National Wrestling Alliance and in holding the Alliance together through legal battles and power struggles between and among its individual promoters, Muchnick had greater stature in the Alliance than any other promoter in the United States except, perhaps, for Vince McMahon Sr. Muchnick enjoyed the trust and respect of his peers around the country—a rare thing in a profession that was often characterized by precisely the opposite.

St. Louis was also a territory unlike any other in the Alliance in that it did not have a traveling circuit. The territory fed off of its famed television program, *Wrestling at the Chase*, which was taped at the studios of KPLR-TV in St. Louis on Saturdays, and its twice-monthly live cards at the Kiel Auditorium in St. Louis on alternate Friday nights. This setup permitted Muchnick four things not shared by any other promoter in the Alliance.

First, other than the person he chose to hold the Missouri State title, Sam had no static stable of wrestlers. Consequently, every two weeks, he was able to pick and choose which wrestlers from around the Alliance he wanted to bring in and feature both on television in one of the country's major media markets, and at the Kiel.

Second, because he booked only one card every two weeks, Sam was free to concentrate his creative energy on developing storylines that were simply directed at filling the Kiel every two weeks by showcasing talent from across the Alliance. Sam always had someone coming up the ladder and getting on a roll, either on the babyface or heel side—usually both. Almost all of the wrestlers on the card were either masters of their art, or the best of the up and coming young talent in the Alliance.

Any wrestler invited to wrestle in the St. Louis Wrestling Club knew he was being looked at by the most influential eyes in the Alliance. It also meant that he would be paid well, so when working for Sam, everyone would turn up his work-rate a notch and make sure everything was crisp.

There were *very* few preliminary matches on a Kiel card—most Kiel cards were like an All-Star Game in professional wrestling.

Third, in many parts of the rest of the country, even back then, professional wrestling was viewed with a sort of bemusement and was not regarded as a sport. Because of the strong relationship Sam maintained in the business community and sports media outlets in the St. Louis area, however, in St. Louis, the activities and events of the St. Louis Wrestling Club were given equal billing to the NFL and Major League Baseball. The St. Louis papers covered wrestling religiously and treated it like any other sport. The Friday St. Louis papers almost always carried a teaser about that night's card at the Kiel, and the Sunday edition would often feature a detailed article about the matches and the results.

Finally, because of Sam's sterling reputation in the business and his relationships with promoters from "rival" organizations like Verne Gagne's and Vince McMahon Sr., Muchnick was able to secure talent and champions from these other federations and put together dream matches and dream cards that no other promoter in the NWA could attract. There was really no other territory anywhere in the Alliance where all three world champions (NWA, AWA, and WWWF) would appear and defend their titles against talent from other wrestling organizations. Only Sam Muchnick had the esteem and trust of his fellow promoters necessary to pull that off.

What all of that meant was that when you wrestled in St. Louis, you were wrestling the very best talent in the world at that time. It also meant that the person Sam chose to be the Missouri Champion held a special stature in the NWA—and was generally regarded as the number-two man in the Alliance behind whoever held the NWA World Championship at the time. Being given a run with the Missouri Championship was widely regarded as the industry's biggest tryout—since that title was frequently a stepping stone to a run with the NWA World Heavyweight Championship.

The fans in St. Louis responded to all of this by turning out in droves. Several thousand fans bought a "season ticket" to the matches for an entire year, which, of course, gave Muchnick the working capital he needed to keep the promotion running and to secure the talent he needed to keep the houses full. On many nights, the Kiel, which held about 10,000 people for wrestling, was filled to capacity.

So with all of this as a backdrop to establish just how important the territory was, and what it meant to be invited to wrestle there—I had a tryout on the undercard of the December 5, 1975, Kiel Auditorium show where I was booked in a ten-minute time-limit match against Bulldog Bob Brown. Brown had been in the Kansas City/St. Louis territory for almost his whole life—he wasn't a really big guy, he was maybe five-eleven and 220 pounds, but he was a good hand. The whole card that night was made up of people who were at the top of their game at the time: Terry Funk was less than a week away from winning the NWA World Championship from Jack Brisco. Stan Stasiak had been the WWF World Champion a couple of years earlier. Nick Bockwinkel was the newly crowned AWA World Heavyweight Champion—having just defeated Verne Gagne a month earlier. Dick the Bruiser was an AWA legend. That snapshot just gives you a little flavor of what the St. Louis territory was like.

The Kiel Auditorium was a terrific venue for wrestling because it was a round arena that allowed everyone to be seated close to the ring. The crowds there were always into the action, making the atmosphere there as good as it was in any place I ever wrestled in except, perhaps, for Madison Square Garden.

When I got to the Kiel for my tryout that night, however, I was surprised to learn that Muchnick was asking me to lie down and take a clean pin from Brown. Sam gave me the finish and told me we'd be going just shy of the ten-minute time limit. I knew from talking to Jim Barnett that Sam was pretty high on me—so I definitely wondered whether there had been a mistake or miscommunication somewhere, or whether I had already done something to sour my relationship with Sam. I definitely thought it odd to be asked to job in my debut.

Nevertheless, as I had always done, I said nothing, listened to what I was being asked to do, went out and had the best match I could with Bulldog, and delivered what Sam was looking for.

As it turned out, that choice became a defining moment in my career.

Sometime later, I learned that because I was a shooter, Sam and his group wanted to make sure, before they made any kind of commitment to working with me, that I wasn't someone whose ego would get in the way of doing business. They wanted to be sure that, if I was asked to "do the honors" for someone, that I would do what was asked of me without complaint. Being asked to do the honors to Brown was a test.

I passed.

The match with Brown went off well, and shortly after the tryout, I got the message through Jim Barnett that Sam wanted me back for a string of dates in St. Louis, beginning on March 26, 1976, at the Kiel. My opponent that night was to be none other than the current Missouri Champion, Harley Race. Because I was still an unproven commodity in the territory, the match was scheduled to be a "non-title" event.

Harley, who remembered me from our match in Omaha, was part of the St. Louis office at the time and wanted to work with me again. He had a lot to do with my being booked into that match with him. We took the crowd on a ride for about fifteen minutes that night, and eventually, I went over Harley by DQ when, per the prearranged storyline, Harley had all he could handle of me and threw me out over the top rope.

The St. Louis fans really liked the match, and particularly liked the finish. Harley drew huge heat for getting himself disqualified and preventing me from scoring the upset. Just by doing that, Harley got the near-capacity crowd that night solidly behind me. The booking of that match was designed to re-establish my standing with the fans after my debut loss to Brown three months earlier, and to get me started on the right foot.

It worked.

On the next Kiel card two weeks later, Sam matched me up with Gene Kiniski, which was another huge honor for me. Kiniski was someone I had heard about for years and years and who was a legend in the business. Kiniski had defeated Lou Thesz for the NWA World Heavyweight Championship in the Kiel ring a decade earlier and then held the belt for three years. He was tall (six foot three or four) and a great athlete, and a very well-respected guy. He was also very tough. Before becoming the NWA World Champion, he had spent most of his career up in Canada.

The match with Kiniski was another big test for me in the eyes of the promoters. At the time of that match, Kiniski was being built up for a match with new NWA World Champion Terry Funk, so Sam asked me to do the honors for him. In the pre-match discussion, however, Muchnick instructed us that he wanted the match to be a see-saw contest that came down to the wire at the end. To his credit, Kiniski honored that request, sold a number of my high spots, and made me look great in defeat. When the match was over, I remember shaking Gene's hand in the back and thanking him for giving me so much of the match, and Gene just clapping me on the back of the head with a big paw and smiling at me. It was a nice moment that conveyed to me that he thought that I belonged.

In St. Louis, Sam Muchnick watched almost every match. Although he was watching, what he was really interested in was feeling the people's energy and how they were reacting to certain guys and certain booking ideas—which guided what he would go on to do in future weeks. Sam could sense that the people were solidly behind me in the Kiniski match, cheering on the edge of their seats, which was exactly the kind of see-saw affair that Sam had asked for. He was looking to see whether I could capture the hearts and minds of the people, get them in my corner, and keep them there, even if I wasn't being booked as a winner in every match.

I guess I passed that test too, because on the card after that, on April 23, 1976, I was booked with Harley again, this time in a title match for the Missouri Heavyweight Championship. The build-up for that match in the local *Wrestling* mailer and at *Wrestling from the Chase* was that Harley had desperately wanted a rematch after our March 26 non-title match that I had won by disqualification, but that I had held out for a title match and gotten it from the promoters. It was a fun little booking twist that increased fan interest in the rematch.

An hour before the match that night, Sam came into the dressing room, and pulled me aside.

"Bobby, you're gonna go over Harley tonight for the belt. When it's time, he's going to try and suplex you, but you'll flip over him and give him the O'Connor finish."

Had Sam Muchnick really just said that?

I was going over Harley Race for the Missouri Heavyweight Championship!

I had been wrestling in Georgia while all of the back-office discussions about this were going on in St. Louis, so I truly had no idea that I was even under *consideration* for this honor, especially considering the way I had been booked in my first three matches. The match itself wasn't the typical long Harley Race–Bob Backlund affair that we would later be known for. We had the people at their emotional high spot at around the twelve-minute mark, so Harley called for the finish. He tried to lift me into the vertical suplex, but I slid over his shoulder and pushed him into the ropes into my rolling reverse cradle and held him there for the three-count. It all happened so fast that it was almost surreal—but I do remember listening to the count, and when the referee's hand slapped the mat for the third time and the bell rang, that there was an explosive cheer from the crowd, as if a year of pent-up frustration had been suddenly released.

In some ways, it had been. Harley had been a very effective heel in St. Louis—hated by the fans for his conniving ways, but managing to hang on the Missouri title for fourteen months—longer than anyone else in the history of the promotion. And then, he and Sam had chosen me to be the man to break that streak. I wouldn't find out until much later how much of an influence Harley had been in getting me a run with the Missouri belt, and in many other ways.

A Backlund High

Bob Backlund had been earning early praise for his potential while he wrestled in Florida. Like me, Sam loved what he saw of Backlund's personality and ability. Pat O'Connor too, was high on Backlund, and Harley simply raved about him. . . . Everyone was amazed at how serious Backlund was. He regularly put in sixty minutes, working out and running the steps before he even stepped into the Kiel ring. He wanted to learn, and he valued constructive criticism . . .

—Larry Matysik, from *Wrestling at the Chase: The Inside Story of Sam Muchnick and the Legends of Professional Wrestling*

Becoming Missouri Champion meant that I always needed to take part in the *Wrestling at the Chase* television tapings, so from that point on, my trips out to St. Louis from Georgia and Florida would involve both the Friday night event at the Kiel followed by the Saturday tapings. My first television appearance with the belt was against Ed Wiskoski—a large, well-built guy who was best known as Colonel DeBeers in the AWA. I went over in that match by disqualification when Lord Alfred Hayes jumped into the ring to interfere in the match—which, of course, was done to create some additional interest in my first defense of the Missouri Championship at the Kiel on May 5, 1976, against none other than Lord Alfred Hayes.

Hayes played the part of an English Nobleman and a snob, so the Midwesterners hated him intensely. He was legitimately from England and was a friend of Billy Robinson, Tony Charles, and Les Thornton—three guys whom I knew well and had trained with in Florida and Georgia. The English guys were all trained in a great wrestling school in England— one of the best in the world—and they were experts at chain wrestling.

Hayes and I had a nice match that was put together pretty well—he had a lot more experience than I did, so he called most of the match, enraging the fans with his heel tactics and hiding them from the referee—building the fans up to a crescendo, where I surprised him and caught him in the small package for the pin. I think that was the first time I met Hayes in the ring—and we had a lot of fun with it.

A couple of weeks later, I caught up with my old friend Terry Funk at what would prove to be an historic *Wrestling at the Chase* television taping. Funk was the reigning NWA World Champion at the time, and was in the territory building up to his upcoming title defense at the Kiel against former champion Gene Kiniski. When Terry saw me in the locker room, he teased me immediately.

"Shit, Bobby. What are you doing up here? You're supposed to be back in Amarillo!"

It was a nice moment.

Sam booked Terry and me into a tag-team match on television against Kiniski and an arrogant blonde and muscular Kansas City heel named Roger Kirby. To my knowledge, that match was the only time the NWA World Heavyweight Champion and the Missouri Champion ever joined forces in a tag-team match.

Pursuant to the booking plan, Kirby and I "had words" and got into it several times in that match, but the real key was that the match ended with Kiniski catching a pin on Terry—all of which, of course, had been cleverly arranged by Sam to generate main events for the next couple of Kiel cards. If Kiniski was capable of pinning NWA kingpin Terry Funk in a tag-team match on television, then clearly he was more than a legitimate threat to take the world championship back in a title match at the Kiel!

Meanwhile, at the next Kiel card on May 21, 1976, I defended the Missouri title against Kirby. The buildup to the Kiniski-Funk NWA title match continued, as the main-event tag-team match that night pitted Gene Kiniski and Jack Brisco against Terry Funk and Dory Funk Jr.

The Funks were over as a monster heel tag team in St. Louis, and the storyline here was that the Funks were "protecting" Terry by trying to take out Kiniski before he could get a world title match with Terry. This was another fun and creative bit of booking by Sam that gives you some insight into the care that went into building these matches.

The energy in the building was amazing that night. Kirby was the master of the piledriver—which was a feared hold in St. Louis at the time—so we worked around him trying to get that hold on me. Eventually, I finished him off after about twenty minutes of back and forth action. Meanwhile, the main event went two out of three falls with the Funks trying and failing to "injure" Kiniski, who was the only guy not to get pinned in the match, and who caught the deciding fall against Junior for the win.

Kiniski had survived the Funks' attempt to injure him. Now there was nothing standing between him and his world title match against Funk.

That match would occur on the next Kiel card. On June 4, 1976, former AWA World Champion Verne Gagne served as the special referee as Terry Funk and Gene Kiniski waged a fierce battle that went to a third fall before Kiniski threw Gagne out of the ring, Funk hit Kiniski with a chair, and the bout ended in a wild double disqualification that absolutely delighted the fans. On that card, I defended the Missouri title against the challenge of Killer Karl Krupp—the latest entry into the Nazi officer typecast. Krupp, who was actually a Dutch guy named George Momberg who hated the Germans for occupying his homeland during World War II, saw this character as a way of ridiculing the Germans, and in doing so, had taken the gimmick over the top. He was a big man with a shaved head, a thin black beard, and a monocle and whip. He came to the ring sneering and goose-stepping in a black cape and shiny black boots, and even though World War II was thirty years in the past by then, the gimmick was a heat machine.

Interestingly—that match with Krupp was the first match I can remember where my opponent no-sold my finisher and the booked finish of the match. Sam had called for me to demolish Krupp with the atomic kneedrop, but when the appointed time came and I hit the fin-isher, Krupp did not go down. Instead, he just staggered around the ring sneering at the fans—which I took as a sign of disrespect both to Sam and to me. I immediately went into shoot mode, slapped him into a standing front facelock, choked him out, and whispered to him that I was going to suplex him for a revised finish, and that he better stay down.

The shoot hold had its desired effect, as Krupp did not test me fur-ther. He stayed down for the three count, but I was not pleased that he had no-sold my finisher in my last match before the summer recess.

We reconvened the *Wrestling at the Chase* television program on July 31, 1976, with a tag-team match where I teamed up with Guy Mitch-ell (later "Gentleman" Jerry Valiant in the WWF) against Harley and Ox Baker. As usual, this tag-team match served a dual booking purpose. First, it set up my next Missouri title defense against Ox Baker at the Kiel. More importantly, it served to reignite my "feud" with Harley Race.

I was thrilled that Sam wanted to book me into an extended program with Harley, because I loved working with him and learning from him. Being in the ring with Harley was so easy—we were nearly always on the same page about where to take the match and how to grow the energy. Harley was *always* focused on making the match the best it could be, and was never concerned about his own ego. The plan that day called for a double disqualification finish, and for me to then demand a singles match with Harley on television at the next *Wrestling at the Chase* program.

The plan went off beautifully. Harley countered that he would not "agree" to wrestle me in a singles match unless I was willing to put up the Missouri title. Of course, I immediately agreed to do so, which brought an outpouring of concern from the fans fearing some sort of double-cross. Sam, however, knew that actually delivering on that double-cross would be too predictable, so he planned another swerve to keep the storyline one step ahead of the fans.

During the televised match, Harley pinned me after illegally using the ropes for leverage and the referee counted to three and raised

Harley's hand. The fans, seeing their worst fears confirmed, were furious. But Sam, who was at ringside watching the match, went to the ring and told the referee what happened, and ordered the match to continue. In a fury, I attacked Race with a vengeance to the delight of the fans, and then, pretending to be totally out of control, threw both the referee and Race over the top rope, leading to Harley's victory by disqualification. I kept the title, Harley was screaming about how the promoters and the referees were "protecting me," and the intensity of our feud ticked up another notch.

Back in the dressing room, Harley and I joked about Sam's booking genius and looked forward to our next chance to entertain the fans at the Kiel.

On August 13, 1976, Terry Funk and Gene Kiniski had their much-anticipated rematch at the Kiel for the NWA World Heavyweight Championship—which was contested, as Sam called it, in a "fence match"—St. Louis's version of the steel cage match. Steel cage matches didn't happen a lot back then in St. Louis, so when Sam scheduled one, it really meant something. To the fans, a cage match meant that there would be a certain winner that night one way or the other. To the workers in the match, a cage match blowoff was a testament to the fact that they had been able to work fan interest in their feud to the highest level. To the other hands on the card, it signaled that the feud between the two wrestlers in the cage match had been milked for everything it could provide, and that a big house (and consequently, a bigger payday for everyone) was in the offing.

That night, Terry turned back Kiniski's challenge in a bloody encounter that gave the St Louis fans something very different from what they were used to. Meanwhile, working off of our previous tag-team encounter, I defended the Missouri Championship against the giant Ox Baker in another all-out brawl.

Ox's pre-match interviews were always good enough to talk the fans into the seats, but unfortunately, they were also almost always better than his actual in-ring performance. To those who don't know Ox Baker—it is worth putting this book down for a moment and YouTubing him to get a sense for what the man looked like in his heyday. Ox stood about six feet six inches tall and weighed about 350 pounds. He was bald, and had a giant black muttonchop beard and wild black eyebrows that framed his face in a permanent scowl.

Ox's interviews were pretty notorious. He would yell and scream and threaten the lives of everyone within earshot. And then he would look into the camera and tell the fans how much he liked to hurt people, all the while ominously tapping his taped left fist that he used for his lethal finisher—the heart punch—which was applied by simply raring back and punching his opponent directly in the heart. Baker enjoyed the additional infamy of having two of his opponents actually *die* (for real) shortly after their matches with him—and although neither wrestler's death had anything to do with his heartpunch, Baker did not hesitate to play up that fact to the fans for maximum effect. In the world of professional wrestling—anything—even another wrestler's *death*, was exploited to create heat.

Baker wasn't the kind of guy you could easily take off his feet or put in wrestling holds. He was a wild brawler—and so we had a fast and furious eight-minute match where he just charged into the ring and beat the heck out of me and got the sympathy of the fans firmly behind me, only to have me pull out a miracle in the end by getting behind him and stunning him with the atomic kneedrop long enough to get the three count and get out of the ring before he realized what had happened. The match with Ox was pretty entertaining in terms of its buildup. He was a terrific-looking and-sounding heel—but once we were in the ring, we were pretty limited as to what we could do.

At the next set of television tapings, Harley attacked me during a televised match against Roger Kirby, again drawing the ire of the fans and setting us up for another tilt at the Kiel on August 27, 1976, for the Missouri Championship. That match was set to be a best two of three falls encounter with Pat O'Connor as the guest referee. Interestingly, there was no NWA World Title match, and no star-studded undercard with talent from Florida and Georgia and Texas supporting us. The undercard that night was filled mostly with standard Kansas City talent, so it was left to Harley and me to draw the house. As I would later find out from Harley and others, Sam was evaluating drawing power as he began to search for Terry's successor as the NWA World Heavyweight Champion.

There was still so much heat associated with Harley's and my feud, that Sam felt that he could milk one more match out of the series—so this one was booked to tease a decisive finish as Harley and I each traded falls, with Harley taking the first one with his finisher—the vertical suplex—and me storming back to take the second fall with mine—the atomic kneedrop. In the third fall, I threw Harley over the top rope and out to the floor, leading, once again, to a disqualification. The fans, however, had gotten enough seeing each of us pinned once, that the indecisive ending only took the energy up that one final notch. We had wrestled for about half an hour and had the people in our hands from the opening bell.

There was only one problem.

The Kiel was only half full.

I remember at the time expressing some concern to Sam that we weren't drawing the kind of houses that St. Louis had grown accustomed to—and Sam just patted me on the shoulder and told me to just worry about putting on a good match in the ring, and not to worry about the houses. I took Sam at his word.

Sam was building toward an October main event where I, as the still-reigning Missouri champion, would face the seemingly insurmountable Terry Funk for the NWA World Heavyweight Championship. To get us there, though, particularly after the fans had just seen Terry defeat the giant former champion Gene Kiniski in the cage, Sam needed to give me a decisive victory over a meaningful opponent.

Once again, Harley Race answered the call.

The match would happen at the Kiel in the territory's first-ever lumberjack match on September 10, 1976, where the other fourteen men on the card surrounded the ring to ensure that neither Harley or I could leave the ring until a definite winner was declared. As before, Sam asked us to trade falls. Harley won the first fall with a vertical suplex, and again, I came back to win the second fall with the atomic kneedrop. In the third and deciding fall, per the booked finish, Harley got into it with Pat O'Connor, who was serving as one of the lumberjacks, and I took advantage of the moment, grabbed Harley from behind and rolled him up for the pin.

The crowd went nuts—and I had my decisive victory over Race. The problem, again, though, was that there just weren't enough people in the seats. Once again, we had no undercard, and our blowoff match for the Missouri title had only half-filled the building. In the dressing room after the match, Harley congratulated me for what he thought was a great match, and I thanked Harley for doing the honors for me. Sam, too, appeared to be very happy with the way the match had come off. Based on what the boys were talking about in the dressing room, I think the problem with the undercard had something to do with a continuing difference of opinion between Muchnick and O'Connor about who to book.

The next Kiel card on September 24, 1976, saw the return to St. Louis of Jack Brisco, the former NWA World Heavyweight Champion. Brisco had beaten Harley for the world championship in Houston on July 20, 1973, and other than an unauthorized and very controversial double-switch with Shohei "Giant" Baba in Japan in December 1974, he had defended the title across the world for over two years until losing it to Terry Funk on December 10, 1975, in Miami Beach.

Jack's return to St. Louis heralded change.

On September 24, 1976, Sam tested Brisco's standing with the fans by immediately putting him into the main event against another former NWA World Champion—Pat O'Connor. He was also building Jack up toward a possible matchup with me for the Missouri Championship. As I would later learn from both Harley and Terry Funk, this was a "test" match, because the NWA Board was taking a look at the former champ knowing that Terry wanted to come off the road, and that the search for Terry's successor was underway.

Interestingly, I was not asked to defend the Missouri title on that card, but instead, was booked on a "dream team" in a six-man tag-team match where my partners were the former WWWF World Champion Pedro Morales and US Champion Wilbur Snyder. Our opponents were a somewhat mismatched team of Baron von Raschke, Tank Patton, and Bob Geigel. Sam kept me looking strong by giving me the pinfall victory over Patton in that lengthy semi-final event. Harley did not appear on that card at all. The fans did not really respond to that booking either—as once again, the card drew a poor house of just over 3,500 fans.

On October 8, 1976, Sam rolled out the card he had been working toward since August—putting me, as the Missouri Heavyweight Champion, into the NWA World Heavyweight Championship main-event match against the world champion, Terry Funk. I was excited to get the chance be in the ring working with Terry again. In light of how much I appreciated the Funks for all that they had done for me, I was bound and determined to make that match with Terry the very best match of my career to date. Happily, we drew a good crowd to the Kiel that night—and the energy in the building was the best it had been in several months. There was definitely electricity in the air, and I think the people could sense that change might be afoot, and that something historic might be in the offing.

Back then, most of the NWA World Championship matches were scheduled for the best two out of three falls to allow for greater booking flexibility—and this match was no different. When Sam brought Terry and me together for the pre-match instructions in the dressing room, he told us that we were going to do a "Broadway" (sixty-minute time-limit draw), and that Terry would capture the only fall in the match. I was thrilled to be given the honor of going Broadway with the NWA World Heavyweight Champion, and shook hands with Terry and shared a few nice words with him before we parted ways prior to the match. Terry and I had worked together so much and so well back in Amarillo that we were totally comfortable being in the ring with each other, and I knew that the fans would be in for a great match that night! There was no mention of a rematch the following month or any booking plans beyond the match that night, but I do remember that Sam was pretty excited about the house we had drawn, and about Terry and me headlining the night.

I can't say enough about how the match came off that night. Terry put over a whole series of my best moves and made me look sensational. As the booking required, Terry took the first fall with a surprise rolling sunset flip, but he waited to take that fall until nearly the entire match had elapsed and he had convinced the fans, beyond doubt, that I had the ability to beat him. Terry did not have to do that. He could have called for the first fall at the fifteen-minute mark and made himself look strong. Instead, he chose to make me look like a world champion.

In the ring with Terry that night in a match for the world championship on the NWA's biggest stage—I realized, for the first time, that I had made it as a professional wrestler. I was totally comfortable, and having the time of my life. It also crossed my mind more than once that Terry was again demonstrating for me the lesson he and Junior had first taught me during my days in Amarillo: when you are the champion, it is your job to make sure that your opponent looks as good as you can possibly make him look. I worked hard in the ring that night—but Terry gave me a lot more of that match than he ever needed to.

It would prove to be the match that made my career.

Making Backlund

Backlund had an excellent one-hour battle with Terry Funk for the [NWA World Heavyweight Championship] gold belt on October 8. Since Funk won the only fall within the sixty-minute time limit, Terry's hand was raised, but Backlund was "made" as a major national player.

After the Funk match, Sam and I were both laughing at how Bob had grabbed each of us, separately, to ask: "Was the match any good?" All I could say was, "Relax—it was great!"

—Larry Matysik

Good People, Good Guys

I wrestled Backlund for the NWA World Heavyweight Championship twice—once in St. Louis and once in Miami. We had a near sellout in St. Louis, and a sellout in Miami, and memorably great payoffs both times. It was such a pleasure for me to step into the ring with Bobby—someone who was an old friend that I had helped to train who, by that time, had already established himself as a credit to our business, and someone that you were proud as hell to be in there with. That's how I felt about Bobby. You wanted good people and good guys to do well in this business—and I'll tell you something—the sixty-minute match that Bobby and I had in St. Louis was one of the very best broadways I ever had as NWA champion—and that's high praise for Bobby, because believe me, I had a lot of them.

—Terry Funk

At the next Kiel card on October 22, 1976, Dory and Harley tangled in the main event, and I was paired with Jack Brisco against Moose Cholak and Buddy Wolfe in a two out of three falls tag-team match. Pairing Jack and me seemed like Sam was angling toward the creation of a "Dream Team" of two former NCAA National champions—but in fact, he was preparing to swerve the fans once again. With the fans expecting us to crush Cholak and Wolfe, we took the first fall easily when I hit the atomic drop on Wolfe for the pin. But Sam was preparing to spring his trap—as he had directed Jack and me to get heat with each other in the second fall.

At the designated time, with all four men in the ring, I "mistakenly" threw Cholak into Brisco, leading to Brisco getting pinned. Brisco popped up and started jawing at me, and bingo—we had heat! Jack then took the third fall by himself without letting me into the match, and I jawed back at him for not "forgiving" my "mistake." The setup for my match with

Jack had now evolved from a pure babyface match, to something with some real additional intrigue! Of course, the unspoken history we had stemming from the Thunderbird incident in Atlanta added some real-life intrigue to this matchup as well.

Once again, just terrific booking by Sam Muchnick.

On November 26, 1976—the seeds of dissension that Sam had sewn a month earlier came home to roost, as Jack Brisco challenged me for the Missouri Championship in a one-fall match. Although billed as a "scientific" encounter, Jack played the tweener brilliantly—skating perilously close to the heel line on several occasions. The end came when I attempted a big splash on a springboard over the ropes from the apron, and Jack lifted his knees and then rolled me over for the pin—bringing an end to my seven-month reign as the Missouri State titleholder.

The main event on that card had Terry defending the NWA World Heavyweight Championship against Harley Race—with Terry going over Harley in what I would later discover was yet another showcase match for the championship committee.

I had my rematch with Jack on December 10, 1976, in the main event at the Kiel. The match was scheduled for the best two out of three falls. Sam's booking called for Jack to retain the belt, but Sam wanted to leave the shine on me—so he had me "injure" my knee in the first fall, allowing Jack to catch me in the figure-four leglock and get the submission. I rose for the second fall and gamely tried to continue the match, but with my knee too badly injured, the ref waived it off about a minute into the second fall and awarded the bout to Jack on an injury stoppage. It was a good way to end my run—making Jack look good, while at the same time, allowing me to get out with my reputation intact. Jack and I worked together very well, and we had no personal differences with each other notwithstanding what had happened in Atlanta. Business was business—and we were both professionals about it.

Backlund as NWA World Champion?

I first met Bobby when he was just breaking into the business around the Minneapolis area in the AWA. He was always a very, very athletic kid, and always in tip-top shape. Actually, in all the years we wrestled, I can never remember seeing Bob not in great shape. I can't remember how many times I wrestled Bob over the years—truthfully, it was quite a few—and he could do virtually anything in the ring.

Given where I was in my career at the time, when I went in the ring, I called 90-plus percent of what was happening in my matches. When you are putting your body at risk with virtually everything that went on, you'd want to make very sure that you knew what was happening at all times. But I never had to worry about any of that with Bobby. When we got in there, we'd just go with the flow.

Anyway, Bobby and I had been together on cards in two or three different places before Sam brought him in to the Missouri territory. At that time, I had already been the NWA World Champion and was, at that time, the Missouri Champion. St. Louis was the dominant city in wrestling for at least fifty years. The NWA was headquartered out of there and spanned from Charlotte to Portland Oregon.

The territory was controlled by Sam Muchnick, Gus Karras, and Bill Longston. Then when Gus passed away in January 1976, Bob Geigel, Pat O'Connor, and I bought Gus's share of the St. Louis promotion, which made the three of us equal partners with each other, and collectively partners with Sam and Bill. By the time Bobby got out here, it was Sam and O'Connor on that side of the state (St. Louis) and Sam and Geigel and me on this side of the state (Kansas City).

I was involved in the decision to put Bobby over for the Missouri title. But we knew that for Bobby to best capitalize on becoming the Missouri Heavyweight Champion—the obvious person for him to beat for that belt would be me. Our thinking was that if he beat the founder of it, the guy that had it the most times, and the guy who was recognized all over the Midwest—that would allow him to jump right out in front of everybody. So when they brought Bobby in, we immediately had a series of matches that ended up with him beating me for the Missouri State Championship. They were great matches. Bobby was a native Midwestern boy. He had such an outstanding look about him—his body and his earnest, innocent face—he just had a look about him that made everyone want to root for him. He was a true babyface, and an underdog-type character who just brought the empathy of the fans right to him. But if you tried to fuck with him for real, believe me, he could handle it. And he got over pretty damned good with the fans out here in the middle part of the country.

Bobby was the type of guy whose personality and work ethic and love of the business just kind of combined to make you want to go in the ring and have a great match with him. I did, anyhow, and I know the other guys in the group felt the same way.

But Bobby's run in Missouri almost didn't end there. He beat me for the Missouri title on April 23, 1976, and then after some rematches, he went on a tear where he was built up for a match with Terry Funk for the NWA World Heavyweight Championship at the Kiel while he was still the Missouri Champion. Those kinds of matches didn't just happen by accident. The person who held the Missouri Championship was widely understood to be a person who was being groomed for a possible run with the NWA World Title.

At the time this was going on, we knew that Terry's run with the belt was coming to an end, and that we were going to need to switch it to someone else soon. But we needed a switch of that title to somebody who both looked the part, and someone who was capable, should someone decide to go into business for themselves and attempt to double-cross him, to put a stop to it in the ring. Bobby certainly looked the part, and he had the shooting skills to protect the belt if necessary. By that point, O'Connor and I had both been in the ring with Bob, and had experienced his skills firsthand.

At that point in 1976, there were three people being considered to become the next NWA World Heavyweight Champion after Terry Funk: Jack Brisco, Bob Backlund, and me. Backlund was very much in that mix. Both Sam and Eddie Graham were very much behind Bobby, and Eddie, in particular, who had been working with Backlund in Florida, was pushing very hard for Bobby. Eddie had worked a lot with Bobby down in Florida, and Bobby had proven himself to be very popular and very reliable and had made Eddie a lot of money down there. Barnett was a big supporter of Bobby's also. But there were others on the Board who were not as familiar with Bobby who wanted to see the title go to Brisco, and there were others that wanted me to get it back.

Back in those days, before his operation splintered off from the NWA to become the World Wide Wrestling Federation, Vince McMahon Sr. was on some of the NWA Boards of Directors. Vince Sr. wasn't on the NWA championship selection committee at the time, but he had a lot of very good friends among the promoters in the NWA that made up that committee, and believe me when I tell you that Vince Sr. wasn't afraid of using his influence to lobby people when he felt strongly about something. Because he controlled some of the largest venues in some of the largest cities in the United States, he had a lot of influence. There were nine members of the championship committee, so you needed a vote of five of the nine to become champion—and that committee didn't have a majority. The group was split three ways between Backlund, Brisco, and me.

Some of the dispute in the office about who was going to get it next was that if the title was going to go back to Jack, it would be a babyface taking it from a babyface, which would run the risk of pushing either Terry or Jack over into the heel role. That would also have been the case with Bobby, but with Bobby, there was the additional concern that he was just too much of a pure babyface. Getting a run with the NWA World Title meant that you had to travel the territories and wrestle the top guy in each territory, whether that person was a babyface or a heel. If you were a babyface champion, in some territories, that meant you'd be wrestling as a babyface against a top heel, while in other territories, you might be wrestling as a babyface against other babyfaces. Sometimes, you could have a straight scientific babyface match, but that wasn't always the most interesting thing for the fans to see, so the booking in those matches often required that, as the champion, you had to cut a corner, or exhibit some more heelish behavior—and that really wasn't in Bobby's nature to do. Bobby Backlund didn't cut corners. That just didn't match up with who he was.

In many of the places I went as the World Champion, I had to play the worst asshole on the face of the earth, and to be honest with you, that came easy to me. Of the people on the championship committee that weren't in favor of putting the NWA World Title on Bobby, that was the knock on him: a perceived inability on his part to play the asshole. Bobby's look and his personality really didn't fit that role. Had Bobby been more of a verbal guy who could talk about himself in arrogant or cocky terms, or if he could have expressed himself more forcefully on the microphone, that might have been enough to overcome those concerns . . . but to be honest with you, that was the one thing about Bobby that was holding some of the members of the committee back from endorsing him for an NWA World Title run.

If you think about the three people in the running for the belt at that time, I was a total asshole and had played one as the champion. I'd beat the hell out of anyone and cheat when necessary whether I was wrestling a face or a heel in any territory in the world, it didn't matter a bit. So I could wrestle anyone without having to radically change my style. Brisco was a babyface, but he was more arrogant and cocky than Backlund—he was better equipped to come on your TV and jump out at you on an interview, and he had just enough swagger to make him better able to walk the line between babyface and heel. Backlund was kind of the opposite of that. He had always been a very humble guy who could cut a convincing straightforward interview and make you love him for being the pure babyface or the underdog—but it was hard to see Bobby playing heel to any babyface in the Alliance at the time. Shit, when he wrestled Dusty Rhodes in Japan for the WWWF title several years later, the fans turned Dusty into the heel. Let's face it—in the world as it was back in the mid-70s, who the hell wouldn't want to see a guy that looked and acted like Bobby Backlund kick the shit out of a cocky asshole like me? Bobby Backlund was the ultimate fucking babyface.

The other concern that a couple of the guys in the office had was that if they put the NWA belt on Bobby, and then he didn't want to lose it when they told him to, who the hell were they going to put in there to take it away from him? If Bobby didn't want to lose, trust me, there were very, very few people in the wrestling business at the time who could have taken it from him in a shoot. That was part of the thinking that went into asking him to lose to Brown in his debut match in St. Louis. It was a test to see whether Bobby would cooperate—and he did, without the slightest hesitation. I don't think that anyone was really worried that he wouldn't cooperate, but that was always something that the committee thought about in those days before they put the big belt on somebody, so why not test him?

Anyway, that's where things were in November 1976—with Terry looking to come off the road and give up the title, and the NWA championship committee undecided as to who should get it next. And that's when, if you can believe it, Vince McMahon Sr.

showed up looking for an "All-American Boy" to be his next babyface champion up in New York.

Vince Sr. came to St. Louis and talked to the committee, and explained that Bruno Sammartino was wanting to come off the road up in New York, and that he was looking for a non-ethnic, All-American Boy to be his next champion. Well Eddie Graham, Jim Barnett, and Sam all recognized at that moment that Vince's opportunity was the perfect shot for Bob. The New York model had always been built around a babyface champion keeping the belt, and getting a cycle of heel challengers coming in from the territories to have programs with him. It had been that way since the territory was founded, and frankly, it was the perfect answer for Bobby, who wouldn't then have to worry about wrestling babyfaces. So Vince Sr. decided to take Backlund to New York, and told the rest of the committee that he thought I should get to run with the NWA World Title based on the way things had gone during my two-month tryout with the belt when I served as the crossover champion between Dory and Jack Brisco.

Vince Sr.'s involvement broke the three-way deadlock and led the committee to choose me to become the next NWA World Champion—and for Bobby, well, that sealed his fate too. He would become the next babyface champion up in New York. Everything pretty much fell right into place after that. I won the NWA World Title from Terry Funk up in Toronto on February 6, 1977, and Bobby went up to New York for his first set of TV tapings for Vince right around the same time.

What happened in that meeting in St. Louis was part of the reason why Vince was always so loyal to Bobby. Vince Sr. had pulled Backlund out of contention to become the NWA World Champion in order to bring him to New York, and had promised the WWWF title to Bobby right down to the day he was going to get it. Vince Sr. was a man of his word, and one of the few people in this business that you could trust on a handshake. So he honored his promise and put the belt on Bobby when the day came regardless of how over Graham was. That's pretty much the way it happened. Vince Sr. was the type of guy that if he really liked someone, he would do just about anything to help him. And Vince Sr. felt that way about Bobby.

—Harley Race

A Committee Divided

I had held the NWA World Title for over a year, and that's about as long as I wanted to have with it because it takes a tremendous toll on your body wrestling long matches night after night, and also on your family because you're traveling all the time. So when I told people that I wanted to come off the road, there was a real question about who was going to carry the title next. Bobby was very much in that mix—in fact, he was the Missouri champion at that time. He had just had a great match with me for the NWA title at the Kiel, and it was between Jack getting it back, Harley, and Bobby. Bobby was being groomed by Eddie Graham, and being groomed very well. Eddie and Sam Mushnick were both pushing pretty hard for Bobby, and he was definitely right in the middle of that discussion. But there was also a group of promoters that liked Jack, and a group that wanted Harley.

The championship committee could not agree, but then we heard that the top spot in New York was about to open up and Vince McMahon was talking to Eddie Graham and looking for an All-American Boy, and Eddie told Vince that Backlund was his guy. Bobby had wrestled for a long time for Eddie down in Florida and for Barnett up in Georgia. Credentials, you see. Why did Bobby end up where he did? Because of his wrestling ability and hard work and honesty. You get up into that group of people who were being trusted to carry the world championships of these different wrestling organizations whether it was in the NWA or for Vince Sr. or for Verne Gagne, and you're talking about people with serious credentials. Bobby was right in there in the mix for a run with the NWA World Championship because of his credentials and his honesty and his integrity.

The committee was split—not because they didn't like Bobby or because Bobby wasn't drawing or anything like that—they loved his look and his ability to take care of himself and the belt, but Bobby would have had to have been purely a babyface champion. And that was their primary concern as it related to Bobby—it was a necessity for the NWA World Champion to be able to be a credible heel in some territories—and back then especially, Bobby didn't look anything like a heel. He looked like the biggest babyface of all time. So ultimately, Eddie pushed Bobby to Vince, because Bobby was exactly what Vince Sr. was looking for—and the glove fit him perfectly in New York, because New York always had babyface champions.

You know, this is probably the craziest business in the world—and yet, the people we are talking about loved this business dearly. And let me tell you something—Vince McMahon Sr. loved this business—make no mistake about that. He cared deeply about getting the right person to carry the WWWF championship—someone who would have the right image for his fans. We talked to him a lot about that.

Junior and I knew what the plan was for Bobby basically from the time that Vince McMahon came to St. Louis to meet with the NWA Board and broke the deadlock in the championship committee in favor of Harley. We knew what would happen as soon as we saw Bobby head for New York. And yeah, we were aware of what happened up there on that February night in 1978 in New York—everybody was. We were thrilled to death for Bobby. Junior and I both were. Bobby was destined to be the champion of the world. But why was that? Because Bobby went to school. He was a great wrestler and a great athlete, and a great student of the game. He learned the ways of this business everywhere he stopped along the way up, and learned how to draw money. And he drew a lot of money for Eddie in Florida. That was very, very important—if he hadn't drawn money, all the other stuff wouldn't have been enough. He wouldn't have had the opportunity. Champions had to have all of the credentials. But really, the one guy who really loved Bob more than anyone else, and who thought the sun rose and set on Bob Backlund, was Eddie Graham, and he was the reason, other than Bobby's own efforts, why Bob Backlund became a world champion.

—Terry Funk

I have to confess that when all of this discussion was going on in the St. Louis office, I had no idea about any of it. I was wrestling down in Florida for Eddie Graham, and I had no idea that I was being considered for a run with the NWA World Heavyweight Championship, and I had no idea, until Vince McMahon Sr. spoke to me in April 1977 in Allentown, Pennsylvania, that I was going to become the WWWF World Heavyweight Champion. Some people will undoubtedly think me naïve, or simple-minded for having come so close to something so important career-wise without even realizing it . . . and consequently, without having had any opportunity to influence the outcome. But that is the way I always lived my life in the wrestling business—and I think that turned out to be much more of a positive for me than anything else.

In any event, that brings the story of my life to the end of the beginning, as the saying goes, and to the place where, at the age of twenty-eight, I made my first trip to New York and prepared to meet my destiny.

I was in the Sportatorium office in Tampa, getting my next set of bookings from Jim Barnett, when Barnett told me that Vince McMahon had called and asked for some dates that I could come up there. We went into Barnett's office and he called Vince Sr. at his home over in Palm Beach. Barnett actually reached Vince Sr. on the phone and I talked with him right then and there. Vince Sr. introduced himself, and he said that he'd like me to come up and have some TV matches for him. He told me to look at some dates and figure out what would work and that he would work it out with Jim.

That was that.

It was a very short, polite conversation—maybe a minute in total.

But as it would turn out, at least as it related to my career in the wrestling business, it was the most important minute of my life.

12

The Six Words That Changed My Life
(WWWF, 1977)

"You are where you are, and what you are, because of your established habits."

—Napoleon Hill, "Use Cosmic Habitforce"

———•◦•———

On the appointed day, I flew commercial from Atlanta to Philadelphia for my first TV taping with the WWWF. Vince Sr. paid for the ticket. Once I got to the Philadelphia airport, I rented a car and began to hunt around Center City Philadelphia for the Philadelphia Arena. This was 1977, long before anyone had ever heard of GPS, or cell phones or the Internet—so I had to stop in at a couple of gas stations, and got lost in some of the seedier parts of South and West Philadelphia, but I eventually found my way there.

I got to the arena at about 6:30 p.m. or so that first night, met the people who were putting up the ring, and they pointed me to the dressing rooms. As soon as I walked in, I saw an older man in a three-piece suit with silvering hair sitting at a table and I knew immediately that it was Vince McMahon Sr.

Vince Sr. got up from the table enthusiastically, and with a big toothy grin, came over and shook my hand. It was definitely the warmest reception I had ever received from a wrestling promoter, and I remember wondering at the time if it meant something. Vince Sr. and I talked for a while, and he explained to me how their TV tapings worked, and what I should expect once the people were let into the building.

Basically, back in those early days at the Philadelphia Arena, the boys got there at around eleven in the morning with Vince McMahon Jr. to start taping three weeks of house show interviews. They typically spent the whole day laying those down, because each card would require three different sets of interviews (one for each week of TV) for at least two and sometimes three of the feature matches. Nothing was scripted, so it often took a few takes to get the interviews right and to make them sound different enough so the fans wouldn't catch on that they were all recorded on the same day. Add in the hijinx and the ribbing and the guys standing just off camera goofing around and trying to make Vince Jr. or each other laugh while they were recording, and you had a recipe for a pretty long day.

That night, I met most of the wrestlers on the WWWF roster, all the managers, and a bunch of the office guys. Captain Lou Albano, Arnold Skaaland, Freddie Blassie, and Ernie Roth (the Grand Wizard of Wrestling) were all sitting there talking with Vince Sr. when I walked in. I also met Domienic DeNucci, Mikel Scicluna, Johnny Rodz, and Gorilla Monsoon. A bunch of them were playing cards. Scicluna was smoking a long, curled pipe and really had the look of a Maltese Nobleman. It was a strange new world—as I had never set eyes on any of these guys before in any of the other territories where I had previously wrestled.

I knew no one, and I definitely felt like an outsider.

I went over and found a corner, put my bag down, and started changing into my wrestling gear to get ready to have a match. The Captain (Lou Albano) was the first guy to come over and engage me.

"Where you from, kid?"

I spoke to him in my normal voice, with my eyes down, looking at the floor.

"I'm from Princeton, Minnesota, sir," I said quietly. "But we're living down in Georgia right now."

"Speak up, mumbles! You sound like you gotta mouthful of mashed potatoes. You need to enunciate. You got that?! E-nun-ci-ate! E-nun-ci-ate! Bwa-ha-ha-ha!"

The Captain was pretty well lubricated with alcohol by that time of the day, and he was yelling and laughing and carrying on with his big belly hanging out of his shirt, which was all the way unbuttoned. He was loud and I certainly wasn't used to that kind of brashness. I hadn't met anyone like him before that, and it caught me off guard. There were people in that dressing room, like Albano and DeNucci and Scicluna and Chief (Jay Strongbow) who had all been in the territory for a long time and knew each other well. I was an outsider—but I think everyone sensed, even on that first day, that I was there for a reason. I don't know whether Vince Sr. had discussed it with anyone before I got there, or told some of the people that I was coming in, or what—but there was definitely a kind of stand-offish curiosity among the boys about who I was and what I was about.

There was a definite clique in that dressing room, comprised of Bruno, DeNucci, Rodz, Garea, Chief, and Scicluna. They were a strong and tight-knit group. Fortunately for me, Vince McMahon Sr. went out of his way to make me feel welcomed and at home.

At the time, the Capitol Wrestling Group ran the WWWF, and that group was comprised of Vince Sr., Phil Zacko, Arnold Skaaland, and Gorilla Monsoon. I think Angelo Savoldi also had a small piece of the action also. He helped on the administrative side and it seemed like he was always around. Vince Sr. had the book, and was very definitely the man in charge. As I would learn later, that group used to gather in their little New York City office across from the Garden on the Monday afternoon before the Garden show and brainstorm about booking ideas—who to bring in, what had been hot on the house show circuit, and what feuds or angles might be started to kick-start some new box office interest. Sometimes, the same group would gather at the TV tapings as well—and you'd see them sitting at a table talking, smoking cigars, and playing gin rummy.

There were locker rooms in the Philadelphia Arena, but the building was a dump and its owners were charging Vince Sr. a lot of money for rent. It wasn't long after I came in for the first tapings that the WWWF moved its television tapings out of the Philadelphia Arena and up the road a bit to the little arena at the Allentown Fairgrounds, and the next day at the Hamburg Fieldhouse. In addition to saving money and getting us out of that decrepit building, I think ownership also wanted the fans from inner-city Philadelphia to come out to the larger and more lucrative Spectrum cards instead.

The Allentown arena was just a large, open agricultural hall with no dressing rooms or showers. One corner was cordoned off with a big blue curtain, and all of the wrestlers, both babyfaces and heels, were just sitting around in folding chairs behind that blue curtain or hanging around outside in the parking lot. Both buildings were very small steel and aluminum structures that actually reverberated with fan noise, and the people there were always very animated, so they worked out well for TV.

We would tape three one-hour shows sequentially, one after the next, with many of the guys wrestling two or three times each night against enhancement talent who would make them look good. There would also be one "dark match" main event at the end of the night, not broadcast on television, which was used to draw the crowd.

Because each of those arenas held only about 750 people, it was basically the same people who were there all the time. There were two different TV shows, Championship Wrestling, which was generally regarded as the "A" show (meaning that if a market got only one show, it was usually this one) and All-Star Wrestling, which was the "B" show (and was often broadcast on another channel serving the same market). Joe McHugh was the ring announcer for Championship Wrestling and Gary Capetta was the ring announcer for All-Star Wrestling. Vince McMahon Jr. and Antonino Rocca were the television announcers who called the action. Rocca was later replaced by Bruno Sammartino after Rocca died. When Sammartino retired, Pat Patterson took over for Bruno.

Those hour-long televised wrestling shows were basically just ads for WWWF wrestling. In any given hour, there might be fifteen to twenty minutes of actual wrestling, nearly all of which would be "squash" matches pitting a popular babyface hero against an enhancement guy to make him look invincible, or the new vicious heel against an enhancement guy to make the heel look like a complete madman or a killer. Of course, the purpose of those TV tapings was to get the people interested in seeing either the invincible babyfaces or the vicious heels battle *each other*, and of course, those matches weren't shown on television. You'd have to pay to see those matches in your local arena.

Each media market would get the appropriate promotional interviews I spoke of earlier, which would be spliced into each market's copies of Championship Wrestling or All-Star Wrestling, and shown after each squash match to whet the people's appetites to come out to the arenas and see the "real" matches.

Although I can't remember exactly, I'm pretty sure I wrestled Johnny Rodz first. Rodz was an excellent hand—and more than anyone else on the roster, Rodz was the guy that Vince Sr. put in the ring with new incoming talent to figure out how good they were. Vince would watch those matches pretty closely, but when the match was over, Vince Sr. would go over and talk to Rodz, and see what Rodz thought of the match—that's how much he thought of Johnny. It is no accident that when he retired, Johnny opened a successful wrestling school. His timing and in-ring skills were just terrific.

I also wrestled a guy named Prettyboy Larry Sharpe, another of Vince McMahon Sr.'s trusted guys whose talents and opinion he respected. Sharpe was in the waning days of his wrestling career at that time, and, at the time, often wrestled in a pretty entertaining tag team with a guy named Dynamite Jack Evans. Sharpe's primary role in the company at the time, though, was to test out the new guys, work on their timing, and see how well they could sell his offense. To a lesser degree, Larry would also work with guys in the local house shows around his home in

Paulsboro, New Jersey. When Larry hung up the boots, he, too, opened a very successful wrestling school.

I also wrestled Pete Doherty, a true character from Dorchester, Massachusetts, who had scraggly blonde hair, mismatched gear, and was missing about every other tooth. Doherty, who was known as "The Duke of Dorchester," looked like a longshoreman, kept himself in really good shape, had really good timing and knew how to work the crowd to get a rise out of them. Doherty kept doing this little gimmick where he would hold his hair up and show the crowd, as if to suggest that his babyface opponent had pulled his hair, which of course, he hadn't. Doherty was especially popular up in Boston, and on the local house show circuit up in that area around Massachusetts, Rhode Island, New Hampshire, and Maine, where he was often used to jerk the curtain and warm up the crowds. He also got a push working under the hood as "The Golden Terror" around this time. Doherty was a very good hand in the ring, and a very funny guy. I liked wrestling him a lot.

That first time up in Philadelphia, people truly didn't know me from Adam, so my job was simply to go out there, show some of my amateur moves and my speed and quickness, and try to get over with the people. The WWWF roster at the time was more of a brawling roster, so I knew that my more refined amateur style was going to be a big change for the fans and might be an acquired taste that would take some getting used to. Each wrestler had a different way of trying to get over with the fans in a new territory. I had already had enough high-profile work, so I was very confident in my in-ring work—so it really just came down to executing my moves and playing to the crowd.

There is no doubt in my mind that Vince Sr. could have recruited any wrestler from any territory anywhere in the world into the WWWF with the promise of making that person the next babyface world champion. He could have taken Dusty Rhodes or Steve Keirn out of the Florida territory. He could have had David Von Erich from World Class. He could have had Tommy Rich from Georgia. But Vince Sr. had a vision—a plan—for what he wanted that next great "character" to be, and he wanted that person to look and act like the "All-American Boy." In choosing me, Vince Sr. obviously gave up an opportunity to put the belt on someone more senior, or someone with a longer track record of making money and putting people into seats in the business—but it seemed that he was completely convinced that his new character would work, and that I was the right person to play the role.

I know, both from chatter I overheard in the dressing rooms in those early days, and from things people have told me over the years, that there were guys in the WWWF at the time who were trying to talk Vince out of giving me the belt. There were different reasons for that—some fair, and some not. I was a complete unknown in the territory, and there were a lot of people who were better known to the WWWF crowds. There were a number of guys already on the roster who had shown that they could reliably draw money and put butts in the seats—whereas no one knew whether I would be able to do that or not. Since the dawn of the territory, the WWWF crowds had grown accustomed to their champion espousing a more brawling, take-no-prisoners style. I was coming in, not only with a more amateur, scientific style, but as the perpetual underdog to boot.

No matter what anyone else thought, though, Vince McMahon Sr. stayed true to his vision, and there is not a day that goes by in my life that I don't think about him and the faith he took in believing in me.

At the end of that first set of tapings, Vince Sr. also put me into the ring in a six-man tag-team match with a couple of other babyfaces, Tony Garea and Larry Zbyszko. The purpose of that was to put some extra shine on me with the fans to help them define me as an upper-level babyface. Both Garea and Zbyszko were very good, so putting us together would showcase the three of us for the crowd, and for the WWWF ownership group, who could then easily compare our skills in the ring, the way we looked, and the way the crowd reacted to us.

I knew from the little bit that Jim Barnett had told me that this was an "important tryout"—and I wasn't about to fail it.

At the end of the tapings, Vince McMahon Sr. had just a quick chat with me. He thanked me for coming, shook my hand again, told me that he thought my matches had gone "well," and invited me to come back for the next taping in three weeks. And with that, I flew back to Georgia and continued to wrestle there for Jim Barnett.

I returned to Pennsylvania in March, and it was at the end of that second set of television tapings that Vince Sr. pulled me into the bathroom and delivered the news that he had decided to put the championship on me. I don't think it really hit me until I was sitting on the airplane flying home from that second set of tapings exactly what that meant economically to my family, what it would mean with respect to my celebrity, and most of all, what it would mean with respect to stability. We would finally be able to settle down up there and not move around from territory to territory every few months.

Bruno on Backlund

McMahon and Junior had made me a deal when I agreed to come back for a second run with the title. They asked me to come back for one year to give them time to find somebody, and then I could retire. They promised me that I would only have to wrestle two or three times per week. They did keep their word—but it went from one year to four years until Stan Hansen bodyslammed me on my head at the Garden and broke my neck. At that point, I told Vince that I had been more than fair with him, and that he had to get someone ready. I didn't want to have the responsibility to be featured in all the major clubs—I wanted to pick my shots, and I wanted to leave on top.

You know, the first guy I wrestled in my career when I was twenty-three years old in 1959 was Gorgeous George. The match happened in Convention Hall in Philadelphia. I was excited—I was 275 pounds, I wrestled amateur but I was also a weightlifter. I was so nervous about wrestling this guy, because I was a rookie, and he was a big name, you know? He had been really big in the '40s and part of the '50s, but in 1959, he was no longer a star. People were catcalling him saying, "Hey, Bruno, don't hurt the old man." It made me feel sad for George. I made myself a promise that I would never let that happen to me—and that when it was time for me to go, I would leave on top.

They asked me who I wanted to drop the belt to the second time, and I didn't want anything to do with that decision. I had nothing against Billy Graham personally, but I did not like the drug use. The younger people weren't thinking long range—they just wanted to take the shortcut to be the next guy. I even spoke to him a couple of times and told him that what he was doing with the drugs could leave a very negative lasting effect on him. But Billy didn't take my advice. They all acted like I was from the Stone Age. You know, you get results when you train hard—but by taking the chemicals, you get twice the result for half the effort, and it seemed like everyone was willing to make that tradeoff.

Vince never asked me about Bob Backlund or about making him the next champion. Shame on me, but I had never even heard of Bob Backlund before they mentioned that he was coming in for TV. When I first saw him, though, I could tell that he was not on the juice, and that he was a legitimate athlete who trained hard. I remember saying to DeNucci how happy I was that Backlund was not a chemical freak. Skaaland spoke well of Backlund too. He was of the same ethnic background as Backlund (from Sweden), and he told me that he was going to be Backlund's manager the same as he had done for me. As I got to know Bob, it became apparent to me that we actually had a lot of things in common, one of them being that he and I were two squares who were still playing by the rules and coming by our bodies legitimately, which of course made me happy to see.

I liked the way that Bob was built—he was very athletic looking and possessed a very good knowledge of amateur wrestling. When I first saw him, I thought that he was going to be a high flyer who did dropkicks and flying head scissors, which he didn't do that much, but I liked that he was using real technical wrestling. And he did, in fact, look like the All-American Boy. You know, the previous baby-face champions had both been ethnic stars. Pedro was from Puerto Rico, and I was from Abruzzi, Italy. Backlund was a change—he was the All-American Boy from Minnesota. It was good. It was different. Backlund represented a change from the norm, and it worked out well for the organization.

The model in the WWWF had always been to have a babyface champion. You see, a heel can go on television with a manager, wreck a babyface and say, "That's what I'm going to do to Bruno or Backlund"—and bingo, you have a draw at the box office. But it takes a babyface a lot longer to get "over" and to see if the people are willing to accept him and rally behind him. So it was a lot harder in the WWWF to have a heel champion for any sustained period of time because it took too long to develop babyface challengers. You could do it in the NWA, because the heel champion traveled from territory to territory wrestling the top babyface in each of them. But in the WWWF, there were no other territories, so the champ was a babyface, and the heels were imported from outside for short runs.

The guys in the locker room understood that McMahon needed to bring in new blood and wanted someone fresh and new and different. After Backlund won the title, I wasn't around regularly anymore, so I can only tell you some of the things I heard. Some of the guys thought that Backlund might have lacked a little bit of charisma, and some of the heels, at least in the very beginning, felt that they had to wrestle his match, as opposed to their match, because Backlund wasn't a natural when it came to brawling. But to be honest, there really weren't a lot of complaints. Some of the guys in the dressing room were wondering whether Backlund could fill the Garden. But McMahon and Junior were both very much behind Backlund.

Much has been made over the years about Backlund having more support on his undercards, but I'll tell you, someone like Andre the Giant was not the kind of attraction they made him out to be. Andre was a novelty guy—he couldn't be in a territory for very long and couldn't be used a lot. Andre wasn't a hell of a lot of help to Backlund—Backlund did what he did mostly on his own. The facts are the facts, and the facts show that Backlund was able to fill the Garden. If Backlund hadn't been able to get over, believe me, Vince would have switched horses like he did with Buddy Rogers. Buddy Rogers was killing the territory as champion, so Vince switched the title. You never really know who the people are going to buy until you see it with your own eyes. If Backlund had not drawn well, he would have been out of there, no matter what promises might have been made to him. McMahon might put someone over, but if the people don't end up coming out to see him, his headlining days would be over quick. The name of the game was selling tickets.

—**Bruno Sammartino**

They Had Plans for Backlund

I was around at the time that the transition away from Bruno began. Bruno was tired of the grind and had wanted to come off the road for some time, and he really wanted me to have the belt. There was a big, big fight with the old man about it because the old man wanted Superstar to get the run, and Bruno wanted me to have it. He put the belt on Billy mainly because Eddie Graham wanted him to do that and the old man and Eddie were very close. Right after he did that, the old man said to me, "Well, we'll figure out who the real heel is between you and Superstar," and he booked a couple of test matches in some small towns mostly up in Maine, away from the big cities just to see what would happen. The one match of those that I distinctly remember was up in Portland, Maine, in the old expo center up there. Billy and I had a hell of a matchup there, I think we went about twenty or twenty-five minutes and we wound up out on the floor in some sort of a double countout with blood all over the place, but three minutes into the match, I had turned Superstar stone cold babyface. The crowd was cheering Billy like crazy, and I don't think the old man liked that at all. Anyway—the experiment proved to the old man that I was the bigger heel.

I remember I was up in Portland and Bangor, Maine, on the northern swing with the kid—Junior–Vinnie—we used to call him Vinnie or Junior—I'm talking about Vince McMahon Jr. now. We were riding back from the show in Bangor down to New Haven, Connecticut, and he was telling me that they had big plans for Bobby Backlund. Vinnie told me that they were going to have Superstar drop the belt to him at the Garden, and that the plan was to run with Backlund for at least five years. And I looked at Vinnie and said, "Five years?! What about me?" The old man had more or less been promising me for some time that I would get a run with the belt at some point. I mean, he never really came out and promised me that in so many words, but it was pretty much the plan for about a year and a half, that I was going to be the one to take it off of Bruno when the time came—and that's what everybody thought.

So Vinnie looks at me and says, "Well, you know Kenny, things change, and this is the direction we're going in." I talked to his dad a day or two later at the Garden and asked him about it, and he said, "Well Kenny, you know, I talked to Eddie Graham, who is a good friend of mine, and Eddie wanted me to put the belt on Superstar." Superstar had been doing a lot of wrestling down in Florida for Eddie Graham and had been the Florida Heavyweight Champion, so I guess Eddie thought it would be good for business to have

Superstar get the WWWF title for awhile. And I guess it turned out that way, because after he won it, he went down to Florida with it and defended it down there, and people knew him, so he drew some pretty nice houses.

Anyway, I reminded the old man that the expectation had been that I would be the guy to take the belt off of Bruno, and now that wasn't going to be the case, and on top of that, I'm hearing that Bobby Backlund is going to have the belt for five years, so where does that leave me? You know? So I asked him, can you give me some idea of what my future looks like here? Do I need to go somewhere else? So the old man looked me in the eye and told me straight up, Kenny, you don't need a belt to draw—but I told him I thought that was a line, because everyone knows the champion gets the main events and gets the big checks, and I told him that I thought I had proven myself.

Anyway, the old man wanted me to stay two more years, but I told him I wasn't going to stay two more years if I wasn't going to get a chance to carry a belt. I was living down in North Carolina at the time, and so I told him I was going to take off and head down there and work for Jimmy Crockett and Crockett promotions. Well I'll tell you, he was pissed. He really got pissed about that. The old man also suggested that during the next two years, he would set me up to go over and work for Inoki in Japan because the old man was trying to work out a reliable relationship with Inoki and New Japan. Well, I stayed for a little while longer, but after that, I did go down and work for Jim Crockett down in Mid-Atlantic, and while I was there, I went over and worked for Baba in All-Japan—which was Inoki's big rival. Well that really pissed off the old man, let me tell you. He was really big time pissed. But what the hell? He fucked me out of the goddamned belt!

—Ken Patera

Corki became pregnant with Carrie in February 1977 and shortly after that, we headed back to Minnesota because we wanted our daughter to be born there. I called Verne, told him that my wife was going to have a baby and that after that, we were going to be moving to the New York area to work for the WWWF. I asked him if he wanted to book me while I was in the area, and he said that he would see what he could do.

As it turned out, Verne kept me pretty busy. News traveled quickly in the territories back then, so many of the promoters knew what the plan was—and Verne had a very good relationship with Vince Sr., so I wouldn't be surprised at all if the two of them had a conversation about "protecting" me while I was home in Minnesota and working in the AWA. Even though there was no crossover television between the two territories at that time, I was now a "made" man in New York, and I'm sure Vince asked Verne to respect that. Given their relationship at the time, and what ended up happening to me while I worked for Verne, I'm pretty sure that Verne did what Vince asked.

Even though I was wrestling in the AWA at the time, I had my first match at Madison Square Garden in New York City on April 25, 1977, against Masked Executioner II (Killer Kowalski) on the undercard of Bruno's final title defense at the Garden against Baron von Raschke. The Garden almost always had at least 20,000 people in it, and it was a very strange feeling going from wrestling in a little high school gym in a tiny town in the middle of nowhere in Minnesota to wrestling in one of the largest venues in the world in the middle of New York City. It was odd just being in New York, getting recognized, having people wishing me luck, and recognizing me from the TV tapings—I could actually feel the amount of exposure I was getting from the TV time. It was rewarding but sort of scary at the same time because it became pretty evident that I was losing my anonymity and my privacy.

Wrestling Kowalski in my debut match at the Garden was quite an honor, although I wouldn't have minded being in the ring with someone who could have moved around a little more so I could have used a few more of my moves. Kowalski was really slowing down by then, and I wasn't able to have my best match with him. It was still great being there, though, and the energy in that building was like nothing I had ever experienced.

With Bruno Sammartino making his last ever WWWF title defense in the Garden on that card, he was a big presence in the dressing room area that night. Bruno didn't really know me, and I didn't know him at all, so we didn't speak much at that card. To be completely honest, because I hadn't grown up watching him, I didn't idolize Bruno like many of the other young guys. He wasn't a hero of mine—and I don't mean that at all in a negative way, I just didn't know a whole lot about him. I knew Bruno only by reputation—that he was a fitness fanatic who worked hard, ran hard, trained hard, and put a lot of miles on his body investing in his craft. I knew that he worked way above and beyond what the average professional wrestler did—and I definitely respected him for that, because I shared those values too.

Bruno and I shook hands in the dressing room that night. It was just a quick handshake—but in reality, it was an important moment there in the back hallway of Madison Square Garden. Both of us knew what the future held, so in effect, that moment represented something of a passing of the torch. A few nights later, Bruno would go to Baltimore and lose the title to "Superstar" Billy Graham and set into motion the events that would eventually lead to my becoming the next babyface WWWF champion.

Shortly after that first appearance at the Garden, I learned another important lesson about professional wrestling that would stay with me for the rest of my career. It was Harley Race who really accentuated the critical importance of respecting your opponent's body in the ring. Professional wrestling might have predetermined outcomes, but it is also a very athletic pursuit, and when you are in the ring in front of thousands of people executing high spots like suplexes and piledrivers with adrenaline coursing through your veins, it is critical to remember that the high spots you are doing can cripple your opponent in an instant if you aren't careful. When you call a spot, you are responsible for making it look good, but even more importantly, you are responsible for your opponent's body and for making sure that your opponent makes it all the way back down to the mat safely and without getting injured.

I knew my time in the AWA was going to be short-lived and that I wasn't going to climb the ladder there toward a shot at the AWA world title. My job was to just keep my skills sharp and stay in shape wrestling in the middle of the cards there. I was grateful to have a place to do that so close to home, and to get paid for doing it. My ticket had already been punched for New York—and this was just a stop on the way to allow Corki to be in Minnesota when our daughter was born.

While I was in the AWA, I liked working with Jim Brunzell and Billy Robinson. Robinson was one of the best shoot wrestlers in the world, and he was there because of that. If Verne was having a problem with someone, he'd book the person into a match with Billy Robinson and tell Billy to "stretch" the guy, and that would take care of the problem. These were the guys that I watched while I was growing up—so it was a real pleasure to be able to get into the ring with some of them, or even to share a spot on a card, or be in the dressing room with them.

Life, however, had one more curve ball to throw at me.

Right before I went to the WWWF, I bought a brand new 1977 gray Buick Electra in Cambridge, Minnesota, and I was showing it off back in Princeton. We had all had a few beers, and I was going home late at night and went to make a right turn onto Silver Lane, lost control of the car in the gravel, slammed into a telephone pole, and put my head through the windshield.

There was only 58 miles on the car at the time of the accident, and frankly, I was lucky to have lived through it.

As the police approached the scene, I jumped down into the grass and pretended to be looking for the keys. I figured that the police couldn't arrest me if they couldn't find the keys to prove I was driving the car. They eventually locked me in the back of the cruiser, but they never found the keys. That's because they were buried deep in my inside pocket the whole time. Things certainly might have turned out very differently for me, and for Corki, if anything about that accident had gone a different way. Given the lateness of the hour, Corki eventually came out looking for me and came upon the accident scene. She was very pregnant, and about to give birth to our daughter at the time, and she was not at all happy with me.

That was the last time I ever drank and drove an automobile or got into the car with anyone who had been drinking. I was very fortunate to learn that lesson and to be able to live to tell about it.

I went back to Philadelphia for the first set of May TV tapings for the WWWF. By that time, Billy Graham had the title, having just beaten Bruno at the Baltimore Civic Center, and they were showcasing him as the new champ. I was wrestling in individual matches but also teaming with Chief Jay and Billy Whitewolf to keep the focus on me as an up-and-coming babyface who was allied with the other, more established heroes in the territory.

At the second set of May TV tapings, I wrestled only in singles matches as Vince began the process of establishing me as a singles wrestler. At those tapings, I wrestled Buddy Wolfe on television. Buddy was a very good performer from Minnesota, and was a lot of fun to work with because he was energetic and had very good timing. Buddy also grew up about 30 miles from Princeton, so we tended to see a lot of things the same way.

On May 27, 1977, I went back to St. Louis for Sam Muchnick, and had my first WWWF title match against "Superstar" Billy Graham at the Kiel on the top of that card. St. Louis was a very safe place for Billy and me to meet in our first match to begin to get familiar with one another and to get our timing down. There was no cross-pollination of St. Louis television anywhere in the WWWF territory, so at the time, very few people outside of St. Louis knew that the match even happened.

Frankly, I was surprised to be getting a match against Billy so soon, but apparently, Sam was anxious to be the first promoter to put the two of us together in the ring. Because Sam had been right in the middle of the NWA World Title discussions a year earlier that had resulted in Vince McMahon Sr. taking me to New York, he already knew that I was the one who was eventually going to beat Billy for the belt—so he wanted to get ahead of other promoters and be the first to book us together.

The fact is, Billy Graham *looked* like a professional wrestling champion, and as everyone knows, he was also terrific on the microphone, but when it came down to actual execution, there was really only so much that Billy could do in the ring. That first match in St. Louis evolved into a fight in and out of a few basic wrestling holds, and Billy won and retained the title, beating me by countout. The countout ending was frequently a pretty unpopular one with the fans and almost always left everyone wanting more—which, of course, was the whole point of having that kind of a finish. Winning or losing a match by countout never really hurt anyone's standing, but it also didn't really do anything for anyone either. It was essentially just a way to tread water until the next card, where the inconclusive finish could help to draw the next crowd if we were coming back against each other.

Fortunately, I had learned from Harley and Jack and Terry how much offense I should take in a match and how much I should give to my opponents. During my days wrestling in the NWA territories, that was never really a problem, as it seemed that most of the guys I worked with were on the same page about that and willing to give and take based on what the crowd was reacting to. When I got to the WWWF, though, things were different. I became very grateful for my amateur background, because there were times that I needed to rely on it. There were definitely people there in the early days that tested me and tried to take advantage of my good nature by taking more of our matches than they should have.

The reality is, in the wrestling business, you never really know what people are thinking, so you always have to be on your guard—especially when you're the guy on top, or on the way to the top, and needing to protect yourself or the belt. All it takes is one quick unexpected move— intentional or not—or one failure to permit an escape while the referee is counting, and the referee will count you out. Even though the out- comes were predetermined, there was an unwritten rule in the wrestling business that the referee needed to make things look legitimate. If you failed to get your shoulders up when you were supposed to, the referees were always directed make the three count, even if it was against book- ing, or against the wrong man, because failing to do so would expose the business.

In the late summer of 1977, Vince Sr. called me and invited me to do a spot house show out on the Boardwalk in Wildwood, New Jersey, against Ken Patera. Up to that point, Vince's plan had been to build me up to the WWWF audience slowly on television, but not to overexpose me out on the house show circuit, since there was still so much time before I would be taking over as champion, and only a few legitimate heels in the territory to wrestle. This match with Patera was to be my first real test in the WWWF, out on the house show circuit in a main event where my opponent and I were being relied on to draw the house. Vince wanted to see how well his experiment in getting me over with the WWWF crowds strictly on television was working. He also wanted to try me out in an arena setting and see how the crowd would react to me and how the match would go.

In Wildwood, the arena was right off the Boardwalk—I think it held something like 1,000 people—and most of the people who would come to the matches were down at the shore on vacation. Wildwood didn't get a steady diet of professional wrestling, so when the WWWF held a spot show there in the summer, it was something of a happening. Gorilla Monsoon, who was in charge of most of the New Jersey spot shows on behalf of Capitol Wrestling, would set up a table out on the Boardwalk and sell tickets, and the wrestlers would typically all be out on the beach working on their tans during the afternoon before the matches.

I remember it being stiflingly hot and humid in Wildwood that night. The people were packed into that place and were very enthusiastic. I was excited to be out on the road, and to be working with a guy like Ken Patera, who was the biggest monster heel in the WWWF at the time, and who was also someone who could really work a terrific match. I knew there was a lot that we could do. Vince didn't want to hurt Patera, for whom he had some big plans, so the match was booked with a DQ finish, but the people were roaring, and I think the experiment was a pretty big success. Arnold Skaaland and Gorilla Monsoon both had nice things to say to me after the match.

Debuting in Wildwood

Other than one or two Garden shows, that match in Wildwood was Bobby's first house show match out on the WWWF circuit after about six months of just being on TV. I'll tell you, he was so fucking wound up and nervous for that match he couldn't sit still. They had just opened up the new building there on the Boardwalk, and the place was packed. I remember it was in the 90s that day and there was not a cloud in the sky, so there were thousands and thousands of people out on the beach and in town. The matches were advertised on posters out on the Boardwalk, and apparently, the ticket office just kept selling more and more tickets until they didn't have any place left to put people.

They didn't have any grandstands or anything—it was just a big empty building with rows and rows of folding chairs around the ring, so at the last minute, about two hours before the show, someone had the bright idea to go down to the playing fields in town with a pickup truck and a trailer and haul back all of the portable seating that they could find in the whole fucking town. Without that, they could only have put about 600 or 700 people in the place, but with those portable bleachers, they jammed about 1,000 people in by selling general admission tickets. So there we were—the building had just fucking baked in the heat all day long, and there was no air conditioning. Bobby had just done all of this promotional TV with the WWWF but had not yet appeared live anywhere, so the fans were just completely insane to see him in person.

The promoter, old man McMahon, had talked to me at the TV taping immediately before this happened and said "Kenny, I want you to take Bobby down there and have a really good match with him to get him off on the right foot with the fans." I knew Bobby's background, knew he had been the Missouri Heavyweight Champion, and knew him a little bit from TV, so when McMahon asked me to break him in, I said, "Sure—I'd love to." So Bobby and I went down there and we had a hell of a match. My body still remembers that match to this day, though, I'll tell you. Bobby got me into the rowboat and he almost tore my arm off he was so excited. Then he got me in a headscissors and brought one leg down across my face and smashed my nose, then about ten minutes later, he potatoed me and gave me a fat lip, and he squeezed his headlock so tight that both of my ears were burning.

We had some kind of a screwjob finish where I got frustrated and hit him with something or hit the referee or whatever, and the fans just fell in love with Bobby. After the match, though, I was joking with him in the locker room and I told him, "Hey—I've had easier street fights than this—you need to learn to settle down and remember that this is for show!"

—**Ken Patera**

After that spot show in Wildwood, I came back off the road in the WWWF again for about a month until I went back to the Garden on September 26, 1977, in a match against "Prettyboy" Larry Sharpe. Larry had been an amateur high school wrestler in New Jersey, and he had blonde hair and a beautiful red robe and a cocky attitude, all of which made him a good foil for me. He was a good hand, and he was pretty good at developing a story. He was a good person for me to wrestle on my way up the ladder at that time because he was capable of having a fast-paced wrestling match, with lots of fast sequences of chain wrestling holds and counters, which was my strength and was becoming my calling card with the fans in the WWWF. Larry was another one of those guys like Johnny Rodz and Jose Estrada who could really work, and who Vince Sr. would use to test people out and see how they could work. Vince would also frequently put these guys with good workers from other territories or from New Japan if Vince wanted to make them look good at the Garden.

That night, Billy and Dusty were on top for the world championship. In retrospect, I think those two guys, individually and collectively, also helped cement Vince Sr.'s decision to put the belt on me. At the time, Dusty and Graham were at the forefront of a group of guys around the wrestling business looking to organize themselves, seize power from the promoters, and have more influence over their lives in the business.

At the time that this match occurred, Dusty had a pretty good grip on the Florida territory to the point where he could control the booking, veto the promoters' plans, and do nearly anything he wanted to do, and there wasn't much Eddie or Jim Barnett could do about it. Although Eddie Graham was the owner and promoter of Florida Championship Wrestling, Dusty really controlled that promotion. Dusty was "everyman"—the self-professed blue collar son-of-a-plumber who the fans could relate to. He was an artist in the ring, and he had the talk and the dance to go with it, and the people down there just went nuts for him. It was genius. People used to dream about finding a character like Dusty Rhodes and being able to do it that well. But Dusty was a one of a kind because it was authentic.

Dusty Rhodes and Billy Graham were very, very good friends. Dusty didn't come up to New York very often when Bruno was champion, but he did come up a fair amount when Graham was champion and in the early years when I was champion. I think that Graham and Dusty were interested in trying to take greater control of Vince's promotion in much the same way that Dusty had done with Eddie's promotion down in Florida. When you get that "over," with the people, you have a lot of control, and the promoter can't get rid of you without damaging his own financial future.

Eddie Graham and Vince Sr., however, were *also* very good friends and they talked a lot, and I think Eddie warned Vince not to let Superstar become his Dusty Rhodes, or to let either or both of them take root in New York. I know that Eddie communicated a lot with Vince Sr. about what was going on in Florida, and that they discussed that often. Vince Sr. understood that my passion was in doing the work *in the ring*, and that I had no interest in trying to influence the bookings or to be involved in any way in any of the back-office stuff. Vince knew that I would listen to him and that I wasn't going to try and take him over, or give him any headaches by no-showing dates or challenging him about gate receipts. We trusted each other, and I think that certainly contributed to his decision to pick me to lead the federation.

At the time this all happened, I was a young and naïve twenty-seven-year-old kid. I didn't have an entourage of friends in the business, or a group of guys around me who I wanted to have come in to wrestle me, or to get bookings in the territory, or to get favorable treatment from Vince Sr. I never went to the booking meetings and I really didn't care to be involved in that at all. I didn't care about who I wrestled. I was happy to let Vince Sr. have that power.

After I defeated Larry that night at the Garden with the atomic drop, I did an interview at ringside with Vince Jr. about being undefeated in the territory and being really excited to have the support of all of the fans. That just served to further cement me as a rising babyface, and to plant the idea in people's minds that I was an up-and-comer who might some-day be worthy of challenging Billy for the championship. Right after that Garden show, Billy came down with a pretty serious staph infection and he was hospitalized for a period of time, which caused Billy to miss many of his shots around the territory in the month of October.

By the time of the October 1977 tapings, I was doing more interviews and getting ready to start my revolutions around the house show circuit. It was also around this time that I began to really develop a friendship with Andre the Giant.

I think I talked to Andre more than most of the guys. I liked him a lot, and I know he respected my amateur background, my training sched-ule, and my work ethic in and around the ring, which was part of why we got along so well. Andre himself had been a pretty serious athlete and had played competitive soccer in Europe before becoming a professional wrestler. Andre took the wrestling business very seriously and didn't have much patience for guys who didn't respect the business.

Andre was a big, big man—but for a big man, he could perform well in the ring. A lot of people only know Andre from his match with Hogan at Wrestlemania III, but the Andre who went to the ring that night in the Silverdome to pass the torch to Hogan was a man in serious pain, and a mere shadow of his former self. The Andre the Giant that I knew in the late '70s and early '80s could throw suplexes, and get up and down off the mat with relative ease—which made his matches that much more enter-taining to watch. I think at the time I knew him, he was legitimately about seven feet tall and about 450 pounds, but he was a really down-to-earth person who just wanted people to treat him like a regular guy.

If Andre bought us a round of beer, as he often did, then I bought him a round back—and when he tried to refuse my offer, I told him that if he wouldn't let me buy him a round back that I wouldn't drink with him anymore. Well that stopped him cold, and after that, we had an under-standing. I was one of the few people who Andre would allow to buy him a drink. Generally, Andre was uncomfortable letting other people buy things for him because of how much he consumed—so he was happy to just go around taking care of the tabs for people. I think the way he thought of it, adding other people's tabs really didn't add too much to what his tab looked like anyway.

Andre and I had a lot of fun together. I liked to drink beer with the boys after the matches when I wasn't driving back home to Connecticut, and I could drink with the best of them. A lot of times, I had to tell Andre that I couldn't stay up drinking with him all night because I had to get up and train in the morning. At a lot of the hotels and motels where we stayed, Andre had a great deal of trouble getting a comfortable night's sleep or even taking a hot shower in the little tub/shower combos that those places had—so he preferred to just stay up most of the night drinking. On those nights, I would tease him and tell him that I'd stay up and drink with him as long as he promised to get up with me at five in the morning to train with me.

Whenever I would say that to him, he would clap me on the shoulder with one of his giant hands and just give me one of those deep, booming Andre "HOGH, HOGH, HOGH" laughs and flash that infectious ear-to-ear smile of his that you'd see when he was having a good time. We had a lot of good times together, but when it was time for me to leave him at the bar, he knew why, and he always respected me for it.

In the wrestling business, your ability to drink beer a badge of honor. Being good at it was important, and it was important to be drink with the boys to keep up relations. We had a place, in almost every town that was a regular stop on the circuit, where we could go to drink after the matches, and where the owner would either close the place to protect us, or where, given the hour, there wasn't going to be a lot of walk-in traffic. Some of the places I remember were Cloud Nine at Bradley Airport, where we would go after Hartford or on the way back from Springfield. In New York City, it was usually the Lone Star Café or the Savoy. Up in Boston, there was a motel behind the old Boston Garden where we used to go. And there were many others—but you get the idea.

A Perfect Role Model

In those days, we'd check into a hotel and before an hour or two went by the television would be laying in the swimming pool, that chair would be out the window, that one would be broken into pieces, there would be naked girls running all around, there would cocaine sitting on that table over there. There would be someone sitting in the bathroom over there rolling joints, and the bathtub would be full of ice and beer. The promoters in the '70s used to tell us that they didn't care what we did on our own time—so as soon as the matches were over and we got back to the hotel, well it was party, party, party.

But Bob wouldn't do that stuff. I can remember one night, we were wrestling in Portland, Maine, and the next night, we were going to be wrestling in Boston. Well as soon as the matches in Portland were over, we were partying it up in the hotel room all night, slept a little bit, and then drove down to Boston for the matches the next day. But not Bob—Bob drove home to Connecticut after the matches, slept at home with his wife and his daughter, and then drove back up to Boston the next night. That's how we all should have done it. But instead, we would just set up shop in the hotel bar, or someone's room—get set up with the local guy who was bringing the weed or whatever else we wanted that night, and the guys would stay up until three or four in the morning partying all night. Then the next morning, everyone would wake up feeling like crap and need to go the matches, and Bob would show up at the arena having had a good night's sleep, feeling good, and be there doing his squats and push-ups. He felt like an outcast because he didn't get involved in the reckless side of pro wrestling, and some people resented him for it because they figured he thought he was too good for everyone else. But in reality, all he was doing was the right thing.

> We lived a real wild life and luckily for us, there were guys like Bob in this business who didn't choose that route. They were the example setters. Some guys would get a brand new car every year, buy a house, get married, divorce the lady two years later, lose the house, pay child support and alimony, and then go off three or four years later and do it all over again. And some of the guys did that two or three times! Those were the guys we thought we should be following, but in reality, the guys that we needed to be following were the guys like Bob Backlund. To me, Bob was the perfect role model. He was a great athlete and a perfect gentleman.
>
> — "Mr. USA" Tony Atlas

Unlike the way things had been in some of the other territories where I wrestled, in the WWWF, Vince Sr. wasn't a stickler for kayfabe, so heels and faces could drink in the bar together. In a lot of the smaller territories in the NWA, doing that would have been cause for immediate dismissal from the territory. In the WWWF, though, it was permissible.

Remember that the WWWF was located in the northeastern United States. Vince Sr. was selling to the masses, so having a few people see heels and faces together wasn't that big a deal to him. There were ten million people in the New York City metro area alone—so it was pretty easy to be anonymous once you got a few blocks away from the Garden. If three or four wrestling fans happened upon us, it wouldn't have had any appreciable effect on the business because there was really no way for them to spread the word. This was in the days before camera phones and the Internet and Twitter and Snapchat and twenty-four-hour cable news shows, so no one could snap a picture of me having a drink with George and do anything significant with it. It wasn't like *The Times* was going to publish it.

I didn't attend the first set of TV tapings on November 8 and 9 because our daughter Carrie was about to be born. I talked to Vince several times on November 8 from Minnesota and he insisted that I just stay put there and be with Corki at the hospital. That was the kind of man Vince Sr. was. He was a serious businessman who was not to be trifled with, but he also understood the importance of family and family harmony in his wrestlers' lives. I'm happy I made that decision, because Carrie was born later that day, and I was there to see it. To anyone who is a dad—you know that there is no greater moment in this world than being present for the birth of your child.

Eleven days after Carrie was born, we packed up our things into a U-Haul and moved our family to Hamden, Connecticut, outside of New Haven, to a rental unit at the Howard Johnson's on the Merritt Parkway. On the phone, Vince Sr. had told me that my time appearing only on TV was at an end, and that the final push leading up to my win over "Superstar" Billy Graham for the belt was about to start in earnest out on the house show circuit.

13

Carrie Me Away

". . . make your prayers an expression of gratitude and thanks-giving for the blessings you already have."

—Napoleon Hill, "Use Applied Faith"

———◆———

As my life was changing inside the business, it was also changing a lot outside the ring. On November 8, 1977, our daughter, and our only child, Carrie, was born. It was a miracle and—as you might expect—one of the greatest moments of my life. There is nothing quite like bringing a child into the world to remind you of your responsibilities!

Corki and I are very private people, and from the very beginning, I have always insisted that our family stay outside the business. I had been given some very good advice by Dick Murdoch during my time in Amarillo that if I wanted to work in the wrestling business and keep my family together, the best way to do that would be to keep the two totally separate. The fans and the groupies who tend to hang around the wrestlers were destabilizing factors for a marriage. So from the very beginning, that is what we did.

Fortunately for me, Corki is a very independent woman, with her own life as a teacher and a gymnastics coach, and while I was on the road she did those things and was a great mom to Carrie. Shortly after Carrie was born and Corki was out of the hospital, we moved out of the Howard Johnson's and east into a little apartment in West Haven, Connecticut, on Greta Street right off of I-95, but near the West Haven beaches on the Long Island Sound where Corki and Carrie spent their days while I wasn't around.

Vince Sr. had told me that I would be keeping the championship long enough to justify buying a house in the territory, so Corki spent a lot of time scoping out towns in and around central Connecticut to try and figure out where we might want to live. I was flying out of Kennedy and LaGuardia and Newark airports a lot for any trip longer than driving distance, and for anyone who familiar with driving in the New York area, you know that traffic is an issue—so doing anything to make those commutes easier was definitely a priority.

Corki spent much of her time in those early days traveling up and down the highways of central Connecticut looking at houses with a realtor. She looked at over two hundred homes between New Haven and Greenwich, until eventually, because there was so much traffic and congestion in that area, we gave up on that idea and started looking north of New Haven into the bedroom communities around Hartford.

Eventually, Corki found a house that we loved in South Windsor, which would have allowed me pretty easy access to Bradley International Airport, which had either direct or connecting flights to any of the major national and international cities where I wrestled. That spot also allowed me pretty easy access to the northern part of the WWWF territory, because it was far enough north in Connecticut to avoid most of the New York–area traffic when trying to get to Massachusetts, Rhode Island, New Hampshire, Vermont, and Maine. The house also had an indoor pool, which would have been great for Corki and Carrie because it would have allowed them to swim year round. We signed papers and put a down payment on it, but as we approached the closing date, the seller not only changed his mind and refused to sell the house to us, he also refused to return our deposit.

To a couple of young and naïve Midwesterners, that was a pretty unkind introduction to doing business in the New York area. We were forced to retain a lawyer, went to court, and although we got our deposit back, we never did get the house.

The story, however, gets a lot stranger from there.

The guy selling the house in South Windsor was a public relations and advertising executive named Richard Shenkman, who later became infamous in the area for kidnapping his then-estranged wife from a Hartford parking garage, forcing her to drive him to the house we tried to buy from him, handcuffing her to him, and threatening to kill her. She eventually escaped, but Shenkman ended up blowing up the house and burning it to the ground. He was ultimately found guilty of first-degree kidnapping, first-degree arson, third-degree assault, possession of an unregistered firearm, and attempted assault on a police officer and sentenced to seventy years in prison.

Maybe it was a good thing that we didn't actually get the house.

After that experience, Corki kept looking until we finally found a three-bedroom house, with a good-size yard and a backyard stream on Slater Road in Glastonbury, a bedroom community just south of Hartford that featured great schools, good athletic programs, a good parks and rec program, and easy access to Bradley Airport.

We knew we had finally found our home.

When we first moved in, the neighbors obviously didn't know us, and they had no idea who I was or what I did. They were definitely a little suspicious that I was always arriving home in the middle of the night, and they certainly couldn't figure out why Carrie and I were always up playing at 2 in the morning, sliding in the snow, or throwing a ball outside. The truth is, on many days, given my travel and workout schedules, that was the only time I could be home and playing with her, and I didn't want her to miss out on time with her dad—nor did I want to miss out on my time with her.

With the exception of the nights I was wrestling in southern New Jersey, Pennsylvania, Delaware, Maryland, and DC, or up in northern Maine or Vermont, I almost always drove back home to Glastonbury after the matches rather than staying in a motel out on the road. There were several reasons for that. First, over time, it saved us a substantial amount of money to not have to pay for all of those motel rooms.

More importantly, though, I wanted to get home to be with Corki and Carrie. Some of the boys in the business teased me for being such a "straight arrow"—but I made no apology for wanting to be a good husband and a good father. It was hard to be away from home as much as I already was—so whenever it was possible to reach home after the matches, I made the drive.

Heading home after the matches also made it easy to resist the many temptations that go along with life on the road as a celebrity. Suffice it to say that the roads of the wrestling territories were littered with the shattered remains of broken marriages, wrestlers' kids who became addicted to drugs and alcohol or made other bad choices, and wrestlers themselves who kept looking for happiness in places other than at home with their families.

I had no use for any of that. I had found the woman I loved, and I married her, and I was in the process of raising my daughter with her, so the choice to drive home whenever I could, rather than to seek fleeting companionship out on the road, was an easy one for me.

Corki had started teaching gymnastics in the parks and rec program in 1979—when Carrie was eighteen months old. The little gymnasts in her program knew her as "Corki" and not as "Mrs. Backlund" (which we did on purpose to keep people off the trail of who she was). She also taught school in nearby Bolton, and over there, she *was* known as Mrs. Backlund, which did give rise to at least one funny story.

One day, as I was about to go overseas, I had to go into Corki's classroom during the school day to get something from her. The next day, a young student in her class who had been giving her some problems all year approached Corki all excited and said to her, "Do you know who that was that was in here yesterday?" For the life of her, my wife couldn't figure out what the boy was talking about, so she thought and thought and eventually gave up. The boy, all wide-eyed said to her, "Bob Backlund—the world wrestling champion! Bob Backlund was here yesterday! Can you believe that? In our school!"

My wife smiled at him and paused for a moment before looking down and saying to him, "Billy, what's my name?"

He thought for a minute and said, "Mrs. Backlund"—and suddenly his eyes bugged out as he put two and two together.

She never had another problem with him after that.

———◆◆◆———

I'm happy to say that in all my years in the wrestling business, I *was* able to keep my family sheltered from all of the fuss and commotion of the life on the road. I don't think Corki saw me wrestle more than a handful of times in my entire career, and I don't think she regrets that one bit.

Corki and I are still married—and just celebrated our fortieth wedding anniversary. It hasn't always been easy, of course. We have suffered from the same troubles, and disagreements, and ups and downs that any couple that has tried to coexist for forty years together will have. That said, we made ourselves a promise a long time ago that we would stick it out, for better or for worse and through thick and through thin—and so here we are. Our secret to success has been to give each other the space to be ourselves, to have our own lives and our own friends and our own dreams, but to support each other and give each other the foundation of a solid family to operate from.

The wrestling business provided us with a good life—and because we were smart with our money—didn't spend what we didn't have, invested wisely, and saved our pennies—unlike a great many of my colleagues, we are in a good place today. But wrestling was only one part of our lives—the business part. The rest of our life was the part we lived privately, within the four walls of our home, with our daughter.

Forty years later, and I wouldn't have it any other way.

———◆◆◆———

A Daughter's Perspective

When they first met, my mom was the lifeguard at the pool and my dad was the football player. He thought his legs were too skinny so he would always wrap a towel around himself until he got to the steps of the pool because he didn't want her to see his chicken legs. She always thought that was funny—that this big, hunky muscular guy was ashamed of his body. Well they hit it off, and were pretty much inseparable after that. My mom helped with a lot of Dad's schoolwork in college because he was always busy with football and wrestling. He was a star athlete—so that was his focus. She was more of the student. Theirs really was the kind of All-American love affair that you see in the movies.

After Dad won the NCAAs in college and then decided to become a professional wrestler, Mom followed him, but she was careful to make her own dreams along the way too. She is a very strong and independent woman. I know that she hated all of the travel in the early days, but she developed her little method of dealing with my dad's lifestyle—she had twenty crates that everything they owned would fit in, and she would just pack them and then unpack them again and again as they moved from territory to territory.

Mom and Dad made a promise to each other a long time ago to respect each other's worlds, but to keep those worlds separate. And that's how it has always been with the two of them for as long as I can remember. It's a different kind of relationship, borne in some part out of necessity, but it works. They do things on their own without one getting mad at the other. They are not joined at the hip, and do not need to get permission from each other to do things. They each do what they want to do. That is how it has always been. A lot of people put a front up for people—they don't—they just do their own things. It never bothered me—that is just how it always was.

Now that I am an adult looking back, I am happy it was that way, because divorce terrifies me, and I feel like if my mom had been forced to try and coexist in the world my dad worked in, they never would have made it. Professional wrestling's circus atmosphere and lifestyle is about as opposite of what my mom is as there can be. I think that is why she always took such pains to avoid being drawn into that world in any way.

Dad kept his life very separate from us—I knew he was gone all the time, and I didn't really understand what he was doing when I was young, I just thought that every other dad was gone too. It wasn't until I got a little older that I fully understood what was going on. My dad really sheltered me and my mom from his world because of the way that world was. Keeping us away from the business was very, very important to him. I'm very happy that he did that because, in retrospect, I would not have wanted to be in the spotlight as the "daughter of the world wrestling champion," or anything like that. I wanted my privacy and to be able to grow up a normal kid and live my own life. Despite my dad's celebrity, he was still able to give that to us, and both Mom and I were very grateful for it. I still never willingly tell people know who my dad is—because I want people to like me for me not because of who my dad is.

My mom loves to read, loves to knit, she kayaks all the time, and she loves to be outside. She will be outside in the yard doing yard work or tending to the garden until it is too dark to see anything. She is always active. She leaves for work at 6:30 in the morning, goes to school, then goes to gymnastics, then does her swim workout for ninety minutes every night, and then she gets home at 9:30 or 10:00 at night. Other than for Thanksgiving, I don't know that we've ever sat down as a family and eaten a meal together, because Dad was gone nearly every night. Thanksgiving, though, was the time we were always together. We would get a condo and go skiing in Vermont.

That was a tradition for us—and something we have done for twenty-five years. I think that is what I missed most about our family—that we never had more of that kind of together time.

My mom is set in her ways. I love her to death and we have a great relationship but we don't have the kind of relationship that a lot of other moms and daughters have. We would talk every Thursday night and Sunday night. We both hate talking on the phone, so to this day, we can go months without talking on the phone. She doesn't have a cell phone—so it's hard to catch up to her sometimes.

Mom was my gymnastics coach forever, which really brought us close because my dad wasn't there. She is still coaching gymnastics for girls all the way from infants to high school. She has always been the balance beam coach—and all the kids just love her. She of course, doesn't need to be a gymnastics coach—I am long gone, and she doesn't have a child on the team, but I think they see her as a mother figure. They all just crowd around her. She is very supportive of them and positive and encouraging—where a lot of the parents are critical of their kids these days. In some ways, I think some of those kids are closer to her than I am.

Mom and I also always traveled together. We have been to France and Spain and Aruba. We would always travel somewhere for Christmas. Dad, on the other hand, traveled every day for most of his life, so on the rare occasions when he was home, he wanted to be home, and if he could drive somewhere, he preferred to drive. On my twenty-fifth birthday, for example, he drove all the way from Connecticut to the Florida Keys to take me out to dinner, stayed overnight with me, I cooked him breakfast, and then he drove all the way back home. He was never able to be around for my birthday parties when I was a kid, so he told me that now that he had the chance, he wanted to be with me. That meant a lot to me. People might read this and think that driving to Florida from Connecticut is crazy but

Dad would rather drive anywhere and be in control of what's going on than have to sit on a plane next to someone who would talk his ear off for the entire flight.

People are always curious about my dad's level of physical fitness, given that he is now in his mid-sixties, but looks a lot younger, and is still incredibly fit. For as far back as I can remember, Dad always juiced fruits and vegetables and was constantly drinking the juice he made—and he always worked out at least twice a day in our home gym. He would work out first thing in the morning and then he would drink juice. He was always very healthy and very in shape and interested in physical fitness. I remember when he had Lyme Disease a few years ago, my mom didn't want me to see him because he had lost so much weight. His clothes just hung on him. We live in the middle of the woods—and from what I can remember, my dad doesn't really go to doctor's and he thought he was just getting older—after all the years of being in the ring, his joints were creaky and it was just getting more painful. Eventually, though, things got bad enough that he had to go to the doctor and they told him he had Lyme Disease. It really affected his knee and his leg and he walked with a limp for a while and it really debilitated him. But he fought his way back from that, and really focused on his diet and exercise, and seems to have made almost a full recovery.

To be honest, I don't have a lot of childhood memories of my father because he was always gone. I know that back in the very early years of my childhood, when dad had just come to the WWWF and Vince McMahon Jr. was the television announcer, we all lived in the same area, and I used to play with Stephanie and Shane McMahon a lot. I met them again at the Hall of Fame induction last year and it was fun—we took a picture together and had a lot of laughs recalling those early days. Our lives have certainly changed a lot since then!

When Dad was home, it was always at two or three o'clock in the morning, but whenever he would get home after being away on the road, he would always wake me up and we would turn on the lights in the yard and go outside and play no matter what time it was. I would always try to impress him with what I was doing on the trampoline. I know that he felt really conflicted about being away from home so much—which is why he would drive through the night so often just to be able to wake up home in our house instead of in a motel somewhere out on the road.

When I was little, I was a huge fan of E. T. the Extra Terrestrial—the character from the Spielberg movie. I had everything—the E. T. sheets, pillowcases, stuffed animal, sleeping bags, anything with E. T. on it. I was totally smitten by E. T. Well, one day, Dad arranged for one of the young wrestlers that he was working with to dress up as E. T. and knock on our front door. I couldn't believe it! I didn't know what to say. I was about six years old, and I thought that my dad actually knew E. T. and had arranged for him to come and visit me. That's the kind of thing my dad would do. I will never forget that.

I always saw Dad with his red wrestling boots on and his briefcase that he used to carry with him, so whenever I went anywhere with him, I would always want to be like my dad—so I would always put my little red rain boots on and carry a little lunchbox and try to be just like him. I played the violin—and I didn't think my dad could really relate to that—so when my recital was over, I would always do a couple of cartwheels at the end because I thought that's what my dad wanted to see. He was always so active and working out, so I thought that's what he wanted me to be doing to—not sitting still and playing violin!

We didn't have a television in our house when I was growing up—so I didn't ever see my dad wrestle on TV when he was the champion. Even today, it is hard for me to watch a match from back then where he got beat up and bloodied because it's my dad—and even though I know it was all a show, it's still hard to see that. Of course, the people I grew up with in Glastonbury knew that my dad was a professional wrestler, but he lost the title when I was six, so we didn't talk about it much. In junior high and high school, though, when my dad was back in the business, we would have parties at my house and the girls would all be downstairs dancing and waiting for the guys to come down, and the guys would all be upstairs talking to my dad about wrestling. They weren't intimidated by him or anything, they just wanted to talk with him about it because so many of them were fascinated by it.

I can remember one day when I was young I pulled open the drawer to my parents' nightstand in their bedroom and saw the gold belt in there. I was definitely interested in that! When my dad was home, that was where he kept the belt because it was obviously valuable and important to him.

Whenever we went out in public to a restaurant or just out and about when he was around, people would always come up and pat him on the back or the shoulders or shake his hand and ask for autographs. People always went crazy around him, and I didn't understand it and I didn't like it because I only got to have a couple of hours at a time with my dad and when I had him I didn't want to have to share him with anyone, especially a crowd of strangers that I didn't know. But my dad was always polite and accommodating to everyone, and kept reminding us that it was the fans that were providing us with the good living that we were enjoying, and so it was important to give back to them. To this day, I don't like to go to restaurants because I still associate eating out with the memory of the three of us getting accosted by people trying to get my dad's autograph and taking some of our precious time with him away from us.

I do also have some memories from childhood that involve wrestling. I can remember one time Andre the Giant came over to our house and was laying on the floor playing with me. I think he was traveling with my dad. He was enormous, but he was very gentle. I remember The Iron Sheik coming over to the house also. Those are the two guys that I can remember seeing at the house. My dad had a very good relationship with both of them, and they were two of the only guys that my dad ever let me be around.

I did see some wrestling on television at my friends' houses— but I would never watch my dad. Whenever we were watching, they would always tell me when his match was over. I went to a few live matches with my guy friends around junior high or high school time—and that's when I started hearing people in the arena saying bad things about my dad. That was during the "Mr. Backlund" days in the mid-1990s. I knew that it was predetermined and that my dad was just playing a role—but I was definitely scared for my dad's safety because there are all kinds of crazy people in the world looking for their fifteen minutes of fame—and what better way to get that than to attack a wrestler who was trying to incite you anyway? Those were the things that I worried about most.

To be honest, thanks to my dad, and the limits and boundaries that he imposed for us, I had a pretty normal life growing up. My dad was a wrestler from day one in my life, and that was just something we had to deal with. One week, when I was in eighth grade we were down at Walt Disney World and one night we went to Pleasure Island and we were dancing together at a nightclub and when my dad left the floor to get a drink this guy came over and said, do you know who you were dancing with? That was Bob Backlund, the world champion wrestler! And I said, "Yeah, he's my dad!"

I know now that Dad gave up a lot for me by not becoming a bad guy after he lost the championship in 1983. He didn't want me to have to face my little friends on the playground at school telling me that my dad was a jerk. Dad was always known as the "All-American

Boy"—and the fact is that it wasn't really a character he played. The character he portrayed in the ring and the person he actually was as home and in our community were one and the same. Dad knew that he was a role model and a hero to a lot of kids, and that was a role and a responsibility that he held as a sacred trust. Even though the wrestling part of his job was predetermined, the role model part wasn't. It wasn't just about the wrestling to my dad. It was the whole package. My dad wasn't the kind of person who would even consider letting those people down just so he could make a buck. It may sound old fashioned, but Dad was, is, and always will be a man guided by his principles.

To this day, I still can't go anywhere with my dad where we don't get stopped by someone looking for an autograph, or to tell a story, or to connect with him in some way. A couple of years ago, we were walking on Duval Street in Key West and got stopped by a guy who called his friend on his cell phone and pushed the phone into Dad's face just wanting to put him on the phone with his friend, who he said was a huge fan, and I was like—my God, we're just trying to live our lives here, can you give us a break and let us have a little privacy here? Whether it's pumping gas, or in the grocery store, or whatever—Dad is always getting stopped. And he always seems to make time for those requests. Growing up, I used to hate when that happened because it took away from what little time I had with my dad—but now I understand that if it wasn't for the fans, he wouldn't have been who he was.

I always looked up to my dad, and I still do, to this day. I always wanted to emulate him. He was always so positive—whenever we sign letters to each other, we always sign off with "PMA"—which means Positive Mental Attitude. As my dad taught me, even if you're having the worst day, putting a smile on your face or just saying hello to a random person can make you and them both feel better. I try to be pretty positive about life, just like he is.

A lot of people will know this now, now that this book is out, but Dad had to work very hard for everything he got. Nothing was ever handed to him. A lot of people climb the ladder in life, but they use people and contacts and favors to get where they are going, and then they forget about the people that they've climbed past. My dad has never forgotten where he came from, and instead of climbing over people, he was very generous with his time. He was always visiting sick kids in the hospital trying to cheer them up, or working with kids in area schools to try and repay the favor done for him while he was in high school. Dad always remembered his past—and the fact that it was one or two people who made the difference in his life and put him on the right path. And I think he saw it as his responsibility to pay that forward in everything he did.

—**Carrie Backlund**

14

The Build-Up

"Enthusiasm takes the drudgery out of your work and makes it a labor of love."

—Napoleon Hill, "Control Your Attention"

———◆———

At the November 1977 TV tapings, Vince Sr. booked me into three different singles matches and then into a six-man tag-team match with the tag-team champions Jay Strongbow and Billy Whitewolf. The idea was to keep me at the front of people's minds as a still-undefeated young wrestler who would eventually get a chance at the gold. My presence was like a pressure building up, more and more each week—with the people eagerly anticipating what the explosion would look like.

I saw Vince Sr. at that taping, and he pulled me aside and confirmed to me that I was going to get the championship from Billy at the Garden in February, and that he was going to build my push both at the Garden and out in the territory with that schedule in mind. I did ask him about Billy and whether that plan might change because Billy was so red hot in the territory at the time. Vince Sr. explained to me that unlike the NWA, the WWWF was a babyface territory, where the heels cycled in and out as challengers, and only served as transitional champions to get the title from one babyface to another, and didn't ever keep the title very long. He told me that Billy was already scheduled to get the longest heel reign in the history of the company, but the time was rapidly approaching to make the change because he had pretty much run through the roster of credible babyfaces to wrestle.

I started out full-time on the house show circuit on December 1, 1977, in Asbury Park, New Jersey. At the TV tapings in Allentown and Hamburg, Vince Sr. had a little area with a table where he would sit, and he had a calendar ledger for the year with all of the dates ahead for at least the next three weeks. In some of the bigger arenas, the dates were scheduled out for the entire year. At that time, the WWWF ran on a three-week schedule—so the full schedule of who would appear on what cards was fully known three weeks ahead of time. I would go into the office, look at Vince Sr.'s ledger, and copy down my schedule into my own ledger for the upcoming three weeks so I would know where I needed to be, and when I needed to be there. My first time going around the territory, I didn't know where any of the buildings were, so I'd just head to each town and find my way. This, of course, was well before GPS or iPhones, so you'd have to simply stop at a gas station or something and ask a couple of times to find the way to the building. If we were wrestling at a spot show in a smaller town somewhere, the matches were usually held at a community college or high school gym, and in those cases, the town was usually small enough that you could find the place without too much trouble. Once you'd been to a building once or twice, it became almost second nature to you. I could probably still find my way to most of the buildings in the WWWF territory—if they still exist.

In most of the big hockey and basketball arenas, with the exception of Madison Square Garden, we changed and showered in the same locker rooms that the pro teams changed in—which meant that the accommodations were clean and bright and well-defended. My first time around, I'd just find the side door where the most people were hanging out and go in there. Since the arena security guys didn't really know me at first, they'd check my ID and then point me to the locker room area.

Once I found the locker room area, the dressing rooms would be designated—one for heels and one for faces—and you'd just go where you were supposed to go and get ready for your match. In the dressing room, you'd usually see Monsoon and Skaaland and Blassie and maybe a couple of the other guys in there playing cards. I usually got to the venue one hour before the matches were scheduled to start.

Vince McMahon Sr. was in charge of deciding the booked finishes, but the agent in charge of each building would decide the order of the matches and how much time to give to each match. The agent, whether it was Gorilla Monsoon, Phil Zacko, Abe Ford, Angelo Savoldi, or Arnold Skaaland, would post the night's lineup card somewhere on an interior wall of the dressing room out of sight to any members of the general public who might be walking around backstage. The card had the order of the matches circled right next to it. They'd also post the approximate amount of time they had designated to each match so that the whole card would last for the right amount of time.

In most of the arenas and gyms, we typically aimed to have a card to last somewhere between two hours and ten minutes and two and a half hours to correspond roughly with people's attention spans. Anything longer than that, and the people started to get restless and unruly no matter how good the matches were. The matches were also ordered to keep the energy flowing. The card was carefully orchestrated so each match would finish at its peak, and to have the night build to a crescendo in the same way—so the night ended on a high and sent the people running to the ticket windows to buy tickets for the following month's card.

Where you were on the card, and who you were, determined how much you got paid. In the WWWF, the guys in the opening match on a Tuesday night in a high school gym might take home $100, and the amounts would go up from there to my match, with the title, which might have been worth $800 to $1,000 for my opponent and me. Our payouts, of course, depended on the size of the building and the size of the gate, from the smallest high school gyms and fieldhouses to Madison Square Garden, which provided the biggest paydays in the territory. At the Garden, the opening match typically earned each guy $300 to $500, and then up from there through the card to the main event, which might have been worth $5,000 to $10,000 to each of us, again, depending on who was on the card, how many people were in the building, and whether the Felt Forum, and its additional seating, was open for a closed-circuit broadcast of the matches.

In the NWA, the championship match was usually at the end. But in the WWWF arenas that we visited monthly, they would announce the matches for the next card before people left. That usually required my match to happen before the intermission so if I was coming back the following month in a rematch or against a new opponent, they could announce it in the building that night and get everyone excited to buy tickets.

I was excited to finally arrive in the WWWF full time. I was excited to get to know the guys on the roster a little bit better by traveling the circuit with them, and to go out to the arenas, introduce my style to the people, and to be able to build a match, tell a story, and show the fans what a good, competitive wrestling match looked like. Obviously, the goal was to make the people in every town and every gym and arena believe that what we were doing in the ring was real, and to draw them into the emotion of it.

It was very valuable for me to finally get out and travel the circuit. I have never been the most naturally charismatic guy—that part of the business just didn't come naturally to me, so it was something I had to work on. I have always been a soft-spoken, humble, and frankly, pretty shy person. In order to connect with people emotionally and to get them to know and appreciate me, I had to spend time in the ring wrestling in front of them and tell them stories through wrestling. I knew I wasn't going to be able to talk them into the seats as well as some of the other guys could. I had to do my talking in the ring.

When I arrived in the WWWF, I also resumed my tradition of going to hospitals and kids' wrestling clubs. I started connecting with high school coaches and interacting with people around the territory. I recognized pretty quickly that on my first time around the circuit, I wasn't getting the same kind of consistent adulation from every crowd in every town that I had gotten in St. Louis. In some places, the crowds were hot—but in other places, their reaction to me was a little flat. That told me that I still had some work to do to get the people in my corner.

It also meant that I needed to be in the ring with opponents with whom I could tell a story, draw the people in emotionally, and whenever possible, make my opponents have the kind of matches that I wanted to have. I liked to have matches where I could showcase my speed, chain wrestling moves, and counters, and have my opponent fight the match with me move for move. I knew from all of the good experiences that I had already had wrestling in the various territories where I had been that the more the people felt they were emotionally invested in my match, move for move, the better it would be. So that was my goal the first time around.

To be honest, though, it was difficult. Unlike in Amarillo, Florida, Georgia, and St. Louis, where the talent pools had been so incredibly rich, back in 1977, the WWWF roster was noticeably sparse on talent— and particularly heel talent. Because there was currently a heel WWWF champion (Graham), there wasn't a lot of fresh and excellent heel talent in the federation to feed to me. There were a bunch of older guys like Baron Mikel Scicluna and Professor Tanaka, who were all well into the back nine of their careers and who really didn't have the spark for the business anymore, so it was hard to develop a hot program with any of them. There were no hot young heels in the territory, because with Graham in the top spot and no other secondary title to compete for, there wasn't any place for those heels to go. I quickly realized that this was why Vince didn't want me out on the road earlier getting stale wrestling these guys month after month.

If you take a look at the WWWF cards from 1977, and compare the matches that occurred, say, at the Kiel Auditorium in St. Louis, or the Bayfront Center in St. Pete, or the Omni in Atlanta with the matches at Madison Square Garden during the same time period, the comparison is stark. You will see a really profound difference in work rate, crispness of execution of moves in the ring, and consequently, in the number of good wrestling matches. The WWWF looked tired and old, and the NWA had it all over the WWWF at that time. I think that was definitely one of the things that Vince Sr. was looking to change.

I think that at least during the nine months that Billy had the belt, with the exception of Sammartino and Graham and their opponents in the main events, and maybe a couple of other exceptions, people had largely gotten fat and happy in the WWWF. I think that for too many years, people had grown accustomed to relying on Bruno (and then Billy) to draw the houses, and had gotten a little lazy with the work rates and creativity in the semi-final and mid-card matches. If you go back and watch some of those matches today, some of them are so bad that they are almost unwatchable. There is no story being told, the in-ring execution is bad, and many of the wrestlers themselves really just seemed to be mailing it in.

Stan Stasiak, who was one of the true gentlemen in the sport, was *not* one of those guys. Vince Sr. had chosen Stan to be the transitional champion between Pedro Morales and Bruno's second reign. Stasiak took the title from Morales in December 1973 in Philadelphia and lost it nine days later to Bruno at the Garden. Even though his reign was short, for the remainder of his career, which would entitle him to be announced as the "former World Wrestling Federation Heavyweight Champion," which gave Stan some extra shine and better positioning on the cards around the territory. That transitional run was a reward from Vince Sr. to Stan for his loyalty and decency.

When Vince went to Stan and asked him to put me over across the territory, Stan accepted that role with grace. We went around the horn together and wrestled a lot. Each night, the promoter would come to us and tell me that I was "going over" in fifteen minutes or so, and then we'd figure out what we were going to do for a finish. In many of the smaller buildings we were allowed to call our own finishes, so it was up to us to either agree to it ahead of time, or simply call an audible in the ring to correspond with what the people in the building on that particular night were looking for.

At the time, the promoters were pushing two finishes for me—the atomic kneedrop, and my reverse rollup and bridge, which Vince Sr. called the "Pat O'Connor finish" (because O'Connor was the first to use and popularize it). Monsoon and Zacko and a lot of the other local promoters liked that move because it was pretty dramatic and looked very realistic, so they wanted me to use that a lot. The problem is, when you put that move on, you have to be working with someone who was flexible enough to be rolled up backwards or the whole thing would fall apart and leave you both lying in a heap in the middle of the ring looking ridiculous. To apply the move properly, I had to push my opponent face-first into the ropes fast enough to maintain speed while then pulling him back, rolling over him backward, and then keeping enough momentum to roll me back over to a standing position and then into a bridge. In the wrestling business, fast was not necessarily better. Timing was everything. You had to give the people time to react to each move that you were doing so that they could register it—and the people certainly registered a reaction to that move when I had a heel wrapped up on his shoulders and then bridged out to lock him in.

I loved traveling the circuit in the WWWF. We worked a full and varied schedule—you could be in front of 22,000 people at Madison Square Garden one night, and in a high school gym in front of 800 people in a New Jersey suburb the next. That made things really different. Each building had a slightly different vibe, and each crowd had a really different personality. It was a thrill going to these different places every night. You'd get in the ring, perform, and try to really connect with the people, whether it was in front of 2,000 people, or 20,000 people.

One of the buildings I enjoyed most on the old WWWF house show circuit was the old Worcester Memorial Auditorium, in Worcester, Massachusetts. In that arena, the people were hanging right over the top of you in a balcony that went all the way around the ring, and the acoustics were really good—so when you had the people roaring, the entire building shook. Wrestling in a building like that certainly helped keep the wrestlers' adrenaline high. If the people were into what you were doing, they were screaming and yelling, cheering or booing, and the building was rocking, which made it hard to have a bad match there.

The acoustics were also pretty good at the Zembo Mosque in Harrisburg, Pennsylvania, another monthly stop on the WWWF house show tour. The reverberations were always pretty good in there as well. I had a pretty good warm-up match with Billy Graham there on a night of a raging snowstorm on January 14, 1978. The crowd that night was small because of the storm, but they were boisterous.

Jack Witschi's, a little club in North Attleboro, Massachusetts, was probably the smallest place that we went regularly on the house show circuit. It was a little barroom that hosted a small pro wrestling card (usually four or five matches) every Friday night. The place was a real dive—the dressing rooms were falling apart, the ring was squeezed in there, and the ceiling was so low that it was impossible to climb up to the top turnbuckle and execute anything from up there without hitting the lights. If the place was sold out, there were probably 300 people in there, but they would usually be pretty well lubricated and really into it, and of course, the more the crowd was into it the more you got into it.

I didn't wrestle at Jack Witschi's very often, and I don't think I ever defended the WWWF title there, but Vince had me beat the then-tag-team champions Mr. Fuji and Professor Tanaka there in consecutive main events as I began my run to the championship. When you wrestled in some of those smaller venues, it was easier to connect with the people, because you could actually make eye contact with many of them and draw them in to your battle.

Finally, and without rival anywhere in the world, there was Madison Square Garden. The Garden was the WWWF's showcase building, and in the monthly cards held there, everything was more closely controlled. Every match at the Garden had a purpose—whether it was to warm up the crowd, showcase a new guy, pay off a favor to another promoter by giving one of their guys a match at the Garden, build a feud, or set something up for next time. There was a lot to "accomplish" on the Garden card each month, so Vince Sr. needed the matches to run to predictable lengths to ensure that they could get everything in before the curfew at 11 p.m. Running beyond the 11 p.m. curfew meant paying the Garden staff overtime, which ate into profits—obviously something they wanted to avoid at all costs. In the Garden, the match listings would be hanging on the wall inside the dressing rooms—and there, Vince Sr. would not only tell us where in the card we were and how long the match was to go, but also the finish he wanted us to use.

Out on the house show circuit, I didn't hide after my matches or try to just rush out to my car. I signed autographs for people at the arena door, out in the parking lot, or basically wherever they found me—which was something that a lot of wrestlers, most notably Pat Patterson, later warned me not to do. The thinking at the time was that big celebrities should not be accessible, so that when you were actually seen coming into the ring in the arena, you had more of a mystique, which created a bigger burst of excitement.

"Don't let the people get close to you," everyone always said, "or they'll realize that you're really just another person like they are . . ."

I rejected that advice and went completely in the opposite direction. I understand the argument that someone with the persona of an Andre the Giant or a Dusty Rhodes might want to do that, because those guys were larger-than-life characters. But I was different. I wasn't Dusty Rhodes or Andre the Giant. I came from the people. I was the underdog who represented their hopes and dreams, and I was someone for them to identify with and cheer for. So it wouldn't have made any sense for me to be aloof and unavailable to them. At least that's the way I saw it.

When I was champion, there were a lot of times when I stood outside the side door of Madison Square Garden late into the night and didn't leave until everyone who wanted my autograph got it. I appreciated the fans, and I wanted them to know it. In my own mind, I wasn't a celebrity—I never thought of myself as a star. I thought of myself as Bob

Backlund, the "All-American Boy" from Princeton, Minnesota, the person I had always been.

———◆———

In the WWWF territory, northern Maine was the "experimental" area where Vince Sr. liked to try things out before he brought them to New York or put them on television. If you look at old arena results from Portland and Bangor and Waterville and other little towns up that way, you will often find little gems and surprises that were a clue as to what Vince was thinking about for booking ideas. Vince could try things up there because, in those days, the news didn't really travel from there to the territory's big cities.

As we headed toward the title change at the Garden in February, we all recognized that, before we took the big stage, Billy and I would need a couple of "warm up" matches to get our timing down, figure out what we could and couldn't do together in the ring, and then figure out what we wanted to do at the Garden. We needed to get used to each other. We had wrestled just that one time in St. Louis right after Billy won the title, but that was already many months in the past. So it was no surprise that Vince chose December 6, 1977 in Portland, Maine, for our first title match in the territory.

I know a lot has been said by people, including by Billy himself, about whether he liked the idea of me as the champion, or whether he wanted to give the championship to me or not. Billy has suffered a lot in his older years, both physically and psychologically, and I understand it. Psychologically, at least, I went through a lot of the same things that Billy did after I lost the title and was forced to leave the WWF. Having said that, I never got the sense in any of my matches with Billy that he was holding anything back.

The Exposition Building in Portland wasn't a big venue, but the people up there were passionate about wrestling and because of that, that place was usually a good bellwether for how fans elsewhere in the territory would react to certain booking ideas and finishes. This was a warm-up to help us figure out what kind of a match to plot out to maximize the drama for the title change. The idea we settled on was for me to try to keep away from his strength, outmaneuver him at the beginning of the match, wrestle in and out of his bearhug which he would use to try and wear me down, and have that be the focal point for most of the match. We would paint the picture that he was the "stronger" man and I was the quicker man—and to make the match about which of those attributes would prevail. In reality, although Billy had the body of a Greek god back then—I was actually both quicker *and* stronger than he was.

In a typical heel versus babyface house show match, the heel would "call" most of the match (direct the in-ring action and call the high spots and the finish), because he knew best how he wanted to build heat with the fans. As the babyface, I would typically just follow along, interjecting on occasion if I noticed something about what the crowd was reacting to, or if I felt like the heel was trying to take too much of the offensive side of the match. If we needed to communicate with each other during the match, we'd either discreetly whisper to each other while in a front face-lock or some other hold, or speak Carny. On the occasions where I felt like I wasn't getting enough spots, or if I thought the match was lagging or we were losing the people, I'd step in and call a few things. I generally didn't have much trouble with that—most of the guys I wrestled had the best interests of the match in mind and didn't try to pull anything.

Bruno mentioned to me one night in the dressing room at the Garden, just before I won the championship, that as a babyface in the WWWF, I needed to try to work to the style of my opponent and adapt more to him, rather than trying to make him adapt to me. That was because in the WWWF, the babyfaces—particularly the world champion—would be in the territory a long time, and the heels would cycle in and out—so working to the different heels' styles would keep things fresh. Before I became the champion, I had been resistant to doing that because I wanted to try and dictate the style and pace of my matches. Once I became the champion, though, it became clear to me that Bruno's advice was right on point.

Bruno and I didn't talk much initially. When I came into the territory after having worked in Florida, Georgia, Amarillo, and St. Louis in the NWA, he didn't really know me. I think Bruno was initially stand-offish with me because he wanted to take a long look at me, and see how I conducted myself in and out of the ring before he would really accept me. I understood that—the man had essentially built the company over the previous twelve years and had given everything of himself to it. If I had been in the same situation, I would have done the same thing.

Bruno had the appearance of a rugged Italian brute who looked like the toughest guy on the street. I was the complete opposite of that—the guy people thought they could beat up, but then found out that they couldn't. As it turned out, Bruno and I had a lot in common in terms of training and nutrition and commitment to the craft, and over time, Bruno warmed up to me. I hadn't grown up watching Bruno, but as I got to know him, I developed the utmost respect for him, both for the way he conducted himself in and out of the business, and for his commitment to training and keeping his body fit the natural and honest way.

Over the years, people have occasionally asked me, "so why didn't Vince Sr. use Bruno to put the shine on you during your run up to the title?" I'm not certain why Vince opted not to do that, but I have learned that Vince never even asked Bruno to help pass the torch to me. I suspect it had something to do with the fact that by choosing me, Vince was trying to create something totally new, and to move in a totally new direction, and using Bruno in any way to help put me over would have worked at cross-purposes to that idea.

What Vince did do, though, was accomplish the same end using Bruno's longtime manager Arnold Skaaland. Vince ran a storyline on television where I came out and talked to Vince Jr. on TV and told him that

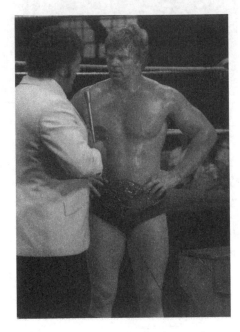

I was going to choose a manager. During the course of the next couple of weeks, all of the WWWF's managers—Blassie, the Wizard, Albano—made their pitch to work with me. Arnold Skaaland did too, and in the end, of course, I picked him. Being courted by all of the heel managers, of course, teased a potential heel turn for me, and when I ultimately chose Bruno's manager and he agreed to manage me, it not only reinforced my standing as a babyface in the eyes of the fans, it linked me to Bruno even if that link wasn't directly acknowledged. The optics were obvious. Bruno and I were the only two men that Skaaland managed—and I was the only person, other than Bruno, that Skaaland deemed "worthy" of his time. We were also the only two babyfaces in the federation, and, I think, in the United States at the time, to have a manager. It was an elegant and successful solution—and one that Skaaland, as a part-owner of the company at the time, was happy to participate in.

During my travels through the territory in the months leading up to winning the belt, there were a couple of other guys I wrestled a lot who are worth a mention here. The first guy was The Golden Terror, who was managed by Captain Lou Albano. The Golden Terror wore a yellow lycra body suit and a yellow mask, and could do some good things in the ring. For those that don't know, the guy under the hood back then was "The Duke of Dorchester" Pete Doherty. I really enjoyed working with him. He moved well, was pretty flexible, was good at inciting the people, and his timing was very good.

Doherty was one of the first people I did the short-arm scissor with in the ring. I loved doing that particular maneuver because there were very few people in the world who were strong enough to do it because it is impossible to get any help. Your opponent catches your arm in a short-arm scissor with his legs and you roll him over and just deadlift him up onto your shoulder and place him up on the top turnbuckle. The short-arm scissor is a credibility move—both inside the business and with the fans. If you can perform that move in the ring, your opponents instantly understand that you are the real deal. When the fans see it, they understand that they are seeing a pretty unusual feat of strength, and always really appreciate it.

The other guy I want to mention is Mr. Fuji. My last singles match at the Garden before my title match with Billy was on December 19, 1977, against Mr. Fuji, who at the time was the co-holder of the world tag-team championship with Professor Tanaka. Fuji had been in the business a long time and had already had a very successful career—especially in the tag-team business—and was someone the fans at that time were not used to seeing get pinned. I was excited to get in the ring with another heel with that kind of experience.

Fuji held himself out to the fans as the "master" of karate and judo and nerve holds, and he was vicious about it, and as good as anybody at what he did. He also played off a gimmick where he always had a packet of salt hidden somewhere in his tights that he would throw in your eyes to blind you if he got the chance. So there was always the opportunity to play off the foreign object when you got in the ring with him. Fuji had his formula down, and was hated by the fans, so you didn't have to do much to him to make the people respond. And you didn't have to limit what you could do with him, because Fuji could do anything in the ring. He understood ring psychology, could take any bump, and was very committed to making the match—telling the story and making it work.

I got a clean pinfall victory over Fuji at the Garden in November 1977, using the atomic drop, to maintain my undefeated streak. As I recall, it was a good ten-or twelve-minute match, where we got in there, got a lot done, and got out. Getting in the ring with Fuji was like having a night off—nothing was mapped out in advance but everything always fell into place. We didn't know what we were going to do until we met the people and found out what they wanted. He was a real pro—he'd hear things and call spots based on what people were hot for, and I would follow along. When I was in the ring with such a clear heel as Fuji was back then, that's all I had to do: do a few speed moves at the beginning to establish my credibility, fall to the blows of his karate and judo, suffer in his nerve holds, and then get fired up, get the crowd behind me to support my comeback, and then, when we had them at their peak, take it home.

By the way, I should mention here that I refer to Mr. Fuji by his wrestling name, and not by his given name, Harry Fujiwara. In the business, wrestlers generally referred to each other by their wrestling names—not their real names. It was easier—and it both protected kayfabe and your family identity. So we called Sergeant Slaughter "Sarge," not Bob Remus. I called Bill Eadie "Superstar," and Khosrow Vaziri "Sheik." Nobody called anybody by their real name unless, as I was, they were using their real name. I was "Bobby" to just about everybody.

The final angle that was used to build up to my title match with Billy at the Garden was my appearance as a "second" in the corner of challenger Mil Mascaras during his title match with Billy Graham in January 1978. The plan was to use that match to set up my match with Billy the following month. The only problem was that Mil Mascaras was really only in it for himself—as opposed to being in it for the good of the match or the angle. Your job as a wrestler is to help get the *match* over, not to help get yourself over. It is supposed to be about telling a good story and entertaining the people. If everyone in the business worked the way Mascaras worked, the business wouldn't work. It is very hard to work effectively with someone when what they're thinking most about is what is good for them as opposed to what's good for the match.

In Mexico, where Mascaras came from, the business was different, and people wrestled in a much different style. The promoters were less involved than they were in the United States and wrestlers there needed to be more of an in-ring advocate for their characters to protect their images and reputations. Mascaras was a legendary character down there, but I think he had trouble adapting to the way things were in the WWWF.

I remember defending the WWWF championship against Antonio Inoki in a bullfighting arena in Mexico City once. It was a disorganized affair backstage—there was much less promoter control over what the wrestlers did in the ring. I worked in a couple of smaller buildings down there on that trip too, and one night was more chaotic than the next. It seemed as if no one was in charge. I had gone down there by myself on that trip, I don't even think I had Arnold with me, and I certainly didn't go with a bodyguard like Ric Flair did. When Flair was the NWA Champion they always sent Harley with him when he went to Mexico just to make sure nothing ever happened to him, because Flair would likely not have been able to protect himself in the ring if the match became a shoot. It was a very roguish place where you really had to be on your guard and protect yourself in the ring at all times.

Anyway, Mascaras got his double-shot at Graham in December 1977 and January 1978, and although he was happy to take the main-event payday from Vince Sr., Mascaras wouldn't do the honors for Graham, even though Graham was the WWWF World Champion. Because of this, Vince Sr. had to concoct a screwjob finish that would allow Graham to win and keep the belt but not actually pin Mascaras or make him submit. There is only one way to do that—and that is to have the babyface challenger lose the match either by count out or disqualification. So that is what Vince Sr. chose to do—but he also decided to build in a little extra push for me while he was at it!

Vince sat down with me and explained how the angle was going to work. In a departure from the usual routine at the Garden, the Grand Wizard would be allowed to remain at ringside with Graham for the match against Mascaras. That would prompt Mascaras to run back to the dressing room and bring me back to second him at ringside. During the match, there would be a couple of false finishes with Graham's feet on the ropes, and it would be my job to interfere in the match by pushing Graham's feet off the ropes to stop the illegal pins. Eventually, Graham would take a swing at me and pull me into the ring, thus getting Mascaras disqualified, and Billy and I would then have an all-out brawl to set up the match in February.

This little gimmick also had the side benefit of upstaging Mascaras in the ring during his title match, which I think Vince Sr. enjoyed doing since Mascaras, in a total break with protocol, had refused do the honors for Graham. The angle was designed, in part, to give Mascaras a little taste of his own medicine.

Mascaras understood that this was a way to get him in and out of the Garden without having to get pinned by Billy, which was acceptable to him. Graham-Mascaras was just another in a long line of examples of matches that seemed great on paper until you started thinking about what you were going to do at the end. When someone isn't willing to do the honors to make the match, the whole idea fizzles. If Mascaras had been willing to do the honors for Graham, it could have been booked that Graham cheated to win, used a foreign object, or whatever—and the feud between them could have had much longer legs. But because Mascaras was such a prima donna, there was nowhere to go with it.

I trusted Vince Sr. completely to build me up to my title match in the way he wanted to do it. From the day in Philadelphia when he first told me I would be his next babyface champion, Vince Sr. had told me not to worry about the crowds—but just to stay in shape, show up on time, work as hard as I could, and that he would take care of everything else. Vince Sr. always said that if we didn't have a good house, it was the fault of the bookers and the front office—not that of the wrestlers. I was very sure about my ability to make a match the way it was supposed to be, and felt that I had trained with enough great people and enough good experience that I could read a crowd and handle any situation—that was the part I didn't doubt.

The dressing room culture, though, remained a different story.

When I was about to become champ, a couple of the guys (to this day, I still don't know who, although I suspect Graham) in the locker room went to Vince Sr. and asked him to make me put up a deposit on the belt. It was not uncommon, either in the NWA or in the WWWF, for the champion to have to put up some cash as surety to give the front office leverage over him to enable them to get the belt back when they wanted it. I know the people who went to Vince to make that request thought that

I didn't have the money, and that I wouldn't be able to put up any kind of deposit on the belt—and that my inability to put up the cash might keep the title change from happening.

At the TV tapings right before the February Garden show, Vince Sr. pulled me aside and asked me if I would be able to put up an $80,000 deposit on the belt. I told him I could, that it wasn't a problem, and that I could write him a check right there if he wanted me to.

Vince Sr. just nodded and walked away without saying a word.

I actually *did* have the money, but he never brought it up again.

The truth is, Corki and I had lived a conservative lifestyle up to that point. We had both come from modest upbringings, and as such, we didn't have a lot of things and toys that we spent money on. Instead, we had managed to put a lot of money away, because in the world of professional wrestling, you just didn't know how long your run would last. You were never more than one bad injury away from being done in the profession—and there was no union, no insurance, and no worker's compensation protection you if you got hurt. A lot of the guys drank their money, blew it up their noses, or popped pills to dull the physical pain or the loneliness of the road. I felt down on occasion too—don't get me wrong—but when I got down, I just trained harder, and that always managed to pull me out of it.

My final match at the Garden before winning the belt was an eight-man elimination tag-team match on January 23, 1978, on the undercard of the second Graham-Mascaras match. In that match, I partnered with High Chief Peter Maivia, Tony Garea, and Larry Zbyszko against the current world tag-team champions Professor Tanaka and Mr. Fuji, along with former world champion Stan Stasiak and Baron Mikel Scicluna. At the time of that match, I was still undefeated, and this was to be the last, big push to put me in position for the title match with Graham.

The match was booked so I would be left in the ring as the sole remaining member of my team against both of the tag-team champions,

Mr. Fuji and Professor Tanaka. I would go on to pin them both in succession with the atomic drop, and win the match for my team.

Later that night, Howard Finkel would announce that I was now the number one contender for the world championship, and that I would face "Superstar" Billy Graham in the main event at the next Garden card on February 20, 1978.

15

My Night at the Garden (February 20, 1978)

"There are two types of people who never amount to anything . . .
those who never do anything except what they are told to do, and
those who cannot even do what they are told to do. The people
who get ahead do the things that should be done without being
told. And they don't stop there. They go the extra mile and do
much more than is expected of them."

—Andrew Carnegie to Napoleon Hill, "Create Personal
Initiative"

———◆———

My world had come full circle. Just a few years earlier, I had been direc-
tionless, lifting weights in a YMCA gymnasium in Fargo, North Dakota,
when a chance meeting with a wrestler doing curls in that weight room
set me on my career path. Now, that very same wrestler would be standing
across the ring from me in the most revered arena in the world—the only
remaining obstacle left between me and stardom.

There had been whispers in the dressing rooms that some of the
boys were uneasy with the prospect of me taking over as the champion.
They were worried that I was unproven as a draw, and might kill the territory. The fear was that an "underdog" champion was not a successful
model to draw houses in the big cities of the Northeast. In the past, in
those arenas, big, bruising ethnic champions had always told the stories of good versus evil—and reassured their hardworking fan bases by
beating the living hell out of their heel opponents to the delight of the
screaming masses.

It was a risk, for sure.

But Vince McMahon Sr. had taken that risk with me—and I wasn't about to let him down. What the boys in the dressing rooms didn't realize was how much heart, will, and intensity and desire to succeed I had.

Billy's last big title defense in the territory was two days earlier Saturday night, February 18, 1978, in the Philadelphia Spectrum, where he faced former champion Bruno Sammartino in a steel cage match. Over the years, Billy has made no secret that he was not happy to be asked to drop the title when he was doing such good business around the territory—and that he was particularly unhappy to be dropping the belt to me, because he thought I was "boring," and "just a kid."

Billy has also said over the years that he and Bruno talked on the night of their steel cage match in Philadelphia about pulling a last-minute screwjob over on the promoters. According to that story, the plan was for Billy to throw Bruno against the door in the side of the steel cage where the door was, causing Bruno to "accidentally" fall out of the cage and win the match and giving the promoters no choice but to put the belt back on Bruno. Once that happened, it would be impossible for me to win the title at the Garden two nights later, since Bruno would have the belt.

Screwjob in the Works?

In the transition from Graham to Backlund, there was definitely some talk in the dressing room about a potential screwjob in the works at the Spectrum between Bruno and Graham right before the Garden show. The way I heard it, Graham was going to go into business for himself and get the belt to Bruno because he didn't want to drop it to Bobby. That story is a complete lie. Then again, nothing really surprises me that comes out of Billy's mouth these days. I wanted out, to get off

> the road, and to be able to wrestle who I wanted, when I wanted, on my own schedule. I didn't want to be beholden to any particular promoter, or to be the champion anymore—so why would I have conspired with Billy or anyone else to acquire something that I was trying to get away from? It is absolute nonsense.
>
> —Ken Patera

For what it's worth—I believe Bruno's version of the story. I had no doubt that Graham wanted to keep the belt, or at the very least, wanted to keep the belt away from me. He may even have talked to people in the dressing room about pulling something. But I also know from talking to Bruno that Bruno didn't want to hold the belt any longer, and was looking forward to coming off the road—so it wouldn't make any sense for him to have been a conspirator in such a scheme. In the end, I chalk this up to Billy just having a rough time facing the end of his time in the spotlight—something I totally understand from having gone through it myself.

On the night in question, Graham did, in fact, beat Sammartino with the booked finish (Sammartino threw Graham into the side of the cage where he smashed into the door and fell out for the win), and then went to Toronto on Sunday night and beat Edouard Carpentier at Maple Leaf Gardens in his last title defense before coming to New York.

For my part, I would be entering the ring against Graham undefeated in the WWWF, and with as much of a tailwind as the WWWF could have provided to me, given the dearth of heel talent on the roster at the time.

———◆———

"Bobby, I've decided to put the belt on you."

Nearly ten months had passed since Vince McMahon Sr. had first spoken those words to me, but on this, the appointed day, those nine little words were echoing in my mind as if I was hearing them for the first time. I had goose pimples all over my body as I sat in my 1977 Buick Electra, idling in the Stamford, Connecticut, rest area on the side of Route 95 bound for New York City and reflecting on the monumental changes about to happen in my life.

The morning of February 20, 1978, had dawned clear and cold in West Haven. Unable to sleep, I got up before dawn, had a bowl of oatmeal and then took Carrie, then two months old, outside for some fresh air. We had a backpack she liked to sit in, so I put her in there, strapped her onto my back, and took her out for a little walk. It was cold, but nothing compared to the frigid weather we knew from growing up in Minnesota, where it was often 20 degrees below zero at sunrise.

Although I had been appearing on WWWF television programming for about nine months, I was still by no means instantly recognized in public. It was still possible for me to go out for a jog without being recognized, or for us to have dinner in a restaurant in town without anyone knowing who we were. As I walked through the streets of West Haven that morning, though, smiling as I passed people getting into their cars on the way to work, I took a moment to appreciate the anonymity.

All that was about to change.

When Carrie and I got back, I went for my normal training session at the Olympic Gym in North Haven. At the time, I was doing primarily calisthenics and several sets of heavy free weights, training different parts of my body each day. I had a good workout, and I was able to get through it without interruption. That too, I knew, would be different starting tomorrow. The Olympic Gym was about to become known as the place where the world heavyweight wrestling champion came for his morning workout.

I went home and met Corki for lunch. We sat at the kitchen table playing with Carrie and dreaming about the many ways in which our lives were about to change. The many years of living out of boxes in temporary housing and moving every three to six months were finally over.

Given that the outcomes of the matches in professional wrestling are predetermined, when an important "angle" is scheduled—as when you win or lose a major title, or become a "heel" by turning on a babyface, or become a babyface by turning on a heel—you can actually anticipate your future before it happens. There are a lot of surreal things about professional wrestling, but being able to sit with your wife and discuss the real-life ramifications of a wrestling match in New York City that wouldn't happen for another ten hours was very strange.

Although Vince Sr. had not told me specifically how long I would be holding the title, he did tell me that we could plan to be in the area for "quite a while," and that it would make sense for us to start looking for a house somewhere in Connecticut—which was roughly at the geographic middle of the territory. Corki and I were about to have real financial security for the first time in our lives. Not only would this actually allow us to stay in the same place for longer than six months for the first time since we left Minnesota five years earlier, it would also allow Corki to find a permanent job, and for us to set down roots and live like normal people.

As we contemplated these changes, we promised each other that we wouldn't let fame change us, and that we would try our best to hang on to our solid Midwestern values and the basic way in which we were both raised. We also promised each other that we would always remember and appreciate that Vince McMahon Sr. was bestowing an incredible gift upon us, and that we would strive to always be worthy of it in the hearts and minds of the fans.

I had a lot of pent-up nervous energy and excitement that my walk and my workout that morning had failed to dispel, so I kissed Corki and Carrie goodbye, got in the car, and decided to set off for New York City.

And that's when the doubts started.

As I sat there in the car in the Stamford rest area, I began to think about Vince McMahon Sr., and his vision of an "All-American Boy" underdog champion—someone who could represent the dreams and hopes of the average American. Someone who the people sitting at home watching on television could identify with, and most of all, someone that those people would want to buy a ticket and come out to the arenas to cheer for. Vince Sr. had just seen the way the world was captivated by and rallied behind the young Romanian gymnast Nadia Comaneci at the 1976 summer Olympics in Montreal, and his idea was that he could catch that same lightning in a bottle using an "All-American Boy" as the model for his next champion.

I thought about where I was in the business, where I had come from, and why Vince Sr. had decided to pick me. I didn't doubt my wrestling ability—I knew that my strong amateur background combined with the five years of training I had in the professional rings with some of the best guys in the business—would serve me well. I knew how to tell a story in the ring, read the crowds, listen to their reactions to what we were doing, and make the appropriate adjustments.

It wasn't the technical things I was worried about.

Sitting there in the car, I was thinking about "Superstar" Billy Graham—the man who had invited me into the business, and the man I had been booked to beat at the Garden in a matter of hours. I thought about his 22-inch arms and 55-inch chest, and his rippling muscles, tie-dyed outfits, and remarkable charisma. I thought about the interviews he had given during his time as the world champion that channeled Mohammed Ali and drove the crowds wild. The way the words just seemed to roll off his tongue as he claimed to be made of "T-bone steaks and barbell plates" and described himself as "the reflection of perfection and the number one selection" or "the women's pet and the men's regret."

Graham was a heel and someone the fans loved to hate because he was so over the top, but he was also a showman who entertained the fans and created incredible interest in his matches. Billy had been doing remarkably well as a heel in a company that had always had a babyface champion. He was selling out buildings across the territory—but he was running out of babyfaces to wrestle. I would be supplanting him as the world champion, not when the people were tiring of him, but at the absolute height of his drawing power. *I* would now be counted on to main-event every building that I wrestled in, and thus, to carry the top of the cards all across the territory. And this was no ordinary territory. This was *the* territory—the WWWF—with the largest buildings and the most lucrative schedule in the business.

Vince Sr. was obviously very committed to his bet that an underdog "All-American Boy" world champion would sell in the Northeast. And Vince had dropped me—a shy, fresh-faced, twenty-eight-year-old farm boy from rural Minnesota into his urban world of larger-than-life characters.

I was a reluctant interview, at best. I didn't have the muscles of a Superstar Graham, the easy charisma of Dusty Rhodes, the incredible survival story of Bruno Sammartino, the tough-guy appearance of Harley Race, or a reliable ethnic fan base like both Sammartino and Pedro Morales had. I also wasn't a brawler, which had been the model for the WWWF's babyface champions since the very beginning. Sammartino and Morales were both known for their no-nonsense roughhouse style. They gave the crowds what they wanted to see—namely, their hard-nosed heroes throwing haymakers, kicking and stomping and beating the life out of the villains who were trying to take the championship away from them. There wasn't much subtlety to it, but the crowds had been eating it up for nearly two decades.

In contrast, I would be booked as a vulnerable, athletic young kid in a place full of monsters, winning the fans over with my courage, hard work, and superior technical skills. There was nothing about me or that model that fit the WWWF's prior image of professional wrestling's world heavyweight champion that it had been selling to its fans since 1963.

But in just a few hours, that is precisely what I was to become.

As I sat there imagining the people who would be sitting in the Garden that night, I thought back to when I had been told that Vince

McMahon Sr. had called his fellow promoters Jim Barnett in Atlanta, Eddie Graham in Florida, the Funks in Amarillo, and Sam Muchnick in St. Louis and had asked them to recommend someone to become his "All-American Boy." Someone who was reliable, could protect the belt, and could be counted on to fill the top of the cards.

Every one of them had recommended me.

My confidence somewhat restored, I came out of my daydream and started to put the car into gear. But then my mind suddenly shifted to the other decision-makers in the WWWF's front office—guys who had been with the WWWF for nearly their entire careers, like Arnold Skaaland, Gorilla Monsoon, Freddie Blassie, Lou Albano, Phil Zacko, Ernie "The Grand Wizard of Wrestling" Roth, and Angelo Savoldi. Many of these guys were minority owners in the business, or were at least part of the WWWF's creative brain trust. I knew they got together and had card games at Madison Square Garden every month before the matches to discuss angles, talent, and new booking ideas with Vince Sr. I wondered how many meetings they must have had about who was going to take the title from Billy Graham. And after Graham became such a box office hit, I wondered how many of them lobbied for Graham to be given a "face turn" so he could continue to run with the title and bring in the big houses for all of them.

Thinking about the meeting where Vince McMahon Sr. first threw out my name, I wondered what kind of response the suggestion must have received from that card table. Most of those people wouldn't have been afraid to tell Vince what they thought. It was a very tight-knit group, and I was a complete outsider who had no relationship with any of them. Vince Sr. told those boys that Sammartino had given his notice that he wanted to come off the road, so he had decided to put the belt on Graham while he searched the world for a new babyface to take over the federation. And when he did that, I'm pretty sure that none of those people was thinking of Bob Backlund. I'm sure they were thinking of in-house guys like Jay Strongbow, Tony Garea, Ivan Putski, or Bruno's protégé, Larry Zbyszko.

So I started to wonder whether I might be walking into a hornet's nest of internal politics where everybody, both in the front office and in the dressing room, would be rooting for me to fail.

In the NWA territories like Amarillo, Georgia, Florida, and St. Louis, where I was trained, the NWA World Champion would come into the territory for a few days a month to face the main guy in the territory. The visiting champion, of course, had to win—but the main guy in the territory had to be left with the shine, or he would lose some of his power to draw houses in the territory. Were it any other way, instead of drawing a huge house for the title defense and helping the territory shore up its fan base, the world champion would end up weakening the territory's main talent, which would have precisely the opposite effect.

Coming up in the NWA territories in the Midwest, the South, and in Texas, training under guys like Harley Race, Jack Brisco, and the Funks, I had been taught how to have longer, more balanced matches. We were trained to start off slow, draw the people in, trade offense with your opponent with the action see-sawing back and forth until you had determined what the particular crowd was into that night, and then try to deliver a healthy dose of whatever it was that the crowd wanted. We'd work up to a particular high spot and then back off, work up to another, and back off—and then maybe work in a near fall or a false finish until the energy in the crowd was as high as we could possibly get it—and then "go home" with the booked finish.

When I was booked to win a match decisively by pinning my opponent, simply winning the match that way and getting my hand raised by the referee in the middle of the ring was enough for the people to get their high from my match. So in matches where I was booked to "go over" my opponent by pinning him, I saw my job as making sure to leave something for my opponent so he could "keep his heat." I might be the champion and the guy on top of the card who was being relied on the most to draw the house, but there was no reason for me to want to do that alone. If I could beat a heel, but leave him with his heat intact, he would be better positioned to help draw the next house by appearing to be a bigger threat to whatever babyface he was booked to wrestle next. If I beat him too decisively, he would lose his heat, and the fans' interest in his next match would be diminished, making him less of a draw for the fans to want to come and see.

As I sat there in the parking lot thinking about the business—I realized that just because something had always been done a certain way in the WWWF didn't mean it had to continue to be done that way. I realized I was bringing to the table a whole new approach to the business of professional wrestling—and an approach that, once understood, ought to be popular both with the front office and with the boys in the locker room. By implementing more of the NWA's model of leaving most heels with their heat so they could maintain their drawing power and longevity in the territory, we would have more options in booking feuds or interesting semi-final matches for the undercards, and, as a consequence, do better business because of it.

With more people working to draw the houses, the houses should consistently be better, which would allow all of us to be more successful. During the time I spent as a regional champion in Amarillo, Florida, and Missouri, I had seen this approach work—and I realized that it could work in the WWWF as well—even though it was not the model currently in vogue.

Vince McMahon Sr. must have recognized this too. The fact that the "All-American Boy" archetype was set up to be an underdog played perfectly into this business model. It would allow me to take that approach with nearly every match I had. It was at that moment that I realized that Vince McMahon Sr. had thought this all out—that his choice of having an underdog "All-American Boy" as his champion would not only allow for a different "look," but also a more robust business model to take the federation forward, and that my look, my background, and my training were all perfectly suited to it.

I pulled my car out onto Route 95 south, and headed on to the destiny that lay ahead for me in New York City. I recognized that it might take a while for people—in the front office, in the dressing room, and in the crowds—to adjust to our new way of doing things. But now that I understood how it all fit together, I was very confident that we were going to make it work. I knew that at the outset, there might not be a heck of lot of people behind me, but I was also confident that given the time to do so, I could win them over.

―•―•―

I arrived safely in New York City around six o'clock, and parked in a public parking lot on 48th Street. I grabbed my gym bag out of the trunk, breathed deeply, and began the fourteen-block walk through midtown Manhattan down to Madison Square Garden. It was a pretty nice evening for February in New York City, and I took my time walking through the streets, passing the crowds of people leaving work for the day, inhaling the ever-present smell of roasting nuts and pretzels being sold by the street vendors, and began to get butterflies in my stomach. I had arrived New York City—the heartbeat of the world—and was about to become its newest hero.

As I got closer to the Garden, I was recognized by a few fans on their way to the matches.

"Good luck tonight, Bob!" a group of them yelled and waved to me from the opposite corner of the street.

"Bobby! Bobby! Bobby!" a group of them chanted, pumping their fists in the air.

"Graham's gonna kick your ass, Backlund!" someone else yelled.

Suddenly, a couple of breathless fans caught up to me on the sidewalk.

"Do you think you can take Billy Graham?" one of them asked.

"Don't let him get you in that bearhug," another of them offered.

"And don't let him cheat you out of it," another said. "Remember what he tried to do to Mascaras."

"I'll do my best!" I said to them, smiling to myself and giving out high fives and handshakes before peeling off onto 35th Street. I stood there for a moment and looked up at the giant marquee lit up in front of the Garden across from the Pennsylvania Hotel.

TONIGHT:
WRESTLING
Graham vs. Backlund
SOLD OUT

There it was—my name in lights in midtown Manhattan, on the marquee of the most important arena in the world. I had come a long way from the farm fields of Princeton, Minnesota, from my life as a young derelict and a near high school dropout. From sleeping in the trunk of my car with a baseball bat eating tuna out of a can.

This was my moment, and I resolved to make it count.

I jogged to the side entrance to the Garden, slid in the door, took the elevator to the main floor, and walked into the dressing room assigned to the babyfaces. There, I shook hands with the Chief (who was neither a Chief, nor even an Indian, but actually an Italian guy named Joe Scarpa), Tony Garea, Peter Maivia, and a few other people, and then tossed my bag onto the bench in one corner and began to change into my wrestling gear. Although news of the title change had spread among the boys, no one said anything to me, which reinforced my suspicion that it wasn't a popular choice in the dressing room. There were guys in that dressing room like Strongbow and Garea who had been in the WWWF for a long time, and must have felt badly about being passed over for a run with the title. But as I stood there changing, I reminded myself that Vince Sr. had faith in me, and that of all the people he might have chosen for this role, he had chosen me, and he had done so for sound reasons. He had a long track record of success, and it was not for me to second-guess him. I promised myself as I stood there changing into my black trunks and black wrestling boots that I would work hard to win the hearts and minds of the fans, the boys, and the front office. I would be a champion they would all be happy to have at the top of the card.

The dressing rooms at the Garden were nothing fancy—they didn't let us use the Rangers' or the Knicks' dressing rooms—so we were in the auxiliary rooms on either side of the great hallway that led to the ramp into the middle of the Garden. They were just large rooms with a few lockers, some folding chairs, and some benches, and an attached room with showers, toilets, and sinks. The faces and the heels had separate dressing rooms on opposite sides of the hallway to keep up appearances.

Belltime was scheduled for 8:30. This would also be the first time that kids from eight to fourteen years old would be allowed to be at the Garden for a wrestling show. Before then, no one under fourteen was admitted for wrestling. But that night, the era of the "All-American Boy" would begin—and with it, the era of cheering kids began as well.

Vince Sr. truly did think of everything.

After I finished changing, I left the dressing room and went down the hallway and out into the big open area at one end of the arena where they housed the animals during the circus. It was a very large room and there was nobody there, so I stretched and limbered up and did some exercises. Billy and I were scheduled to go off late in the card that night—I think it was scheduled to be the sixth or seventh match—so I had plenty of time to wait and burn off more nervous energy.

As the time for our match drew near, I definitely felt the butterflies. Eventually, word came that Vince Sr. wanted to see me, and that's when I got the goose pimples all over my body. I returned to the dressing room area, and Vince motioned me into the men's room where Billy was waiting. Vince Sr. brought us together, riffling the ever-present stack of quarters in his hands. He pulled his glasses down to the end of his nose and looked us both in the eye.

"Well, this is it, Billy. Bobby is going over tonight. I want you guys to work around the bear hug and wait until the time is right. When it is,

Bobby, you get behind Billy, pick him up and really hold him up there, carry him around, and then give him the atomic kneedrop—but make sure to drop him close to the ropes. Billy, you're going to put your foot up on the rope, but the referee isn't going to see it, and he's going to make the three-count—and that will be it." (In professional wrestling rules, ordinarily, getting a foot on the ropes would be cause for the referee to stop the count and break up the pin.)

The finish was intentionally designed to be a mirror image of the way Graham had been booked to win the title over Sammartino in Baltimore. That night, the referee hadn't "seen" Billy's feet on the ropes in the corner of the ring when he used them to get extra leverage to pin Sammartino for the title. Tonight, the referee wouldn't "see" Billy's foot on the ropes to save him from the three count that caused him to lose the belt.

Wrestling promoters did love irony . . . Billy nodded somberly and said nothing. He had the championship belt draped over his massive shoulder, and I could tell he was disappointed at being asked to surrender it. Even though he had known for almost a year that this day was coming, I think Billy had held out some hope, until the very end, that his great performances and his surprising drawing power would change Vince's mind.

There was little doubt that Billy had wrestled some fantastic matches and had given some great interviews—and over the past few months I had been a witness to the way the fans had reacted to him. Some people loved him, and a lot more hated him, but there was no one who was agnostic about "Superstar" Billy Graham. When you get that kind of rise out of the fans, you know that your character has gotten over. It had been a great recipe for business that had lasted nearly ten months—tenfold longer than any heel had ever carried Vince's world title in the history of the promotion to that point.

That was the extent of the conversation. Vince gave me a little wink and a nod, and before I knew it, he was gone. Billy retreated to the heels' dressing room without saying anything further either to Vince Sr. or to me, and I headed back to my spot out in the holding area.

Vince had booked the finish to the match that way because he didn't want to destroy Graham's "heat" with the fans. By allowing Billy to get pinned with his foot on the ropes, Billy could claim, in his post-match interviews, that he had been "robbed." We didn't want the title win to look like a fluke—because that would have weakened my title win, which needed to be strong to put me over with the people—so it was important that I dominated a lot of the match before the pin. But we also wanted the finish to look like an upset that might not happen again in a rematch, which the foot-on-the-ropes finish provided.

Two months of rematches, ending in a steel cage "blowoff" in April, were already booked for the Garden on Vince's calendar and storyboard, and he had high hopes to draw huge sellout crowds to pay off that storyline. So it was critical that we delivered just the right touch with the booked finish, so I would come out of the match with a decisive victory, but Billy would come out still looking like a strong champion who had just been upset.

That would be the key to drawing well for the rematches.

Back out in the hallway, I did some final pre-match stretching and got mentally set to go out into the ring. At the appointed time, we were summoned, and my "manager" Arnold Skaaland came to my side and walked me down the hallway. I had wrestled several times in the Garden by this point, but I was grateful to have Arnold at my side that night because the nerves were definitely getting the best of me. We turned left down the runway, past Vince Sr. who winked at me again as went by, and then through the curtain and out into the arena.

As soon as we came into view, the people just started cheering wildly. I had goose pimples all over my body and shivers racing down my spine. There were 22,000 people out there that night in the Garden. There wasn't an empty seat in the place—which was a tribute to Billy's ability to draw as the champion, but also a tribute to the booking that had been done to get people interested in seeing my match with him. I remember thinking that you could have fit the entire population of Princeton into the Garden ten times over.

No words can ever really do justice to the feeling of the vibrations and the energy of the people roaring for you as you stand out there, in the middle of the greatest arena in the world, about to wrestle for the WWWF championship. It is something I will never forget.

As I climbed up the steps and into the ring, the emotion of the people showered down on me. I remember thinking that life really couldn't get any better than that moment—it just doesn't get any higher. I stood there jumping around and trying to stay loose and recognized that this was everybody's dream in the business, to be in the position that I was in at that very moment.

And then, suddenly, the moment passed as the roar of the crowd turned to a chorus of boos, and I knew instinctively that Billy was making his way down to the ring. I looked over at him as he climbed the steps alongside his manager, Ernie Roth, known as "The Grand Wizard of Wrestling." Billy's face was blank and emotionless—quite a change from the usual. I could tell he was really struggling with it all.

The bell tolled several times to bring the noise level in the arena down as ring announcer Howard Finkel stepped to the microphone.

"Ladies and gentlemen, *this* is the main event of the evening. It is for the World Wide Wrestling Federation's Heavyweight Championship, one fall with a one-hour time limit."

The bell rang again as the crowd cheered, and I felt the hair on the back of my neck stand up. My heart was pounding in my throat. People I didn't know were giving me thumbs up from the crowd, or nodding and smiling and pumping their fists. All around the ring, flashbulbs popped as the photographers angled for their pre-match shots.

"First, I would like to introduce the respective managers. In the corner to my left, here is the Grand Wizard of Wrestling!"

Ernie Roth, his identity hidden by his green turban, wraparound sunglasses, and colorful, bejeweled cape, spread his arms out and soaked in the chorus of boos. Roth had the worst set of crooked and yellow teeth you have ever seen—the product of decades of chain smoking—and he showed every one of them to the fans as he gestured defiantly to the crowd and then pointed admiringly at the gold championship belt around Graham's waist.

"And in the opposite corner, the Golden Boy, Arnold Skaaland!"

Arnie, standing beside me in his trademarked dark jacket and tie, smelled of the cigars he had smoked earlier in the day while playing gin rummy with the front office guys. He gave a little wave and smiled at the crowd, which roared its approval. For the eleven years that Bruno held the world championship, Skaaland had served as Sammartino's "manager." Now he stood beside me as mine—and that commonality was not lost on the crowd.

During my buildup to this night, Bruno and I had never appeared together on television, or in an interview, and we had never wrestled together in a tag-team match. I was certainly not positioned as Bruno's protégé, which would have been an easy way to get me over with the fans. But as I was standing here next to Arnold Skaaland, it suddenly occurred to me that such an overt gesture wasn't necessary. I was the only other wrestler to be represented by Bruno's manager—but I would not start my reign in Bruno's shadow.

The torch had, in fact, been passed.

"And now, ladies and gentlemen . . . the challenger. From Princeton, Minnesota, weighing in at two hundred thirty four pounds, the All-American Boy, Bob Backlund!"

The bell tolled again, several times, as an even louder roar from the crowd rained down upon us from the upper decks. I thrust my arms up into the air in a gesture of greeting, and then shielded my eyes from the glare of the lights as I looked around at the crowd in the arena. They were packed in to the rafters, up to the last rows in the nosebleed seats in the corners of the building. As I jumped up and down to stay loose, I looked across the ring at Billy, who still wore a blank look on his face. I wondered what was going through his mind as he stood here in the ring at the end of his days in the spotlight. I wondered if he was regretting that brief talk we had in the YMCA in Fargo, North Dakota, and thinking about how ironic it was that I would be ending his reign as champion when he had been the man who had ushered me into the business.

"And his opponent. From Paradise Valley, Arizona, weighing two hundred seventy eight pounds, the World Wide Wrestling Federation's heavyweight champion, "Superstar" Billy Graham!"

Graham pulled his t-shirt over his head and gave a couple of little jumps in place with the title belt around his waist before slowly unsnapping it, carefully folding the straps inside, and handing it to the referee, who held it aloft for the crowd to see. Graham was careful not to look at the belt for too long to give away what was about to happen, but I could tell that if he could have, he would have hung on to that moment forever.

Flashbulbs sparkled all around the seating bowls and upper decks. The Garden was buzzing with electricity and nervous energy, as the roar of the crowd subsided slightly and the fans, nearly all of whom had been standing for the introductions, began to take their seats.

Arnold Skaaland put his arm around me in the corner, leaned closely into my right ear, and spoke exactly four words to me.

"They're all yours, kid . . ."

Graham and I stepped out of our corners and into the center of the ring for the last-minute instructions from the referee.

It was showtime.

The bell rang, and the crowd buzzed with anticipation as Billy and I circled each other in the middle of the ring. Billy immediately caught me in a reverse bearhug and squeezed until his triceps rippled. I worked into an escape by slipping my arms through, and then reversed the hold, and Billy reached for the corner and a break—the fans booing heartily. I took the cue, and instead of breaking, deadlifted Billy's 275 pounds into the air and placed him back into the center of the ring as the crowd roared its approval.

Playing his role perfectly, referee Terry Terranova forced a clean break, admonished me, and pushed me into a neutral corner, claiming that Graham had reached the ropes and I had failed to break cleanly. I argued and gestured at the referee, and a cascade of boos descended from every corner of the Garden as Graham played to the crowd that I had pulled on his tights. In unison, the crowd began to chant an obscenity at Graham, and he jawed with the ringsiders as I jumped up and down in the ring and pumped a fist to rally the fans.

We had the crowd less than a minute into the match.

We teased a headlock into a near fall, as Billy threw me into the ropes and I leaped over his backdrop attempt and caught him in a sunset rollup. The referee counted to two, and Graham escaped into the ropes again. Again the referee pushed me back away from Graham, and again, the boos descended on Graham.

This time, Graham caught me in a full nelson, and we played off of that for a short while. I sold Graham's strength until I eventually worked my leg into a kick-up escape and Graham complained to the referee and gestured to the fans that I had oil on my body.

Once again, a crescendo of boos rained down on Graham. Although Graham had been popular with a certain segment of the fans at the Garden, on this night, it was clear that the fans were solidly behind the underdog kid. Vince Sr.'s plan was working.

We locked up again, and Graham caught me in a headlock and cinched down on it and jawed at the fans some more. Eventually, I threw him into the ropes, he came off the ropes with a head of steam, and shoulder-blocked me down to the canvas, ran through to the other side and attempted another shoulder block. I ducked behind him, pushed him into the ropes, and brought him back into a victory roll without the bridge, and the referee again counted to two for a near fall.

The fans were screaming as they sweated the count. On the television broadcast that night on Madison Square Garden Cablevision, the announcer, Vince McMahon Jr., observed that "there is a certain electricity here tonight in Madison Square Garden."

I applied a reverse chinlock on Graham to give him a blow and a chance to consider our next series of moves. When he indicated that he was ready, he gouged my eyes to break the hold, got to his feet, and bodyslammed me to the canvas. When he went for a second bodyslam, I blocked him and rolled him up into a small package. By design, the referee was out of position, and took an eternity to get into position to begin to toll the count. When Graham kicked out at the two and three-quarters count, the crowd groaned—recognizing that, had the referee been in position—that would have been a three count. The energy was building.

I spit on my hands, rubbed them together, and beckoned Graham back toward the center of the ring. He put up his hands and begged off— and the crowd booed him deafeningly.

It was time to transition the momentum.

We locked up again, and I swung Graham into the ropes and threw a dropkick. Graham held onto the ropes and I missed him and crashed down to the canvas on my left shoulder. Graham began to kick and stomp and pound on me with forearm blows and elbow smashes. I crawled around the ring selling his power, as he grabbed me by the hair, threw me into the ropes and caught me on the rebound and hoisted me up into his signature finisher—the bearhug—and cinched up his twenty-two-inch python-like arms.

On the television broadcast, Vince McMahon Jr. was selling Graham's finisher to the tens of thousands of people watching on television.

"There it is, the Superstar bearhug—another successful title defense . . . as Graham begins to squeeze . . ."

But then, after a beat of silence with the crowd roaring their support, I used an old amateur move and put pressure on the outside of Graham's elbows to weaken his grip. McMahon recognized the move immediately and called it.

"Backlund is hanging in there—he has the elbows hooked in an effort to take some leverage away from Superstar . . . in trying to find a measure of escape where so many men have not!"

We then intentionally turned to the television camera and I went to the inside, forcing my arms inside his arms as he maintained the bearhug, and Graham beautifully sold the escape, slowly separating his clasped fingers as I applied my leverage against his arms until I broke the hold and took him over with a hiptoss.

The people cheered approvingly.

I dropped to the canvas and sold a back injury to give proper credit to the impact of Billy's finisher.

Billy rushed me, and I tried to give him a double-axehandle, but he grabbed the bearhug again, and this time, I went limp for a couple of seconds to keep the fans on the edge of their seats, and then pushed back on Billy's head and worked back to the inside.

"Backlund knows all the pressure points . . ." McMahon observed on the telecast.

Having worked my arms to the inside, I reversed the hold, and hoisted Billy up into a bearhug, cinched it up, and applied the pressure. Graham yelled something. It was nearly impossible to hear anything over the din.

Maintaining the bearhug, I dropped Billy down, shoulders first, to the canvas and got a two count before he pulled my hair in a desperate attempt to break up the pin. The fans were in a frenzy, so we repeated the move again, and again he pulled my hair to escape being pinned. Acting on the adrenaline coursing through my body, I deadlifted Graham from the canvas back up into the bearhug but Graham stuck a finger in my eye to break the hold. We both staggered for a moment, and with perfect timing, Vince McMahon, on the television broadcast, anticipated the finish.

"In Madison Square Garden here tonight, he is a long way from North Dakota where he won the NCAA collegiate title . . ."

I threw Graham into the ropes, and applied the abdominal stretch submission hold and really sunk it in and stretched Graham. The decibel level in the building was off the charts, and Graham and I both recognized at that point, that even though the match was only about thirteen minutes old, we weren't likely to get the crowd any higher than they were at that moment. The referee gestured at him, and Graham shook his head wildly from side to side to indicate to the referee that he was not going to concede the match. I poured on the pressure. We both listened for another moment, and then recognizing where the crowd's energy was, Graham tapped me on the head to indicate that it was time to go home.

He grabbed my hair and hoisted me over in a hiptoss.

"Every time you think you have Graham, he comes up with something . . ." McMahon lamented on television.

As Graham staggered around the ring, I snuck behind him, waited just long enough for the fans to comprehend what I was about to do, and I then hoisted him up onto my shoulder for the atomic kneedrop.

"Wait a minute! Bob Backlund has "Superstar" Billy Graham up in the air!" McMahon shouted excitedly on the broadcast.

The fans had seen me pin every opponent I had wrestled at the Garden with this very move. They were now all on their feet, jumping up and down, waving their arms, as I carried Graham all the way across the ring to the opposite corner. The one thing going through my mind at the time was to be sure to drop him close enough to the ropes so he could get his foot across the bottom rope.

"There may not be an escape for Graham!" McMahon yelled.

I ran Billy out just *past* the middle of the ring and then smashed the base of his spine across my knee.

"He's in the middle of the ring. Atomic kneedrop! Down to the canvas . . ."

Billy had landed in precisely the right spot.

"Backlund covers Graham—one, two, and three!"

⟶➤•⟵

As one, the Garden crowd sprang to their feet, arms in the air, and bedlam ensued. The fans jumped up and down, throwing programs and cups into the air in celebration. Down in the ring, Graham still lay prone on the canvas, his foot perfectly draped across the bottom rope. He yelled at the referee and pointed at his leg. But the referee hadn't seen it as he delivered the fatal three count from the other side of Graham's body.

The celebration was on!

"Bob Backlund has won the World Wrestling Federation Championship. A dream come true!" shouted Vince McMahon as the bell rang and rang, and the referee paraded me around and around the ring in circles with my arm raised in a token of victory.

Still down on the canvas, Graham was still selling the rematch, gesturing over and over to the referee, the fans, and the ringside cameramen and press people that his foot had been on the bottom rope at the time of the pinfall, and that he had gotten robbed.

I walked over to the side of the ring and yelled "WE DID IT!" to the ringside fans. They were celebrating right along with me. There was jubilation in the Garden as the microphone lowered from the Garden ceiling and announcer Howard Finkel was preparing to make it official.

"Ladies and Gentlemen, the time of the fall, fourteen minutes, fifty-one seconds, the winner—and NEW World Wide Wrestling Federation Heavyweight Champion, Bob Backlund!"

I stood in the ring and celebrated with the fans until I was summoned to return to the dressing room area. There, I shook hands with a smiling Vince McMahon Sr., who met me just inside the curtain.

"Great job, Bobby! Well done. Well done!"

Vince was a man of few words, but he was smiling, and I could tell that he was pleased with how the crowd was reacting to the way the transition had played out. From there, I sought Billy out in the heels dressing room, shook his hand, and thanked him for giving me and the fans a great match. Billy clapped a big paw behind my neck and offered his congratulations. I knew we would meet again in many rematches, both at the Garden and around the horn—so this wasn't a goodbye.

The boys in the dressing room offered their polite congratulations—but I could tell I would now have to prove myself to a dressing room full of guys who had been passed over for the role, and had grown accustomed to having Bruno in the driver's seat. I resolved, again, to work to earn their respect.

I showered, got dressed, carefully placed the WWWF title belt into my gym bag, and headed out the side door of the Garden and off onto the street for the long trip back to Connecticut.

The Garden Was Electric

The night Bob won the belt, the energy in the Garden was just amazing. I would say that the buzz in the Garden that night was electric—it was an atmosphere that was just off the charts compared to anything we had experienced there in the recent past. Bob had been accepted by the fans at that point—and the people were fully behind him. There was a small pocket of people that were still behind Billy—but don't kid yourself—that building was solidly behind Bob.

I actually didn't know the finish of the match before it happened, so I was on the edge of my seat like everyone else! But when Bob picked Billy up for the atomic kneedrop, everyone knew what was coming because that move had been built up so much both in previous matches at the Garden and on television. You could literally see the people all over the arena rising to their feet as one to see what was going to happen. And when he dropped him, and jumped on top of him, and the referee counted one, two three—that building just blew up. I mean the place was literally shaking.

—Howard Finkel

16

Getting Over (1978)

"Teamwork is a never-ending process, and even though it depends on everyone involved, the responsibility for it lies with you."

—Napoleon Hill, "Inspire Teamwork"

———◦•◦———

The morning of Tuesday, February 21, 1978, was a morning like no other in the Backlund house. The WWWF championship belt was now safely stored in the night table drawer next to our bed, and suddenly, I had a whole lot more responsibility on my shoulders. After getting a few hours of restless sleep, I awoke with a start, thinking that I had overslept for a flight to a match. From here on, I would be in the main events every night. Showing up late or missing a date was not an option.

The whole episode seemed like a dream. I had to go back and check the drawer to make sure that the title belt was actually there. I pulled the belt out and sat there at our little kitchen table running my fingers over the gold plating, recalling the way that the Garden crowd had exploded when the referee's hand hit the mat for the third time.

I could do this. I could be the people's champion. I would find a way to earn their respect, and their admiration, and make them want to come out and cheer me on.

The day after the Garden show, we went to Pennsylvania for the television tapings. We'd get there at around eleven in the morning and the ring would already be set up there in the empty fieldhouse and the guys would have lunch and sit around playing cards or reading or goofing around with each other while we shot promos for the local house shows all afternoon. Since this was my first TV with the belt, I was now in all the main events, and for the first time since I had come to the territory, I was involved in most of the promos.

It was my first real exposure to talking a lot on camera, and it just wasn't my strength. I was a pretty shy, and I certainly never professed to have the ability like Graham or Dusty to talk people into the seats. So figuring out what to say, and how to say it convincingly without seeming totally awkward, was a challenge. I decided to handle these promos as if I was talking about preparing for one of my amateur matches — and to just carry that straightforward, plain-talking style through. It was a choice made from a combination of fear and necessity, but I actually think it worked out okay and gave my matches an additional air of authenticity.

Vince Jr. ran these tapings for his father. He had a long list of all of the house shows we were taping promos for, and the matches on those cards for which we would be cutting promos. For each of those matches, to give us some context, Vince Jr. would tell us where the promo was for, who our opponent was going to be, and what had happened there last time. Once the interviews were done, they would incorporate these promos into the tape and then send the tape off to the television station(s) that covered the area where that particular house show was going to occur.

Some of the guys were very good at it and enjoyed cutting these promos. Others had managers like the Captain or Blassie or the Grand Wizard to do most of their talking for them. But that was the basic setup every three weeks — with everyone sitting out there waiting their turn, reading, hanging out, and talking or whatever. The office would bring in sandwiches to give everyone a little break.

There was a real fellowship at these tapings. Everyone on the roster was present. For new blood coming in, the tapings were usually the first place they appeared. The tapings were also the place where most of the hot new angles began, and the place where Vince Sr. handed out the booking assignments for the following three weeks. So taping days were a bit like a company staff meeting.

Initially, I was very uncomfortable at these tapings. I still felt very much like an outsider who was being judged on his every move. But with time and experience, and as I came to be accepted more by the boys as the champion, I actually grew to enjoy them.

After the tapings, we all set off in different directions. I headed down to Jacksonville, Florida, for a WWWF World Title versus NWA World Title match with my old friend Harley Race, and for promoter Eddie Graham in the Florida Championship Wrestling territory.

As I've mentioned before, Vince Sr. and Eddie were good friends and trusted colleagues in the wrestling business. Harley and Billy Graham had just wrestled a Broadway (sixty-minute time-limit draw) in Florida that had drawn a nice gate—and a rematch had already been scheduled. Of course, at the time the rematch was scheduled, both Vince Sr. and Eddie knew that the rematch with Race would be with me and not with Billy—but both Eddie and Harley were fine with that. The real draw for the match was the possibility, in the eyes of the fans, of a unification of the NWA and WWWF World Titles.

I was very enthusiastic to return to the Florida territory for Eddie as the newly crowned WWWF champion and also to have that match with Harley. Eddie and Vince booked us to do another Broadway—which made sense given that the fans had seen Harley go an hour with Billy, but not with me.

Harley was a master of the art of developing a match and telling a complete story in the ring. He understood, in the fullest sense of the word, that the entire purpose of a wrestling match was to entertain the people in the arenas, and Harley entertained them to the fullest. He never put himself, or his ego, or his reputation ahead of whatever would be best for the match, and he would give the people in any particular arena on any given night the very best bang for their buck. That willingness to entertain the people and to put the match above himself made Harley a very special performer.

Harley and I, of course, had been in some wars together feuding over the Missouri title in St. Louis. This match, however, was a special one to both of us because we had both ascended to the very pinnacle of our profession and were now representing our respective organizations as world champions. I didn't know it at the time, but this was also our first meeting in the ring since Vince Sr. broke the deadlock in the NWA championship committee by voting for Harley to become the NWA kingpin and taking me to New York to become his champion. Since Eddie Graham had recommended me to Vince Sr. originally, getting this "Superbowl" match in his territory was also a little bit of a "thank-you" from Vince Sr. to Eddie—as it would virtually ensure a huge gate.

The Ultimate Babyface

Everyone in the NWA watched what happened up in New York because the New York area got ten times more nationwide press coverage than anywhere that we wrestled. So everybody knew that Backlund had gone over Graham at the Garden to become Vince's new babyface WWWF Champion. I obviously can't speak for everyone, but from what I heard, saw, and observed, everyone in the NWA locker rooms that I was in was happy for Bobby.

I wrestled Bobby down in Florida right after he won the belt from Graham. That match was initially booked as me against Graham, but when Bobby beat Graham for the belt in New York, they switched it so that we could keep it title versus title. And that worked out fine because Bobby had just recently worked down in Florida, was very over with the fans there and was well known, so it was kind of like a homecoming of sorts for him. Meanwhile, Bobby's in-ring persona was food for a guy like me. I mean, who the hell wouldn't want to see a guy that looks and acts like Bobby kick the shit out of a cocky asshole that looks and acts like me? So it was a perfect setup for us. I've known Bobby a long, long time now, and I've shared the card with him in an awful lot of places and let me tell you, Bobby Backlund was over with the people. He was a great athlete, a great wrestler, and a person that the people just loved to love. He was the ultimate fucking babyface.

—Harley Race

The match with Harley in Florida went beautifully and drew another very nice house for Eddie, and, of course, a nice payday for us. It was great to see Harley again, and to be in the dressing room with a bunch of the guys from Florida who I hadn't seen in a while. Eddie Graham gave me a huge hug, wished me well in my new role, and assured me that I had the chops to be Vince Sr.'s champion for a long time. The boys on the card were also very nice and congratulated me heartily on becoming the WWWF champion. I felt more welcomed and comfortable in the dressing room in Jacksonville that night than had I had felt anywhere in the WWWF.

After returning from Florida, I settled into the routine of the WWWF house show schedule. Basically, everything was keyed off of the Garden show. With few exceptions, we were in New York at the Garden every fourth Monday night. Television in Allentown and Hamburg was every third Tuesday and Wednesday—with the days consumed with taping the promo interviews, and the nights filled with taping the three hours of squash matches that would comprise the episodes of Championship Wrestling and All-Star Wrestling that people would watch on the weekends. Allentown and Hamburg also each got one competitive "dark" match, not broadcast on television, which was used to draw the crowds.

Every third Tuesday and Wednesday, we would head up to Maine for shows in Portland and Bangor, with an occasional spot show in Waterville or Augusta. Every third Thursday was Poughkeepsie, New York, at the Mid-Hudson Civic Center, or in Worcester, Massachusetts, at the Memorial Auditorium, while Fridays were at the Civic Arena in Pittsburgh (monthly), Jack Witschis (weekly), Harrisburg at the Jaffa Mosque, or in Albany, New York, at the Washington Avenue Armory. Saturdays were at the Baltimore Civic Center, the Boston Garden, the Capitol Centre in Landover, Maryland, the Spectrum in Philadelphia, the Civic Center in Providence, Rhode Island, or the Civic Center in Springfield, Massachusetts. Sundays were at the Veterans Memorial Coliseum in New Haven, Connecticut, the Hartford Civic Center, the Nassau County Coliseum in Uniondale, New York, the JFK Coliseum in Manchester, New Hampshire, a spot show elsewhere, or an off day. There were other buildings we frequented also, and this schedule varied somewhat over the years depending on building availability and the schedules of the professional sports teams that were their primary tenants, but this was generally the way things went.

After I won the title, the first order of business was to have rematches with Billy in just about every building in the territory. In all those many rematches (and there were *many* of them), I never once got the sense that Billy was just going through the motions. Although I know that he was suffering inside from the loss of the limelight, Billy was always professional and gave his all to every match we had.

I now more fully understand, from watching his YouTube videos and seeing some of the interviews that he has given over the years, that Billy took the title change hard. I understand that completely, because I went through the very same range of emotions and the same enduring sadness after I was asked to drop the title. I actually enjoy watching Billy's interviews and hearing him, more than thirty-five years later, still expressing outrage about me and how I handled myself with the championship. He's gotten a lot of extra mileage for himself from that. I don't know if that is Billy still working or if that is how he truly feels. I'm not even sure that Billy knows the answer to that given how many different ways he has expressed himself on that issue. Whatever the truth, I prefer to just thank and respect Billy for the professional work he did in the ring with me the night the title changed, and in the many times we wrestled after that.

In the first couple of weeks out on the road after I won the title — it was announced at the various venues where I would appear that I had won the championship from Graham at Madison Square Garden, and that my match on the card that night against whomever I was wresting would now be a world title match. People were initially very surprised to discover that I had won the title from Graham. Once they learned the news, though, fans were very supportive and enthusiastic when I would meet them and sign autographs outside the arenas after my matches. Doing that was always an honor for me — because I knew it was the people who had put me there. If the people weren't buying tickets to come see me wrestle, I wouldn't have been the champion for very long.

While we are on the subject of the "business end" of the business — payoffs worked differently in the WWWF than they did in the other territories. In the WWWF, in the smaller towns, you could either "bank" the payout and get a draw or get paid in cash that night just by signing for it. You'd get your payoff from the bigger arenas by check every three weeks at the TV tapings. At the Garden and in some of the other larger arenas, for example, we would be paid on a percentage of the gate, which had to be figured out after the fact. A certain percentage of the gate went to overhead like the arena rental fee, police and security, and the like, a certain percentage went to the talent, and the rest went to the owners. Where you wrestled on the card determined your percentage. The main event always made the biggest percentage, and as the world champion, I was always in the main event, and my challengers in the main events would share in that benefit.

Given this setup, as champ, I was primarily relied on, along with my challenger, to "draw the house," which made sense since we got the biggest percentage among the wrestlers. As the main eventers, we had the biggest incentive to do the promotional work necessary to put butts in the seats, and then to put on a great show so we could draw an even better crowd for the second or third match of our series (if we were going more than one month). Beyond that basic understanding of how things worked, though, I didn't really get involved in the office part of the business. In all the years I was champ, I never checked the gate numbers, didn't keep track of monthly attendance figures to see how we were doing, or how certain challengers were doing with me, or anything like that. Those were business concerns for the office to worry about, and I trusted that if there were issues or concerns to be addressed, someone would come to me to discuss them.

No one ever did.

The truth is, Vince Sr. and I didn't have a lot of substantive conversations about the business, and I think he liked it that way. Whenever I saw him, he always asked after my family, and he often checked on my health or any injury I might have incurred in the ring, but other than that, our conversations were always light and brief. We had complete trust in one another. I trusted him with the bookings and the payoffs and everything on the business end, and he trusted me with the wrestling side. It sounds naïve, but it worked, because Vince Sr.'s word was his bond, and in all the years we worked together, he never gave me any reason to doubt him.

For his part, Vince Sr. could rely on the fact that, as his champion and the person being most heavily relied on in the main events every night, I would always be at the appointed building an hour before the card began—so he never needed to worry about having to reshuffle a card, or refund money in a big building because his main event failed to go off. Vince Sr. also knew that I would always worked my hardest to stay in top shape, gave the fans my all every night, and represented his company with dignity and honor behind the scenes. In return, his consistent promise to me was that he would supply me with the very best workers in the business, and that it would be up to him to worry about the angles, the promotion, and the crowds. Generally, I would check in with him once every three weeks at the TV tapings to make sure he was pleased with the way things were going. Without exception, he would tell me that "things were going well," and that he was very happy with my work as his champion.

Vince Sr. never expressed any dissatisfaction to me about the gates we were drawing in any city. To the contrary, he paid me religiously, without fail, and with a smile at every TV taping. In fact, Vince Sr. never told me to do anything differently in the five years and ten months I carried the championship for him.

It was a much different feel coming into the Garden with the belt in March 1978. Just walking down 7th Avenue in New York on my way to the Garden with my gym bag slung over my shoulder, I suddenly had a throng of happy and supportive people walking with me, asking questions, and wondering how it felt for me to be coming into the Garden with the title. New Yorkers, at the time, took their wrestling very seriously and completely bought in to the business as authentic.

For me, it was just like being on top of the world.

In the promos for Billy's rematch with me at the Garden in March 1978, Billy continued to argue that his foot had been on the bottom rope at the time of the pin, that he had been robbed, and that my title victory over him had been a fluke. On the strength of that storyline, we filled up both the Garden and the Felt Forum for the first rematch.

When Billy and I met in the bathroom at the Garden that night to get our instructions, Vince Sr. called for an enraged Billy to beat me within an inch of my life, for me to "get color" (gig myself with the tip of a razorblade to start the flow of blood from my forehead), but to stand there toe-to-toe and take all the punishment Billy could dish out until I was beat up so badly and bleeding so profusely that the doctor at ringside intervened to stop the match due to my blood loss. Although Billy would win the rematch, I would keep the title (because the title did not change on a blood stoppage), and the fans would get to see a new side of me—not the pure technical wrestling side—but the side of me that could survive and thrive in a straight-out, pier-six brawl.

It was a way to draw out the feud for another month.

The fans ate it up.

I appeared, for the first time ever, at the Spectrum in Philadelphia on March 25, 1978, and went to a double disqualification with the latest addition to Blassie's Army, The Iron Greek, Spiros Arion. It was interesting that I had never been booked in Philly during my run-up to winning the title, so the fans there hadn't really warmed up to me at all other than what they saw of me on television. Philadelphia, with its large ethnic Italian population, was very much a Bruno town, and was definitely one of the places, along with Pittsburgh and Boston, where I had a harder time getting over. When I was champion, those places weren't really mom and dad and apple pie towns. They were the home of the hard-knocks, blue-collar fans that were very skeptical of the pure, clean-cut babyface. They would cheer their own ethnic babyfaces, but they also loved the more edgy American heels.

I found it ironic that I had the hardest time winning over those fans, because, in real life, I was one of them. I shared their hard-knocks, blue-collar upbringing, but the image that Vince was building for me was that of the do-right, amateur-trained, collegiate apple pie and Chevrolet All-American Boy babyface. That didn't play as well in Philly and Boston as it did in some of the other cities and in the suburbs. It was harder for me to win over the Philly fans than it was in almost any other place—so when we had the Spectrum banged out and roaring, as we often did in my later years as champion, it made me feel especially good.

Graham and I came back to the Garden in April for the blowoff to our feud in what would be my first-ever steel cage match. Once again, Billy had played the promo interview game perfectly, reminding the fans that he had beaten me to a bloody pulp last time, and that this time, with a steel cage around us and no referee or doctor to save me, he'd be getting his title back. This time, though, I had some fire in my interviews also, and we set up the match as the culmination of a great feud that, by that point, had been roiling in the federation for four months.

Because we went from town to town and wrestled all sorts of different people in different kinds of matches on different nights, it was always important to check yourself and understand where you were in a given feud in a given town on a given night. The specialty blowoff matches, like the steel cage match, the Texas Death Match, or the lumberjack match, were a big part of the WWWF's booking strategy, and I couldn't just go into one of those matches and have my "usual" style of match inside the cage, because that's not what the people were paying to see.

If I found myself in the cage with a heel—it meant we had already wrestled once or twice in that building, or at least in the region, and that we had already done a scientific-style match, and likely a second match that had also ended indecisively. So if the people were buying a ticket to see you wrestle the same opponent for a third time, it was time for one or the other of us to finish the job. You needed to be meaner, use different tactics, and settle the feud in the minds of the people. It nearly always meant that one or the other (or both) of us would get color. And because, as I have mentioned before, Vince Sr. was very big on marketing hope, the man with the white hat almost always came out on top in the end.

Neither Billy and I nor Vince Sr. and I had much of a pre-match conversation that night. We just went into the heel locker room, into the bathroom, as was Vince's custom, and listened as Vince Sr. explained the finish. The plan was that, at the appointed time, when the fans were at their peak, Billy would fall off the inside wall of the cage and get his leg caught between the cage and the ring, allowing me to escape the cage and retain the title, but, again, allowing Billy to lose with some dignity.

Billy nodded, and we dispersed. That was the extent of the conversation.

The match went off as planned, and Billy hit his spot perfectly. When I walked out of the cage, the Garden crowd erupted in cheers, and it felt like I had secured them in my corner. After the match, I went over to Billy's dressing room, shook his hand, and thanked him for a great series. He clapped an arm around me, playfully slapped me with his towel, and wished me the best. It was an emotional moment between us—a changing of the guard.

⬥

After my thee-month feud with Graham at the Garden, Vince wanted me to get some decisive wins in quick succession in defense of the championship. This, he explained to me at the next television taping, would allow me to establish myself with the fans and prove to them that my pinfall victory over Graham had, in fact, not been a fluke. Once again, Vince Sr. first turned to Ken Patera.

Vince Sr. thought very highly of Patera both as a wrestler and as a person, and because we had wrestled so many good matches before I won the title, Vince Sr. knew that Kenny could be counted on to provide a credible box-office threat to the title, solid pre-match hype on the microphone, and a great match in the ring. Patera was an American Olympic weightlifter and the first man on Earth to press 500 pounds over his head. You would think that someone like that would be clumsy and heavy-handed, but when you were in the ring with Patera, although you could tell that you were in the hands of a very strong guy, he was actually very gentle. He looked like a bodybuilder, though, and he was a fearsome heel and very over with the people.

Most of our matches were structured similarly to the Graham matches—with me using speed and technical wrestling moves, Kenny fighting his way out of those, and then using a lot of strength moves and me selling those. We'd go back and forth like that, with the threat of his swinging full nelson submission hold that had "crippled" so many wrestlers up to that point always looming in the minds of the fans. The difference between my matches with Graham and Patera was that Patera was very skilled in the ring, and had a wide repertoire of moves. You could do just about anything you wanted to do in the ring with Ken.

Patera was agile, and arrogant, and the people just loved to hate him. One night when we were battling outside the ring in a match at the Civic Center in Springfield, Massachusetts, an elderly lady rose from her seat at ringside, took a full backswing, and smashed Kenny over the head with her cane. He just seemed to inspire that kind of emotion in people.

In May 1978, I faced Patera at the Garden. We teased his swinging full-nelson throughout the match until in the end, he got it on me, but before he could lock it in and swing me around into unconsciousness, I slipped out of it, got behind him, hoisted him up, and hit the atomic kneedrop for the finish. That move continued to have a lot of drama because it allowed me to lift my opponent up in the air, parade around the ring with him, and make sure that the fans all knew what was about to happen and were paying attention before I dropped him down over my knee in the middle of the ring and covered him for the pin.

Getting a clean win over Patera in the middle of the ring at the Garden definitely helped to get me over the "fluke" problem, since Kenny was the premiere heel in the federation at the time, and someone who had given Bruno Sammartino a lot of trouble in their previous feuds over the WWWF title. I was certainly grateful to Kenny for being so willing to put me over so strongly. Fortunately, I got a chance to repay that favor by having a longer series with him when he came back to the federation in 1980.

After Patera, the next challenger at the Garden was Spiros Arion—a big, legitimately Greek heel who was not particularly wild or colorful, but was a very solid-looking guy and a very good performer in the ring. Arion, who was managed by Freddie Blassie, was hilarious on the microphone in the promos, speaking in his ominous, heavy Greek accent and trying to convince the fans that I was a flash in the pan, and that he, Arion would, in fact, break me in half.

A couple of years earlier, on his last tour of the territory, Arion had incurred the wrath of the fans by turning from a babyface to a heel when he attacked his partner, Chief Jay Strongbow in a tag-team match. During that attack, Arion destroyed the Chief's ceremonial headdress (which, of course, was really just a set of feathers acquired from a costume shop), and got the better of the feud that followed, so Arion had credibility and legitimacy as a challenger to the world title.

I'd never met Arion in any of the other territories where I had wrestled because he spent most of his time wrestling in Australia and New Zealand. Because Arion had also worked with Bruno in a previous run in the WWWF a couple of years earlier, he knew the drill about how to work a main event at the Garden. Arion was actually a very nice guy, and I got along well with him because he was all about the match rather than his own ego. Arion worked hard, knew what he was doing in the ring, and was not at all limited in what he could do in the ring like Billy had been, so there was a lot we could do to entertain the fans.

Around this time, I also made my second trip to Florida as the WWWF champion—again at the request of Eddie Graham. This time, I flew down to Tampa and wrestled former WWWF champion Ivan Koloff at the Bayfront Center in St. Petersburg on April 29, 1978. Over the years I was champion, I worked with Ivan twice—for a run in 1978, and then for another run when he came back as a smaller and more agile heel in 1983. I always liked working with Koloff. His character ("The Russian Bear") was very strong, and was easy for me, as the "All-American Boy," to play off of. These matches were always about Ivan, as the Russian strongman, trying to prove that Russians were superior athletes, and me trying to defend American honor. It was a ready-made feud right out of the box, and a box office success anywhere you booked it. Ivan always worked very hard, and he too could do basically anything in the ring, so our matches were always interesting.

There was a much stronger sense emphasis on kayfabe down in Florida, so unlike in New York, where Vince would bring us both together in the bathroom to discuss the match, down there, Eddie just came in, shook hands and said hello, and gave each of us the finish, independently, and that was that. The heels and faces were not allowed to be seen together, or to be mixing with each other before a match, so it was up to us to figure it out in the ring.

Because Vince Sr. and Eddie Graham had such a strong personal relationship, they traded talent a lot. Eddie sent Dusty up to New York regularly to have matches at the Garden and once in a while, he'd even spend a week in the territory and wrestle in some of the other major arenas. Likewise, I made a number of trips down to Florida to defend the WWWF title around the Florida territory.

During those first couple of months elsewhere in the territory, I faced several different heels that were fed to me in one-and-done matches to establish my credibility as the champion. "Crazy Luke" Graham was one of those guys—although I only faced him in a few of the smaller buildings in the secondary towns. Graham was a brawler, and he was getting up there in years, so we were somewhat limited in what we could do. He acted like he was insane, and that was the pitch of those matches—finding a way to beat the unpredictable "crazy guy." Crazy Luke was a good guy to help me introduce myself as champion to the crowds in some of the secondary towns, though, because we could have a quick, fast-paced, high-intensity match that impressed the people and left them happy.

George "The Animal" Steele was another one of those guys, and I also faced him quite early in my reign as champion in 1978. Steele had an entertaining gimmick back then—which had evolved quite a bit over the years that Bruno was champion. A lot of people don't know this, but initially, Steele played a hipster character that spoke on the microphone, called people "daddy-o," and knew how to wrestle. By the time I got to the WWWF, though, the character had evolved into "The Animal"—a hairy guy with a green tongue who ate the turnbuckles, rubbed the stuffing in people's faces, used a foreign object, and just stomped and punched and kicked people—then put them into the flying hammerlock to try and "break" their arms.

In real life, Steele was a high school teacher and very successful football and wrestling coach from suburban Detroit, and a heck of a nice guy. Because WWWF television did not reach Detroit, nobody out there really knew what he was up to on the weekends and in the summer months when he would come in to the WWWF to do television and a quick ten-week tour of the territory. George was actually a very smart man with a great mind for the business, but he absolutely loved playing the role of this "missing link" type creature.

Steele and I had a few matches in the summer of 1978, but we had our biggest series in 1981—when I actually wrestled him for a couple of months in a row in a lot of the bigger towns. The foreign object that he was always hiding in his wrestling pants was a bottle opener wrapped in medical tape. Before the match, he'd use green food coloring or a lozenge that would turn his tongue green and then he'd come out and wave his arms around and make these guttural noises and throw his jacket and chase the referee out of the ring, and eat the turnbuckle, and the fans were really and truly afraid of him. Heck, if I let myself believe that his gimmick was real, I would have been scared of him too.

Steele was also very big in Japan, and he loved to scare the heck out of the Japanese fans, who took their wrestling very seriously. One time when we were in Japan together, Steele went in to get his hair cut at a salon. The Japanese women, who didn't like to show a lot of emotion, were giggling and wondering how they were supposed to give him a haircut when he had no hair on his head. Then, all of a sudden,

Steele took off his shirt, pointed at his back, and said "no ladies, back here!"

Slowing the Pace Down

The first time I met Bobby we were over in Japan. This was well before he became the champion, and he gave me a picture of himself, which was one of his early, early pictures that he wanted me to give to Mr. McMahon because he wanted to come to the WWWF. The picture really did not look like he was physical enough to do the kind of things that we were doing at the time, so I never showed the picture to Mr. McMahon because I just didn't think it would work.

I taught school and coached, so I only wrestled in the summertime. The rest of the year I was back in Michigan. Well wouldn't you know, the following summer when I got to the TVs for the first time, Bobby comes in, and Mr. McMahon introduces me to him and tells me that this guy is going to be the next champion! Well Mr. McMahon wanted to get some heat on Bobby and make him look good. Bobby was wearing a denim suit that his wife had made by hand that they both loved, and Mr. McMahon said, "Jim, Bobby is going to be out there in the ring wearing that suit doing an interview and I want you to tear it off of him!" Well I ran out there and ripped that suit off of him, and it gave him a good start. They didn't show that tape right away, they saved it and aired it later while I was still away teaching, but when I came back that summer, our first run in 1978 was over that incident.

In his first year as the champion, Bobby was a very excitable guy in the ring; maybe even a bit overexcited, but he was very good. He was hard to hold down because he was a very good amateur and he was trained to get right up, but in the pros early on, his timing was almost too quick. Sometimes you need to slow down and let the people digest what you just did—and Bobby had to learn to slow the pace down from what he was accustomed to doing in the amateurs.

—George "The Animal" Steele

On May 15, 1978, I made my first trip north of the border to Toronto and faced "Superstar" Billy Graham at the Maple Leaf Gardens. Frank Tunney, the promoter up there, was also very close to Vince Sr., so there were never any worries about issues with finishes or payoffs. I wrestled in Toronto a fair number of times as the WWWF champion. When we wrestled in Toronto, we used to stay at a hotel right across the street from the arena, so it was a pretty easy travel day—fly in, clear customs, workout in the city, and then go over to the arena. Frank Tunney was another one of the highly respected and trusted promoters in the NWA, like Sam Muchnick, who had the standing to put together "dream cards." If you look over some of the results from cards in Toronto over the years, you will see appearances by all three federations' (NWA, AWA, WWWF) world champions, and a number of unification matches. Only the most respected and trusted promoters had the kind of influence to arrange those inter-promotional matches. I always loved wrestling in Toronto because Frank Tunney was one of those guys, and you knew when you wrestled on a card for him, that you'd be surrounded by some of the best talent in the business.

I took my first tour of Japan as the WWWF champion at the very end of May and beginning of June 1978. By this point, I had been over there a couple of times and knew the routine and the odd bookings, which were a nice break from the norm. In Japan, because WWWF television programming was not generally shown on television, Japanese promoters were not concerned with who was a heel and who was a babyface back in America, or what angles might be going on between guys in a territory. Because of that, Japanese results often didn't make sense when viewed against what was going on in the United States.

If a wrestler hadn't spent a lot of time over in Japan, he wasn't "established," so a heel could play face, and a face could play heel, and American heels and faces could end up as tag-team partners over there against a couple of Japanese guys. The second-to-last night of that tour was the first time I recall teaming with Andre in the little town of Gifu. I remember feeling like a little baby standing next to him in the ring, and as Andre's tag-team partner, I didn't have to think too much about what I would do. The formula when you were Andre's tag-team partner was always the same—get in a few moves at the beginning, take the heat from your opponents for a while, tease an inability to tag Andre in for a while longer until you had the crowd at its peak, then tag Andre in, and let him clean house and take it home.

Everything about Andre was larger than life. To give you a sense of his size, you could pass a silver dollar through the inside of his ring. In his prime, there was nobody in the world that was going to stop Andre from doing something in the ring if he didn't want to be stopped, and when you're that big, it didn't make a whole lot of booking sense to have him doing crazy moves in the ring. If you think about it, there is no need for you to throw a dropkick or use aerial moves if you can just use your immense strength and size to bully and overpower your opponents. That said, when Andre was lighter and still relatively pain free as he was back then, he could throw suplexes and get up and down quite a bit.

You knew that Andre liked you and trusted you if he let you bodyslam him. Although a bodyslam was a pretty generic move for most of us, for Andre, who legitimately weighed well over 400 pounds, taking a bodyslam was a significant and legitimately painful bump. Dropping him anything other than perfectly could have seriously injured him and ended his very lucrative career. As such, over the years, there weren't too many guys let into that club. Hogan did it to him on television in 1980 at the start of their feud, which had pretty good shock factor, since most people had not seen Andre slammed before. Andre graciously allowed that to happen to help get Hogan over with the people as a credible threat to Andre's undefeated streak, and to help sell their feud that summer. He did it again at Shea Stadium and a few other times around the circuit—but if Andre didn't want you to slam him, you weren't going to get him up there without his cooperation. Harley and Ken Patera and Don Leo Jonathan, El Canek down in Mexico, and Otto Wanz over in Germany were among the handful of guys who had been allowed the privilege of bodyslamming Andre.

I liked Andre very much—and he was always very good to me. I liked to drink beer with him, and after the matches, on nights when I was too far away to drive home, there were many times that he and I would end up in a bar drinking together. He'd want to keep me up all night—and I always joked with Andre that I would stay up all night drinking with him if he would come out and train with me in the morning. Somehow, that conversation always ended with him clapping one of his huge hands across my shoulders, laughing his deep laugh, and then saying, "Okay, Bobby," and letting me go to bed! I was in a bar with Andre one night where he drank 112 bottles of beer and remained coherent enough to line all of the empties up on the windowsills of the bar.

That was a truly amazing sight to behold.

Sometimes I would team with Andre in a tag-team match because a particular promoter decided it would be interesting to try. At other times, they would put us together to set up something for the next town on the tour, or for the next time over there. My match with Andre against Inoki and Sakaguchi on that tour was a perfect example of that. That tag-team match was used as a platform to build some intensity between Inoki and me for my title match the next night, on the last night of the tour, when Antonio beat me by countout at the Budokan Hall in Tokyo, the largest sumo wrestling arena in Tokyo, which held about 22,000 people for wrestling.

Wrestling Inoki was always easy—it was almost like working with someone in America. He didn't speak much English back then, but he was so fluid and smooth in the ring that we didn't really need to talk. We could anticipate each other's moves, and just flow off of each other. Antonio was New Japan's featured performer, and we knew that we'd be working together pretty much every time I was over there, so we needed to leave the fans with something that would bring them back next time. Having me get counted out of the ring was the choice for this first tour, which would allow him to win, but me to keep the title, and leave the resolution for next time.

Back stateside, I rode the circuit for the next couple of months finishing the feud with Billy in the secondary and tertiary towns in the territory. Vince Sr.'s booking in 1978 ensured that everybody in the territory had a chance to see me with the championship, and allowed me to start building face-to-face relationships with the fans in all the regular tour towns. Billy continued to be a true gentleman in all of these matches. Even though he knew that his time in the territory was growing short, and even though he was *still* getting great crowd reaction everywhere he went—he never let that disappointment detract from his performance in the ring.

At the end of July, I went back over to Japan to Budokan Hall for the rematch with Inoki. That was an unusual trip in that I went over just for this one match with Inoki, and the trip was memorable as one of the biggest travel nightmares of my reign as champion. I arrived at the international airport in Tokyo and had to clear customs, and then, even though Inoki had sent a driver for me, it took two and a half hours to fight through the incredible traffic in downtown Tokyo to get to the venue.

The match was scheduled for the best two out of three falls, and the plan this time was for us to go Broadway, with each of us taking a fall on the other during the sixty minutes, to show the fans that either of us could beat the other. The Japanese fans were not used to seeing either one of us lose cleanly—so the thought was that seeing that would be a big deal and raise interest for future bouts.

We decided to give Antonio the first fall, to perpetuate the illusion for as long as possible during the match that he might actually win the WWWF championship. As I recall, Inoki used something he called the "octopus hold," which was one of the new finishers he was trying out, to win the first fall. It was basically a version of a standing crucifix where he was up on my back twisting my head one way and my arm another using both his arms and his legs. It was a visually dramatic move, and the fans were stunned when I sold it for him and submitted to give him the first fall. It was one of the very few times in my career that I lost a fall by submission.

We battled hard in the second fall, until eventually, I was able to foil a suplex attempt and get behind Antonio, hoist him up, and apply the atomic kneedrop, which allowed me to pin him cleanly in the middle of the ring to win the second fall and tie up the match. The fans were equally stunned to see Inoki pinned cleanly in the middle of the Budokan Hall ring—something that almost never happened. The time limit then expired before either of us could win the third and deciding fall, so the match was declared a draw. At the end of the bout, the fans were already calling for another rematch. We had done our jobs well.

At the time, the NWA was doing a lot of things with Baba and All-Japan, including scheduling the NWA World Champion for full tours of Japan. As a result, Inoki—as the head of the New Japan promotion was trying to compete with Baba—wanted to do more with me.

I showered in the locker room at Budokan Hall, and then it took us another two hours fighting traffic to get back to the Tokyo airport, where I then flew straight to Los Angeles to wrestle Roddy Piper in the Olympic Theater. That was the match that Roddy describes in the Foreword to this book.

Mike LeBelle was the promoter in Los Angeles at the time, and he thought the world of Roddy and wanted to showcase him in a long match with a world champion. Mike, however, knew that I had just flown in from Japan after doing a Broadway with Inoki, so he was very reluctant to ask me for that kind of a favor. I hadn't wrestled Roddy before that day, but I had heard a lot of good things about him, and remembering the lessons from those who had taught me—I knew that, as the champion, I had a responsibility to come into the territory and give Roddy as much as I could. We decided that I would go over with a quick pin late—but that in the meantime, we would showcase Roddy.

Roddy was a young but brash tweener at the time. He had torn up a picture of me on television and talked some trash to get people interested in the match, but we were still able to have a pretty nice babyface match. We did the double bridge, we did the short-arm scissor, and we did a lot of amateur stuff and fast-paced mat wrestling and switching, and Roddy, who was still very young back then, stayed right with me for the whole match.

I liked wrestling in the Olympic Theater, because the ring was in the middle and the building was round, so the people were in close and you could feel the intensity of their emotion and enthusiasm. The crowd that night loved what we were doing, so we went virtually to a Broadway— 59 minutes—and had the people on the edges of their seats in a pretty good frenzy before I finally caught Roddy in an inside cradle and got the pin just before the time limit was set to expire.

It was a great match—and I knew right then that if Roddy could put on a little more size, he would go places in this business because the man could flat out work. His mic skills, of course, for which he is perhaps best known, were already among the very best in the business.

Back in the dressing room after the match, both Roddy and Mike LeBelle thanked me profusely for the near-Broadway. The honor, though, was mine. I then hopped on a plane and crossed the country to Pittsburgh where I would finally catch some sleep before facing "Superstar" Billy Graham at the Civic Arena in the main event the next night.

No rest for the weary—but to be honest, I would have given anything for that life to go on forever. I was loving life as the champion, traveling around the world, and wrestling the very best and most talented guys that each territory had to offer. It was a totally exhilarating experience.

In the wrestling business, wintertime was the boom time, and although it may seem counterintuitive, summer tended to be our slower time. In the northeast, particularly in the big cities where we drew some of our biggest houses, people took their vacations in July and August—to the shore, to the lakes or the mountains or the state parks—to escape the heat of the large urban centers. As they did, they fell out of touch with the wrestling storylines, and also missed the house shows. Overall, the WWWF houses were typically down in the summertime, and so we tended to run smaller and cheaper shows to compensate for that. Vince would also slow down the storylines, playing off the feuds that were already established and taking those feuds to the secondary and tertiary towns, while the Garden frequently got a couple of one-off challengers who weren't part of a big program. He would then ramp up the new angles in the fall, when people were reliably back in front of their television sets on the weekends.

If you look at my schedule in the high summer of 1978, you will see examples of this booking strategy. I faced Graham in cage-match blowoffs in the bigger cities, concluding an angle that had started in December 1977, and otherwise found myself facing Arion, or in one-offs with guys like Steele or Luke Graham.

On August 28, 1978, though, we started ramping up for the fall season, and I ended up in the ring at the Garden for the first time with the returning former WWWF champion Ivan Koloff. Koloff, of course, was the man who only a few years earlier had shocked the world by pinning the previously unbeatable Bruno Sammartino, putting an end to his seven-year title reign and stripping him of the world title in this very same ring. This was the quintessential Vince McMahon Sr. match—with the upstart young All-American Boy champion facing the challenge of the chain-swinging, Russian flag-bearing former WWWF champion. Koloff, who was nicknamed "The Russian Bear," had become white-hot with the fans for berating everything American, and "crippling" a number of young American wrestlers. He was, once again, a seemingly insurmountable monster heel. He also had Captain Lou Albano as his manager, which of course, only helped to increase the frenzied vitriol that the fans showered on them both.

Behind the scenes, Ivan was actually a terrific guy, and someone that I liked very much. I had wrestled him once earlier in the year down in Florida for Eddie Graham, and we had worked out a few nice high spots during that match that we repeated in New York. Ivan was a great worker and had an impeccable sense of timing. At that time, he was around 285 pounds, and we did the short-arm scissor that night at the Garden which saw me dead-lift him to my shoulder out of the short-arm scissor, walk him over to the corner, set him on the top rope, and slap him in the face.

The fans were immediately into the match, as you might imagine given the ready accessibility of the Cold War–inspired hatred between America and Russia at the time. Vince Sr. called for Ivan to ram me into the ring post and for me to draw color and then, despite me battling on valiantly, to have the doctor at ringside stop the match due to my cuts and award the decision to Koloff. That, of course, would set us up perfectly for the rematch in September just as the fall season was heating up.

Blood stoppages were another common booking tool in the WWWF, particularly in the major arenas where I was scheduled to have multi-month runs with a particular heel. Whenever the promoters wanted an inconclusive end to a match to draw the next house, and the heel was generating more heat than usual, they used the "blood stoppage" to amp up fan interest in the rematch. There was an old saying in the business that "red means green"—meaning that any match that had color at the end would draw an even better house the next time. The promoters didn't pay more for color—they just asked for it when discussing the finish with you in the dressing room before the match—and when they asked for blood, you obliged.

Getting color was just another part of protecting the business—people needed to see blood every once in a while to keep them believing that what they were watching was real. You couldn't bang someone's head against the iron ring post or smash someone over the head with a chair without it causing someone to bleed—or it would begin to seem suspicious. The people wanted to believe that what we were doing to each other was real—it was just like watching a movie or a television show—people wanted to suspend reality and be drawn into the story. We had to make it possible for them to believe—and "getting color" every so often as part of the storyline was part of that process.

I got bloody noses very easily, and used to get them all the time in amateur wrestling—so oftentimes I would just give myself a bloody nose and let that bleed all over everything and get the job done without actually having to gig myself with a blade. Other times, I would cut the very tip off a razorblade and bury the "gig" sharp side up in a piece of athletic tape on the inside of my wrist or finger. Some guys even kept the gig in their mouths, although I could never understand how anyone did that without swallowing it or gashing the inside of their mouths during a high spot.

Anyway—at the appointed time, you would take the bump (such as, for example, a shot into the iron ring post outside the ring) and crumple to the ground where you would then gig yourself with the hidden piece of blade by dragging it quickly across your forehead. That would open a cut, and the running sweat would take care of the rest, giving you the "crimson mask" effect of streams of blood pouring down your face that the promoters were looking for.

I didn't like blading, and I tried to avoid it as much as possible—but you knew that it would help you make money by drawing more fan interest in the return match, so you just did it when they asked you to. It did make you ask yourself, though, if you were willing to slice open your own face for the business, just how far were you were willing to go to draw money?

Once I drew color, the doctor in attendance at ringside, who *was* a real doctor, but who was also typically in on the booked finish, would jump up, examine my cuts, and determine that I was losing too much blood to safely continue the match. He would then call for the bell and waive off the match, and award the decision, but not the championship, to my opponent.

Over the years I worked for Vince Sr., I was grateful that he didn't ask me to gig myself too many times.

A "full" Garden title series with an able challenger was a three-match program that would begin in New York at the very beginning of the challenger's stay in the territory—often after the new heel had only one or two television appearances. That was why pairing the heels with Blassie, The Grand Wizard, or Albano was so important—it was a placeholder to alert the fans that this "new guy" was a heel and was someone they were supposed to hate, even if the new heel's character hadn't yet been fully developed on television. The challenger would get a convincing victory over me in the first encounter, either by blood stoppage or countout to show the fans that he had a legitimate chance to win the belt.

We would then come back in the second match and increase the intensity of the action, often resulting in a disqualification, a double disqualification, or some kind of double-countout or pull-apart finish. That would set up the third and final encounter, which was usually a gimmick match like a steel cage match, a Texas Death Match, or a lumberjack match, where I would go over.

Arnold Skaaland always encouraged me to take more of offense and sell less in the blowoff matches in order to appear more powerful, but I always wanted my heels to leave our blowoff match at the Garden or anywhere else with as much heat as they could keep—because that's what was good for business. For part of the time that I was champion, Pedro Morales was the Intercontinental Heavyweight champion, and he would often be booked to face the heel that I just beat on the next Garden card. Given that, I wanted to make sure that I left those heels with enough credibility in the minds of the fans to still pose a legitimate threat to Pedro, or to whomever else they might find themselves in the ring with.

While doing that might have not made me look like an unbeatable champion, I had been taught that it was always good to have a strong heel or two that I hadn't totally chewed up on the undercard. If it looked like any one of those heels could beat me on any given night, it was good for them and would continue to be good for the business as a whole. That became my way of doing business, and, I think, why a lot of people in the business ultimately came to respect me.

On September 25, 1978, Koloff and I came back to the Garden for our second match. The booked finish that time was a swerve by Vince Sr. intended to continue to build my credibility with the fans. Remember that Koloff had shocked the world by pinning the seemingly unbeatable Bruno Sammartino at the Garden to win the WWWF title, and he hadn't been pinned much at the Garden since then, so when I hit him with the atomic kneedrop and pinned him cleanly in the middle of the ring in the *second* match of our series, the fans were amazed. It was a really big deal to pin Ivan Koloff at the Garden, and I think that finish really shocked the fans and earned me a lot of credibility in their minds.

After that match, I showered and, as was my custom, headed out the side door of the Garden to walk to my car. That night, however, I was mobbed by a large group of fans and ended up standing there, outside the side door of the Garden, talking with fans and signing autographs until the sun came up the next morning! I think the second Koloff match at the Garden was the tipping point that put me over in the hearts and minds of the fans. I had now truly been accepted as their champion—and they now believed in me, and were firmly behind me.

In October 1978 up in Maine, we tested one of the angles that Vince Sr. was thinking about running the following year—namely pairing me with the Paramount Samoan High Chief Peter Maivia and making us tag-team partners. On October 18, 1978, on the proving grounds in Bangor, where many of the WWF's angles were tested, Peter and I took on (and lost to) the WWF tag-team champions the Yukon Lumberjacks. The fans, however, had reacted favorably to our team, and that gave Vince the information he needed to plan the federation's primary angle for the first half of 1979.

On October 23, 1978, though, I faced "The Big Cat" Ernie Ladd at the Garden. Ernie was managed by the Grand Wizard and had returned to the federation as a huge, "arrogant," and well-known football personality.

Standing six feet nine inches and weighing 350 pounds, Ernie had, at that point, been one of the biggest men to ever play in the NFL—where he was an All-Pro defensive tackle who played for the San Diego Chargers, the Houston Oilers, and the Kansas City Chiefs. This was another marquee matchup for the fans at the Garden, as it pitted me—their former NCAA collegiate wrestling champion All-American Boy—against a very legitimate NFL football star. This would ultimately take the form of another "big guy" match, although Ernie Ladd could move around as well as any big man I ever got into the ring with. Ernie was a great talent with a silver tongue and a fearsome appearance.

When Ernie and Vince and I met for the pre-match discussion in the bathroom in the heel locker room at the Garden, though, Vince was riffling his quarters as he always did, looked Ernie in the eye, and explained that I would be going over Ernie by pinfall with the atomic drop. I remember Ladd towering over both Vince and me looking disappointed, but he just smiled at both of us and said, "Okay, boss." I think Ernie was hoping for more than just one match with me—and frankly, I think we could have done more with me trying to figure out how to break down a man of Ernie's immense size and losing the first match by countout—but Vince Sr. wanted to keep me strong.

Unlike some other professional football players-turned professional wrestlers who I wrestled during my time as champion, Ladd was in total control of his body and a complete and total gentleman in the ring. Ernie used his huge size and tremendous athleticism to beat on me for the better part of fifteen minutes, with me trying to stay away from him and tire him out.

Eventually, at the end of my comeback, when the time came for the finish, I hoisted Ernie and his 350-pound frame high up in the air, walked him around the ring, backed into a corner, and then ran him out into the middle. Ernie was so big, he could have either made me work really hard to execute that move well, or could have shown bitterness about asking to do the honors in his first match at the Garden by making the move look pretty bad simply by letting his legs hang limp. But Ernie Ladd was a true professional, and was about making the match look good—so he held his legs up straight up in the air to make it look good, and sold the atomic drop like a million bucks.

When we got back to the dressing room, Ladd told me that he would never have believed I could carry him around for all that time unless he had seen it himself. Ernie was not a guy who had been picked up off his feet very much in his life, and he was legitimately impressed with my strength, conditioning, and physical appearance. Vince Sr. liked Ernie Ladd a lot, respected him for what he accomplished in his football career and for the legitimacy that he brought to the WWF by being part of the federation. I liked him too.

On October 29, I made another trip to Florida for Eddie Graham for the return NWA-WWWF title match with the still-reigning NWA World Champion Harley Race at the Orlando Sports Arena. We did *another* Broadway, continuing the mystique of the irresistible force meeting the immovable object theme that had characterized our matches. The allure of the double title showdown helped to bring in another good house for Eddie—and continued the back and forth talent exchange between Vince and Eddie that would persist for the next few years.

On November 4, 1978, the experiment that Vince had tested up in Bangor got off the drawing board and onto television as Peter Maivia and I were paired in a main-event tag-team match on television against Freddie Blassie's combination of Spiros Arion and Victor Rivera. Arnold Skaaland was, of course, in our corner.

Peter and I started teasing dissention in our ranks almost immediately by having a little disagreement about who would start the match—with Skaaland eventually settling the "dispute" by deciding that Peter should start first. Later in the match, as I was getting double-teamed in the heel corner, Peter did not come into the ring to help out. Arion then started getting the best of me and Maivia was wandering away from the corner not paying attention, or giving me the short-arm from the corner and refusing to tag into the match.

The fans started chirping, and Skaaland starting getting on Peter. Then suddenly, out of nowhere, Peter attacked Skaaland, ripped Skaaland's shirt off, and pounded away on him while Arion and Rivera double-teamed me.

The angle was on.

People were screaming at Maivia in disbelief as he left ringside with Freddie Blassie and Arion and Rivera, his shocking heel turn revealed. On cue, Skaaland was carried back to the dressing room by Tony Garea, Larry Zbyszko, Dino Bravo, and others, which left me to come out of the ring to cut my first truly "incensed" promo of my tenure as champion in the WWWF. These spots, which were not scripted ahead of time, were not easy for me.

"What happened?!" I screamed into the microphone, doing my best to seem truly shocked and enraged.

"Why did that happen?! Is the whole world against me?!"

Vince McMahon Jr. just stared at me blankly, feeding me nothing to work off of, but the fans were buying it, so I just looked around at them and then said the next thing that came to mind.

"I'm going to kill that son of a bitch!"

Oops.

Some of you probably know that Peter Maivia was movie star The Rock's (Rocky Maivia/Dwayne Johnson's) grandfather, and Rocky Johnson's father. He was also a good friend, and one of the truly toughest men in the wrestling business. He was legitimately a Samoan High Chief, and the ceremonial tattoos that he displayed around his waist and upper legs were a sign of his status. Apparently, they were painfully applied with bone and shell over a period of weeks. No one in the wrestling business ever had anything bad to say about Peter Maivia. He was a good man with a huge heart and was a truly nice person who I loved working with.

The heel turn we did on TV with him attacking Arnold, however, was an early indication of just how powerful television could be—and how critical television exposure was for territorial wrestling. Just that one short ten-minute segment was enough to get the people to hate Peter, and these were fans that had loved him and had cheered him when he tried to get the championship away from Billy Graham only a year earlier. Peter soaked up their hatred and played it up like the pro he was.

Peter and I drew some nice crowds together all around the territory after his turn. To give you some idea of how much heat Peter got from that angle, one night in Springfield right after the angle aired on television, I was scheduled to appear in the main-event title match at the Civic Center with "Superstar" Billy Graham. Billy didn't show up for the match, and the promoters were scrambling to figure out what to do. After talking with the office, they decided to sub Peter into the main event for Graham. Ordinarily, the crowd would have gone nuts to have lost a Backlund-Graham main event, and the office would have been flooded with demands for refunds. When the ring announcer told the crowd that Billy was unable to appear, as expected, they booed and started throwing things at him. But then he announced that a replacement challenger had been found, and that that person was "none other than the Samoan High Chief, Peter Maivia!" The thunderous boos turned on a dime.

The people hated Peter so much, they didn't even miss Billy. And that is really saying something.

———◆———

There were a couple of other interesting stops on my itinerary in November, 1978. First, Vince Sr. had gotten a call from old friend Ken Patera, who by this point, frustrated that he was not going to get a chance to carry the belt, had made good on his promise to leave the WWWF and return home to North Carolina. Patera was wrestling down in Charlotte for Jim

Crockett in the NWA, and had already won Crockett's big regional belt, the Mid-Atlantic Heavyweight Championship. Crockett was hoping we could do a champion versus champion match down in their signature building—the Greensboro Coliscum. Vince asked me if I'd be willing to do that, and of course, I was happy to help out Kenny, given how strongly he had put me over in our matches in the WWWF both before and after I won the belt.

So I drove back to my home from Boston on Saturday night after wrestling Koloff in the Boston Garden, and then hopped on a plane the next morning and headed down to Greensboro for what would be my one and only appearance with the belt in Jim Crockett's mid-Atlantic territory. Patera and I had worked so much by this point that wrestling him was like a night off—we could practically anticipate each other's moves before they happened. We had a good match down there, I went over by DQ, they drew a nice house, and everyone was happy.

The other interesting guy I wrestled a few times during that month was Crusher Blackwell. Jerry was a really thick, massive guy—he was legitimately well over 400 pounds—but he could move around better than just about any other man of that size in professional wrestling. He could get up and down, climb the ropes, and even throw a decent-looking dropkick, but he wore a pretty bad-looking full body suit in the ring, and had a lot more blubber on him than most of the men I would wrestle.

Jerry had made good money for Verne Gagne up in Minneapolis and was involved in a number of angles up there, so Vince Sr. brought him in for a short stint in the WWWF. He didn't hang around long, but I did work with him a few times. I wrestled him once at the Spectrum, and after wearing him out for ten or twelve minutes, got him up in the atomic kneedrop, and carried his 400-pound body around the ring before dropping him on my knee and covering him for the pin.

Even the tough Spectrum crowd popped for that one.

On November 20, 1978, I climbed into the ring at Madison Square Garden for my first head-to-head matchup with Peter Maivia after his televised heel turn. This was also the first time I had someone in the ring with me at the Garden who had done something to me on television—so there was an extra element of psychological drama associated with the match. Before the match, when we met with Vince in the dressing room, Vince told us that given how much heat our feud was drawing, we would definitely be coming back the next month—so Peter and I knew that Vince was looking for this match to just set that up.

I don't remember much about the actual match that night other than the fact that the crowd was so hot that it took us less than ten minutes to get the people to their emotional high point. Despite the brevity of that first match, the fans were so all over Peter that I was convinced that he couldn't get them any higher than the where we were at the nine-minute mark—where we spilled out of the ring and finished it with Peter jumping into the ring just before the ten count and going over by countout.

<hr/>

Maivia and I had our first rematch at the Garden on December 18, 1978. We had again drawn a strong house, and the heat between us was still so strong that when Vince brought us together, he informed us that we'd be going three matches, culminating in a steel cage blowoff the following month. Consequently, he wanted this one to end with me chasing Peter all over the building, and for the match to end with Peter getting counted out.

It is worthy of mention here that the December holiday cards at the Garden were always special, because Vince Sr. would always bring in extra talent to give the people who had supported his promotion throughout the year a little something extra. This time was no different, as Vince had Harley in to defend the NWA World Title against Tony Garea.

The NWA promoters always wanted Harley to look good at the Garden, and Vince put him in there with Garea because he knew that Tony was a good hand who would give Harley a solid match, but would ultimately make Harley look good and put Harley over well. Antonio Inoki was here for that card as well, and was being billed as the "Martial Arts Champion," as the front office was trying to figure out what to do with him to make him a draw in America, where he was still virtually unknown.

Antonio wanted to be more involved in the WWWF, but he never got over with the New York fans because he didn't really have an identity or a personality when he appeared in New York. Antonio couldn't speak much English, so he had no real opportunity to connect with the American fans as a babyface. Because he was the head of the New Japan promotion and wanted his matches in New York to be seen in Japan, he didn't want to adopt the usual formula and become a "foreign heel" managed by Blassie, the Wizard, or Albano.

This was a struggle that the WWWF and New Japan would continue to have as we turned the calendar to 1979.

17

Taking Flight (1979)

"A *positive mental attitude attracts success.*"

—Napoleon Hill, "Learn from Adversity and Defeat"

———————

1979 began with my second cage match ever at Madison Square Garden. This one, of course, was the culmination of my bitter "feud" with Peter Maivia, now the most hated man in the federation. Peter and I had drawn strong houses at the Garden and all over the territory in each of the first two months, so Vince Sr. saw reason to go with a cage match blowoff to this feud.

Booking wrestling is an interesting art—part storytelling, part psychology, and part business. The people are different in each city, and even sometimes from month to month in the same city. They want to be entertained, so you have to give them a steady diet of something different. Taking a look at my history as champion at the Garden up to this point will illustrate this point.

In New York, the people had seen me win the belt from Graham in February, lose to him on a blood stoppage in March, and win the cage match blowoff in April. They then watched me score three solid pinfall victories in a row, over Ken Patera in May, Spiros Arion in June, and George "The Animal" Steele in July. By August, it was time to give the fans something different, so we did a long match with former champion Ivan Koloff and gave him a blood stoppage victory. We then came back with the rematch in September, which I won with a surprise pinfall when everyone in the building was expecting something different. As the promoter, it is always critical to zig when the fans expect you to zag. In professional wrestling, predictability was a business-killer.

Next, I scored another surprise pinfall victory over Ernie Ladd in our first contest in October, and then battled Peter Maivia to a countout loss in November, and a countout victory in December—both of which ended in brawls that settled nothing between us. The Garden crowd hadn't seen a specialty match since my cage match with Graham in April—so after eight months, in Vince Sr.'s mind, enough time had passed to do that again.

Though I much preferred to work the psychology of a crowd using chain wrestling and a series of high spots and near falls, when I wrestled in a cage match, I knew that I had to work with the cage, bring it into the match, and give the people what they came for—vindication and catharsis. When you were in a cage match, the cage had to be the third man in the ring that you were telling the story with, and at the end of a cage match, there had to be a definite winner and a definite loser. Because we were selling hope, no matter how bleak things might have looked up to that point, the winner of the cage match had to be the man wearing the white hat.

Sometimes to mix things up the blowoff match was a Texas Death Match or a lumberjack match. Which match was chosen for the blowoff had a lot to do with who the people were in the match, what had been done recently, and what would sell the story best. But the steel cage match was definitely the biggest draw in the minds of the fans. Just seeing the cage getting erected around the ring in the middle of the Garden was enough to get the crowd buzzing with anticipation—so by the time you made your entrance from the dressing room and started "testing" the cage and looking it over, the people's energy was already high, and growing by the moment.

Peter got over incredibly well as a heel, which made wrestling him very easy. He was seasoned, set a very easy pace to work with, and had been in the business for a long time. We also had a story to tell that people had seen multiple times on television. The cage match with Peter was pretty long—going twenty minutes in the cage was pretty unusual—but we had some great heat going in this series, and we both enjoyed working together so much that we decided to get the crowd totally lathered up that night. We teased a few false finishes until the crowd was emotionally at their exhaustion point, and then finally gave the people their catharsis.

I remember the ending of that match well — Peter and I were fighting on the top turnbuckle at the corner of the cage, when I eventually got the upper hand and threw a haymaker that knocked Peter down and got his leg caught in the turnbuckle. The people were screaming and waving at me to climb out over the top. Their energy was sky high. So I gave them what they wanted and climbed out over the top and dropped down to the arena floor, rather than going out the door, with Peter still hanging there from the turnbuckle on the inside.

I don't think that had *ever* been done at the Garden before. The people went home happy that night.

That night was the second time, I signed autographs by the back door of the Garden until the sun came up.

In February, 1979, I had my first match at the Garden with Greg Valentine, managed by the Grand Wizard. Valentine was a new type of heel challenger for the WWF (The World Wide Wrestling Federation was renamed The World Wrestling Federation right around this time, so for purposes of the book, from here on, I refer to the federation as the "WWF" and the title as the WWF title), a slimmer, meaner, cocky heel, with long, golden hair, who wore beautiful floor-length sequined robes, and who could also chain wrestle. Greg came into the territory featuring a potentially crippling finisher known as the figure-four leglock, which he resulted in a number of his television opponents being stretchered out of the ring. Greg also had a perpetual scowl on his face that just made him look mean, and he played that up, frequently telling people in his interviews that he had sympathy for no one.

The fans legitimately feared him, and the son of the legendary Johnny Valentine became an instant and credible threat to my championship.

I knew Greg from my time down in the Florida and Georgia territories, and I had been in the ring with him enough to know that he was someone that I could really work with. Greg was highly skilled in the ring, and had good stamina. I was also pretty confident that, after I had done so many Broadways with Dory and Terry and Harley and Jack Brisco back in the NWA, that I could go an hour in the ring with Greg. Of all the guys I had wrestled in the WWF up to this point, Greg was the guy who could tell the story with me that I wanted to tell.

It would be the first time, to my knowledge, that a Garden crowd had ever seen a title match go Broadway—so it would be something new for them, and something I very much wanted to introduce to them. So in a rare moment where I actually got involved in the booking, I asked Vince Sr. to let me go Broadway with Greg in our first at the Garden. Seeing the same potential that I saw, Vince Sr. immediately agreed to the idea.

Greg and I did a lot of chain wrestling, mixed in some high spots, worked in and out of the ring, and took the crowd on exhausting emotional rollercoaster ride. We were both drenched and exhausted, but as the minutes ticked on, the crowd realized that they were seeing something epic that they had never seen before. The fans were on the edges of their seats, exhausted themselves, waiting and wondering what was going to happen.

It was good booking for me, because I was going toe-to-toe with this devastating new heel who had destroyed all his previous competition on television, and who, in his pre-match promos, had promised not just to beat me, but to break my leg and put me out of wrestling for good. It was good for Greg, obviously, because he was taking the young WWF champion further than any challenger had ever taken him—and appeared to be someone who had the stamina and physical toughness to go toe-to-toe with me.

At the appointed time, just before the time limit expired, and after I had blocked the application of the hold all match long, Greg finally caught me in the figure-four leglock in the center of the ring. I was struggling to escape the hold when the referee called for the bell. The crowd was aghast—many of them thinking that, like everyone else before me, I had been forced to concede to the devastating finishing hold. The bell continued to ring, but Greg refused to release the hold—trying to make good on his promise to break my leg. Finally, Arnold Skaaland jumped into the ring and smashed Greg in the head with the championship belt, causing him to unlock our legs.

I sold the hold to the moon, struggling to get to my feet after the hold was broken and holding onto the turnbuckles and then to Arnold as Howard Finkel announced to the exhausted Garden crowd that I had, in fact, *not* submitted, but that the match had gone to the one-hour time limit, and was a draw. It was a great swerve that worked perfectly. With Greg seemingly injuring my leg at the end of the match, we had left a great new foundation at for the next match to be built upon, and we were all set up for the following month.

Around the rest of the territory, I finished up feuds in some cities with Ivan Koloff, including a couple of memorable cage matches with him, and in other cities and towns with Peter Maivia. I also wrestled in some tag-team matches with Chief Jay Strongbow and with "Polish Power" Ivan Putski against the WWF Tag-Team Champions the Valiant Brothers, managed, of course, as all heel tag-team champions were, by the "Guiding Light" Captain Lou Albano.

Vince Sr. was again testing out booking ideas by putting me into these tag-team matches—a strategy he had used in past years either to set up feuds for Bruno Sammartino, or to establish the credibility of new challengers when Bruno was champion. Vince Sr. would put Bruno into a tag-team match with a couple of monster heels—and have one of those heels either pin Bruno in the tag-team match, giving that heel the "credibility" to beat Bruno one-on-one, and immediately propelling that heel into the "number-one contender" position out on the house show circuit. Alternatively, he would have one of the heels do something to Bruno during the tag-team match that would start an angle that would lead to a championship match between the two.

Unlike Bruno, I didn't love working in tag-team matches. Although I had done a fair amount of tag-team wrestling for Eddie Graham down in Florida when I worked with Steve Keirn, it wasn't my favorite. That was especially true with a partner like Ivan Putski.

Although the people loved Putski, and he was popular and reliable enough to main-event some of the smaller buildings in the territory, I just didn't enjoy working with Putski. Like Mascaras, any match involving Ivan Putski could not be a tag-team match, or a match to highlight one or both of the heels. A tag-team match involving Ivan Putski always had to be about Ivan Putski. He just wouldn't have it any other way.

Ivan was a legitimate Polish strongman, and a very stubborn guy with intense national pride. In the ring, he wanted to be the dominant guy and wasn't interested in sharing the spotlight with anyone else. There was no cooperation or storytelling in any match that involved him. When I tried to talk to him about that, he would kind of give me the "yah yah" as if he were listening, but then he would do what he wanted to do in the ring, and not do a lot of selling for the opposition, which did nothing to build drama. You can't have drama without tension, and he provided no tension because he never wanted to appear vulnerable.

Vince Sr. saw that and he killed the tag-team idea pretty quickly.

Of course, the same scenario played out with the rest of Putski's matches, whether he was on the undercard or being used to main-event a small building on the house show circuit. If you were a heel in a match with Putski, you were either going to end up in a war with him over him taking too much of the match, or you would end up getting chewed up because he wouldn't sell for you.

There was no doubt that Ivan was a reliably good draw in some of the towns though—and consequently, he was a good guy to have on a card, particularly in places where his Polish heritage was a draw. The office knew the towns where Putski drew well, and they deployed him there in main events or semi-final matches against heels that I had finished with and who were on their way out of the territory anyway—and fed those heels to Ivan.

And Ivan inevitably chewed them up.

Of course, the name of the game was not necessarily great wrestling, great storytelling, or unselfish sharing of the spotlight. The name of the game was putting people in seats. And in a lot of places, Ivan Putski could put people in the seats, so Ivan Putski remained an important player in the WWF both in this run, and when he returned as a slimmer version of himself in 1982.

On March 25, 1979, I traveled up to Toronto for my first WWF title vs. AWA title world championship unification match with AWA World Champion Nick Bockwinkel. Nick was the son of Warren Bockwinkel, who was a heck of a wrestler in his own right. When I was growing up, I once saw a match between Warren and Wilbur Snyder where the biggest offensive move in the match was a forearm smash—which tells you that Warren was all about storytelling through *wrestling*. Nick definitely learned his craft very well from his dad.

Frank Tunney, the promoter in Toronto, was a close friend of both Vince Sr. and Verne Gagne, and wanted to bring Bockwinkel and me together because he thought that the two of us could put on a great *wrestling* match. Of course, with Gagne successfully running the AWA and Vince Sr. successfully running the WWF, there was no chance of ever actually unifying the world titles by having one of us go over the other cleanly, but the fans didn't know that—and these inter-federation unification matches were always historic and virtually guaranteed sellouts wherever they occurred. Even though the card in Toronto was totally stacked with talent that night, Frank Tunney gave Bockwinkel and me no time duration for our match. Given the historic nature of the match, his instructions to us were to simply "let the fans decide."

The fact that we took the main event to the thirty-nine-minute mark on a card with that much talent tells you a lot about how the crowd was responding to what we were doing, and what a great worker Nick Bockwinkel was.

Nick had a great head for the game, a wonderful sense of ring psychology, and an uncanny ability to use his intelligence and cockiness to get under the people's skin. He was a terrific representative for the AWA and was *the* key player in the success of the AWA for a long time. I didn't know Nick very well outside the ring, and we only crossed paths a couple of times during our careers, but I had grown up watching him on television, and I had always wanted to work with him. He was a very intelligent, well-spoken, and cocky heel, and his in-ring skills were right up there with the very best in the business.

I always wished I had gotten the chance to do a unification match with Bockwinkel at the Garden. Given the chance to do a few interviews and a couple of television tapings, I think that match could have been as hot with the people as any series I had in New York.

The following night, Greg Valentine and I returned to the Garden for the return match after our Broadway. The rematch was billed as something of a specialty match in that it would have "no time limit"—meaning that Greg and I could wrestle all night if that is what it took to declare a winner. We would also play off of the leg "injury" that I had sustained at the end of the last match, with Greg immediately testing the stability of that leg, and me trying to keep him away from it. In the end, though, it did not make sense for this match to go to a specialty third match, because the strength of the Backlund-Valentine series was in the *wrestling*, not the brawling.

Consequently, I went over Greg by pinfall after about thirty minutes of excellent wrestling, putting an end to the Grand Wizard's threat. Valentine did a wonderful job in that series with me both at the Garden and all around the territory, and quickly became one of my favorite opponents. Vince Sr. liked him too, and gave him a subsequent series with Chief

Jay Strongbow where Greg "broke" Strongbow's leg using the figure-four leglock and then, after Chief returned, battled him all over the territory in one of the most memorable feuds of the era.

✦

After Valentine, we had a bit of a soft spot in the schedule while Vince Sr. was readying the next big angle—so I ended up wrestling a couple of one-off matches at the Garden. The first of those matches was against an aging veteran named Dick "The Bulldog" Brower. Brower was one of the hardest guys I ever had to work with in the ring, and probably the least favorite man I ever had to wrestle for the WWF title. Brower's nickname was the "One Man Riot Squad"—and on this trip through the territory, he was paired with Captain Louis Albano—so the idea was to portray him as a crazy and completely unpredictable wild man who was capable of doing absolutely anything inside or outside of the ring.

The problem was that Brower was looking very tired, old, and out of shape at the time he came into the territory. He wasn't the hardest-working guy in the ring to begin with, so many of his televised matches leading up to his title match with me at the Garden had been sloppy and unconvincing. Our title match at the Garden wasn't drawing well, so the front office had to do a rescue job for Brower on television to manufacture some heat for him.

First, they ran an angle where he snuck up from behind me and waf-fled me with a folding chair while I was standing in front of the empty ring taping a promotional interview. That was the first time *that* had ever been done, so that accomplished the goal of getting him over a little bit better as a totally unpredictable madman. It also served to create a little bit of personal "animosity" between the two of us.

The second thing that the front office did was give Brower an unheard-of pinfall win over Ivan Putski on television—which served three differ-ent purposes. First, it gave Brower a marquee match on television that enabled him to better establish himself as a wild heel that was capable of beating anyone at any time. As I recall, Brower, knowing that he was on thin ice, showed up to play in that match, and displayed some of the skills and mayhem that had made him a big star in the '60s and '70s. He was all over the arena scattering the people, battering Putski with a chair, upending the doctor at ringside, lifting up the entire set of ring steps and breaking them apart, and chasing Putski around the ring with a broken board from those steps.

Second, by beating Putski by pinfall on television, it gave him instant credibility, since Ivan Putski never took a pinfall anywhere—even in the larger arenas on the undercards. Pinning Putski on television was a big deal. If he could pin Ivan Putski—Brower was capable of pinning anybody. Or so the story went.

Third, the angle forced *Putski* to be a team player by requiring him to put someone else who needed a push over on television, which was something Ivan did not ever want to do. He was very upset about being asked to do this—particularly for a guy like Brower, who wasn't fond of foreigners, and wasn't very popular with the boys. I'm sure the message from Vince Sr. to Ivan was intentional—a reminder of who was boss, and who was ultimately in control of all our characters, and all of our storylines. It was a reminder to Ivan to play nicely with others.

Brower was not an up-and-down, tell-a-story kind of opponent, so we were clearly going to be one and done at the Garden. There was only one story to tell with him: me trying to avoid getting killed or seriously injured by the crazy man, but still needing to get close enough to him for long enough to pin him and then get out of there as quickly as possible. My match with Brower fell into the same kind of booking scenario as my matches with George "The Animal" Steele—except that Steele was much more intelligent and a much nicer guy who actually cared a *lot* about telling a good story in the ring.

Brower and I played cat and mouse for a while until I got too close and Brower pounded away on me with punches and kicks and threw me out of the ring. He then used some items on the arena floor to further enrage the fans. When it looked like Brower had me in peril, I made a quick comeback, pinned him, and got the heck out of there before he injured me, either as part of the storyline, or in real life.

The match with Brower was one of my shortest and least favorite title matches at the Garden.

As a study in contrasts, my next opponent at the Garden was one of my favorites of all time, but at the time the card was announced, no one knew who it was going to be.

For the June 1979 Garden card, Howard Finkel announced that the winner of a twenty-man over the top rope battle royal would win a match with me for the WWF title later that evening. It was a pretty interesting concept—because in the minds of the fans, *anyone* was capable of winning the battle royal and getting the title match with me. Gorilla Monsoon and Ivan Putski were both in the match, so what if one of them won it? The WWF never really had babyface title matches, so that alone was cause for significant fan intrigue.

I didn't like battle royals, and tried to avoid participating in them whenever possible. I got injured in the first one I ever took part in when I wrestled for Leroy McGuirk in Baton Rouge. That night, I hit the ropes the wrong way on the way out and slammed my hip hard into the apron of the ring on the way down. I felt that injury for weeks afterward. There are just too many ways to legitimately get hurt in a ring with sixteen or twenty guys in it. With everyone in there moving around, flying off the turnbuckles, coming off the ropes, or trying to execute moves, it is just too easy to get a wrist or an ankle stepped on, to inadvertently bang heads, or end up with all sorts of legitimate bumps and bruises from accidental contact with another wrestler that can dog you for days afterward.

Fortunately, in the WWF, the champions typically didn't have to wrestle in battle royals because the promoters understood that there was too much risk. I also enjoyed the science of crowd psychology, responding to the fans and how they reacted to each move as you progressed through a match, and brought the crowd to a peak. None of that was available in a battle royal.

They way that battle royals were booked, you'd simply be told who the person was that was going out before you, and who was going to be throwing you out—and so all you really had to do was keep an eye on the guy going out before you, and then work something out with the guy slated to throw you out so you knew what move he was going to use to eliminate you from the match. Only the last three or four people in the battle royal needed to work out a spots to tease an outcome and figure out how they were going to get to the end.

I know the fans liked battle royals because of the novelty of seeing sixteen or twenty wrestlers all in the ring at the same time—but if you've ever watched one closely, you know that there really isn't a whole lot going on in the match. There is really just a bunch of pushing and shoving, rest holds, headlocks, and front facelocks as the guys going out later in the match bided their time and waited for the guys ahead of them to get thrown out. Next time you watch a battle royal on YouTube, notice how quickly the eliminations happen once the first few people go out. That's because every wrestler in there wanted to get out as soon as he could to avoid getting hurt.

Anyway—to my knowledge, this was the first-ever battle royal at the Garden to determine a world title challenger, and it was "won" by my old friend Khosrow Vaziri—best known as The Iron Sheik, but at that time, known as "The Great Hussein Arab." Of course, this had been the intent all along. Khosrow and I had wrestled a test match somewhere up in Maine just before the Garden card, and a dark match at the television tapings, both of which had gone very well, so I was looking forward to getting in the ring with him on the larger stage.

Given the diplomatic tensions between the US and Iran at the time, Vince Sr. was nervous about promoting and advertising a world title match between me and the Sheik at the Garden, or in any of the other major urban arenas, for fear of riots. I know that Khosrow found himself a little bit hamstrung, as he could not play up the politics as much as he otherwise would have, because the real-life political situation between the United States and Iran was just too hot. At the time of the match, the United States, which had supported the Shah, had just evacuated most of its people from Iran, and even though the hostage crisis would not begin for a few months, relations between our two countries were rapidly worsening. It was all over the nightly news, so I think if Sheik had played out his support of the Ayatollah (which would have been especially ironic given that he had been at one point a real-life body-guard for the Shah's family), and used the act he would later employ in 1983, it might have put him at serious risk. So this was the creative way that Vince Sr. opted to give Khosrow the match he deserved at the Garden without advertising it in advance and risking a riot or danger to Khosrow's well-being.

Given that I had just had a short, wild match with Brower the month before, the match with Khosrow was a refreshing change of pace. We had a terrific thirty-minute match that was almost entirely amateur chain wrestling. Sheik was also a suplex artist, so we highlighted many of his different versions in that match. There was very little kicking and punch-ing—and I think the fans truly enjoyed the bout. In the end, I pinned him, and sent the decidedly partisan New York City crowd home happy and without a riot.

Our paths would memorably cross again at the end of my reign in 1983. But this match with Khosrow was one of the best *wrestling* matches I had as the WWF champion, right up there with my matches with Har-ley, Valentine, Pat Patterson, and Don Muraco. I wish we could have had a two-or three-match series at the Garden, as there was certainly a lot that we could have done to entertain the fans. Had the political situation between our two countries been a little less "hot" at the time, our first match could certainly have been a Broadway. Khos was definitely one of those guys who was more than capable of going an hour and telling a compelling story.

Around this time, there were also a couple of memorable mishaps out on the house show circuit. The first one occurred in Poughkeepsie, New York. Several of the boys were late getting to the building because they were coming from a venue some distance away and had become snarled in traffic. There were enough people involved that we really couldn't even start the card, so I went out into the ring, and invited a few of the kids from the crowd into the ring, lined them up, and put on a little wrestling clinic right there in the ring in front of the fans. I had the kids wrestle each other, and I had them wrestle me, and I explained the moves and escapes to the crowd on the microphone, and the people got into it and we burned an hour that way until the rest of the boys could get to the building. The people never even knew that the wrestlers were late.

You do what you have to do to let the show go on.

Another night, we were scheduled to wrestle in a high school in Elizabeth, New Jersey, and there was some sort of miscommunication between the office and the ring crew, so the ring never showed up. So there we were in the middle of this high school gym with 1,000 or 1,500 people in the building and no ring.

What do you do with that?

Well, the name on the marquee is wrestling, right?

Fortunately, the high school wrestling coach was around that night, and gave us access to some wrestling mats, so we just laid the mats out on the gym floor as they would have been in an amateur meet, and we had the pro matches right there on the gym floor on the amateur mats. I remember I was scheduled to defend the WWF title that night against Khosrow, so he and I put on a mat wrestling clinic. It was fortunate that I was scheduled to wrestle Khosrow and not someone like Brower, who would have been nearly impossible to engage in a mat wrestling match like that. We obviously couldn't do any real high spots, but the show went on, and we found a way to entertain the people!

Many people have asked me over the years why during the early days of my title reign, I didn't appear very often in Boston. First, the promoter for the Boston Garden was Abe Ford—and Ford was a Bruno guy. Boston was also a town with a very strong blue-collar Italian heritage, and that was Bruno's sweet spot in terms of his drawing power. Given that, I don't think that Ford was very happy about Vince selecting me—a collegiate-looking Midwesterner—to be the next champion, and I don't think Ford was convinced that I could draw in Boston.

Ford had done business with Bruno for a long time, and had gotten comfortable with having Bruno at the top of the card, and for Abe at least, as long as Bruno was still around, he wanted Bruno headlining Boston. That also meant that Bruno was asking for main-event money, and Ford probably wouldn't have wanted (or needed) to pay both of our matches main-event money. That is why if you look at a lot of the earlier Boston cards, I was used sparingly—and Bruno was often inserted into the main-event matches with the heels that I was wrestling against elsewhere in the territory.

The other reason is that there were several cities other than Boston that wanted Saturday night bookings for their big buildings, including Philadelphia (Spectrum), Baltimore (Civic Center), Landover (Capitol Centre), Uniondale (Nassau County Coliseum), and Springfield (Civic Center). So Vince was willing to allow Ford to use Bruno at the top of his cards in Boston because it freed me up to be used in whatever other Saturday-night card was being booked opposite Boston, or to book me in Japan or Toronto or other NWA territories during that week.

I spent the rest of the first half of 1979 traveling the larger buildings of the WWF territory, primarily finishing up different series with Valentine, Ladd, and Brower depending on what the local promoters were doing. All this was to prepare for the feud that would consume the rest of 1979—the WWF's first-ever title versus title tilt between me and the soon-to-be North American Champion (and then Intercontinental Heavyweight Champion) Pat Patterson.

A new young babyface named Ted DiBiase had come into the WWF territory at the beginning of 1979. Ted had played football at West Texas State University, but had sustained an injury his senior year that effectively ended his football career. He had grown up in wrestling was trained by his adoptive father, the legendary Iron Mike DiBiase, and by Terry and Dory Funk and Dick Murdoch. DiBiase had a lot of the same training that I had, and he had become a great young babyface. After leaving Amarillo, Ted spent several years in the Mid-South territory wrestling for Bill Watts, and also briefly held the Missouri State Championship for Sam Muchnick before getting the call from Vince Sr.

When Ted came into the territory in 1979, he was brought in as the "North American Heavyweight Champion"—a title that Vince Sr. created to give DiBiase some immediate credibility, and to create some additional interest in the WWF undercards by giving the boys a secondary belt to fight over. DiBiase defended the belt in the territory for several months until he faced a new brash-talking, cocky platinum blonde heel named Pat Patterson on television in June 1979. Patterson, who was managed by the Grand Wizard, knocked DiBiase out cold with a pair of brass knuckles he had hidden in his trunks and pinned DiBiase to win the belt in front of a shocked crowd in Allentown. In a post-match interview, Patterson and the Wizard went on television and promised the world that I would be next.

On July 2, 1979, the Garden saw its first-ever match between two reigning singles champions, as I faced the challenge of the new North American Champion Patterson. Pat was truly as good as it could get in the ring—he was very smooth, very gentle, and exceptional at developing a story in the ring. By the time he arrived in the WWF, Pat had over twenty years of experience in professional wrestling, mostly in the San Francisco area, where he had wrestled for promoter Roy Shire and formed one of the most famous heel tag teams in wrestling history with Ray "The Crippler" Stevens, and also in the AWA for Verne Gagne.

Pat could get the crowd riled up as quickly and as well as anyone I ever wrestled. He just had a knack for knowing exactly what to do at exactly the right time to infuriate the people, and his gimmick of hiding a pair of brass knuckles in his tights had gotten over like crazy with the WWF crowds. For our first match at the Garden, Vince Sr. brought us together and told us that we'd be coming back the following month — because Pat had become a white-hot heel after waffling DiBiase with the brass knuckles on television, and the fans had come out in force to see the first title-versus-title showdown at the Garden. So Vince Sr. asked for me to get color in this match in to give Pat the victory with a blood stoppage.

Stay Down, Bob!

Vince Sr. called me. I had been working for Verne Gagne in Minneapolis teaming with Ray Stevens when Mike LeBell, the promoter in Los Angeles, called me and told me that Vince Sr. really wanted me in New York, but he didn't want to create any heat with Verne. So I waited about a month and then I called Vince and asked him to give me a date — and that's how I ended up in New York.

When I first met Vince Sr., I told him how much I appreciated the opportunity, and that I hoped I would make him happy and he said, "Pat, all I want you to do is help Bob Backlund." Bob had been a terrific amateur wrestler and Vince wanted to make him a star — but Bob hadn't necessarily had the right guys to work with yet. He worked with some of these guys that were big monsters — but they couldn't always move like you'd want them to, so sometimes, these matches were not as exciting as they might have been. A lot of those guys looked really good — so that the fans would say, "Oh, my God, Bob Backlund is never going to be able to beat this guy," and then he'd go into the ring and beat them, but up to that point, I don't think he had really had the chance to work at the Garden with an old pro who could really move.

So Vince put me with the Wizard, told me I was going to work with Backlund, and started to build me up toward a match with Backlund at the Garden. So I had to think of something to get heat, you know, and I came up with the idea of brass knuckles. It started when I became the North American Champion by knocking out Ted DiBiase on television with a pair of brass knuckles that I pulled out of my trunks. Once I did that, now I had a belt, and it was the first time that Bob Backlund would be wrestling another champion at the Garden. On television, I was destroying all of my opponents, so they were building it up that Bob Backlund was going to have to wrestle another champion. And the people hated me, and the brass knuckles were now part of my heat, so that was the story. I wanted it to be in the minds of the fans that when I got in the ring with Bob Backlund, that was something for the fans to be worried about—so that every time I'd go to my tights, the fans would go crazy because they thought I was going for something.

In the early days, you know, Bob was still a little green, and still had some of that amateur in him, so when you'd start beating the shit out of him, he didn't sell as long or as much as he could have. He'd want to pop right up and start making a comeback—but you can't make a comeback without heat, you know? So I'd say to him, "Stay down, Bob!" I used to yell at him in the ring and say, "Don't move! Stay down!" but after every match we'd have, he'd come into the locker room and hug me and say, "Thank you, Pat. That was good, wasn't it?" And I would say, "Yeah, that was good!"

—**Pat Patterson**

Pat and I came back in the Garden on July 30, 1979. Pat's experience had made him very creative in putting together matches and coming up with angles and finishes. I didn't know it at the time, but he was the one who came up with the idea for the next finish at the Garden. Pat had more than enough ability to work for heat, but the brass knuckles gimmick had gotten over so well with the people, that they just let him run with it. That second match at the Garden was unquestionably one of the best of my career. Pat and I built that match so masterfully and worked it for almost thirty minutes that night that when the finish came, it was one of the most memorable endings Madison Square Garden had ever seen.

The Double Kayo

Vince Sr. would not allow the heel managers to stay at ringside at the Garden. As soon as the bell rang, the manager had to be escorted back to the dressing rooms. Well that night, I begged him to leave the Wizard at ringside, and to just trust me, and that it would all work out beautifully. Well to his credit, the old man agreed—and at the right moment at the end of the match, when we had the crowd just right, the Wizard stood up and the referee turned around and was distracted just long enough for me to go into my tights and boom!—I hit Bob with the brass knuckles and down he went. Well when Bob went down like that, Skaaland jumped up on the apron, and I took a swing at him and missed and he hit me in the head with the championship belt. Pow! and now I'm down. And now Backlund and I are both laying there . . . and the referee starts to count. One . . . two . . . and Bob did not move one finger. He was laying there dead, just like I told him to be. Six . . . seven . . . and the building was shaking, I swear it was so loud in there I thought the roof was going to come off the place. Eight . . . nine . . . and I was almost to a sitting position, and then I fell back down. Ten. And nobody won. It was magnificent. My God, the Garden, that building was going insane. I'm telling you— that's the fun you can have when you really get the people involved. And boy, did we have them that night.

I remember when we came backstage the old man hugged me and he just looked at me and said, "Ho-ly shit!" And the Garden had gotten so loud that everyone else was watching the match in the back, so that when we came through the curtain, they were all congratulating us on what a great match it was. Well when that happened, you knew you had done something—and we did. I'll never forget that. I'd love to see that match again!

— Pat Patterson

By the time our third match rolled around on August 27, 1979, Patterson was now the new "Intercontinental Heavyweight Champion." The office didn't think that the name "North American Champion" had quite the pizzazz that they were looking for, so they went on television on August 22, 1979, with a storyline that Patterson had just returned from a trip to Rio de Janeiro, Brazil, where he had won a tournament and become the South American Heavyweight Champion, and the WWF had now unified the North American and South American Heavyweight Championships into a new "Intercontinental" Heavyweight Championship. Of course, all of this was just part of the storyline—but it added some additional interest in Pat's continuing title run at the Garden. As the story went, he was on an incredible roll. He had beaten DiBiase for the North American title, "won" the tournament in Rio to become the Intercontinental Heavyweight Champion, and now, once again, was coming after my WWF World Heavyweight Championship.

When Vince Sr. brought Patterson and me together in the Garden bathroom before the match, it was the first time since I won the title that anything Vince Sr. said in one of those pre-match meetings actually surprised me. We were going to have a *third* consecutive match without a decisive victor. Pat was going to hit me with the knuckles again, and this time, I was going to fall out of the ring and get counted out—which would set up a no-holds barred encounter in a steel cage the following month. In that match, there would be no referee and no rules, and Patterson could legally use the brass knuckles if he wanted to, and there would have to be a winner.

A New Backlund

Vince was the promoter. Yes, he had Monsoon and Phil Zacko back then, but Vince would ultimately make the decisions. When you are the promoter, you have a feeling for it, and you can do whatever you want. It's your choice of what you want to do. I never thought that I would have four matches in a row with Backlund at the Garden. But it was working. Just imagine that you are Vince Sr., and you are the guy responsible to create the bookings and the kind of fan interest that will put 20,000 asses in the seats at the Garden every month. He had very good relationships with the promoters all over the country, and had access to a lot of talent. But you know there were territories, and then there were territories. Minneapolis was a territory, San Francisco was a territory, Texas was a territory, but the Big Apple—that was where the money was. The northeast was THE territory. It was a big responsibility, and you had to draw money big time, and he did.

I think the thing that really helped me was that right from the first match that I had with Backlund—we saw a whole new Bob Backlund. Our matches were completely different from what had come before. I was lucky. Before me, he had wrestled all of these big guys who really couldn't move all that well. Now I'm in the main event with Bob at the Garden, and I said to him, we're going to have some real fucking action! And we took bumps and had high spots all over the place. So the old man looks at the first match and says, yeah, that was pretty good, and I have to draw a house next month, so I think I'll work a return match with Bob and Pat. And then the return match with the double knockout works and almost takes the building down, and the old man says to himself, "Hey, I'd like to have one more match with no winner, can we do that?" And we said, "hell yeah, we can do that!"

Look, the truth is, if you are wrestling with the champion and you build up a story and the story that you built doesn't sell tickets—forget it, you're not going to be in the main event next month no matter what they might have had planned. You're going to be one and done. That happened sometimes. But this match was selling tickets, and so the old man wanted to stretch it one more time. This time, the referee was going to get knocked down, and I was going to hit Backlund with the brass knuckles, and he was going to fall out of the ring and get counted out.

—Pat Patterson

When we took to the ring that night at the Garden, the fans heard Patterson introduced as the new Intercontinental Champion. And that definitely gave the match some added importance in the minds of the fans. And so there we were, for a third month in a row, slugging it out, and for a third month in a row, Patterson pulled out the brass knuckles and connected with them, and left me laying outside the ring to get counted out. This outcome set the blowoff up perfectly—as Pat would go on television for most of the next month telling the fans that inside the cage, he could knock me out with the brass knuckles and it would be legal and then all he'd have to do is walk out the door, and he'd be crowned the new world champion.

Pat Patterson was the only man in the nearly six years that I held the WWF World Championship to get four consecutive world title match main events with me at Madison Square Garden. That speaks volumes about the kind of business we were doing. And that cage match on September 24, 1979, at the Garden, featuring the federation's two champions going at it for a fourth straight month with no holds barred and no referee brought in so many fans they had to turn people away in droves. There wouldn't have been a building in New York large enough to hold all of the people who wanted to see that match.

Pat and I battled in the cage at Madison Square Garden for nearly twenty minutes in what was certainly one of the two or three best cage matches I had in my career. We both got color, teased finishes all over the place, and "battled to the death." The end came when we were both perched at the top of the cage pounding away on each other when I connected with a wild haymaker knocking Pat down, where he got caught up in the corner. I fell to the canvas and crawled toward the door to get position on Patterson, and then kicked him off of me repeatedly until I fell out the door backwards onto the arena floor.

I'm No Frank Sinatra

You should have seen Bob in that cage match. He was so afraid he was going to be double-crossed. He was trained to keep an eye on that, because you never know. It only takes one move, one accident, one thing that your opponent does that he's not supposed to do, and he's the champion. Some guys might have the balls to do that, you know, and then try and explain it after the fact by saying I'm sorry, I slipped or I fell down, and I'm sorry, but then you have a new champ.

So I told Bob before the cage match began—when I go for the door, or I go for the top, I'm going to dive for it and it's going to be like a shoot Bob—so you better grab my fucking leg, or I'm going over. And Bob was like damn, Pat, are you crazy? And I said no that's what I'm going to do to make the match. But I had a blast with him— because when I'd hit him, he'd go down, but he wouldn't stay down, because while he was down I'd be jumping up over the top trying to get out and he had to pop up and chase me to keep me from going out. We were up on the ropes and I was trying to get over the top and I'd hit him and told him to go down, and he wouldn't fucking go down, and I'd be like, "Go down." So he went down, and as soon as he did, I went right over the fucking cage as quickly as I could and he popped up there and snatched me. Or another time, the door was open, and I was like, "Let go of my leg, let go of my leg," and as soon as he did, I would dive out the door and he'd catch me at the very last second, oh, it was awesome. I was having such a blast—he was like one of the fans—I think he thought I was really going to go out!

Everybody knew that Vince wanted Backlund to be a star. And every once in a while, the word would come back—you know, he's still a little green, but that didn't matter. It takes time to develop that. And that was part of the effort of everyone else who was there—that was the job to be done. Bob had no ego—he was wide open, listened, and I think he had some of the best matches of his career with me, without a doubt. He had some big matches, but exciting matches with good wrestling, where you really felt it . . . ours were hard to beat.

Bob was always a bit of a loner—he traveled by himself and he didn't mix with the boys that much. I think I saw him in the bar once or twice while I was there having a couple of drinks with the boys. When he did, he would come in, and buy a few rounds for the boys, and then he'd be gone. And I couldn't believe how much this guy was training—he would sit in the hotel rooms out on the road during the week and crank the heat on and work out in his room until he was drenched with sweat. He became an animal—he just loved to train and push himself. But you know, I kept thinking to myself, "This guy is missing the boat. He should be relaxing a little bit more and mixing with the boys." But he was doing what he liked . . .

Arnold Skaaland and Backlund would have a few drinks here and there also. Skaaland told me one time that he was convinced that the kid would make it. Arnold always protected Backlund—he was Vince Sr.'s right hand man, and he always made sure that Bob was taken care of and was kept happy. If you think about it, the WWF was the only place you'd ever see a babyface have a manager. And I think Bruno and Bob were the only two babyfaces I can ever think of that had a manager. But again, it worked out for them, because Arnold kept Bob happy—and managing Bob gave Skaaland a job and a steady paycheck long after his wrestling career was over. Vince Sr. was a good man—he was liked by everybody, and he took care of a lot of people.

In watching Bob, as I did over the years, he was really trying hard to get the people to like him. He was friendly and happy and looked like an athlete—but I asked him one time, because I had heard that when he arrived at the Garden, he'd often go through the front door. Typically, when we go into the Garden, we'd go through the back door and go up the elevator but Bob was going through the front door and would shake hands with all the fans. I think Bob enjoyed that so much, because he knew that the people really liked him, and I think that he wanted to thank them personally and wanted to be with them. But when you are going to a big match, my view is you should let them see you first when you are going to the ring. So I said to him one time, Bob I can't believe you're doing that. And he said to me, "Pat, they're my fans." I said Bob, if I'm waiting in line in Las Vegas for half an hour to go see Frank Sinatra, and then all of a sudden Frank Sinatra walks by all of us and shakes our hands in the line— well then I've already seen him before he ever gets onstage. And you know, you lose the mystique. But when I told him that, he just looked at me and said, "You know, Pat, I'm no Frank Sinatra."

—Pat Patterson

I spent most of the rest of 1979 wrestling Patterson to capacity crowds around the horn, where we did various iterations of the double knockout finish that had so wowed the crowd at the Garden, and eventually, blowoff matches that had me going over Pat by pinfall. But there were a couple of other notable matches that I had during this time that are also worthy of mention.

On July 15, 1979, I went back up to Toronto for Frank Tunney and faced the NWA's United States Heavyweight Champion, "Nature Boy" Ric Flair, at the Maple Leaf Garden. This was my first time getting into the ring with Ric, with whom I would have an even more memorable night at the Omni later in my career. I enjoyed wrestling Ric. He was very skilled, worked hard in the ring, was flamboyant, and really knew how to work the people. Ric and I had a great, pretty long matchup there that night that really seemed to capture the people. Toronto was also getting to be a good town for me, as the people had seen me often enough to really be in my corner.

Because Ric was the US Champion and I was the WWF World Champion, even though the match that night was only for my belt, there was no way that the NWA promoters would allow Flair to be pinned by the WWF's world champion. Because of that, there was only one way to go, and that was with some kind of an inconclusive ending, like a draw, or a disqualification or a countout. Tunney opted for a countout.

On August 25, 1979, I traveled to Cobo Hall in Detroit to defend the WWF title against the Sheik, who was the wrestler-promoter for the territory. The Sheik, of course, was, by this point, legendary for creating mayhem wherever he went. He had actually been legitimately banned in several cities because he was so convincing that he had sparked riots in the crowds. Anyway, the Sheik (Eddie Farhat) called Vince Sr. and asked me to come up there and do a match with him.

When you wrestled the Sheik, you knew what he was going to call for—the booking plan was always the same. He was going to try to murder you, and as the babyface, you were just in there trying to survive, get a three count on him, and get out of there with your life. The Sheik's big gimmick was "conjuring up" and then throwing a "fireball" into the face of his opponents behind the referee's back—and so we played off that. When he tried to do it to me, I ducked it, and then we battled outside the ring to a countout ending where I snuck back into the ring to beat the referee's count.

These "babyface-in-peril" bookings weren't my favorites, because they didn't really offer me the opportunity to build fan interest during the course of the match through actual wrestling. Like my matches with George "The Animal" Steele, Abdullah the Butcher, or Bulldog Brower, these matches were just mayhem from the opening bell, with me getting beat up and hanging on, waiting for an opportunity to sneak in a quick finish and get out of there without getting "hurt." But I know that the people loved the variety of seeing a match like this once in a while, so that's why we sprinkled a few of them in from time to time to mix things up.

My last real series of 1979 was against "Cowboy" Bob Duncam. To get things started, we ran a little angle on television where he had been running roughshod over the guys he was wrestling on television week after week—refusing to pin them, and toying with them and trying to "injure" them. So during one of those matches, after I ran out there and tried to "save" one of the young guys he was beating up, and he attacked me and Arnold, and we had instant heat.

Bobby had played professional football and worked very, very hard in his matches. He was a rough-looking and very convincing heel, but he had only one speed—sixth gear—so it was practically impossible to get him to pace himself out there. When you worked a match with Duncam, he would go all out for twelve to fifteen minutes and then blow up. You'd often see Bobby in the dressing room after his matches lying flat on his back on the floor in the dressing room trying to get air.

At the time we had our series, Bobby's wife was very sick with cancer and she was getting treatment in Boston at Massachusetts General Hospital. Bobby cared very deeply about her and no matter where he was wrestling, he would drive back after the matches to sit by her bedside. Obviously, that put a lot of stress on him, forced him to do a lot of night driving and to eat a lot of fast food, so he got pretty heavy. But what's not to love about a man who loves his wife like that?

Duncam worked very hard with me, and knowing his personal circumstances made me want to work extra hard with him and for him.

Bobby also remembered the days back in the AWA when I was putting him over, so he was anxious to be able to have some good matches and return the favor for me.

On November 19, 1979, we met at the Garden and, premised on what the fans had just seen on television, we had a wild brawl that ended in a *double* blood stoppage. I attacked Duncam right away and we just went after each other to play off of the TV angle. Bobby was at his limit at eighteen minutes. You couldn't take him much deeper into a match than that and have things continue to look good. But Duncam would give you an absolutely awesome 100 percent work rate for every one of those eighteen minutes, so we just played off of that and gave the people at the Garden a great pull-apart brawl that had the building really rocking.

On November 4, 1979, I went back to Toronto where I was *supposed* to be wrestling Pat Patterson, but Pat had gone over to Japan to drop the no-longer-existing North American title to Seiji Sakaguchi as a favor to Inoki, so Frank Tunney brought in Baron von Raschke from the AWA to sub for Patterson. Von Raschke and I had also wrestled previously when I was in the AWA, and we worked that match around his "notorious" iron claw submission hold, which was an easy gimmick to play up for the fans.

Von Raschke was fun. He was another wrestler who was playing up the German Nazi gimmick, but in reality, von Raschke had been a great amateur wrestler at Nebraska. He got the crowd lathered up, and we battled to a double countout. The match surprised Tunney in that it drew enough heat that Tunney forgot all about Patterson and brought von Raschke back the next month in a no-disqualification match where I beat him cleanly with the atomic drop.

18

A Favor for Antonio (Japan, 1979)

"Show an alert interest, tolerance and respect for others, and they will instinctively do the same for you."

—Napoelon Hill, "Assemble an Attractive Personality"

———◦•◦———

In the late 1970s, Japan was a hotbed for professional wrestling, and tours there drew huge crowds and were very lucrative for the boys. It was not unusual to make more money on a ten-day or two-week tour of Japan than you could make in a month or more wrestling in one of the territories in the United States.

Shohei "Giant" Baba was the head of All-Japan Pro Wrestling and Baba and his All-Japan promotion were closely allied with the NWA. Baba had a good relationship with the Funks in particular and All-Japan was gaining momentum at the time. Baba had already had his first run with the NWA World Heavyweight Championship—a local switch of the title during a Japanese tour that had been privately arranged between Baba and NWA World Champion Jack Brisco and brokered by the Funks without the knowledge of the NWA Board of Directors. Brisco just dropped the NWA World Title to Baba at the beginning of the tour, and Baba dropped it back to Brisco at the end of the tour before Jack returned to the United States. This, of course, served to put a lot of shine on Baba in the eyes of the Japanese fans, and drew more fans to All-Japan.

Meanwhile, while this was going on, Antonio Inoki, the head of New Japan Pro Wrestling, had built an alliance with Vince McMahon Sr. and the World Wrestling Federation. Inoki was losing face in Japan because Baba had been a world champion, and Inoki had not.

Vince Sr. and Inoki wanted to enlarge their relationship. They had already worked out a deal to bring WWF talent to Japan regularly, which would be great exposure for the WWF and financially advantageous for the boys. The "payback" for this deal, though, was to give Inoki and his promotion a "rub" that would help keep him on par with Baba. The first of these overtures was for Pat Patterson to go to Japan and "lose" the North American title (which Patterson was no longer defending since Vince Sr. had renamed it the Intercontinental Heavyweight Championship) to Seiji Sakaguchi—one of Inoki's best hands.

But there was more to come.

Vince Sr. approached me at the Hamburg television taping on November 14, 1979, and told me I would drop the belt to Inoki on my next tour of Japan, that I would get it back at the end of the tour, and that it would be a quiet little thing he was doing to help Inoki and further the WWF's business relationship with New Japan. I didn't have any problem with Vince's request–Antonio and I had already had several matches in Japan, and there wasn't a whole lot more we could do if we didn't do a title change to keep things interesting. Vince Sr. didn't tell me anything about how I was going to lose the belt, or how I was going to get it back—he simply told me that it would all be worked out when I got over there—that Arnold Skaaland would be coming with me and handling the business end of things, and that I could trust the New Japan promoters to handle things properly.

The chosen night was November 30, 1979, the first night of the tour, in Tokusimaat the City Gymnasium. The City Gym wasn't a very big place—about the size of a small college fieldhouse. There were a few bleachers and then a lot of chairs lined up in rows on the floor. I presume the promoters chose this building because it happened to have been the first venue booked on the tour, and they wanted to give Antonio as much time and exposure with the belt as possible.

Unlike in the United States—where the promoters would usually bring the wrestlers together to discuss the finish—over in Japan, word just got passed along to you. In this particular case, it has all been worked out between Hisashi Shinma, representing New Japan, and Arnold Skaaland, representing Vince Sr. Arnold explained to me that we were going to do a false finish where I caught Antonio in the atomic kneedrop and pinned him for what I thought was a count of three—but he would have his leg on the rope and I wouldn't notice. I was to pop up, throw my hands in the air and let my guard down, as Antonio, who knew he had his foot on the ropes, would get up, get behind me, and deliver a vicious suplex that would catch me off guard, knock the wind out of me, and allow him to pin me for a three count. It was a very believable finish—and one that was very respectful to me, so I was enthusiastic about making it look good.

It felt a little strange to allow myself to be pinned and to give up the WWF title, but I had lost the Western States belt, and had lost the Missouri State Championship to Jack Brisco in St. Louis, so losing a belt wasn't a completely foreign feeling. It would be good for our business over in Japan, which, in turn, would help the WWF overall, so I was happy to do it.

My match with Antonio that night was one of our better ones. Inoki spoke little English—but he was a great performer and was always very attuned to what was going on in the ring, so we never needed to talk about much. He was easy to work with and very loose and flexible, so I could do just about anything I wanted to do with him. We did a lot of back-and-forth and switching, and we definitely had the fans engaged in the match. I hit the atomic drop and pinned Inoki for what I "thought" was a three count. I jumped up and started celebrating—and did not notice the referee waving off the pin, or Antonio getting up. When he suddenly suplexed me hard to the mat and got the three count on me—it was completely conceivable that I would have had the wind knocked out of me, having dropped my guard.

The crowd, of course, was totally stunned—and I worked to sell the pin as a screwjob as best I could. In the ring, I worked to give the impression something had gone wrong, pushing the refs and the other officials in the ring, and imploring Arnold to stop what was happening. In fact, after the match that night, I actually ran around the public areas of the building trying to convince people I had been robbed of the belt. I'm not a good actor, so I needed to convince myself this had actually *been* a screwjob, and to do what I would have done if the title had actually been stolen from me.

Even as I left the arena to board the bus, I was still ranting and raving about how I had been robbed because there were a lot of fans gathered there. It wouldn't have made any sense if those fans saw me laughing with the boys or acting as if nothing out of the ordinary had happened. In their eyes, I had just been jobbed out of the world heavyweight championship, so I had to appear to be very upset until there was no one left to see me. Normally, as you are leaving the ring, you continue to sell whatever happened in the ring until you are out of sight of the fans, and then you can just turn it off and resume your normal life. But that night was different, because we had something serious to sell to people. I carried on yet again once I got to the hotel where I was staying that night. I wanted everyone who came into contact with me that night to be convinced that I appeared to be upset and distraught, and to spread that word to their family and friends in Japan. I've even had some fun toying with people over the years at fan conventions by continuing to play up the idea that the "screwjob" over there was real just to see how far I could run with it.

But I guess this is the time to finally put that old chestnut to rest. There was no screwjob that night in Tokusima. The switch to Inoki in Japan was very much a planned and orchestrated event to give him the same kind of "rub" that Jack Brisco had given Baba by dropping the NWA World Title to him.

After Inoki beat me that night, he ran with the title for the full length of the tour. In his first title defense, Inoki defended the WWF title against former WWF champion Pedro Morales, who was *also* asked to do the honors for Inoki. Like the consummate pro that Pedro was, he graciously agreed to follow suit—which was a pretty big deal as well. You can count on one hand the number of times you saw Pedro Morales get pinned in that era—and to have the same guy pin both Backlund and Morales in the same week gives you a pretty good idea of how committed Vince Sr. was to this new Japanese partnership.

The Japanese tour ended at Sumo Hall in Tokyo on December 6, 1979. The booked finish that night was for me to come off the top rope with a high spot and pin Inoki, who was going to be distracted by outside interference from Tiger Jeet Singh. That would allow Inoki to "lose with dignity" rather than taking a straight pinfall loss in the middle of the ring in his home arena. They also did an additional little swerve with "WWF President" Hisashi Shimna coming into the ring in Japan and "overruling" the referee's decision, declaring the bout a no-contest, and declaring the title vacant. Antonio and I had done great business together over in Japan, and this was a continuing effort to try and set up a little something for later.

Both Inoki and the New Japan promoters wanted Antonio to get a main event to wrestle me for the belt at Madison Square Garden, and this was their effort to set that up. But they hadn't yet sold Vince Sr. on the idea, and Vince Sr. never mentioned to me that anything like that was in the works. They gave me the belt back because they knew I had dates to defend the belt back in the United States, and although they were angling for a match at the Garden, they weren't about to anger Vince Sr. and jeopardize their new partnership by keeping the belt and trying to hijack the holiday card at the Garden.

Inoki was a major star in Japan, but because very few people in the United States at the time had access to Japanese television, no one really knew of him over here. To get Inoki "over" for a main-event appearance at Madison Square Garden would have required Antonio to come over to the United States for a couple of television tapings so they could build him up on television as a challenger who could draw the interest of the fans in New York. That would have much been easier to do if Inoki had come in as a heel with Blassie or the Wizard as his manager, but Inoki didn't want to do that, because he was a babyface and wanted to remain so. Vince Sr., though, wasn't about to put someone that the fans didn't know into the main event at the Garden, particularly on the holiday card. So that was the stalemate that prevented a Backlund-Inoki match from ever happening at the Garden.

Even when NWA World Heavyweight Champion Harley Race came up to wrestle me at the Garden, Vince Sr. had Harley come up to Allentown and Hamburg and do a couple of television tapings first so that the fans would know who he was, and Harley Race was much better known in the United States than Inoki was. If that was what was required to promote a unification match at the Garden with the NWA World Heavyweight Champion, you can understand that it would have been impossible to have just brought Antonio over here for a match at the Garden without first explaining that he had beaten me over in Japan. But as far as Vince Sr. was concerned, the title change in Japan had "never happened." It was just business for the Japanese relationship, and he wasn't going to allow it to be exploited beyond that.

The holiday Garden card that year was on December 17, 1979, and the entire card was broadcast back to Japan. Because Antonio didn't want to come to the United States for the necessary buildup on television, and because Antonio, who was the head of New Japan, didn't want to get beat in Madison Square Garden, there was no way to settle the title "vacancy" in a way that satisfied anyone. I would love to know what the Japanese guys were saying on their television broadcast to try and explain this situation to their fans.

During the pre-match preparations (and despite the fact that I had been defending the belt around the territory since I had returned from Tokyo ten days earlier), Vince Sr. told me that since the broadcast of the card was going back to Japan, I couldn't go to the ring with the belt because in the eyes of the Japanese fans, the title was still vacant. So the "President" of the WWF, Hisashi Shinma, came out to the ring with the WWF World Title at the beginning of my Texas Death Match main-event rematch with Bobby Duncam. Antonio was on the card and was put into a match with the Great Hussein Arab (The Iron Sheik) in a match for

Inoki's New Japan Heavyweight championship, while I took care of Duncam in the Texas Death main event.

Putting Inoki in the ring with the Sheik was the easiest way to ensure that Inoki would be given a hero's welcome at the Garden. Remember that at the time, Iran and the Ayatollah Khomeini were holding 212 American hostages. The Sheik was from Teheran, both legitimately and for purposes of the storyline, and was so hot at the time that a lot of promoters didn't even want to book him for fear that he would spark riots and violence in the arenas. Anyone who opposed the Sheik would be a guaranteed fan favorite at the Garden, so that's what Vince Sr. decided to do with Inoki.

Sheik made Antonio look really good for the Madison Square Garden crowd, but even with that and the whole hostage crisis fueling the fans' hatred of the Sheik, Antonio got only a modest reaction from the sellout crowd at the Garden—reinforcing Vince Sr.'s initial instinct to refuse him a main event against me for the WWF title.

19

An Olympian, a Drill Sergeant, and a Young Hulkster (1980)

"There will be other generations after ours. . . . We must all become bridge builders."

—Napoleon Hill, "Inspire Teamwork"

—◆—

As 1980 began, former WWF champion Bruno Sammartino had healed from the injuries stemming from his many years out on the road and had expressed interest in having one more go-round out on the WWF circuit. At the time, Bruno was announcing with Vince McMahon Jr. on the WWF Championship Wrestling and All-Star Wrestling television tapings and Bruno's old protégé, Larry Zbyszko was back in the territory as a babyface—and Bruno wanted to do something with Larry. So Bruno came up with what was, perhaps, the greatest single angle in the history of professional wrestling. It was, of course, a tale as old as time—an angle with its roots in the Biblical story of Jesus and Judas—and summed up in a single word.

Betrayal.

As the story went, Bruno had taken Larry under his wing and trained him. But Larry was frustrated that he was unable to step out from under Bruno's considerable shadow. So at the television tapings in January 1980, Larry challenged Bruno to an exhibition match, and when Bruno demurred, Larry threatened to retire if Bruno did not agree to meet him in the ring. Bruno relented, and the match that Larry "wanted" took place at the television taping on January 22, 1980, in Allentown.

After Bruno dominated Larry with a series of amateur moves, each time choosing to release the holds and to allow Larry to escape, Zbyszko's frustration began to boil over and he jumped out of the ring to collect himself. As Sammartino held the ropes open in a gesture of sportsmanship to allow Larry back into the ring, Larry hit Sammartino with a knee to the midsection, and then began punching and kicking Bruno. The crowd in the arena was stunned into silence as Larry then went outside the ring, brought a wooden ringside chair into the ring, threw referee Dick Woherlie out of the ring, and then waffled Sammartino over the head three times with the chair. Bruno went down, bladed, and Larry then left his mentor lying in the ring a pool of his own blood.

That angle, of course, immediately turned Zbyszko into the hottest heel in the federation, and the Sammartino-Zbyszko feud was off and running. Those two went around the territory and main-evented or co-main-evented buildings with me from February until August. It was a wonderful way to give Bruno one more big run around the territory, and of course, doing business like that was also great for Larry, and for the entire troupe. That feud defined the year.

Meanwhile, my old friend Ken Patera had returned to the territory, managed by the Grand Wizard, and was once again being built up on television as a monster heel. At the time, Kenny was legitimately still one of the strongest men in the world, and was one of those perfect heels who had a great look, excellent in-ring skills, and a cocky persona that could talk people into the seats. Patera had worked hard in the territory before main-eventing with Bruno when Bruno had the belt, and although he was disappointed that he hadn't gotten his promised run with the heavyweight championship when it came time to take the title off of Bruno (that honor, of course, going to "Superstar" Billy Graham in large part due to the insistence of Eddie Graham), Patera had done me the great honor of making me look so good in our matches in 1977, and again by selling for me so convincingly in one of my first title defenses in the Garden in 1978. Vince Sr. also liked Patera a lot and admired his professionalism enough to reward him with another long run in the WWF. I was determined to return the favor for what Kenny had done for me, and to do everything in my power to make our series together in 1980 a huge box office success.

We had our first match at the Garden on January 21, 1980. Patera had been injuring people on television with his swinging neckbreaker submission hold, and that, coupled with the great job he did in his interviews, led to the Garden selling out well in advance of the night of the match. We knew we would be coming back in February, so Vince Sr. booked our first bout to end inconclusively with the referee getting knocked out and the bout being declared a draw.

I met and talked with Kevin Von Erich in the Garden that night. Vince Sr. brought him in as a favor to his father Fritz and to give Kevin the exposure that came with having a match at Madison Square Garden and getting photographed by the national and international press that was always at ringside there. It was the goal of virtually every wrestler in the business to have a match at the Garden because it was the biggest stage in our industry. Fritz owned the World Class Championship Wrestling territory in the Dallas–Forth Worth area of Texas where his sons, David, Kerry, and Kevin were the resident and extremely popular babyfaces. Kevin was a very nice young man who was very personable and very respectful to everyone in the dressing room, and to the business as a whole. I welcomed him to New York and tried to make him feel comfortable since he didn't know any of the guys in the dressing room. Kevin was good for the business—he looked great and could really move in the ring.

On February 7, 1980, in Worcester, at the War Memorial Auditorium, I had my first match with the newest member of Freddie Blassie's army—a man who had debuted on television a couple of months earlier, and who had been built up on television to be an insurmountable heel. He was put together, standing about six feet ten inches tall and weighing 320 pounds. He had massive quads, a huge chest, twenty-four-inch biceps, bleached blonde hair, and a deep California tan. And he was not only undefeated, he had been virtually untouched since his debut in the federation.

This man, of course, was Hulk Hogan.

Hogan had been the bassist in a band down in Florida in the early '70s when he was discovered by Jack and Jerry Brisco. He had absolutely no wrestling experience then, but with his height and physique, he had the "look" that promoters longed for, so the Briscos arranged for Hiro Matsuda to train him. Contrary to what a lot of people have said about him, by the time he got to me in 1980, Hogan was actually decent in the ring—he was not clumsy or awkward, and, most importantly given his strength and size, he was mindful of taking care of his opponents in the ring. You could tell that he was still green, but knowing that Matsuda had trained him, I was comfortable working with him.

Hogan followed instructions well, and we told a pretty good story together that night in Worcester. It was a good crowd to have him learn in front of because of the way the place was constructed, with a balcony that put people right over the ring, so we could easily tell what they liked and didn't like. Hogan didn't have a wide variety of moves in his repertoire, so there wasn't that much that he could do—but he had a few go-to moves that he could use to draw people in.

For the most part, our matches together were novelty acts for the promoters, pitting me, as the champion, against the seemingly insurmountable giant heel. Given Hogan's relative lack of experience and his limited array of moves, our matches in 1980 followed the quintessential "big man" blueprint: him trying to beat me into oblivion, and me trying to avoid him and tire him out with whatever amateur moves I could get on him.

Although I was happy to work with Hogan, Vince Sr. saw only one real commercial purpose for Hulk Hogan in the WWF in 1980—and that was to feed him to Andre. Consequently, because Vince Sr. wanted to leave the heat on Hogan so he could draw in his feud with Andre, I wrestled Hogan only sparingly, mainly to continue to train him and to teach him how to work longer main-event matches. Where I did wrestle him, we generally went to countout finishes to leave him strong for his upcoming series with Andre.

One of those nights was on April 12, 1980, at the Spectrum in Philadelphia. That night, I was teaching Hogan how to listen to the crowd and develop a match. I called most of the spots, but I took him twenty-nine minutes deep into the match, showed him how to set the pace, and how to trade the lead. The match was well developed and we actually did a lot of wrestling maneuvers. To Hogan's credit, he was in shape and did not blow up, and per the booking, as he had done in Worcester, he went over me when I was counted out of the ring, permitting him to keep his heat, but allowing me to keep the title.

Hulk looked good, the crowd was into it, and we actually had a lot of fun in there together. After the match, I found Hogan in the dressing room and checked in with him. He shook my hand and thanked me for a great match. I remember that night clearly because Hogan wrestled in a style that wasn't his own—it was mine—and he followed my lead really well. It was a long match for him—a lot longer than he had ever been in the ring before—and he carried through it very well. The fans responded well enough to the match that Phil Zacko ordered up a rematch for the following month.

Meanwhile, after Patera and I had our second match at the Garden in February, which I won after special guest referee Pat Patterson counted Kenny out of the ring—Patera and I took a two-month hiatus from our series at the Garden. Bruno and Larry's feud had developed from that angle on television into the hottest feud the WWF had ever seen. I was in those arenas on the nights when Bruno and Larry wrestled, so I know how white hot the crowd reaction was. Bruno was adored by the vast majority of the people, and Larry's actions made Larry the most hated person in the building every night. It was a beautiful thing for Bruno to go out on, it was great for business, and it made everyone a lot of money.

Bruno and Larry's feud was a reliable enough draw to sell out any building in the territory, and they had been booked into the Garden for both March and April, so Vince saw no need for me to kill off Patera on a Garden card that was going to sell out anyway. Meanwhile, Vince had decided to put the tag-team belts on the Samoans later in the spring, so he decided to break up Afa and Sika into title matches with me in March and April 1980 in order to give each of them a nice payday on the March and April Garden cards (as well as in most of the main events around the horn) during the months when Bruno and Larry would be headlining.

Despite their wild and frightening appearance, Afa and Sika were kind and warm-hearted people. No matter what was happening around them, they were always calm and relaxed, and would do anything for you. Legitimate Samoans, they still had a lot of the worry-free island mind-set. They were most interested in enjoying today and would worry about tomorrow, tomorrow. They traveled in a converted van with a door on the back that gave them access to a sleeping area, and they also kept a pet python in the back of the van that they would bring out on occasion when they wanted to get a laugh.

The Samoans were booked as monsters. Over 300 pounds each with huge, wild afros, they were both very powerful and very credible. The fans were scared to death of those guys. You could see the fans shrink away when Afa and Sika would walk into an arena, or especially when one of them ended up out of the ring and out in the ringside area near the fans — but when you tied up with them in the ring, they were among the gentlest guys in the business. Afa and Sika were a great and very convincing heel tag team, and were very "over" with the fans.

On March 7, 1980, I had the privilege of traveling back out to St. Louis for Sam Muchnick to defend the WWF Championship at the Kiel Auditorium against my old mentor "Captain Redneck" Dick Murdoch. I was very happy to have this match, and to finally be able to return a favor to Dick after all that he had done for me back in Amarillo.

It was great to return to St. Louis to have a match with Murdoch in a place where he was well known and didn't need any buildup or any introduction. It was booked as a title match for the WWF championship, which gave Dick a nice payday. I had gained a lot more experience and wisdom both inside and outside the ring since we had last been together, but getting back into the ring with my old mentor and teacher brought back a lot of good memories for me. We had a great match together that ended with Dick getting disqualified. Back in the dressing room after the match, Dick and I visited for a little while and reminisced about our days together in Amarillo. He still seemed sad to me, but try as I might, I could never get him to tell me why.

The month of April 1980 saw a lot of changes in the WWF. First, at the April 12 Spectrum card that Hulk Hogan and I co-headlined with Bruno and Larry, the Samoans beat Tito Santana and Ivan Putski for the tag-team titles to begin their first run with those belts. Then, on April 21 at the Garden, Ken Patera beat Pat Patterson for the Intercontinental Heavyweight Championship on the undercard of a bill that featured Bruno beating Larry by countout and me defending the world title against Afa—who was now a champion in his own right as the co-holder of the world tag-team championship.

Jim Crockett's prized new tag team of Ricky Steamboat and Jay Youngblood came in for a shot on that same card. I knew Ricky Steamboat from my time in Florida. He was a very good performer in the ring and did a lot of terrific business for the Crockets down in the Carolinas. Steamboat was a big draw, and he and Ric Flair had some tremendous matches down there in the Mid-Atlantic region. Having these guys get some national and international exposure the Garden and go over a couple of our more aging heels (Kamata and Brower) was another one-time thing that Vince Sr. did as a favor to the Crocketts at a time when there was still a pretty open talent trade between the territories.

I was likewise being sent to defend the title in St. Louis and Florida a lot, where the fans were familiar with me, and their talent was coming out to New York, both for one-off matches, and in the case of heels, in regular rotations to give me a continually fresh supply of guys to wrestle. Vince was still on the NWA Board at the time, and as I have mentioned before, he had a lot of friends in the wrestling world because he was so willing to trade talent, or send me down to help draw a house or lend prestige to a card by defending the WWF title.

Five days after *that*—on April 25, newly crowned WWF Intercontinental Champion Ken Patera and I traveled out to St. Louis for Sam Muchnick. There, Patera defeated Kevin Von Erich to become the Missouri State Heavyweight Champion on the undercard of the Harley Race—Ric Flair NWA World Title match. On that same card in St. Louis, I defended the WWF title over Bulldog Bob Brown in a match that got me a little bit of revenge over the man who had beaten me in my first-ever appearance there.

So now, with Patera in place as the new Intercontinental Champion in the WWF (and the NWA's Missouri Champion at the same time, although that fact was never mentioned in the WWF), our rematch at the Garden would take on added importance. The match would be again be a clash of the federation's two top singles champions—the first time that had happened since I defeated Pat Patterson in the steel cage at the Garden back in September 1979. The match was booked as a Texas Death Match three months in the making because we had already done two inconclusive finishes at the Garden in January and February.

Kenny and I went at it full force that night, and together, we had the Garden rocking. As it was with a steel cage match, in a Texas Death Match, where there were no countouts, no disqualifications, no blood stoppages, and no holds barred, you had to give the fans what they came to see. That meant that you had to be out of the ring, punching and kicking and brawling and ramming each other into the barriers and ringposts and steps, and hitting each other with chairs. At one point, Kenny grabbed the title belt from Arnold Skaaland and hit me with it and I went down and bladed pretty deep and got a lot of color. Later in the match, after we played off a couple of near falls that had the fans screaming, I mounted a comeback and threw Kenny over the top rope, banged his head into the steel barrier, and rammed him into the ringpost. He went down and bladed also — causing his bleached blonde hair to go crimson red with his blood and sweat. That was what a Texas Death Match was about — it was a battle until one man could not continue, and it brought out the sadistic side of the wrestling fans and really got them going.

I don't know if that match is available on the WWE channel, but if it is, watch it and see how loud the Garden crowd got that night. That was the sign of the culmination of a really hot feud. When you can get the fans that high just through the story you are telling in the ring, well, it just doesn't get any better than that!

When we had built the crowd up to a total frenzy, Patera called for the finish. He climbed to the top turnbuckle, but I caught him up there and threw him off the top turnbuckle and down to the mat. We then went outside the ring, where we fought over a chair. One of us threw the chair into the ring. Once back in the ring, we fought over the chair, each of us getting an exhausted swing at the other with it, as we teased the fans and tantalizingly drew out the finish for another minute.

Up to that point in my career, I don't think I had ever heard the fans that into a match before. The people that night were climbing the walls, and reacting to our every move. I finally got the chair away from Patera and waffled him with it. Patera's knees buckled and he crumpled to the mat and I fell on him and the referee counted to two and a half before Patera slipped the shoulder out the back door teasing the fans one last time. Kenny had put on an absolutely masterful performance, and it was only fitting that a great wrestler and a great champion like Patera should be allowed to keep his heat that way. Even a direct shot to the head with a chair couldn't stop him.

But now it was time to go home.

I climbed up to the top rope as Patera staggered around the ring, and with the fans jumping out of their seats, jumping up and down, and gesturing wildly at me, I hit him with a bodyblock off the top rope and came down hard on top of him. The referee and about 22,000 fans all counted "one, two, three" in unison as I pinned him in the middle of the ring for the three count, and then the place just erupted.

I had given Kenny a lot of that match. He had me bleeding from the head and the nose, beat me from pillar to post, and, in the eyes of the fans at the Garden that night, took me to within an inch of winning the belt. It had been the greatest war that the fans at the Garden had seen me in, and there was no question that Patera left the ring that night, not just with his Intercontinental title, but with his heat still fully intact.

Patera and I took that feud around the horn, and the promoters and the fans just ate that series up. Kenny was one of my all-time favorite guys to wrestle, and we drew some great houses all over the territory. He is also

a very funny guy and one of the few guys in the business who I still keep in touch with and talk to from time to time.

It's Howdy Doody Time

McMahon Sr. and the other office guys created a new belt—which they called the Intercontinental Heavyweight Championship. They gave it to Patterson to start off with. He was the North American Champion, but somehow, that name just didn't have the same ring to it—so they got him a beautiful new belt and renamed it the Intercontinental Championship, and claimed that he had won it in some tournament in Rio De Janeiro or some such thing. Well Patterson had just come off his long series with Bobby, split with the Grand Wizard, and had become a pretty hot babyface as a result. And I, of course, was managed by the Grand Wizard, so that added an element of revenge to the whole thing. The plan was never to have Patterson hold that belt for long—they created that new belt for me to appease me and to give me the title run that I had been promised back when Sammartino was still champion. I left after they put the belt on Billy Graham and then switched it to Bobby and screwed me over. So I went down to work for Crockett in the Carolinas for a while, and then one day, Vince Sr. called me with this plan to put a new belt on me, and promised me a good run with Bobby, so I came back. So as I said, I had the Wizard as my manager, and the whole thing had a nice setup, and I was booked to destroy Patterson at the Garden and take the Intercontinental Championship belt from him, and then to be booked to seem unstoppable to set up my series of matches with Bobby.

Bobby had had the belt for a couple of years by that point, and you know what? He had really gotten himself over with the fans. I know that some of the boys in the locker room liked to try and say that Bobby wasn't over with the fans, and he wasn't a draw, and all that sort of stuff, but I can tell you, Bobby was over. People were just jealous. You know how it is? Let's say there are three or four guys in the running to become the CEO of a large company. Only one of them is going to get it. So the other two or three are either going to immediately start to try to undermine him, or they're going to leave the company and go elsewhere. That's just the way it is. It's human nature. And it's the same thing in the wrestling business. I never got involved in that stuff, because that's a dead end road—if you start to go behind people's backs and start knocking them in a serious way—not in a kidding way like we did with the whole Howdy Doody thing—but in a serious way, you wind up being the loser. So I never got involved in that shit.

I'll tell you what, if Bobby wasn't over, he wouldn't have been selling out all of the big buildings in the territory—and we were selling out everywhere. I was in a lot of those buildings with him, and you know, when Bobby would come out, he had that habit of jumping around in the ring and stuff, and the crowds would really pop for him. Meanwhile, back in the dressing room, every time Bobby would go out, there were a couple of people who would start singing, "It's Howdy Doody time, it's Howdy Doody time." And I just couldn't keep a straight face because it was funny. The Wizard was the one who started that—and that's all he had to say to get people going. But where the stories tend to go off the rails a little is that it wasn't a malicious sort of thing against Bobby—it was more just the boys ribbing Bobby a little bit because of his squeaky clean golly gee aw shucks Midwestern image. But believe me, everyone was grateful for the business we were doing.

I remember at our first show at the Civic Center in Baltimore in 1980, Larry and Bruno had main-evented the building in their first match down there and hadn't sold out the building. Then Bobby and I were scheduled to main-event the building the next month. So Zbyszko was running his mouth to me in the locker room somewhere talking about the next show in Baltimore and he guaranteed me that Bobby and I wouldn't come close to selling that place out. I reminded him that he and Bruno hadn't sold it out either. Well wouldn't you know, when Bobby and I went in there, Phil Zacko told me there were something like 35 tickets left in the entire building. I asked him how many had been left the month before with Bruno and Larry's first match, and he told me it was 600 anyway. And it was that way all over the place. Bruno and Zbyszko would go in and do their routine, and they would draw well, don't get me wrong, but

when Bobby and I would go in the month after and start our series, we outdrew them every time.

—Ken Patera

Asses in the Seats
There were a lot of guys in the business who if you had a top position—they wanted it. Bob was young, and some of the old timers

didn't love the idea of Bob coming in and getting a big push and getting the belt and making a lot of money. Some of the guys thought they should have gotten that run simply because they had been around longer. Bob also never partied with the boys, he never took drugs, he was always reliable and didn't cause any trouble, and they resented all of that, and the inner strength that he had. What they didn't realize was that the promoters didn't base your position on the card by your age — they based it on how many asses you could put in the seats. You can be the greatest athlete in the world, but if you can't put asses in the seats, the promoter had no use for you.

When I was in the WWF, Bob was the champion because he sold out buildings. That's why he was champion. If nobody was paying to see Bob Backlund, he would never have gotten the belt — and if people didn't keep paying to see Bob Backlund wrestle, he would never have kept the belt. The reason why Bob Backlund was

champion for six years was because he was consistently and reliably putting asses in the seats.

— "Mr. USA" Tony Atlas

After that match with Patera, I took off for a two-week tour of Japan. This was the one and only trip I took to Japan where Corki joined me — something she regretted almost immediately. That was the tour that featured one of the craziest and most interesting matches of my wrestling career — the night that I defended the WWF title against "The American Dream" Dusty Rhodes. It would also be the last time that Corki ever attended one of my matches.

Hisashi Shinma (the booker for Antonio Inoki's New Japan promotion) decided to put Dusty and me together in a main event for the WWF championship in Osaka on May 27, 1980. New Japan's bookers could always be counted on to pair two American "Gaijin" (outsiders) together, either in a tag team against two Japanese wrestlers, or against each other, regardless of whether that matchup would make any booking sense in the United States. This was the one and only time Dusty Rhodes and I ever wrestled each other. We were also on neutral ground, which made what happened that night especially fascinating.

Dusty and I didn't get together to talk things over before the match that night, but we'd watched each other a lot both in our days in Florida and Georgia and on previous Japanese tours, so we both knew what we wanted to do. The Japanese fans had always appreciated my scientific, amateur style in the ring, and had supported me wholeheartedly. Dusty, likewise, was hugely over as a babyface in Japan. So that night, we resolved to listen to the crowd in Osaka and let *them* determine what they wanted to have happen.

Japan was a funny place. You just didn't know what to expect. We were both anxious to see what the fans would do with us.

When our match was called, Dusty came charging through the crowd into the ring in his beautiful black and white robe, and he had the fans all over him, patting him on the back and reaching out to touch him. He got a big, roaring ovation. There was no doubt that the fans viewed Dusty as a babyface at the beginning of the match. I came out to the ring second, displaying the WWF title belt around my waist, and got a similar reception from the crowd.

We came together in the center of the ring, and our hosts played the Star-Spangled Banner and presented us both with huge bouquets of flowers, as was the Japanese tradition prior to the main event of the evening. During the pre-match announcements, it was very hard to tell who got the bigger ovation from the crowd, Dusty or me. We shook hands enthusiastically in the middle of the ring, the crowd cheered in appreciation, and we were off.

For the first couple of minutes of the match, we did a nice sequence of amateur moves, with go-behinds and switches, with both of us returning to our feet in the ready position. From the very beginning of the match, though, you could sense a strange sort of tension in the building. I don't think the fans were entirely happy to see two of their biggest heroes facing off against each other. As we went on, working off a series of armholds, I got the upper hand, and Dusty feigned frustration. There was a point, still early in the match, where Dusty pushed me into the ropes and instead of giving me an immediate clean break, as the fans might have expected him to, Dusty held me there for an extra beat and I threw my guard up. It was a tease, and just for a second, but with that very subtle little extra beat of time, we dramatically increased the tension in the crowd. You could almost hear the fans draw and hold a breath. When Dusty then broke clean, the relieved fans exhaled, applauded in appreciation, and the match continued. Shortly thereafter, I pushed Dusty into the ropes and likewise broke cleanly.

We were testing the fans to see which way they wanted us to go.

They hadn't decided yet.

We then took it to the mat for several minutes, with Dusty taking control with a series of leg holds, elbowdrops to my legs, and leg scissors, with me trying to escape. It was a pretty good display of mat wrestling that had the fans watching intently, so we kept that going. Eventually, I escaped the leghold and reversed things, and took command with a series of legholds of my own. Dusty, however, couldn't break out of these holds by using counters as I had done, and again showed his "frustration." Since he couldn't escape using a counter, he poked me in the eyes instead, which made me break, and then we rose to our feet.

The fans saw that Dusty had cut a corner, and a few of them began to jeer. He showed them a couple of bionic elbows, which made them cheer temporarily, since they had seen him use that move so many times as a hero. He followed with a series of punches, and we went back to the mat with Dusty in control using a chinlock to wear me down. I rallied, shaking my arms to see if I could get the crowd behind me, and suddenly, the crowd was cheering and chanting, "Bob-by! Bob-by!" as I rose to my feet. Dusty played off it perfectly, jerking his head from side to side, looking at the crowd with a look of complete betrayal on his face, as if he could not understand how or why the fans would be cheering for someone to make a comeback on him.

The crowd in Osaka had made its decision.

We clinched closely, head-to-head and called a high spot. Dusty threw me into the turnbuckle, I came out, and he caught me in a body-slam, but I kicked my feet furiously and fell on him for a count of two and a near fall. The crowd cheered, confirming what we thought was going on.

They wanted Dusty to play the heel.

I got to my feet before Dusty, who was pretty gassed by that point, and got behind him and picked him up for my finisher—the atomic kneedrop. Dusty, who was around three hundred pounds at that point, sold it perfectly, waving his arms around as I hoisted him up and carried him around the ring before smashing him into my knee. He dropped next to the ropes and clung to them like a baby would cling to a blanket, preventing me from going for the pin.

The crowd was roaring.

I got up and hit a piledriver on Dusty in the middle of the ring. He slipped out at the count of two and a half. We criss-crossed into the ropes and slammed into each other. I fell backward and Dusty wobbled before crashing down himself, but managed to drape an arm across my shoulders as the referee counted. Another near fall, as I kicked out at two.

Three more false finishes followed in quick succession. First, Dusty tried for a vertical suplex, which I spun out of. Next, I got behind Dusty and pushed him into the ropes for the rolling reverse with the bridge— which I had used to pin many opponents in Japan—but Dusty hung on the ropes causing me to crash backward onto my head. Then Dusty went for his figure-four leglock, and I kicked him off at the last second—and he ran right into the referee and knocked him down.

Had Dusty struck the referee on purpose? Had I kicked him off into the referee by accident? The spot had come off perfectly, so it was nearly impossible for the fans to tell.

I rose, dropkicked Dusty out of the ring, and went over to "check" on the referee. As I did, Dusty pulled me out of the ring by the leg, and declared himself a full convert to the heel side (at least for that night) by slamming me into the ring steps, and then smashing my head into the iron ringpost that held the ropes and turnbuckles together. The fans watched in stunned silence as I collapsed to the arena floor, my head hidden in my hands so I could "get color." Dusty showed the blood to the fans by holding my head back and dropping an elbow right on the cut and helping the blood to mix with my sweat to give me a better "crimson mask."

Dusty threw me back into the ring and the crowd cheered, relieved that the match wasn't going to end on a countout. Dusty threw his hand in the air and the crowd cheered momentarily—but he then swerved them and played another heel card, scooping me up, trapping me upside down in the cornerbuckles, and kicking and stomping away. The crowd jeered. The referee stepped in to break it up, and Dusty threw him aside and down to the canvas. The ref signaled for the bell and called for the disqualification.

Dusty raised his arms in the air and the crowd met him with . . . silence. The crowd in Osaka was totally stunned by their hero's heel turn. He walked around and raised his arms to another part of the crowd.

Silence.

Meanwhile, I slammed the mat and rose to my feet with fists clenched, and the crowd roared in approval. Dusty backed off into the corner and threw his arms in the air.

"Hey, Bobby . . . Bobby . . . whoa now . . ."

Far too late for apologies, I kicked Dusty hard in the gut, tossed him out of the ring and returned the favor by slamming his head into the ringpost and he likewise collapsed to the floor to get color.

I picked him up and we battled outside the ring, both of us now bleeding profusely and mugging for the legion of Japanese photographers who were blinding us with their flashbulbs—two of the biggest American babyfaces beating the living daylights out of each other and bleeding like stuck pigs in Japan. It was definitely a moment for the magazines. What in the world would they say about this back in the United States?

We brawled in the ring until we were pulled apart—both of us asking the referee for five more minutes, and teasing a restart. The cheering crowd implored the referee to allow it, but then Dusty bailed out. I grabbed the belt and held it out for him to see and yelled, "Come on Rhodes—come and get it!" and the crowd roared again.

Dusty and I had the place eating out of our hands.

Dusty then retreated from the ring area to a chorus of boos and the ring announcer made the announcement that I had retained the world title on a disqualification. The fans rushed the ring as I was presented with the winner's trophy and cheered wildly as I lifted it above my head and played it up to the fans.

The match had gone wonderfully, due largely to Dusty's brilliant swerve in adopting the heel role mid-match with such conviction. Not everyone would have been willing to risk their fan base in Japan to make a match—but Dusty was confident enough to do so—which is a huge credit to him. It certainly made for one of the most memorable matches of my career.

Dusty and I would cross paths wrestling on the same cards both in the WWF and in other places many more times in our careers—always with a kind word, a fond recollection of that night in Osaka, and a healthy respect for one another. But we would never wrestle each other again.

Corki found it particularly distressing that Dusty and I were bleeding all over the place. On that same tour, Andre the Giant and Stan Hansen wrestled and caused a near riot in the crowd. Corki was sitting near the announcer's table when Andre and Hansen spilled out of the ring and started brawling in the ringside area. The match ended with Andre outside the ring running around throwing chairs and chasing Hansen through the ringside seats, which caused the people to jump all over each other to get away from him. Corki got caught in the chaos out there and nearly got trampled. So suffice it to say, Corki stayed back at the hotel for the remainder of the tour rather than coming to the matches, and she never went back with me to Japan.

Upon my return to the United States, I faced Larry Zbyszko in a world title match at Madison Square Garden on the June 16, 1980, card. I liked Larry a lot—he was great in the amateur style and could really move in the ring, and he was a master of ring psychology. There were few people better at getting the fans truly aggravated with him than Larry—which made wrestling him all the more fun. As I recall, we started by just having a really good wrestling match with good pacing and mirroring what Bruno and Larry had done on television with Larry getting frustrated that he "couldn't keep up" with my amateur moves, and resorting to cheating and jumping in and out of the ring. He eventually rammed my head into the ringpost, and stole a cheap win via a blood stoppage so he could keep his heat for his main-event Shea Stadium cage match with Bruno in August.

I was looking forward to working more with Larry at the Garden after the Shea Stadium card, but it never happened. Larry and Vince Sr. had some kind of a dispute about the payoff from Shea Stadium, I think Larry said some things to Vince Sr., and after that, Vince Sr. just moved on and wouldn't give Larry another night at the Garden. I did have some great matches with Larry elsewhere around the territory, most notably in Philadelphia, where promoter Phil Zacko (and the Philly fans) liked the matchup enough to go with it three times.

On July 23, 1980, I headed down to the Convention Center in Miami to face Eddie Graham's Florida Champion, Don Muraco. Eddie explained to me that he was about give Muraco some pretty big exposure by putting him in a WWF title match with me at the Last Tangle in Tampa supercard at the football stadium, so he wanted to give us the chance to work together a little bit before that big card. The finish in Miami, with me winning by countout, allowed me to keep the title and Don to keep his heat. They didn't film that match, so the only people who saw that "rehearsal" were the people in the building that night. Don and I worked well together, though, as Eddie knew we would, and I looked forward to going back down there for the big supercard in August.

On July 30, 1980, I made a special trip to Honolulu, Hawaii, to defend the WWF championship against Wildman Austin at the Blaisdell Arena. My old friend Peter Maivia had purchased the Hawaii promotion and had almost immediately gotten into financial trouble because people had stopped coming to the matches. Peter called Vince Sr. and asked him if he would be willing to send some people out there for a big show. It was just a one-shot deal, out and back to try and help Peter out. Nick Bockwinkel defended the AWA World Title on the same card, as Verne Gagne had also responded to try and help Peter get out of financial trouble.

Two supercards were held around the wrestling world in August 1980—and I had the good fortune to be part of both of them. First, on August 3, 1980, at "The Last Tangle in Tampa" supercard promoted by Eddie Graham at Tampa Stadium in Tampa, Florida, I defended the WWWF title against Florida Champion Don Muraco. This was the rematch from our bout in Miami ten days earlier. We wrestled outside and drew just under 18,000 people—which, at the time, set a new attendance record for wrestling in the state of Florida. On the same card, Dusty Rhodes challenged Harley Race for Harley's NWA World Heavyweight Championship.

Muraco and I had another great wrestling match, which I won by disqualification after a dramatic, see-saw battle. Eddie obviously thought a lot of Don, not just because he chose to put the Florida Heavyweight Championship on him, but because right after that event, he recommended Don to Vince Sr. for a run in New York. Eddie certainly had an eye for talent. Muraco went on to be one of the very best heels to ever challenge me for the WWF title, and was the number-two man in the federation (as the Intercontinental Champion) for most of the next three years.

Even though Eddie drew a great crowd that night, I never enjoyed wrestling outside as much as I did inside. Even with 18,000 enthusiastic people packed into the lower tiers of Tampa Stadium, we didn't feel the energy and the emotion of the fans as much as we would have even in a much smaller venue because the fans were farther away. Also, in an open-air stadium, the crowd noise just dissipates up into the air rather than echoing off the walls. You also had to worry about the intense heat from wrestling in the hot Florida sun, or rain or humidity making the mat slick, which was a big injury risk for the wrestlers. That night, the card started when the sun was still out, and it was in the '90s and incredibly humid. By the time Harley and Dusty came out in the main event, the sun had set, but it was still very, very warm out, and they were scheduled to do a Broadway. I don't know how much water weight those two guys lost in that main event, but it must have been a lot. Rain was probably the biggest concern for a promoter of a big outdoor card, though. Eddie Graham had a lot of guaranteed money invested in the talent for a stacked card like the Last Tangle in Tampa. If it had rained and he didn't draw a good walkup crowd

on the night of the event, it would have been a financial disaster for the promotion. Luckily, however, the weather was good, and the event was an unqualified success.

Bleeding the Hard Way

I knew Bob from his early days down in Florida when he was down there getting some experience, but not really more than a handshake and a hello. Our first big match was at the Last Tangle in Tampa, the big outdoor show at the Tampa Stadium, and I think we drew as much of that crowd as the NWA World Title match that night. The really memorable thing about that night, though, was that Bobby and I were working hot and heavy and I was spinning around coming out of a move and I accidentally hit him just above the eye with the tip of my elbow and it split his eye open and he just started gushing blood the hard way all over the place and I was like, "Oh shit . . . there goes my chance of making it to New York!" That was the thing I remember most about that match—having the opportunity to get into the ring with the WWWF champion on the top of the card at a big show like that with all kinds of people watching and then splitting his eye open. But Bob was great about it. He just kept going like it was all part of the show.

—Don Muraco

After the Tangle, I flew back up to Connecticut and appeared on the WWF's Shea Stadium Supercard on August 9, 1980. I had first learned about that card when I picked up my bookings at the TV tapings three weeks earlier. There has always been a rumor floating around that the original plan was for Harley Race and me to meet in an NWA-WWF title unification match on the Shea Stadium card, but if that *was* ever part of the plan, neither Harley nor I ever knew anything about it. Given that Vince Sr. had Bruno and Larry in the cage on top—which could have probably drawn the house nearly by itself, I think it is very unlikely that Vince Sr. ever seriously considered that plan, because he wouldn't have wanted to "spend" a match like that on a card where he was already guaranteed a huge house. There were also eleven other matches already scheduled for the Shea card, including the big grudge match between the undefeated Andre the Giant and the undefeated Hulk Hogan, the Intercontinental title match between Patera and the undefeated "Mr. USA" Tony Atlas, and matches featuring guys from other promotions to whom Vince Sr. had promised time and exposure. The amount of time that Vince Sr. would have had to devote to a world title unification match between Harley and me that night would have made that card far too long. I found out at the television taping about a week before the event that Pedro and I would be working as a tag team at that event and challenging the previously undefeated Wild Samoans for the WWF World Tag-Team Championship.

Vince Sr. drew a terrific crowd of about 36,000 for the event at Shea—maybe 10,000 to 12,000 more fans than he could have put into the Garden and the Felt Forum. Everybody was pretty excited about the night, but there was also some friction from an ongoing disagreement that Bruno and Larry were having with Vince Sr. about the gate. There were a lot of things going on, there was a lot of press, and because of the new venue, everyone was out of their usual routine.

On the typical wrestling card, there is no one match that draws all the people—but it seems like the guy on top always gets the blame when the gate is bad. But when the gate is good, everyone gets credit. Other guys in the dressing room would comment when the crowd wasn't the best, but more often than not during the days when I was in the WWF, the crowds were good. When they were, people rarely thanked you or credited you for that outcome. I want to change that a little bit here by saying this, and hopefully putting some myths to bed.

I have read and heard Hulk Hogan say that it was his match with Andre the Giant that drew the house at Shea Stadium, and that he should get the credit for putting 36,000 butts in the seats that night. Make no mistake about this—it was Bruno and Larry's cage match fueled that tremendous gate at Shea Stadium. There were *definitely* people who came out to see the battle of the giants between Hogan and Andre, and there were a lot of people in the crowd hoping to see the unbeaten "Mr. USA" Tony Atlas win the Intercontinental Heavyweight Championship from Ken Patera. And the match pitting Pedro and me against the Samoans, two seemingly unbeatable teams in a best two out of three falls tag-team title match was interesting as well. But Bruno and Larry were the story that night, and anyone who says otherwise is just trying to re-write history.

To be completely honest with you, I would have been perfectly happy being off that night, and having an unheard-of Saturday night off to be with my family. Vince Sr., however, felt that I was his champion and since this was the WWF's Supercard, I had bet on it. Harley and I *could* have followed all of this and still gotten the people, but the name of the game is putting butts in the seats, and the fact is that the culmination of Bruno and Larry's feud in the steel cage was so hot, a world title unification match between Harley and me wasn't necessary to draw the crowd that night. The incremental gain from having that match that night would not have been worth the additional cost, nor the opportunity cost. That crowd was coming to Shea regardless, so why not hold off the world title unification match for another day when you needed it to draw?

Like September 22, 1980, at the Garden, for instance.

※

Vince never mentioned to me that Harley was coming into the territory for a world title unification match until I saw Harley walk in to the Ag Hall in Allentown for the television tapings. I was genuinely happy to see him, and very excited to learn of Vince Sr.'s plans to hold a world title unification match between us at Madison Square Garden. Harley, more than any other individual wrestler I'd been in the ring with, had helped me to hone my skills and to become what I had become in professional wrestling. I was thrilled to be able to get in the ring with him, now with both of us at the top of our profession as champions, on the greatest stage in our sport.

Whenever I got into the ring with Harley, other than knowing the booked finish, we never knew how the match was going to go, or what we were going to do, but I think both of us knew that we going to have a great match. By that point in my career, I was very confident about my

ability to control the ebb and flow of a match, and to know if someone was trying to take too much. That never happened with Harley, of course—we had known each other for a long time and trusted each other completely, so we could just settle in and focus on putting on a great match for the fans.

Never Heard a Crowd Pop Louder

The reason for the match at MSG was that Vince Sr. knew that if he brought me to the Garden, that I would go out there and have as good a match with Bobby as he could possibly have with anybody. Bobby trusted me enough, and I trusted him enough so that we could have that kind of match together without either one of us having to watch our backs or worry about the belts.

I know there have been rumors that our match was supposed to happen at Shea Stadium, but as far as I know, that match was always planned for the Garden. That was where Vince Sr. wanted his top match. The Garden always came first. He called Sam, and Vince and Sam had their discussion of how it was going to be paid, and from that, what we were going to do. From there, I got a call saying you can do this, but you can't do that, so that neither title was diminished. On the night of the match, Vince just called me and Backlund together in the dressing room at the Garden and told us to have fun out there.

Just being there in front of a crowd like that and with all the press that was in the house for that event—I knew that when I left, I was going to leave in a much better position than when I arrived. Back then, two thirds of the national press and publicity for our industry was headquartered out of New York. The people in the New York area didn't know much about who the NWA World Heavyweight Champion was, because not much of our television penetrated the New York market at that time—so that match definitely raised my credibility in the New York area. For Bobby, it got him worldwide recognition across the NWA to have a title versus title match with the NWA World Champion in his home arena. Even though we went to a finish with Bobby going over by a disqualification, the feedback after the match was exactly what I thought it would be—the way the press handled it—it was a huge positive for both of us.

And let me tell you this about Bobby—when I went into the Garden to wrestle him, I went out to the ring first, and when he came through that curtain, I don't think I have ever heard a crowd pop louder for anyone. I don't think that I have ever wrestled anyone anywhere in the world who was more over than Bobby was at the Garden. He did a great job up there during his time as champ. As to Bobby and Sammartino, it was a flip of the coin as to who was more over at the Garden. In all the places we were together, and there were a lot of them, I can never remember the people not just loving Bobby Backlund. He was always the people's favorite.

As the heel, I called every match we had. I like to look at it as devotion to the business. If I don't make my opponent look good, how the hell am I going to look good? My whole ballgame as the NWA World Heavyweight Champion was the have the best possible match I could have with anyone, everywhere I went. In most of those matches, I was going over, so why would you not want to beat someone that the people were left thinking had an excellent chance of beating you? That's what sells tickets.

I've known Bobby Backlund virtually since day one of his career. Speaking of him as a person, I don't think I've ever met a kinder, nicer person. The guy would literally do anything for you, and like me, he was all about the match, and giving people the very best wrestling match he could give them. He was a true professional. As for all of the golly gee and aw shucks stuff, don't let that fool you. I know Bobby as well as anyone in the business knows him, and Bobby Backlund was the smartest dumb-fuck you ever saw. In the ring, I don't think I've ever met anyone any tougher than Bob. He could

really take care of himself in there. I know that there have been a few people during his career who have tested Bobby out there, particularly early on, because they were deceived by his baby-faced good looks and didn't think that he could actually take care of business . . .

But I can't think of anyone who tested him twice.

—Harley Race

I could not have been happier to share the stage with Harley at the Garden and to show the fans in my home arena what a truly great wrestling match looks like. As expected, the match came off brilliantly, the fans loved it, and when it was over (I went over by disqualification when Harley hit the referee), our respective reputations had been enhanced that much more—as each of us had pushed the other to the very brink of defeat.

On October 20, 1980, I was back in the Garden facing the challenge of a new heel who had burst upon the scene in the WWWF. Managed by the Grand Wizard of Wrestling, Sergeant Slaughter had the perfect look. Standing nearly six and a half feet tall and weighing in at just shy of 300 pounds, clad in his wide brimmed hat, sunglasses, a whistle, and carrying a riding crop, Slaughter had the jaw and the nose and the look of a drill sergeant. He was the first wrestler in the WWF to come to the ring with entrance music—playing the Marine Hymn "The Halls of Montezuma" every time he would come forth from the dressing room. He also featured a hold called the "Cobra Clutch"—a form of a sleeperhold that he had been using to decimate his opponents on television. He and the Grand Wizard were also using a gimmick known as the "$5,000 Cobra Clutch Challenge" where a wrestler would sit in a chair in the ring and allow Slaughter to apply the hold, with Slaughter promising to "pay" any wrestler $5,000 if he could escape the hold.

Of course many tried but no one succeeded, the hold became one of the most feared finishers in the sport, and Slaughter quickly rose to the number-one-contender status in the federation. The fans had grown to hate Slaughter so intensely that they had taken to chanting "Gomer" at him (a reference to the bumbling marine portrayed by Jim Neighbors on the television show *Gomer Pyle, U.S.M.C.*) and carrying "Gomer" and "Sgt. Pyle" signs into the television tapings and into the arenas where Slaughter wrestled. This, of course, was manna from Heaven for Slaughter, who fed the fans' fury by putting his hands over his ears, gesturing wildly at the fans, and demanding in his interviews that they stop calling him "Gomer," which, of course, just made the fans yell it louder and with more commitment than ever. There were some arenas that we wrestled in where the chant of "Go-mer" was deafening when Slaughter came to the ring. Slaughter was absolutely the most interactive heel, in terms of his relationship with the fans, which I had wrestled to date.

Slaughter was so hot, and the Cobra Clutch was so over as a threat to my championship, that the setup for this first match didn't take very long. With Slaughter getting the title match at the top of the card, the Garden had sold out long before the night of the event, so we knew we would be coming back for a second match the following month. I think even Vince Sr., who was rarely caught flatfooted, was a little surprised at just *how much* heat Slaughter was getting with the fans. Vince thought highly of Sarge, and really wanted to go places with him. When he brought Sarge and me together for the pre-match discussion in the dressing room, Vince asked me to put the hold over cleanly.

"Bobby, Sarge is going to ram you into the post outside the ring and then take a shot at Arnold. He'll then throw you back into the ring and get you in the Cobra Clutch. It's going to look like the end, but he's going to get a little too close to the apron of the ring, and when he does, Skaaland is going to hit Sarge over the head with a chair, get you disqualified, and save your belt."

It was kind of a heelish finish for me, but justified enough by Slaughter's swipe at Skaaland to make it passable without it causing me to get heat with the fans. The match went only sixteen minutes, a very short time for a title match at the Garden, because we had the crowd in a frenzy that night. The people told us that at sixteen minutes, they were as emotionally invested in the match as they were going to get—and once you have them at that peak, there is no sense in going any further. You want to go home just at the point where you believe you have the fans' emotional reaction to the match as high as it can get.

Naturally, this finish gave Slaughter the ability to go back on television for the pre-match interviews for the following month and claim that he had been "robbed" and that I was "protected" by Skaaland, and that he would be the champion were it not for Skaaland. In fact, his comments were pretty accurate—and all of this served to draw an even *larger* crowd to the New Jersey Meadowlands arena for our eventual Texas Death rematch.

Sarge was originally from Minnesota, and was an excellent all-around athlete who played a lot of sports in high school and college, from golf to wrestling to football. He was all about the match and entertaining the people and was a truly exceptional performer in the ring. Slaughter did a lot of things well—in particular—his run into the turnbuckle, which

was just tremendous. He took good care of himself physically, stayed out of trouble, and always showed up on time ready to put on a great show. For all of those things, Slaughter got rewarded with two great tenures in the WWF in 1980–81 and in 1983–84 where, both times, he had extended main-event runs with me, and then subsequent headlining feuds with others in the federation (Patterson in 1981 and The Iron Sheik in 1984).

Call Me "Gomer"

I was brought to Allentown in late 1979 to do television tapings and promos for the WWWF TV program knowing that my first match in the territory was going to be at Madison Square Garden against Bob. I was playing a tough drill instructor, a 300-pounder who could dropkick and armdrag and telling people in the promos that I meant business and was going to take the title. Mr. McMahon just loved the Sgt. Slaughter character—he told me I was one of his favorite heels of all time. When I first got there, Mr. McMahon asked me to go out and do a promo with his son, and he asked whether there was anything he could do to help put heat on me. I went to my bag and got a cassette tape out and gave it to him. He said, "What is this?" I told him it was the Marine Corps Hymn and I asked him to play it when I went out there. He said he'd never thought about someone walking out to music before, but that he was willing to give it a try—so we tried it, and the response was overwhelming. The people didn't know me, but I walked out to that music and did the promo, and when I got back, Mr. McMahon was jingling his quarters in his hands, and said,

"That was the greatest promo I have ever seen—even my son hates you!" And that's how we started it out.

The other thing we did was during the promos, I told Bob that he should call me "Gomer" and he was like, "Gomer?" And I said, "Yeah, that's what they call a misfit in the Marine Corps—they call him Gomer." So he was doing a promo, and pointed into the camera and said, "You're just a Gomer, Sgt. Slaughter, you're a Gomer!" And then the people started chanting that, and of course, I played along, and told the people to stop calling me Gomer, and that they better not show up to the arenas with Gomer signs, and that got great heat.

The first time that Bob and I wrestled was at Madison Square Garden in the main event. I had been beating everyone on television with the Cobra Clutch, and I had promised the people that when I got it on Bob Backlund it wasn't going to be any different. Well when we got there, we had sold out not only the Garden, but the Felt Forum also. We had the match, and I got it on him at the end, and Backlund was fighting it like crazy. I had done something to "antagonize" Arnold Skaaland just before that, so he climbed up onto the apron and hit me from behind with a chair so I won that first match by disqualification.

The one thing I noticed when I first started working with Bob was that he seemed very worried that someone would try and pull a fast one on him—but after we'd had a few matches, he came to trust me, and let me be the ring general and dictate how I was going to get my heat, and that meant a lot to me. It also made for much better and high-quality matches and storytelling.

Bob was a wrestler that was a lot like John Cena is today. Most people loved him, but there were some people who hated him. But whenever I wrestled Bob, 100 percent of the people were for him, because everyone hated Sgt. Slaughter so much. Bob enjoyed that, because it allowed him to be the true babyface that he always liked to be.

Bob Backlund was also one of the most physically in-shape wrestlers of all time—he took it very seriously, worked out very hard, and was one of those guys you could really go out there and tell a great story with as a villain. We drew a lot of pretty big crowds; whether

it was in the Garden or a high school down the road, Bob and I packed them in and gave them their money's worth, entertained them and had a lot of very compelling matches. If we were on before intermission, our matches were hard for others to follow. I can remember thinking to myself on of occasions when Bob and I were on before intermission—I'd never broadcast it, but I thinking to myself, "Follow that one, boys!"

—**Sergeant Slaughter**

Meanwhile, on November 7, 1980, I had the less-well-known rematch from the September 22, 1980 Madison Square Garden world title unification bout with Harley Race. This time, the match was held in the NWA's home arena—the Kiel Auditorium in St. Louis. This match was arranged by Vince Sr. and Sam Muchnick and was intended to give Sam the reciprocal honor of hosting the world title unification match on the NWA's home turf.

St. Louis had been a key territory in my training, so I felt at home there, especially with Sam Muchnick promoting and being in the ring with Harley.

The match at the Kiel was, like many NWA World Title matches on their turf, scheduled for the best two out of three falls with a one-hour time limit. Structuring a world title match with those stipulations definitely gave the bookers more flexibility. Since the champion would have to be pinned or submit *twice* within the one-hour time limit to lose his belt, it was possible for Harley and me to trade falls during the hour, which allowed the fans to see one or both champions get pinned or submit, and greatly increased the dramatic tension for the fans.

We decided to sell each other's finishers. Harley pinned me with his vertical suplex in the first fall—which really got the people going thinking they might be watching the unification of the world championship. Harley had the background and the skills to shoot or hook if he wanted to—so this kind of match obviously required a level of trust to pull off. Because I trusted Harley and Sam completely, however, it never even entered my mind that either of them would try to put anything over on me or Vince—so allowing Harley to get the first fall on me was not a problem. With a different champion than Harley, or in a different venue with a promoter other than Sam, we might not have agreed to do that—because losing the first fall cleanly does put you at the mercy of the promoter the referee, or both, in the subsequent falls, and makes it much easier for a screwjob to actually happen.

Harley sold my finisher in the second fall with no problem, and the fans at the Kiel that night were delirious having watched two world champs pin each other on the same night. Obviously, we weren't going to unify the titles, so we needed to come up with an ending that left the people happy—so my inadvertently backdropping Harley over the top rope provided the answer, giving him the win by disqualification. It gave Harley the win on his turf, squared us up after Harley had given me the win on my turf, and allowed us both to keep our belts and our reputations intact.

After St. Louis, I did another trip to Japan—and my participation in the tour over there was important enough to Vince Sr. to cause him to permit me to miss a Garden show for the first time since I had become the world champion. They were trying to make Inoki and me bond and to be seen as friends in the eyes of the Japanese fans, so on this tour, Antonio and I did a lot of tag-team matches together. December 3, 1980, was a memorable night on that tour, as it was the only night in my career that I can remember being in the ring *against* Andre the Giant, as Antonio and I took on Andre and Stan Hansen.

I remember that Andre put me in a headlock in the match that night, and I felt very small, even though Andre's touch on me was light as a feather. Andre was very good in the ring—he took care of you and worked harder on that than most wrestlers because he was so big that he was worried about inadvertently hurting people. But Andre was a gentle giant who had a very delicate touch in the ring unless he was trying to make a point. I wasn't in there with him for very long that night, as Antonio caught most of Andre's in-ring time. Stan and I started the match, but with Andre, Stan Hansen, Inoki, and me in there, you had four of the biggest stars in the New Japan promotion in the ring, so everybody needed to get a little and sell a little and we needed to settle the issue of who was going to make the comeback. Andre and Stan both played borderline heels in Japan, so that made the match interesting, but with that much to protect in the ring at the same time—a double countout and full-out brawl where everyone looked strong was about the best that we could do.

Inoki and I went on to win the MSG Tag League tournament in the Prefectural Gym in Osaka on December 10, 1980, defeating Stan Hansen and Hulk Hogan in the tournament final when Inoki caught Hogan in a beautiful backslide and pinned him for the three count. Again, this tour was designed to make Inoki and I seem like we were good friends, which, in turn, served to bind our two promotions more closely together. After that win, we took some pictures with the trophy that were widely published in wrestling magazines across the world.

As mentioned, I missed the first December Garden show because I was in Japan—and that was the night that John Lennon got shot in New York City just a few blocks away from the Garden. Pedro Morales went over Ken Patera to win the Intercontinental title that night, and Bruno, who was covering for me in the main event while I was away, wrestled Sgt. Slaughter and beat him by countout in a wild brawl that left Slaughter with his heat for our rematch a couple of weeks later at the Meadowlands.

Pedro still had the standing in the WWF to carry the Intercontinental Heavyweight Championship, and was over big with the Puerto Rican community, who came out strongly to support him on the cards in the major cities. With Patera getting ready to leave, Pedro was the obvious choice to carry that belt.

The year ended with a second card at the Garden on December 29, 1980, with me facing the newest member of Freddie Blassie's army. With both Mr. Fuji and Professor Tanaka gone from the territory, it was time for the federation to add a new Asian heel in its cast of characters, so Blassie introduced his newest "find"—a "terror" from the Orient named Killer Khan who had not been seen in the WWF before.

Khan's gimmick was that of a wild man from Mongolia who was vicious and loved to torture American wrestlers and hurt people. He would contort his face into a fearsome scowl, and he screamed a lot in the ring when delivering chops and kicks and punches. All of this, coupled with the fact that Khan was about six foot four and around 300 pounds, got him very over with the people as a monster heel. Khan had been a legitimate sumo wrestler in Japan, but he was also very flexible. Because of that, I was able to work a very realistic looking leg stretcher move on him that night in the Garden that would have ripped a normal person's groin apart. The move *looked* brutal, the people loved it, and Khan sold it like a champ, but because he was so flexible, it didn't actually hurt him at all. All of this, of course, was designed to make it appear that I was working over Khan's legs to try and take away his finishing maneuver from him. Khan's finisher—a flying kneedrop off the top rope—had already caused a number of guys on television to be "stretchered" out of the ring. Our "plan" was that if he couldn't stand up and balance on the top rope, he couldn't hit the move on me. This was just one of the ways that in-ring psychology could be used to make a match seem more strategic and realistic.

In reality, when performing that move, Khan caught most of his weight on his hands and his other leg, and that finish was much harder on him. Landing on your hands and knees after a five-foot leap from the ringpost night after night, you would develop knee and wrist problems from having to work so hard and so carefully to protect your opponent. That flying kneedrop was also a very dangerous finisher for the guy laying on the mat, because if Khan missed with that move, even by a little, the underneath guy would have caught the full force of Khan's knee on whatever part of his body he happened to hit—and that would almost certainly have ended in something getting broken or crushed.

My match with Khan set up as the typical "babyface in peril" match. I liked Khan, so I sold a lot of his offense and even took his "weakened" finisher from him in the near corner of the ring, but managed to get a foot on the ropes at the very last moment to break up the count. For the finish, because Khan was so flexible, I was able to gut wrench him into a German suplex with a bridge and use his own weight as leverage to get a quick pin on him and get out of there before he could "hurt" me further. It was the kind of quick move, following his giving me a brutal beating for most of the match, that would leave Khan with most of his heat, but would also look great for the fans, and give me a clear and decisive win. By surprising the 300-pound Khan and pinning him in the center of the ring in Madison Square Garden, I was able to send the fans home happy and punctuate the end of what had been a very successful year, both personally and for the federation.

20

Monsters and Broadways (1981)

"Let your manner always be friendly, no matter what the outcome, and people will be glad to have worked with you."

—Napoleon Hill, "Assemble an Attractive Personality"

———◆———

The beginning of 1981 saw the rise of another new member of Freddie Blassie's army—Stan "The Lariat" Hansen. Stan and I had been in the Amarillo territory together, and we had always had a bit of an uneasy real-life rivalry with one another because the Funks had pushed me ahead of him. The Funks had trained Stan, who was from Texas, and I think Stan had thought of himself as their "favorite son." Yet, when I arrived from Tri-States, Terry Funk immediately put me over by taking me to the ten-minute time limit on television, and then put me over in the six-man tag-team elimination match where I was partnered with Stan but was booked to be the last man standing. I think all of that affected Stan a little bit, because he was a pretty competitive guy by nature. I suspect that the Funks were just testing Stan's humility—which might have needed a bit of adjusting—in the same way that Sam Muchnick later tested mine by asking me to put over Bulldog Bob Brown in my first match in St. Louis. In any event, our shared history had placed Stan and me a bit at odds as we came together for this series over the WWF title.

Hansen had been in the territory before, back in April 1976, when he was best known for *legitimately* breaking then-champion Bruno Sammartino's neck with a sloppy, botched bodyslam during their title match at Madison Square Garden. Amazingly enough, after suffering that broken neck in the ring, Bruno had the presence of mind to call for Hansen to hit him with his finisher—a devastating-looking "lariat" slingshot—leading to a finish by blood stoppage. Bruno's quick thinking had allowed Vince Sr. to put Hansen's lariat over with the people by claiming that it had been that move that had broken Bruno's neck. Although a terrible in-ring accident that legitimately landed Bruno in the hospital and shelved him for several weeks, that situation actually helped to make Hansen's career as a vicious, brash, and violent cowboy who could not be controlled in or out of the ring.

When he returned to the WWF in 1980, Hansen was well over 300 pounds, and he had reprised his role as a wild Texas outlaw complete with leather chaps, a leather vest, a bullrope, and, in many of his television interviews, a drooling mouthful of nasty brown chaw that completed the picture. In his early television matches, Stan was bloodying and stretchering out opponent after opponent with the lariat. When he did it to fan favorite Dominic DeNucci, though, the fans really began to see this man as someone who couldn't be stopped. Stan was getting over with the fans to a level that few heels before him had been able to achieve.

In some cities around the territory, Bruno Sammartino took some main-event matches against his old nemesis in an effort to "avenge" Hansen injuring his friend DeNucci. Yet even in these initial matches, Stan was booked to go over Bruno by countout, which continued to build Hansen's heat for his eventual title matches with me. In other cities, he was booked to annihilate WWF tag-team champion Tony Garea. Vince Sr. booked Stan as strongly as he had booked any other heel to set the stage for his title series.

On February 16, 1981, Stan and I had our first match at the Garden. The match had garnered significant fan interest because it would pit a scientific wrestler with amateur skills (me) against a completely uncontrollable wild American street fighter who had steamrolled over everyone, including Bruno. Everywhere Stan went, the lariat was put over as a fearsome finishing move that was crippling people. There was even talk of trying to get the move "banned" by promoters because of how many people he was "injuring" with it. After all, if he had broken Sammartino's neck with it, he could do it to anyone, and that's the way it was sold and promoted on TV.

Something had to give.

Our first match at the Garden had sold through very well at the box office, so when Vince called Stan and me together for our pre-match discussion, we knew we'd be coming back. Vince called for the match to end in a wild, pull-apart brawl, stopped by the referee because both of us were too bloody to continue, and requiring the assistance of other wrestlers from the locker room to restore order. Early in that first match, Stan hit me stiff (i.e., legitimately hit me instead of pulling his punches just short of the mark) in the stomach a few times to try and knock the wind out of me. The word on Hansen has always been that he worked stiff because his eyesight was quite bad and he couldn't execute moves with precision. But since that wasn't *always* the case, I think Stan was actually testing me to see how far he could push me and whether I was prepared to do anything to stop him. He might have also worked me stiff because he was often gassed in our matches and needed to do something to slow me down. This was another virtue of my commitment to training. Stan Hansen could hit me in the stomach all day long, and it wasn't going to slow me down enough to allow him to catch up.

Hansen had been brought in for *two* matches at Madison Square Garden, but apparently, Stan was under the impression that he was getting a three-match series, including a steel cage blowoff, so he wouldn't have to get pinned by me at the end. Hansen had not been pinned much anywhere in the world, and given his wild Texas outlaw character, he claimed that taking a pin would cause him to lose his heat, and that his handlers in Japan did not want him to get pinned during his stay in the WWF. Apparently Hansen raised quite a fuss with Vince Sr. in the office about taking a pinfall loss to me in the second Garden match because he claimed it would affect his standing and reputation in Japan, where he was slated to go for an extended stay after his run in the WWF was over. Arnold Skaaland told me that Hansen had insisted on getting a third match, pushed his connections and relationship with New Japan, and had gotten Vince Sr. to capitulate.

Stan and I had our second match at the Garden in March 1981. The match had *again* drawn well at the box office, so despite his dispute with the front office and the fact that I wasn't wild about having to work with him again, we were told we'd be coming back a third time. Vince Sr. asked me to put the lariat over to create a hot box office push for the third match. Our second match was booked to end with me standing outside on the ring apron, and when the referee stepped between us to try to create some space for me to re-enter, Hansen would come from behind the referee and hit me in the neck with the lariat and knock me off the apron and out into the crowd where I would be counted out. It was a pretty big bump, and would certainly serve to create even more fear and mystique about that move.

The match went off as advertised, the fans were into it, and more than in any other title match to date, they seemed genuinely concerned for my safety and well-being given what they had seen Stan do to so many wrestlers in the WWF up to that point. When we had the fans where we wanted them, I called for the finish and Stan hit me so stiff with the lariat across my neck that the impact rattled all the way through my body and it was all I could do to stay in control as I fell backward off the apron to take the bump onto the Garden floor. Stan was a terrific and a fearsome heel, but his in-ring work was definitely among the stiffest I have ever encountered.

As March turned to April, I learned a little bit more about Hansen's beef with the front office people, and in particular, that he had basically held up Vince Sr. for the third title match at the Garden by threatening to refuse to do the honors for me in the second match. Vince Sr. was second only to my father in terms of the standing that he held in my life, and the thought of anyone trying to hold Vince Sr. up was really getting to me.

Stan must have *really* frustrated the WWF front office people, because even though we did great business at the Garden with the blowoff cage match, selling out the arena and nearly also filling the Felt Forum for the closed-circuit television broadcast, as we went down the Garden hallway and through the curtain to the ring that night, Arnold Skaaland leaned into my ear and told me to "eat him up."

As I have mentioned, it was very much against my style to destroy an opponent in a title match, because normally, I'd be trying to leave the heel with his heat so that he could go on to draw in later matches in the territory. In this case, however, if you watch that cage match, I basically no-sold nearly all of Stan's offense. I was very angry at the way Stan had conducted himself in our territory, particularly after everyone, including me, had bent over backward to put him over as an unstoppable monster heel. I wasn't about to do any more favors for a man who would put himself ahead of the business and defy Vince Sr.'s booking plan.

It was the shortest cage match of my career—clocking in at just under nine minutes. That match was about one thing—teaching Stan Hansen that you don't come into our territory and start dictating the terms of your engagement. I had been the world champion in the territory for three years, and I had never once tried to talk Vince Sr. off the planned finish for even one of my matches—so I didn't appreciate the fact that Hansen, who had been in the territory less than three months and knew that he was just passing through, refused to honor Vince Sr.'s requested finish.

To his credit, Stan took it like a professional. It might be that he was just happy to get the third Garden payday, which, as it turned out, was one of the bigger ones of my title reign—but Vince Sr. made sure I got something more than money out of that third match. Destroying Stan Hansen in a cage match at the Garden in under nine minutes put me over as powerfully as any match could have. The fans at the Garden had watched Hansen break Bruno's neck and give him a lot of trouble, and booking me to go over him *this* strongly in our blowoff match was probably the turning point of my career and the match that really proved my mettle to the fans. The people in Madison Square Garden had never seen me in three flat-out street fights like that before—and I think the booking of that series proved to them that even though I preferred to wrestle in the amateur style and beat people with wrestling—I could also take care of myself when things turned ugly.

Hansen must have totally blown himself out with the office, because it wasn't long after the cage match at the Garden that he was gone from the territory. Ordinarily, he would have stuck around and had some matches with Morales over the Intercontinental title, and maybe even reprised some of the epic matches he had with Andre in Japan for audiences in our territory. I had one or two other matches with Stan in the territory after the blowoff at the Garden, and then he was back in Japan, never to return.

It is interesting to contrast the way things went for Hansen with what was going on with Sergeant Slaughter—a guy who was just as over as Hansen was, but who, in sharp contrast to Hansen, was also a *total* company guy. Sarge was a front office darling because he had proved to be very reliable, always gave a great effort, and had gotten his finisher, the Cobra Clutch, over as well as any hold the company had ever seen. Vince was riding Slaughter as far as he could, and extended his stay in the territory well beyond what was originally planned for him. Sarge was getting main-event matches all over the territory, not just with me, but with Morales over the Intercontinental title, with Andre, with Mascaras, and even with Bruno in a few towns. Sarge was proving the old adage that the Funks, and Eddie Graham, and Sam Muchnick had always told me: if you work hard, are reliable, and get over with the people, eventually the promoters will have to take notice. That is certainly what happened with Sarge, who had come into the territory having really been nothing more than a mid-carder, and made himself into a main eventer who would be box office gold for years to come.

While our series was finishing up around the territory, Slaughter and the Wizard had started holding $5,000 "Cobra Clutch Challenges" at the television tapings. These challenges called for someone to come out, sit down in a wooden folding chair in the ring, and "allow" Slaughter to apply the Cobra Clutch to them and then try to escape the hold. Several guys on television, most notably Rick McGraw, had given it a good show, but nobody had been able to break the hold. The series was so popular with the fans that we even took it out into some of the smaller venues out on the house show circuit, where various "challengers," including Rick McGraw, Pedro Morales, and the tag-team champions Tony Garea and Rick Martel, would put the hold over for Sarge before their matches with him. There was even a card somewhere in Massachusetts where I was scheduled to wrestle Sarge, and I took the Cobra Clutch challenge and put the hold over for him before his title shot. After all, what better way was there to convince the fans that Sarge could win the title than to show them that his finishing hold, should he get it on me, would put me out?

All this promotion reached its pinnacle on television in late February 1981 when Sarge and the Grand Wizard started taunting Pat Patterson, who at the time was doing the color commentary for the television tapings with Vince McMahon Jr. Slaughter would come out and challenge Patterson, and call him "yellow" or a "coward," and Patterson would claim that he was "studying" the hold and wasn't yet ready to step into the ring and challenge Slaughter. In the third hour of the taping, Slaughter and the Wizard raised the stakes to $10,000 just for Patterson and put the bad mouth on him a little bit. Patterson tore his suit jacket and blazer right off then and there and went into the ring and took the Cobra Clutch challenge. The people were really into this story, and that little fieldhouse in Allentown was rocking as Patterson faded at first, but then rallied, slammed Slaughter into the turnbuckles again and again, and eventually slipped inside and was pushing the hold off when Slaughter released it and then waffled Patterson with the folding chair.

A new feud was on!

The Slaughter-Patterson war was a wonderful boost to box offices around the territory during the spring and summer of 1981, as it provided

Vince Sr. with a certifiable main event in some of the smaller venues where I wasn't scheduled, and where the Intercontinental title match might have previously been relied on to carry the house. Sarge and Patterson, who were two of the best workers in the territory at the time, tore it up—taking that feud around the circuit once in matches that were ending in pull-apart brawls, blood stoppages, disqualifications, or double countouts, and then in a second revolution around the territory in no-holds-barred "Alley Fights" where both wrestlers could come into the ring dressed however they wanted.

The Alley Fight that Sarge and Patterson had at the Garden was a classic, as Slaughter took one of his famous flying leaps over the turnbuckles and into the ring post, but then gigged himself too deeply as he flew backward onto the canvas, and ended up bleeding out all over everything. It was a gruesome battle that Patterson eventually won when the Wizard came running back down to ringside and threw a white towel into the ring signaling Slaughter's surrender. The people roared their approval.

Once again, Vince Sr. had box office gold.

April and May 1981 also saw me wrestling out of the territory quite a bit in some notable matches. On April 5, 1981, I was back in the Florida territory for Eddie Graham where I put the WWF title on the line against old friend Hiro Matsuda. If professional wrestling matches had been legitimate athletic contests without predetermined endings, this match would likely have been one of the two or three toughest of my career. Matsuda was a hooker and a trainer for Eddie Graham, and had trained some of the best workers in the business in the mid-'80s. At the time, Hiro wasn't wrestling a full schedule anymore, so it was an honor for me to get to work in the ring with him. Matsuda had a sterling reputation for his wrestling skills, and I was grateful to Eddie Graham for once again giving me one of the best guys in his territory to work with.

I left for Japan right after the cage match blowoff with Hansen at the Garden and spent about a week over there wrestling for New Japan. One of the matches I enjoyed the most on that tour happened on April

16, 1981, in a town called Usa where I teamed up with "Quickdraw" Rick McGraw in a babyface tag-team match against Antonio Inoki and one of his new young talents, Ricky Choshu. McGraw and Slaughter also had a couple of great matches around the territory at the time, one of which happened in Philadelphia at the Spectrum, where the promoter Phil Zacko, who loved McGraw, asked Sarge to give McGraw a lot of their match before finally beating him. The Philadelphia crowd loved it.

McGraw was only about five foot seven, but he looked really good. He was a great athlete and he was a very clean-cut kid when he first got into the business. The people loved him, and he was very talented, and even though he was small, he would have had a really bright future if he hadn't allowed himself to be overtaken by the peer pressure. When we worked together in Japan, I spent some time with Rick, and he explained to me that it was his dream to get bigger. He really thought that having a more muscular body would help him make it in the business. I tried to encourage him to just train hard, eat right, and stay clean, because he was a fast and exciting worker and the people liked him just the way he was.

About a year later, Rick went on to become part of a popular and successful tag team in the WWF known as "The Carolina Connection" with another great young worker named Steve Travis. McGraw and Travis both wore Carolina blue, and did some really great dropkicks, speedwork, and high-flying moves. They were also very popular and very over with the ladies.

Unfortunately, Rick McGraw became one of the first guys in our business to die from the abuse of steroids and other drugs. He just couldn't shake the idea that he wanted to be big, and I guess he just wasn't satisfied with the great body that he already had. He ended up dying of a heart attack in 1985 at age thirty in a hotel room in East Haven, Connecticut. I had already left the WWF at that point—but I remember hearing about it and feeling a great sadness about it. Rick was a wonderful young athlete and a terrific guy with a very bright future in the business—but like so many other guys did after him, he succumbed to the Siren's song of steroids and other drugs in the quest to make it further in the business.

On May 1, 1981, I made my first trip down to Mexico City to a venue called El Toreo de Quatro Caminos, where once again, I found myself in the ring with my old friend Antonio Inoki. This was another match for New Japan, which had some cross-promotional deal with this Mexican wrestling organization that was looking to gain some international statute by booking a high-profile main event with two champions. They packed a lot of people into the stadium that night, and they were very fiery, but they were speaking Spanish, so we couldn't really tell what they were yelling and chanting at us. Sometimes it was hard to tell who there were behind, and what they liked and didn't like, so in the end, we decided to just have more of a clean babyface match and just trade on the fact that we were both champions defending our belts. We both took a pin—I got the first one and he got the second one, and in the third fall, we were both counted out of the ring. Unlike most of my international trips, on that trip to Mexico, I went on my own—neither Arnold nor any other representative of the WWF came with me. I was happy to get to see my old friend Billy Robinson while I was down there. Billy was from England, had come up the hard way, and had learned how to hook people. I watched him a lot in Minneapolis when I was growing up. I talked with Billy at length in the dressing room that night and both of us expressed the hope that one day, we might be able to get in the ring with each other somewhere and show the people an exciting scientific wrestling match.

The next night, May 2, 1981, most of the guys were in Rochester, New York. This was the famous day when Andre the Giant rolled his ankle getting out of bed at the motel and ended up breaking it. Since he was scheduled to wrestle Killer Khan that night anyway, Vince Sr. just worked it into the kayfabe storyline that Khan had landed his kneedrop off the top rope and crushed Andre's ankle—knowing full well that when Andre recovered from the broken ankle, it would make for a ready-made feud and a box office bonanza.

In reality, Andre was transported from upstate New York to Boston for his operation at Beth Israel Hospital. The only problem was that the doctors couldn't figure out how to sedate Andre before the operation. Because they had never dealt with a man of Andre's size, the anesthesiologists couldn't figure out how much sedative to give him. Fearing they might kill him by giving him too much, they erred by giving him too little, and couldn't get him to pass out. Eventually, Andre just told the doctors to get him two bottles of Crown Royal. The bottles were produced, Andre signed a consent form, drank them down, and then told the doctors to just go ahead and perform the surgery on his ankle.

Former WWF referee Mario Savoldi told me that when Andre was released from Beth Israel Hospital, he asked that his girlfriend, a six-foot-five-inch flight attendant from Minneapolis, be flown out for the occasion. The arrangements were made, she arrived in Boston, and Mario drove them both from the hospital to a hotel where they got separate rooms. Andre went to sleep, but when he woke up to use the bathroom, he heard a woman in the next room making noises as if she were having sex with someone. Thinking that there was another man in the room with his girlfriend, Andre flew into a rage, broke through the sheetrock wall separating his room from the adjoining room, and came through that wall with his hair flying all around bellowing for his girlfriend. Well wouldn't you know it, Andre had gotten mixed up as to which side of his room his girlfriend's room was on, and had broken into the room of a totally different couple in the room next door. That couple were so frightened by what happened, they apparently ran out of the room and to the lobby and never came back. Andre was so upset by the incident, and was so intent on calming the couple down that he ran through the door of the adjoining room without even opening it and knocked it flat off the hinges.

On May 4, 1981, we went to Madison Square Garden for a card that was notable for a couple of reasons. First, Inoki was supposed to travel to New York to take part in a tag-team match alongside Yoshiaki Yatsu on that card, but Inoki no-showed the Garden. While this may have seemed like a big deal, it was not high on Vince Sr.'s list of concerns. The fact was, Inoki just wasn't over in New York because he wasn't willing to take the time to come to the TV tapings, appear on television, do interviews, and get himself over as a babyface with the WWF fans.

Second, this was the card featuring my first match with former Canadian football star Angelo "King Kong" Mosca. Mosca and I had just done an angle at the last television taping where he had repeatedly refused to pin one of the enhancement guys, and I rushed into the ring in my three-piece suit only to have Mosca attack me, hang me upside down from the turnbuckles, and stomp and spit on me until other wrestlers came from the locker room to save *me*. This angle came about, in part, because some of the underneath guys had told me that Mosca was a bully who enjoyed working stiff and was having fun in the ring at other people's expense. I figured if he was going to play that way, he might as well try it with me. The television angle had done its job, as we got a good walkup crowd at the Garden in the couple of days prior to the matches, and the house was very close to capacity at bell time. I think that television angle saved Mosca from being one and done at the Garden, as Vince Sr. asked for the match to be an all-out brawl, with Mosca winning by disqualification when he ducked a punch of mine that ended up hitting the referee.

Mosca was a convincing, menacing heel. He had had a long and decorated career in the Canadian Football League, and had then built his reputation in professional wrestling in Canada wrestling in Toronto for Frank Tunney. Where things fell apart for Mosca a little bit, I think, was that my series with him immediately followed my series with Stan Hansen—and Hansen and Mosca were somewhat similar stylistically. The Garden fans had just seen me in three successive brawls with Hansen, and now, I was in another brawl with Mosca—but Hansen had broken Bruno's neck, and Mosca just wasn't as convincing. I was not one to second guess Vince Sr., but this underscored why Vince Sr. only wanted Hansen to get two matches. By the time my series with Mosca was over, it would be five brawls in a row over the WWF title at the Garden, and the fans were ready for something different.

Speaking of Mosca's penchant for taking advantage of people in the ring, on June 5, 1981, he potatoed me in the face during in our title match at the Pittsburgh Civic Arena. That shot swelled up my eye and the side of my face, but I let it go. I remember that throughout the match, all of his moves were stiffer than they needed to be. As Hansen had done, Mosca was testing me to see how much I would let him get away with. When that happens in the ring, the only person who knows it is the guy in the ring who is taking it—and when it happens to me, as it did from time to time, I'd have to do what I needed to do to put a stop to it, because if I took a real beating like that too often, my wrestling career would have been a short one.

Since that was the first time Mosca had tried anything with me, I didn't want to overreact, so I didn't say anything to him in the dressing room, or to anyone else after the match. I just let it go. But when I heard more from underneath guys about what Mosca was doing to them in preliminary matches, I realized that maybe his shot hadn't been a mistake and that something should be done about it. I knew I had a number of other matches with Mosca scheduled in the territory in the coming month, so I resolved to just wait and see if he tried something with me again.

Sure enough, the very next time I was in the ring with him, in Springfield at the Civic Center, Mosca potatoed me in the face again—the same way that he had done in Pittsburgh. This time, though, I was ready for him, and retaliated by hitting him so hard across the side of the face with a forearm shiver that it lifted his 319 pounds right off the mat and into the air. Mosca crashed down onto the mat and was lying flat on his back shaking the cobwebs out, but for real. I stood over him and dispensing with all pretense of kayfabe, just said to him in a voice loud enough for anyone at ringside to hear, "If you want to fight, get up!"

Mosca stayed down.

Eventually, I pulled him up, and he tied up with me, and pushed me into the ropes, and wouldn't you know it, his touch was suddenly light as a feather. And that was the last problem I ever had with Mosca in the ring. This is an example of what happens when someone decides to "go into business for himself," and why, as champion, you have to have the ability to defend yourself against that in the ring. If Mosca had responded to my challenge by actually getting up, the match would have turned into a shoot, and that wouldn't have gone well for him. Fortunately, Mosca was smart enough to get back to business.

When we got back to the dressing room that night in Springfield, I went over to Mosca's dressing room and addressed the issue face to face. He apologized to me, and after that, we had no further issues.

I had earned his respect.

I've seen Mosca a number of times since then at conventions, and we talk and can even joke about that situation now—but back then, it was a pretty tense thing. Tony Garea saw the whole Springfield episode happen in real time, and the moment that I flattened Mosca with that forearm shot is still one of his favorite stories, because he, too, had been roughed up in the ring a fair bit by Mosca.

Mosca and I came back to the Garden on June 8, 1981. After the last month's disqualification finish, though, Pat Patterson was assigned to be the special guest referee for the return bout. Patterson, who had just come off the Alley Fight blowoff to his feud with Sarge, was looking for something new to do, and had decided that a feud with Mosca would be his next adventure. So Vince Sr. and Patterson set up a little angle at the TV taping where once again, Mosca was taking advantage of an enhancement guy—this time, a jobber named Victor Mercado—and repeatedly refusing to pin him. Referee Dick Woherlie finally decided he'd had enough and disqualified Mosca, who then flew into a rage, and threw everyone, including Woherlie, out of the ring.

Patterson, who was doing color commentary for the television broadcast at the time, went to the ring to interview Woherlie, and congratulated

Woherlie for "finally" doing something to stop Mosca's reign of terror. Mosca took exception to Patterson's remarks and waffled him with a metal water pitcher, knocking him out, and the next great feud was on.

All that was used to set up the fact that Patterson had been assigned as the special guest referee for my rematch with Mosca at the Garden. But there was additional intrigue about that since the astute Garden fans no doubt remembered that there was no love lost between me and Patterson either, since less than eighteen months earlier, Patterson and I had concluded our historic four-match battle at the Garden. I ended up going over Mosca with a quick pinning combination and a notoriously quick three-count from Patterson, which caused Mosca to attack Patterson in the ring after the match to perfectly lay their feud on the tee.

———◆———

About a week after that match, on June 20 at the Spectrum in Philadelphia, the WWF created a new superstar. A few weeks earlier, Don "The Magnificent" Muraco had debuted on television, with the Grand Wizard as his manager. Muraco, who had a deep surfer's tan and hailed from Sunset Beach, Hawaii, was a very different kind of heel for the WWF. He was a big man, tipping the scales around 280 pounds, but he was also a good *wrestler* in terms of his knowledge of amateur moves. He was very active, he could get up and down, execute and take high spots, and he was arrogant and loquacious on the microphone—really a complete package as far as a wrestler was concerned. Muraco could fit anybody's style, and make anybody look good.

Muraco had done very well in Florida for Eddie Graham, which, as you have probably now gathered, functioned almost like a development territory for most of the top talent that eventually came to the WWF. Muraco had been on top as Florida Champion, had drawn well, and according to Eddie, was poised to take the next step. As I have explained already, Eddie and Vince Sr., who also had a house in West

Palm Beach, were very close and communicated on a weekly basis about their territories, and when Muraco's time as Florida Champion had run its course, Eddie called Vince Sr. and recommended him for a run in New York.

On that night in June in Philadelphia, Muraco, to the shock and dismay of the sellout crowd, stripped the popular former WWF Champion Pedro Morales of the Intercontinental Heavyweight Championship by knocking Pedro out with a pair of brass knuckles and pinning him in the middle of the Spectrum ring. Fans in the WWF were not accustomed to seeing Pedro Morales pinned—much less by brash "newcomer" like Muraco who was making his first appearance in the building. I was at the Spectrum that night defending the WWF title against George "The Animal" Steele, so I know the way the crowd reacted to that title change—and you could just tell that Muraco was going to be something special. The fans really disliked him, and every time he'd come out to the ring, they'd chant "beach bum! beach bum!" at him, which of course, he played up to the hilt by covering his ears and yelling at them to stop. The "beach bum!" cheers from the crowd were deafening in many places—which, as a heel, is the biggest compliment you can get.

I was very excited to have Don in the territory, particularly as a heel Intercontinental champion and the number-two guy in the federation. You couldn't duplicate Don Muraco—he had evolved into his character from the time he entered the business, and it worked very well for him. Muraco really did live in Hawaii, and he loved surfing and spending time on the beach—and the fact is that the best in-ring character you can have is the one that is closest to something you really are so that there is no pretending. Muraco was a handsome, cocky, athletic guy with all the skills in the world, and the persona he played just came naturally to him. The WWF was also noted for big guys, and Don had shoulders as big as anyone in the business—so he really looked the part. Vince Sr. liked Muraco immediately, and after getting the seal of approval from Eddie Graham down in Florida that Don was reliable and could be trusted not to miss dates, Vince felt comfortable putting him into the federation's second biggest spot as the Intercontinental Champion.

Since I just mentioned him in the context of that Spectrum card where Muraco took the title, I would be remiss if I didn't give some more ink to George "The Animal" Steele, who I faced that night in Philadelphia, at the Garden in July, and all over the territory that summer. Around this time in 1981, Vince Sr. had found a Canadian enhancement guy named Rick Bolton who had a trick shoulder that he could pop in and out of its socket on demand. Since Steele's finisher at the time was the flying hammerlock, this became a wrestling promoter's dream. They brought Bolton in for a one-shot and paired Steele and Bolton on television and had Steele stomp and kick and bite the guy's arm and then put him up in the flying hammerlock. On cue, Bolton dislocated his own shoulder, making it appear that Steele had ripped Bolton's shoulder right out of its socket. It was sadistic, but incredibly realistic—and Vince Jr. and Patterson sold the heck out of it on the television broadcast as Bolton staggered around with his arm completely turned around the wrong way and his elbow facing front and the Animal continuing to chase him around and pound on it. It didn't hurt Bolton at all, but it certainly hurt to look at—and was a totally legitimizing moment for professional wrestling. Had Steele really just wrenched this poor man's shoulder out of its socket? And could he do it to me next?

The people, of course, ate it up—and largely as a consequence of that match, we drew a crowd of over 22,000 people to the Garden for Steele's title match with me in July 1981. Naturally, in his pre-match interviews on television, Steele stared into the camera with his green tongue lashing around and yelling "Backlund! . . . break! . . . arm!" as Vince Jr. kept reminding the fans of what Steele had done to Rick Bolton, and how, that if that happened to me, we'd have a new WWF champion.

Because we couldn't really have a *wrestling* match, Steele and I worked out this little thing where he would come out to the ring first, and then not let me in, so we could play out the first five or seven minutes of the "match" with Skaaland and me on the outside figuring out how to get me into the ring without getting attacked. We did that gimmick over and over again all across the territory and the people believed in it. Once I was in the ring, all I had to do was follow his lead and let him attack me with the taped-up can opener he kept in his tights and sell it like crazy, with the referee checking him repeatedly but not finding anything. Eventually, when we had the people in enough of a frenzy, Steele would miss a high spot (often a charge into the turnbuckle or a botched hammerlock attempt) that would allow me to steal a quick pin on him and then get the heck out of there. That, too, worked like a charm all over the territory.

People loved to come and see The Animal wreak havoc, throw chairs around, and bite open the turnbuckles and rub the stuffing in people's eyes. No one else had that kind of effect on the people or the crowds. George "The Animal" Steele was a very strong character who was completely different from anyone else in the business. He fulfilled another "type" in the business that put butts in the seats. He would come in for a couple of the spring television tapings, get over with the fans immediately, raise hell out on the house show circuit all summer, have a bunch of good paydays, and help us all put people in the seats, then head back to his teaching and coaching jobs in the fall as if nothing happened. Everyone was amused watching Steele work and wondering how he did it. Remember, this was during the territory days—so no one who actually had Jim Myers as a teacher or coach would be able to get the word out to the people at Madison Square Garden that The Animal was really just a normal guy. And who would have believed them anyway?

Before we leave Steele, I have to tell one more story about him. Once, when we were in Japan together, we were walking in an alley near our hotel and suddenly he leaned over to me and said, "Watch this, Bobby" and then he slipped into his gimmick, ran ahead, pointed at a group of people, yelled "You!" and then started flapping his arms all over the place, running toward the crowd, and sending the people scattering in all directions.

George was certainly a lot of fun to be around, had a great sense of humor, and was an incredibly influential force in the wrestling business for many, many years.

Right There With Bruno

When I came back in the summer of 1981, Bobby and I had a great run. That summer, my series with Bobby was squeezed in between a bunch of his hour Broadways with Don Muraco, and I'll tell you, I'm glad I was squeezed in between those and that nobody asked me to go an hour with Bob, because that would have killed me. Bobby had become a superb wrestler and much more comfortable in the role of champion, and he was in tremendous physical shape. Bob was a very unique champion for the WWWF because of his amateur background and his style, but he was one of the very best champions the WWF had ever had. I would put Bruno first, but you know, I would put Bobby right there with him, and then after them, there was Hogan. They might not give Bobby that much credit, but I was in the ring with all three of them and Morales too, so I will, and I mean it. The funny thing about Bobby though, the fans never accepted him as much as they should have. In some cities, the fans would chant "Howdy Doody" at him and if they were taping, the producers let that get on television, and as you know, in this business, television dictated everything. I thought the office should have continued to push Bobby in a more respectful way than they did.

In the second match of that series, Mr. McMahon asked me to go out and put Bobby over in less than a minute—and I would have done almost anything for him, but I said, "I don't think that's the right thing to do, and I'm not going to do it." And Mr. McMahon looked at me, surprised, and asked me, "Why?" And I told him that I thought we would be screwing the people by giving them a one-minute main

> event, and that it would be bad for business. So Bobby and I went out
> and had a shorter match, maybe ten or twelve minutes, most of which
> was done outside the ring, but it had a much better finish, and I think
> the people really liked it.
>
> —George "The Animal" Steele

At the television tapings immediately following the July 1981 Garden show, Vince Sr. decided to switch the tag-team titles back from the heel Moondogs to the former champions, the sensational young babyface team of Tony Garea and Rick Martel, who had previously dethroned the seemingly invincible Wild Samoans. This change occurred, in part, because the Moondog team had changed from "Rex" and "King" (Randy Colley and Sailor White) to "Rex" and "Spot" because White, a Canadian, was having work visa issues and not allowed to reenter the United States. Spot was just not as fearsome or convincing as the 300-plus-pound King had been, and White's visa issues had effectively killed the team.

I knew Rick Martel from the time we spent together at Florida Championship Wrestling. Martel started in the business very young, when he was only sixteen or seventeen years old, and to be exposed to the professional wrestling life at that age—the drugs, women, the politics, and unscrupulous promoters and journeyman wrestlers looking to take advantage of you—must have been very, very tough on him. As a young wrestler, the industry just looks like an never-ending game. Just about everything in the world of professional wrestling is a work, so you start to question whether anything or anyone is actually real. Having said that, Martel did an amazing job of keeping himself on the straight and narrow—and like I did, he managed to run into the right people who helped his career along.

Tony Garea, meanwhile, was a longtime WWF guy, having debuted in the federation in 1972. Vince Sr. had briefly considered Tony for a babyface run with the championship in the early '70s, but by the time I came upon the scene, Vince wanted someone from outside the regulars and was looking for an All-American Boy, not a New Zealander with tattoos and a heavy accent. That said, Tony was a good friend and occasional travel companion for me, and he and Martel worked very well together. They looked good, were good performers, and they could really get the crowd going. Of course, they also had some good talent to work with on the heel side, from Afa and Sika, to the Moondogs to Mr. Fuji and Mr. Saito, in addition to various heels finishing their run in the promotion like Mosca, Khan, Hogan, the Hangman, and others who the promoters would put together to create an interesting tag-team title match to fill out a card.

With very few exceptions, no one match on its own would fill up a big house. If one of the big houses out on the circuit sold out, which many of them did while I was champion, it was because the promoter had put together a good solid card all the way through. Having an interesting and exciting tag-team title match on the card, especially with good babyface champions, definitely helped to accomplish that. The women fans, in particular, loved Garea and Martel, and they played the babyfaces in peril role perfectly. Martel was a fresh and interesting face who injected a lot of energy and excitement into the WWF. He was fast, and a high flyer and constantly in motion. Garea, on the other hand, was the veteran presence on the team—a very solid worker who knew how to pace a match and how to control and build the energy in a crowd. I worked with them a few times in six-man tags, and their energy was truly infectious.

After the Garden show in July and the subsequent television tapings, Muraco and I headed down to Florida for Eddie Graham, and on July 23, 1981, at the Convention Center in Miami Beach, Don and I had our first match together as the WWF's respective champions. Don and I had been in the ring together before when I defended the WWF title against him back when he was the Florida champion, but this was a particularly interesting night because Don, as the WWF Intercontinental Champion, and I as the WWF World Heavyweight Champion, were the main event on the NWA Florida Championship Wrestling card. Vince Sr. sent us both down to Eddie's territory to get comfortable with each other because we were about to start a historic program up in the WWF territory.

Don and I worked very well together. The crowd was familiar with both of us and was very into the match, and the timing, precision, and execution of moves in that match was as good as anyone I had worked with. I could barely contain my enthusiasm in the dressing room afterward. Don was aggressive, focused totally on the match rather than on ego, and was someone who I grew to respect immensely.

When I got back from Miami, I explained to Vince Sr. how well things had gone with Muraco, but he had already heard from Eddie that our match in Miami had been sensational. Then, for the first time in my career as the WWF champion, I asked Vince Sr. for a booking favor. I explained to Vince Sr. that after such a long run of consecutive brawls at the Garden (Hansen three times, Mosca twice, and Steele once), I wanted to show the fans something different—namely a *wrestling*-driven, one-hour Broadway with Muraco at the Garden. Vince Sr. readily agreed, and our first match on August 24, 1981, at the Garden was a one-hour time-limit Broadway.

As a general matter, Vince Sr. wasn't big on Broadways—he was worried about *anyone* being able to properly pace a match to hold the crowd's attention for an hour, because in the history of the WWF, there hadn't been anyone with enough of a repertoire to pull off an hour-long match without having it become repetitive. He was also concerned that a one-hour match would necessarily truncate all the other matches on the card to fit a two-and-a-half-hour package—and, of course, it was the full card, not just one match, which drew the house and made the people happy.

No matter how engaging a card might be, two to two and a half hours is the limit on what people can take. If you're going to have a Broadway on a card, you need to keep the other matches short, or have fewer matches on the card without telegraphing to the people that you were planning for that.

Given his faith in Don and me, though, Vince Sr. was willing to give it a go.

In our first match, Don and I spent ten minutes just playing off a short-arm scissor, and we had the people totally engaged in it. It was interesting to show Vince Sr. that the New York fans had grown to appreciate the more nuanced, strategic style of my matches, and that they weren't just bloodthirsty and craving a brawl. Vince watched that entire first match at Madison Square Garden from his spot at the curtain, listening to the fan reaction. The match went very, very well, and the fact that it was champion versus champion was a nice add-on. That hadn't happened in well over a year (since my match with Ken Patera in May 1980), so that, coupled with the fact that Muraco had steamrolled over Pedro Morales, himself a former WWF World Champion in winning the Intercontinental Championship, added another layer of drama to the match. Many of the fans were seriously questioning whether Muraco might be the guy with the skill set to beat me—which, of course, is *exactly* what you need to build a good house.

When the match was over, Muraco and I were both drenched with sweat. I had lost five pounds in the ring during that hour, and Don, who was about fifty pounds heavier than I was, lost more. We were exhausted but exhilarated at the same time, and when we came through the curtain, Vince Sr. congratulated both of us with more enthusiasm than I had seen him display since the Patterson double knockout. By the time of the television tapings the following week, Vince Sr. had re-jiggered the booking plan and ordered up six more one-hour Broadways in the coming weeks—the first time that had ever been done in the WWF.

On October 17, we actually wrestled *two* one-hour Broadways on the same day. Aside from the sheer physical toll that wrestling two Broadways on the same day would take, the problem was complicated by the fact that because Landover, Maryland, and Philadelphia were only two hours apart by car or train, we knew that the matches needed to be totally different because some people would go to both cards. I remember that we finished the Broadway in Landover, showered and dressed, and then drove to Philly for the nightcap. During the ride, I drank a lot of water and thought about how to change things up to make sure the Philly match was different. When we got to the Spectrum that night, Vince Sr. was there, making a very rare appearance in a building other than the Garden, and the three of us found ourselves standing there together in the back hall. Muraco was laughing with me about being forced to wrestle two Broadways in one day, mentioned how much weight he had lost in the first match, looked at Vince Sr. and jokingly asked him, "What were you thinking?" And Vince joked right back with Muraco telling him, "Well, Don, we need to get this right, so we're going to do it one more time."

Going Broadway

When I got to New York in 1981, they did things a little bit backward with me. Usually they would bring the heel in and you would do TVs and then they'd put you right in with the champion at the Garden. But for some reason I generated a whole bunch of heat with Pedro, so they decided to put me into a series with him over the Intercontinental Heavyweight Championship before I ever got to Bob. And both of those belts were drawing good money for them. So I won the title from Pedro in Philadelphia and then did a series with him before I faced Bob, and once we got together, I had the Intercontinental Heavyweight Championship and Bob had the World Championship, so that really added something to the series. And then once we got together, they decided to put us into a whole bunch of one-hour Broadways to start and you know, those were all good matches but an hour match is always a hard match because you have to mix it up and keep it interesting. We tried really hard to make them all different — and that was easy to do because Bob's incredible athletic ability made it so that there was a lot we could do. He used to love to pick me up in the short-arm scissors, and we'd build that up for awhile until he'd pick me up over his head and put me on the turnbuckle and the fans always loved that. But you had to be in some kind of shape to be out there sweating like that and knowing that you were in it for an hour— or on that day, two hours!

Bob had a lot of fire in his comebacks—it was a lot of fun being in there with Bob. We drew really good money together, and he was always very professional and had great energy. The Philly/Washington night was the one that really sticks out because that was the day we did two on the same day, so we were in there wrestling with each other for hours.

—Don Muraco

I loved doing Broadway matches, because, in addition to the obvious physical challenge that they presented, they also offered a mental challenge to try to build the people's energy over an hour, keep them on the edge of their seats, and build their energy to higher and higher levels throughout the match until we had them at the peak just as the bell rang signaling the expiration of the time limit. You don't get to have a winner and a loser in a Broadway, so at the end, you have to try to get the people's emotions to a place where you have a peak and an abrupt ending or false finish and leave them begging for five more minutes.

The five more minutes would come on September 21, 1981, the next card at Madison Square Garden, where we staged the rematch—which, for the first time in Garden history, the WWF World Title match was scheduled for one fall with a *two-hour* time limit. To create some additional intrigue, and because we hadn't had one in the Garden for a while, the match was booked as a Texas Death Match to signal to the people that even though this was a match that involved two champions, it would have a decisive finish.

This time, because we knew we were going to a finish, and because we were both in such great shape after going for hours and hours all over the territory, we decided to really up the work rate, do false finish after false finish, and try to lather the crowd up into a complete frenzy. At about the twenty-eight-minute mark, after Muraco had pounded me with a ringside chair and a variety of stuff the fans had thrown into the ring, I began to make my comeback. We could feel the energy rising as Muraco gave me the Hawaiian Hammer inverted piledriver, leaving me to kick out at two . . . a suplex with me kicking out at two . . . and a splash from the top rope that saw me kick out at two and a half. Finally, he tried a double underhook, and I backdropped him into a bridge. He put his foot over the bottom rope, the ref didn't see it, and three seconds later, the Garden literally exploded. It was one of my favorite finishes in all my matches in my career, because I'm not sure I have ever had a crowd any higher than they were that night. That is the emotional magic that a great wrestling match can conjure.

For much of the second half of my time as the WWF champion, Muraco was either the Intercontinental Champion, or was chasing Pedro for it. That meant that we were on the cards together in all of the big buildings in the territory. Muraco was one of the very few people whose matches I routinely watched while I was champion, because I respected him and his work so much. The man could flat out wrestle. I am asked many times who my favorite opponent was. I have had *many* great matches, and many great series with most of the very best wrestlers in the world from the late '70s and early '80s—but in trying to answer that question, Don Muraco would definitely be on the short list. He was also one of the funniest guys in the business. When Don was on, no one cut a better or more entertaining promo than he did.

On October 12, 1981, I headed north of the border for a rare baby-face matchup in Montreal with Ray Rougeau. I enjoyed working with Ray, who was very popular in Montreal, and the two of us treated the crowd at the Montreal Forum to a really nice scientific wrestling match that I eventually won with a quick pin, and which ended in a handshake and both of our arms raised to a cheering crowd. I liked having one of these babyface matches every now and again because it was a challenge to try to get the people into the match without the usual love-hate thing going on, and to get them to just pop for the high spots and the story that we were telling in the ring. I never got to have any of these babyface matches at the Garden, and really only had a handful of them anywhere in the WWF territory during my six years as the champion because I don't think that Vince had any confidence that a babyface versus babyface main event would draw money in the territory.

As some of you may know, Vince Sr. tried this once in 1972 when he had Pedro Morales defend the WWWF title against Bruno Sammartino in the main event at Shea Stadium. The match went to a sixty-five-minute curfew draw because what other outcome could there be? Bruno and Pedro were the top two babyfaces in the federation at the time, and if one of them beat the other, you'd be taking drawing power away from the losing babyface. Beyond that, you'd be running the risk that the fans would turn one of the babyfaces into the heel because the crowd was so conditioned to think that one guy had to be "good" and one "bad" that they would want side with one over the other. Given how difficult it was to build up a successful babyface in a territory, as a promoter, neither of these scenarios is anything you would ever want to risk.

It is important to remember, also, that first and foremost, Vince Sr. was marketing hope. He was all about good triumphing over evil in the end, and he thought that was good for society. There were many different ways to tell that story, so I don't think he wanted to confuse things by putting two good guys in there together. A lot of the guys also wouldn't have been good at having pure babyface matches. Chances are someone would have naturally gravitated to the heel role because it was easier, and that could have easily messed up the booking plan going forward. The promoter was always thinking about how to put people in seats, and in a babyface versus babyface match, one forearm shot would sometimes be the only heel move in the match. But it could sometimes be enough to turn the crowd against you. I remember watching Nick Bockwinkle's dad Warren Bockwinkle wrestle Wilbur Snyder in a two out of three falls match that went almost an hour. Snyder threw only one forearm in the entire match, but that was enough to cause him to draw heel heat from the fans.

Many people over the years have asked me whether there was ever any talk of a Sammartino-Backlund dream match, or a Morales-Backlund dream match, and the simple answer is no. There would not have been a good way to end a Sammartino-Backlund match, or a Morales-Backlund match—so there really wasn't any point in having those matches. I took a lot of heat in the wrestling magazines for not putting the WWF title "up" against other babyfaces in the WWF, but there were very good business reasons why those matches weren't booked in the WWF. I loved having those kinds of matches—I just had to have them out of the territory.

The October 1981 television tapings saw an incoming tide of fresh and new heel talent into the WWF. Fresh off a stint in Verne Gagne's AWA, Adrian Adonis and Jesse "The Body" Ventura made their WWF debuts, both managed by Freddie Blassie. The taping also saw the return of Greg Valentine, who had been wrestling in the Mid-Atlantic area of the NWA, managed by the Grand Wizard. This was typical of how things worked in the office at the time. Every three or four months, Vince Sr. would bring in a fresh group of new heels from the NWA territories, the AWA, or Japan. He would have the Garden dates in his book six to nine months in advance, and once he got a look at the new heels at the television tapings, he would determine how many title matches he wanted each to get at the Garden, figure out how to get the new heels over with the fans by putting some heat on them, and then build the cards around that in a never-ending effort to draw fan interest and sell tickets. If a formula proved successful at the Garden, it was then sent around the territory to the other arenas.

This period in 1981 was a period of deep talent, and big business. There were a number of very talented and colorful heels coming and going, a lot of great storylines progressing, and exciting young guys like

Rick McGraw and Curt Hennig on the undercards who were getting beat in long twelve-to fifteen-minute preliminaries, but in the process, building their in-ring skills and getting over with the fans. The fans loved to cheer these guys on, so eventually, the promoters started putting them over more because that was what the fans wanted to see.

The first of these new heels to get his run at MSG was not really a "new" heel, but a retread from 1979 in the person of Greg Valentine. Greg and I had a great two-match series at the Garden in February and March 1979, and now, two and a half years later, Greg was back from a very successful run in Jim Crockett's Mid-Atlantic territory and ready for another run in New York. Vince Sr. liked Greg a lot and wanted to do something new and different with him at the Garden right off the bat, so Vince asked me at the TVs to come up with an interesting finish for our October 1981 title match at the Garden that would get people to come back for the return match.

In response to Vince Sr.'s request, I came up with what has become known as "The Black Trunks Screwjob." That night, Greg and I both came to the ring wearing identical black trunks. When we had the crowd at their high point, Greg got me up in the airplane spin and I kicked the referee in the head, knocking him down. The impact caused Greg to lose his balance. I fell on top of him and the ref counted to three, but then Greg jumped up and pretended he was the guy that was on top and put his hands up in the air. The referee, who was disoriented from being kicked in the head, raised Greg's hand and handed him the WWF championship belt as I lay dazed and dizzy down on the mat.

No one could figure out what had just happened.

On cue, a number of WWF and New York State Athletic Commission officials rushed into the ring. The people coming into the ring was all part of the angle—it was all to sell the idea that the referee had made a huge error and had cost me the belt. The Commission guys were told what to say and how to act to make it all seem totally realistic. Greg, meanwhile, played it perfectly by hurrying out of the ring and taking the belt back to the dressing room. Arnold played his part by arguing with the referee, gesturing wildly, and pleading our case to the Commission officials.

The crowd at the Garden was stunned.

Once we got back into the dressing room area, Greg gave the belt back to me, and we all had a good laugh. Back out in the ringside area, however, it was announced that due to the referee's error, the WWF title had been vacated and would be "held up" pending a rematch the following month. This little angle was created just for Madison Square Garden to add a little intrigue to the series. During the remainder of October and November, the rest of the WWF territory was none the wiser as I continued to hold and defend the belt everywhere else I went.

I enjoyed my matches with Greg, and had a lot of respect for him, so it was fun to do this with him and put a little bit of a rub on him. The way I originally pitched the idea, Greg was going to carry the title for a month across the territory pending our rematch at the Garden where I would get the belt back—but Vince Sr. didn't want to do that. He wanted me to have a title run to rival Bruno's—and he thought that my holding the title for an unbroken length of time gave me more strength—so he didn't want to let Greg get the title, even for just a month. Still, this little angle created some additional fan interest and brought the house back stronger for the following month—so it served its purpose.

This little angle, however, brings into focus how important the referee can be in the success or failure of a match. In my era, most of the time, the referees did *not* know the finish of any given match ahead of time. That information was withheld from them to make their reactions in the ring more realistic—but it also meant that it was up to the wrestlers to pay attention at all times. If you had your shoulders down on the mat and the referee was counting, you had to make sure to remember to kick out so he wouldn't count you out, since he didn't know the outcome. That's why, if you watch closely, a lot of the time, the referees would not only count with their hand slapping the mat, they would also yell the count so the wrestlers would be aware of what the count was.

The referees were also critical in the execution of high spots. If you executed a high spot and got a guy down into a winning combination, and the referee wasn't right on top of the move and down on the mat to make a count, the people wouldn't pop and the entire sequence would fall flat. The referee needed to be right there with you, in the flow of the match, anticipating what you were about to do in order to maximize the pop on each move. Referees like Dick Kroll, Dick Woherlie, Tim White, and Mario Savoldi were very good at that, and you knew they'd enhance the quality of the match. Others were not so good. Some of the referees were WWF guys, and some of them were athletic commission guys. If we drew one of the less-than-stellar commission guys on any given card, Vince Sr. would always ensure that he didn't work the important matches.

People also often ask how it was determined which heel went with which manager. Vince Sr. would figure out which heel's character would "fit" better with whom, and how badly a particular heel needed a talker. "Superstar" Billy Graham, for example, was one of the best talkers in the industry, so he didn't need a talker, and that's why they put him with the Grand Wizard both times. The Wizard was a good talker, but he was not the best of the three. Albano was loud and crazy, and as such, he generally got the crazy or wild heels that fit best with him. He was also known to be the "Guiding Light" of heel tag teams, so he generally got all of those. Freddie Blassie, on the other hand, was diabolical, and gave a great heel interview because he'd been heeling his whole life. He was also the head of "Blassie's Army"—which was usually comprised of the strongest, most muscular heels, and most of the foreign heels, who he would always claim to have "discovered" on his most recent trip to Europe or the Orient.

Albano was a huge asset to the company because he could not only talk people into the seats, he could also still occasionally get into the ring and work. When they put Albano into the ring, it put a lot of people in the seats who wanted to see him get his comeuppance. Although Blassie had been a monster heel in his day, he really couldn't work or take bumps anymore because his knees were shot from jumping off the ropes his whole career while having to protect the down guy. The Grand Wizard (Ernie Roth) was really more of a behind-the-scenes guy who helped the office with booking ideas. Ernie weighed 125 pounds soaking wet, so we weren't about to put any bumps on him.

Whenever I considered taking a bump, I always tried to think about Freddie Blassie, who by that point was already walking with the aid of a cane, and thought about what that bump was going to do to me ten years down the road. Take Hulk Hogan, for example. Think about how many times in his career he had to execute that running legdrop. That became his signature move, and, thus, one that he was expected to execute just about every night. That means that on around three hundred nights a year, Hulk Hogan was jumping up in the air, and dropping his 310-pound frame on his pelvis and his wrists, which he used night after night to break the fall. Any wonder why Hogan has back problems now.

There were definitely a lot of things to worry about inside the ring. Some high spots afforded you more control than others. Consider the bodyslam. If you didn't completely trust the guy bodyslamming you, you could hang onto his trunks or put your lower hand on his quad and at least partially control what part of your body hit the canvas first, and where you ended up. Likewise, on a piledriver, you'd grab the back of the offensive guy's knees and legs and he would then bend his knees as he fell back, and you would either get your hands on the mat, or rotate them around and push up on the guy's knees as you fell to ensure that your head never actually hit the mat. The vertical suplex was a more dangerous move because you had less control and had to trust your opponent to start in the right spot, aim in the right direction, and then drop you onto the mat backward with enough clearance to ensure that you could get your feet to hit first, and that no part of your body would hit the ropes or the turnbuckles on the way down.

I didn't like getting thrown over the top rope, because the drop to the floor was hard to time. Because you also never knew exactly where your opponent was going to throw you, there was always the risk that you would hit a table or a chair or something else in the ringside area on the way down. I got the worst injury I ever had in the business during my first three months wrestling in Baton Rouge when I went over the top rope in a battle royal, and hit my hip on the steel ring apron on the way down. My whole side was black and blue down for days after that, and frankly, I felt that injury my whole career.

A lot of the submission holds, like the sleeperhold, the Cobra Clutch, the Boston crab, or the figure-four leglock would really work if your opponent applied pressure to the hold, so if you actually allowed your opponent to put one of those moves on you, you had to trust that the guy was working with you. Other moves, like the brain buster, had a big "if" factor attached: namely that if the person applying the hold was off by even a little bit or lost his grip on you because of sweat or whatever, you could get seriously injured. Fortunately, with only a couple of exceptions, the guys who made it into the ring with me in the championship matches in the WWF were generally the top performing pros in the prime of their careers.

Typically, my opponents were very careful in the ring with me and didn't *want* me to get hurt because they were usually working multiple dates with me in the territory, so they needed and wanted me to be there to ensure their payday. Obviously, during the years that I was champion, I was the main event on the card, and in any given month would generally wrestle the same three or four guys all over the territory—so the guys I wrestled had a significant financial stake in making sure that we both got into and out of each match healthy and in one piece.

Although the WWF title was "held up" at Madison Square Garden, I continued to defend the belt around the rest of the territory in October and November 1981 against Muraco, and finishing up series with Khan and Mosca in some of the secondary and tertiary cities and towns. During the month, Don and I did our sixth and seventh one-hour Broadways in Binghamton and New Haven, to packed houses at the Broome

County Arena and Veterans Memorial Coliseum, respectively. I think the fans in those two towns were somewhat incredulous to watch the federation's two champions go at it to a one-hour time limit in their towns, and when those matches were over, the people knew that they had seen something special. For our part, Don and I were continuing to enjoy working together as the top two guys in the federation thrilling the fans with our epic battles.

On November 23, 1981, Greg Valentine and I were back in the Garden to decide the fate of the "vacant" WWF title. The angle worked, because the house came back stronger than it had been the month before for our first match. When Vince Sr. brought us together for the pre-match discussion, he told us that since Greg had gotten such a nice rub from getting his hand raised in the first match, he wanted the second match to be a decisive victory for me—so I would be going over by pinfall and regaining (or retaining!) the title, and then Valentine would be entering a feud with Pedro Morales over the Intercontinental title. On that same night, because Don was reaching the end of his run with the WWF and getting ready to leave the territory, Pedro was slated to get his revenge over Muraco and to win back the Intercontinental Heavyweight Championship.

They put the title back on Morales, because after taking a little break, Pedro expressed interest in getting back into a more regular role with the company. Pedro had a pretty reliable fan base of Puerto Ricans who would come out to see him in many of the larger cities and towns in the Northeast. Even though we were both babyfaces, there was no threat of redundancy in our title defenses because our styles were so different. Pedro was a brawler like Bruno was, and I was more of a collegiate-style scientific wrestler, so our matches were always very different making it easy for us to share a card.

Interestingly, Dusty Rhodes was also back in New York on that card. It certainly seemed to me that Dusty was working Vince Sr. pretty hard to get booked and get "over" up here, but the reality was that Vince Sr. was *way* ahead of Dusty and because of what Eddie Graham had warned him about, he really didn't have any desire to see that happen. On the November card, for example, Dusty was matched up against King Kong Mosca in a pretty interesting babyface-heel matchup that could have main-evented many of our secondary towns. If Vince Sr. was interested in building Dusty up to go anywhere in the WWF, he would have put Dusty over Mosca cleanly in that match. Mosca was about to leave the territory and was already doing clean jobs for Pat Patterson all over the territory. Instead, Vince Sr. booked the match to a DQ finish, which tells me that Vince saw Dusty's appearance as nothing more than a novelty act and a favor to Eddie Graham.

At the TVs the next day in Allentown, before the tapings started, they announced to the people that Pedro had won the title from Muraco at the Garden the night before. This allowed them to immediately run the angle with Valentine challenging Pedro and suplexing him on the concrete floor to get that feud off the ground. It had its desired effect—as the people were infuriated by Valentine's actions. It was also the first time that anyone had seen Pedro hurt like that before, so it perfectly set up Pedro and Greg to have a hot feud around the territory headlining some of the smaller buildings, and in combination with my main-event title matches in the larger buildings.

Before that, though, Muraco and I had some unfinished business to attend to over the next ten days in Landover, Boston, and Pittsburgh. I had been booked into return "title versus title" matches with Muraco, who, of course, had already lost the Intercontinental belt to Pedro. But because only the very few people who had satellite dishes at the time would have seen the Intercontinental title change at the Garden on MSG-Cablevision, Muraco came to the ring in those towns *still wearing* the Intercontinental Heavyweight Championship. The promoters in each of those cities wanted to see me beat Muraco before anyone learned that Morales beat him, because that would have affected the gate and taken away the champion vs. champion main-event rematch at the top of the card. So they just held back the TV taping in those three markets, kept Pedro and Muraco on the same routing to make sure that the belt was in the building on those nights, and kept the belt on Muraco in those cities to allow for these remaining matches to play out. Certainly anyone who was at the Garden to witness the title change and then happened to find themselves in the buildings in Boston, Landover, or Pittsburgh during the next couple of weeks would have been very confused—but in the days before the Internet, all of this was possible.

Boston was a rough city—they liked cage matches, and we hadn't done one in a while up there, so they put Don and me into a cage matchup there—with me going over Muraco when he got himself caught up between the ropes and the cage, allowing me to go out the door. In Landover, we did a Texas Death Match much like the one we had done at the Garden.

I was definitely sad to see Don go so soon—as I think he had gotten over with the people even more than Vince Sr. had imagined. I would put Don right up there with Sergeant Slaughter as the two most pleasant heel surprises of my time in the WWF. History will dictate which of those battles was the more compelling one to the fans in the WWF—but I certainly enjoyed working with both of them immensely.

21

The Peak (1982)

"Infect others with your enthusiasm, and teamwork will be the inevitable result."

—Napoleon Hill, "Inspire Teamwork"

<hr>

As we turned the calendar to 1982, I was still battling Greg Valentine around the territory in return matches in many of the major cities—but the storyline on television was the arrival of "The East-West Connection," Adrian Adonis and Jesse "The Body" Ventura from Verne Gagne's AWA. Neither Adonis nor Ventura had ever appeared in WWF rings before, and both were colorful heels who were larger than life in their own way. Adonis, who hailed from New York City (the "East" half of the tandem), was a leather-clad, fast-talking hipster and the master of "Goodnight Irene"—a deadly sleeperhold that had allegedly been banned in many cities because it would render Adonis' opponents unconscious. Ventura, on the other hand, was a tall, deeply tanned muscle man from San Diego (the "West" half of the team), who wore tassels in his bleached blonde hair and dangling earrings, and came to the ring clad in colorful robes. He was the master of the "Body Breaker"—an over-the-shoulder backbreaker that brought a quick submission from everyone caught in its clutches. Both were managed by "The Hollywood Fashion Plate," Classy Freddie Blassie.

Although the "East-West Connection" had been a very successful tag-team combination in the AWA, as the storyline went, Blassie had decided to break them up to run them against me in succession. That way, Blassie explained on television, one could soften me up for the other, and on any given night somewhere in the territory, one of the two would be ready to claim the WWF title for Blassie's army. These battles began at the All-Star wrestling TV taping in Hamburg at the very beginning of 1982, at which Pedro Morales and I wrestled the dark match against Adonis and Ventura just to give the four of us a chance to get our timing down with each other. Pedro was going to be defending the Intercontinental Championship belt against both Adonis and Ventura, and given that none of us had spent much, if any, time in the ring with each other, the four of us wrestled to a pretty entertaining countout in Hamburg to give each of us a chance to get some sequences down.

Around the territory at the beginning of 1982, Adonis and Ventura got staggered title matches, with Ventura getting the first shot in places like the Meadowlands, Baltimore, and Boston, while Adonis got the first crack in places like New York City, Hartford, and Landover. All the while, Blassie explained his strategic brilliance on the televised interviews that were being "bicycled" all over the territory, and the tandem of Adonis and Ventura drew great business with me nearly everywhere we went.

Adonis got the first shot at the Garden on January 18, 1982. Although Adrian and I had not spent any time in the ring together before, something just clicked with the two of us. Adrian was a very skilled worker who could get up and down really well back then. He was flexible and acrobatic, with a good knowledge of chain wrestling, and he was a bump machine. He was also a nice contrast to the parade of monsters I had faced for much of 1981, and consequently, he was a good opponent for me stylistically. Our work flowed well, and we were able to have some nice long matches that kept the fans on the edges of their seats.

Adonis was deceiving and had a great repertoire of moves. He was strong and very quick, and kept a good pace in the ring. Although he had a little extra weight on him, it did not slow him down. The fans had not yet seen a heel challenger to my title employ the sleeperhold as a finisher, so that was another "first" that helped Adonis gain some real traction as a challenger.

Vince Sr. knew right away that he had something in Adonis, and when he brought us together for our pre-match discussion, he had a sold out house waiting for the match. Accordingly, Vince Sr. called for a blood stoppage—and asked me to put over the sleeper as convincingly as possible to sell the possibility that Adonis could take the title in the rematch.

Our first match at the Garden went over thirty minutes, which means the match was paced pretty well, and that the people hadn't yet reached their energy climax by the twenty- or twenty-five-minute mark, where most of my matches usually ended. It took us thirty minutes to get to the blood stoppage—but we were listening to the people, not watching the clock. The fans were riveted by the back-and-forth nature of that match, so we decided to just let them tell us when it was time to bring it home. Adonis had not appeared in the Garden before, but he was being hyped pretty strongly on television—so we also wanted to take the time to develop his character a little more in the match to make his challenge for the belt look strong and convincing.

Unfortunately, the consequence of that match running longer than expected that night was that Putski and Killer Khan ran out of time in their final bout of the evening. Sometimes, the card would run long, either because guys weren't staying close enough to the time allotted to their matches, because my match or one of the other main-event caliber matches would run longer than expected, or because guys were taking too long to down to the ring or back to the dressing rooms. When that happened, the guys at the end of the card would get pinched for time. Sometimes, when that happened, the final match would go to the curfew time limit and the "referee's decision" was used to get the booked finish. That's what happened with Putski and Khan that night, with Putski getting awarded the victory over the departing Khan. On other nights, when they knew they were running way behind and had no *chance* of finishing the card the way they intended to, the 11 p.m. curfew was lifted. When that happened, it would end up costing the WWE a lot of money in mandatory overtime for the Garden employees, so lifting the curfew was a rare occurrence, and usually a pretty good indication that *something* in the card had not gone off as expected.

People often ask why one of the preliminary matches wasn't dropped instead, or on nights when we had a stacked card, why those preliminary matches were still allowed to run twelve to fifteen minutes, or even to a twenty-minute time limit. The answer goes back to my earlier discussion about building the fans' interest in a card. To build fans' interest, you want to start slow, and draw them into the action. That's why the curtain-jerker is usually a slow, methodical, mat-based match with only one or two high spots. You're giving the fans a chance to settle in and get oriented. Likewise, a preliminary match is sometimes dropped in somewhere in the middle of the card—usually right after a title match, or a big grudge match—as a chance for the fans to catch their breath, and a chance for the promoter to build them up again toward the next high spot in the card. None of this was accidental. These matches were all organized with a particular purpose in mind—so you couldn't just "cut" something in the middle of a card without impacting the flow of the rest of the card by doing it.

Between my matches with Adonis at the Garden, I made another trip out to Hawaii to again try to help out Peter Maivia. Peter had bought the promotion in Hawaii in 1980 where he and his wife Lia had retired after he finished wrestling in the WWF, but doing so had cost Peter all the money he had saved up from his years in wrestling. The promotion out there was a member of the NWA, but given its remoteness, it was also one of the smallest territories in the Alliance, and it was faltering economically. Knowing that, many of us, including Vince Sr. and Don Muraco and I, wanted to help Peter out.

One of the main problems was that the promotion was having a hard time getting a consistent time slot—the lifeblood of a wrestling promotion—on television in Hawaii. The one-hour weekly television program was essentially a one-hour-long advertisement to support the promotion, draw fan interest in the wrestlers and matches, and alert the fans to when and where the live house shows would be occurring. Without that kind of consistent and reliable exposure on television, it was very, very difficult for any promotion to draw well.

Peter's business had also been beat up by a lack of booking creativity that had forced repetitive angles on the fans, which led to giving the fans increasingly higher high spots to "shock" the fans into renewed interest. That just made it harder for them to come back, because it is the psychology of the storytelling, not the high spots, that keeps the fans coming back. King Curtis Iaukea had returned to Hawaii from Australia, and he was doing things in the ring night after night that were focused less on ring psychology and more on shock and mayhem. That popped the houses for a little while, but mayhem is unsustainable in the long run and eventually just made it tough to get the fans to come back when the mayhem was missing.

In an effort to help Peter, Vince Sr. sent me out there to defend the WWF title in a two-match series against Don Muraco. The first night, we wrestled at the Honolulu International Center arena—which held about 8,000 people. Because Don and I had done so many Broadways together while we were both champions, we wanted to do one more for Peter—so that's what we did. That was our eighth and final Broadway together in the ring. Unfortunately, given Peter's problems getting exposure on television, even with the WWF title defense at the top of the bill and Muraco and me in the main event, we didn't draw a big crowd at all. The Blaisdell Arena, where we wrestled on the first night was maybe half full. It was really shocking to me to only see 4,000 or 5,000 people in that arena given how well Muraco and I had drawn in the large East Coast of the WWF, and how well the cards had drawn in my previous matches in Honolulu when I would stop over there on my way back from Japan. This simply underscores how *critical* consistent television exposure is to the survival of a wrestling promotion. Vince McMahon Jr. knew that too, which was why buying up the television rights of the small regional promotions around the country was the critical component of the WWF's national expansion in 1983 and 1984.

The next night Muraco and I wrestled in Hilo. That night, I went over Muraco cleanly to defend the WWF title, but we again drew only a lackluster house. After seeing that two nights in a row, it was clear to us that Peter was not going to make it. Peter was a much beloved guy in the wrestling business and always treated the boys very well on our Hawaiian stopovers on the way back from Japan. Let's face it, who wouldn't want to be booked to wrestle in Hawaii? Access to talent wasn't his problem—the problem was in the promotion. Peter needed money to get reliable and consistent television. Without it, his promotion was dead in the water.

Unfortunately, Peter never got the chance to use his creativity and incredible connections in the profession to turn things around. It was around this time that Peter finally sought medical attention after years of ignoring the pain and discomfort, passing it off as simply the byproduct of taking nightly bumps in the ring. The doctor told Peter that cancer had spread throughout his body and he died shortly thereafter, in June 1982. My trip to Hawaii in February was the last time I would ever Peter.

I sure am glad I made that trip.

When I got back from Hawaii, Adonis was waiting for our return encounter at the Garden on February 15, 1982. I would have liked to do three matches with Adrian given how well our first match had gone, but we had a backup of heel challengers forming, so Vince Sr. scheduled this second match to be a Texas Death Match with Ivan Putski as the guest referee. We drew a bigger crowd than in our previous encounter—selling out the Garden. Once again, we played off of Adrian's Goodnight Irene finisher—the killer sleeperhold. We had been playing around with a great possible finish where he got the hold on me, nearly put me out, and then in a final furious comeback and effort to break the hold, I would run Adrian into the turnbuckles backward and then forward, forcing him to break the hold, and then sneak behind him and roll him up backward and bridge for the pin.

It was a high-risk finish that required a lot of agility on both of our parts, and a lot of things had to go exactly right for it to work. Adrian was very flexible and a great worker, so after running it successfully a couple of times in smaller towns, we decided to use it at the Garden. This time crowd was into our battle from the outset, and it didn't take very long to work the crowd into a frenzy—so at just after the fifteen-minute mark, Adrian captured me in Goodnight Irene. I slowly slumped to the canvas and Putski held my arm out, and I let it fall limply to the canvas.

One.

I could see the fans gasping and the ringsiders jumping up and down trying to urge me on. Putski held my arm out again, and I again let it fall limply to the canvas.

Two.

The energy in the building went up another level. Putski again reached for my arm, but this time, with the building rocking, I started to shake and quiver and tense my arms and rally to my feet. The roar of the crowd was deafening as I backed Adrian up and slammed him into the turnbuckle.

He held on.

The crowd continued to scream as I ran him back into the turnbuckle a second time, faster and harder. Adrian sold the move with a yell and an obvious grimace of pain, but still he held on.

I moved my arms to bring the fans one level higher, and then this time, ran Adrian forward, slamming his face into the buckle. He released the hold, and before anyone could see what had happened, I had slipped around him and caught him in the rolling reverse. I could feel his body relax to permit me to complete the roll and then bridge out onto my arms and my head. We had it positioned perfectly, and Putski was ready.

One . . . two . . . three!

The crowd exploded—the bell rang, and frankly, in my opinion, we had one of the best finishes in a title match that I had ever done with a challenger. It took the fans from a frenzy of despair and concern, to the edge of their seats, and then to jubilation all in about a span of twenty seconds. That's the kind of energy and emotion that the best professional wrestling can produce—and we did it without chairs, or tables, or fire, or foreign objects. This finish was simply about wrestling—about holds and counterholds, and knowing when to seize the moment when the crowd was at its peak to take them home.

We liked this finish so much that we repeated it in nearly every arena around the territory that got a Backlund-Adonis title match—and it had the same effect just about everywhere we tried it. Kudos to Adrian for a tremendous series. For those who only saw him in the cartoon years, you really missed something.

At the March TVs in Allentown and Hamburg, the new crop of summer heels, "Superfly" Jimmy Snuka, "Cowboy" Bob Orton, and "Blackjack" Mulligan arrived for their first television matches, which would be broadcast over the next several weeks. This was also the taping where the great new babyface tag team known as the Carolina Connection of Rick McGraw and Steve Travis was born. Rick and Steve were a good combination, and were a big hit with the ladies. They would go on to feud with the tag-team champions, Mr. Fuji and Mr. Saito around the territory in the summer of 1982, and the crowds really responded to those matches. I think they would have been great for a babyface run with the tag-team belts.

I knew Orton from Florida, where Steve Keirn and I had worked with him and his father. Orton was very good in the ring, and I was excited about his run, and about getting to work some interesting technical matches with him as a nice change of pace. Mulligan was the perfect combination of giant and cowboy heel—and, like most of the best characters, it wasn't really a gimmick for him. What you saw on television was the real person. Jack was a legitimate tough guy who knew and loved the wrestling business, and was interested in making the best of every match.

Jack was also a *really* big guy, I think he was six-foot-five or so and about 350 pounds, had a great sneer, an ominous handlebar mustache, a big black hat, and a mysterious black rubber glove on his hand that he would use to administer his "brain claw" finisher—another hold that the New York fans had not yet seen during my tenure as champion. He talked well, and I think he would have presented a really good, powerful, and interesting challenge to the belt. But as I would find out later, as he had with Hogan, Vince Sr. was focused on preparing Jack for a headlining run with Andre, and that was a great thing too — because whenever Andre had someone more his size, he could work with him more, and any clash between Andre and another credible giant was gold at the box office.

I didn't know Snuka at all, and had no real expectations about that series. I fully expected that the highlight of that group was going to be Orton. That's why Vince Sr. did the booking and I did the wrestling!

This latest crop of heels also gives you some insight into how the business worked at the time. At that taping, I had just finished with Adonis at the Garden, but was really just getting started wrestling him around the rest of the territory. Meanwhile, I had not yet wrestled Jesse Ventura at the Garden, although I already had *some* matches with him in other cities around the territory. Although it was unusual for other cities (other than a one-off small town somewhere if a heel and I were unfamiliar with each other and needed to get our timing down) to get a main event before the Garden, in this case there was a real logjam of challengers forming.

Ventura was to be my next opponent. Jesse, who legitimately *was* a bodyguard for the Rolling Stones, was trained, like I was, at the 7th Street gym in Minneapolis by Eddie Sharkey, and was trying to emulate and expand upon the character first used by "Superstar" Billy Graham. Ventura had a very muscular body, a deep tan, and was a good talker. Ventura wasn't as up and down on and off the mat as some of the other guys were, and he wasn't a bump machine like Adonis was, but I hadn't wrestled a strong man–type challenger since Ken Patera and Hulk Hogan in 1980, and it takes all types to make the story work, so this was a logical fit.

Jesse and I only did one match at the Garden because his repertoire of maneuvers in the ring wasn't as broad as some of my other challengers, and at that point in his career in the WWF, he hadn't gotten as "over" as some of the other heels that the people just lined up to hate. Adonis, for example, was cockier on the microphone, and as I have mentioned, his

Goodnight Irene sleeperhold finisher had propelled him into the ranks of heels people really wanted to see. Ventura, at that time, was a cool, beatnik type from the West Coast that the people honestly didn't hate that much. I'm just not sure that the people quite knew what to make of Ventura, whose persona was really part wrestler, and part rock star. I also think that the people didn't really see him as possessing the same kind of "heel credentials" as guys like Stan Hansen or Sergeant Slaughter or Don Muraco—who I think the people really believed could win the world title from me on any given night.

I felt badly that Jesse didn't get more of a run at the Garden because I liked him a lot as a person. He was a pleasure to be in the ring with in that he always protected us both very well. Jesse got the matinee card at the Garden on March 14, 1982. I remember the match well—he came into the ring with Freddie Blassie wearing a really colorful robe and earrings and jewelry around his arms. His entrance, frankly, was among the best of any of my heel challengers at getting the people riled up—and the entrances and Howard Finkel's in-ring introductions were a very important part of getting the people's energy up for the title match. I think everyone knew that Jesse would pull that part off as well as anyone because he loved to play to the crowd and he was as good at that as anyone.

After that, though, Vince Sr. knew that Ventura and I wouldn't match up that well in terms of our in-ring repertoire because Jesse's palette of moves was limited. Given that, Vince Sr. had set up Ivan Putski as the guest referee for the bout, which was unusual given that it was our first match, and there really wasn't a grudge befitting a special guest referee. In reality, Vince Sr. was really looking to find something to do with Jesse. Ventura and Putski started jawing at each other right from the pre-match introductions, and given the finish that Vince Sr. called for, that was all part of the setup.

When you are the champ, and you are facing someone like Ventura in the ring, you have to consider what you can credibly do within the confines of each wrestler's abilities, and given that, how to get the people to the right place to get to the finish. The match was mostly a street fight, with Ventura punching and kicking and choking and trying to soften up my back for his finisher, the Bodybreaker, mixed with Ventura and Putski getting into it over Putski's manhandling him to force clean breaks, and administering a couple of very slow counts when Ventura had me in pinning combinations. The drama in this match was as much about the obvious bias and growing heat between Ventura and Putski as it was about Ventura's quest to unseat me as the WWF champion.

I basically let Jesse beat on me for about eight minutes, during which he got a series of very slow counts from Putski, after which point he got me up in the Bodybreaker for a false finish. I managed to get to the ropes, kick off, and backdrop him into a pinning combination that we held for a two count before he kicked out. The people were buzzing pretty well at that point, and I thought that was the time to go. I didn't want to lose that peak, because you can't hold it for long, and if you lose it, the match can go downhill from there. Given what I knew we were able to do, and how much of it we had already done, I wasn't sure we'd be able to get the people back to that level again.

There had been a lot of long title matches at the Garden in the preceding months, and a lot of long series with challengers, so keeping the people off balance and having some shock value was always important, and that's what this was—something completely opposite of what the people were used to seeing. So Ventura went to put me up in the Bodybreaker again, but I slipped off his shoulder, got behind him, pushed him into the ropes, and caught him in the rolling reverse, which Ventura positioned himself *perfectly* on, allowing me to bridge out in one fluid motion. Putski went to the mat and delivered the fastest three count in Garden history, the people roared, and the bell rang. The finish looked so good, it was used in the intro to the *Championship Wrestling* television broadcast for nearly a year after that. Credit to Jesse for making that happen.

After the announcements, the pot boiled over as Ventura attacked Putski, setting up an instant feud which would main-event the high school and community college gyms and fieldhouses around the territory for much of the spring and summer.

After we finished going around the horn, Adonis went on to have a series of Intercontinental title matches with Pedro Morales while I was wrestling Ventura. Ventura then went on to wrestle Putski and then Tony Atlas in strongman matches in a number of towns. Adonis and Ventura later got back together as the "East-West Connection" tag team, and would go on to have entertaining matches around the territory with Tony Garea and Rick Martel, the Carolina Connection, and the Strongbow Brothers that all did well at the box office.

Mulligan was the next heel up. It had been about a year since the WWF crowds had last seen a heel cowboy (Stan Hansen), and Blackjack, at over six feet eight inches tall and about 330 pounds, was very different from Hansen. He was more of a cross between the "rugged cowboy" and the "giant" types. Mulligan should have been the perfect guy at the time to put some heat into, but, as they had with Hogan in 1980, they wanted to keep Mulligan fresh for Andre without having the Garden crowd see me beat him, so they never booked Jack into a main event with me at the Garden. Instead, they tested the Andre-Mulligan matchup in a few small towns in New Jersey and Pennsylvania, and finding that Andre and Mulligan worked well together and that the people were responding favorably to their feud, they decided to push Jack into a feud with Andre at the Garden right away.

I only wrestled Mulligan in a couple of towns. We did a double disqualification in our first match at the Baltimore Civic Center on April 10, 1982, then followed that a week later on April 17 at the Spectrum in Philadelphia, in a match that almost didn't happen. During that week, while driving from Maryland to Connecticut, then back out to Long Island, and then out to Pittsburgh, I developed a blood clot in my leg. While I was home, I went to see my doctor in East Haven, Connecticut—who was the same doctor who would check the wrestlers for the Connecticut State Athletic Commission when we would wrestle at the New Haven Coliseum. My doctor told me that if the clot came loose and moved out of my leg, I could die. He called Vince Sr. and told him what was up, but with near-sellout crowds waiting in two of the largest arenas on the circuit, no-showing the main events was simply not an option. I gingerly limped my way through the next two nights' main events against Adonis in Pittsburgh and then Mulligan in Philadelphia, where I was limping so badly that I was barely cleared to wrestle by the Pennsylvania State Athletic Commission. I wrestled one of the shortest title matches of my career that night because I was in legitimate pain and had real concerns for my health and well-being. Being the true professional that he is, Jack took especially good care of me in the ring that night to make sure that my condition wouldn't worsen further. I was grateful for that. Vince then gave me a week off to get healthy and ready for my first match with Snuka at the Garden.

I was not privy to the communications Vince Sr. had with Jim and David Crockett of the Mid-Atlantic territory bringing Jimmy Snuka into the WWF, or how much the Crocketts had told Vince Sr. about Snuka or how he was drawing down there in the Carolinas, but I don't think anyone had any inkling of just how over Snuka was going to get with the WWF fans. At the outset, Vince Sr. had set things up so I would end up doing a longer series with "Cowboy" Bob Orton, who, like Don Muraco, was a product of Eddie Graham's Florida Championship Wrestling, and with whom I could have had some great *wrestling* matches. Orton had gotten a run with the Florida Heavyweight Championship for Eddie, and I know that Vince Sr. loved Orton, both for his look and for his substantial in-ring skills. But when Snuka just erupted into a mega-heel at the box office, the office rode that horse all the way to the bank, I unexpectedly spent nearly all of the summer of 1982 wrestling him, which seriously truncated the time I had available to spend with Orton.

For those who are unfamiliar with the Snuka series—which, in terms of box office interest, and general buzz, probably represented the high-water mark of my nearly six-year title run—let me set the scene. Snuka came into the territory as a mysterious, wild jungle savage in leopard print trunks, managed by Captain Lou Albano. The man allegedly spoke not a word of English, but had a body that looked like it had been chiseled from stone. He also possessed one of the most spectacular finishing maneuvers in the history of the business to that point—a signature move where he would climb to the top turnbuckle and then swan dive halfway across the ring before crashing down onto the prone body of his opponent. That move had earned him the nickname "The Superfly," and had also allegedly sent numerous victims to the hospital. The first time that Snuka executed that move on television, everyone watching knew that this guy was something special.

After the first couple of matches at the taping, however, it became clear just *how* special.

Snuka was in his late thirties when he arrived in the WWF, and had a lot of experience in the ring. In the ring, Jimmy was a terrific performer. He knew what he wanted to do at every minute, and after each move, he would pause just long enough to allow the people to respond before he went on to his next move. Jimmy had excellent timing—he was deliberate and never rushed anything—and that's part of what made him so successful. He got the most out of every move in terms of the people's reaction. His level of experience in professional wrestling made Snuka one of the most polished heels I ever had the pleasure to step into the ring with.

The combination of the seemingly savage and uncontrollable Snuka with the wild and unpredictable Albano also really helped to strike fear into the hearts of the fans. The two of them fit together brilliantly and they played well off each other. It was just a great combination. At the beginning, the fear in the hearts and minds of the fans was palpable. Because television from Crocketts' Mid-Atlantic area did not reach into much of the WWF territory, few WWF fans had ever laid eyes on Snuka before. He got a heck of a response when he came out—one that just sparkled a little bit more than most other heels. And then he started stretchering the TV job guys out, one after the next, with that devastating swan dive — and the fans' response to him become increasingly intense. I can clearly remember the reaction everybody had at that first television taping — both the people in the crowds in Allentown and Hamburg, and the office guys in the back. Vince Jr. *really* liked Snuka, and Vince Sr., also liking what he saw, started reshuffling the book to accommodate an unexpected box office hit in the making.

Snuka's title match with me in the Garden on April 26, 1982, was his first arena shot in the territory. Nobody had gotten to see him in a WWF arena before, so when he emerged from behind the curtain at the Garden with Albano, it was definitely a special moment. Flashbulbs were popping and the crowd was buzzing with anticipation, and Snuka, for his part, was really playing it up — looking around quizzically at the large number of people gathered around the ringside area, and then wide-eyed as he surveyed the thousands and thousands more in the first and second decks as if to communicate the thought that he was thousands of miles from his jungle home and had no idea where he was.

Back in the dressing room area before the match, Vince Sr. had taken me into the bathroom separately, *without* Snuka, which was very unusual. I deduced pretty quickly that something was up.

"Bobby," Vince Sr. said to me, "this guy is really getting over . . . and he could really be something. He's going to go over tonight by disqualification. But after that, I'd like to have Snuka hit that splash, hurt you, and send you out of here on a stretcher. Would that be alright with you?"

We wanted to get Jimmy's amazing finisher over with the people as strongly as we possibly could, and what better way to do that than for me to get carried out of the Garden on a stretcher for the first time ever? I was very pleased, however, that Vince Sr. thought enough of me as his champion to pull me aside, and *ask* me for this booking rather than simply telling us to do it. Of course, I had so much respect for Vince Sr. that

I would have done just about anything for him, and frankly, I agreed with him that it made a lot of sense to do that finish. The people had seen Snuka stretcher a number of people out on television, and that splash was the kind of maneuver that, in reality, could break ribs or collapse a lung—the kind of damage that, if it were real, really *would* cause you to be taken from the ring on a stretcher. The idea was to put in the minds of the fans that this guy had the potential not just to beat me for the world title, but to actually injure me so severely that I wouldn't be able to wrestle again for a long time.

I was all for it.

That first match definitely had its desired effect, as Jimmy and I brawled all over the Garden for about twelve or fourteen minutes. The purpose of that first match was to deliver the impression that I was not in a wrestling match with this guy—but was actually in a fight for my life against a savage who was seemingly impervious to pain. That was why my choking Snuka out and not heeding the referee's warning until he disqualified me made sense as a finish. If you were in a fight for your life, you would use whatever means were at your disposal to try and protect yourself, wouldn't you? That was exactly the feeling that I was going for in that first match.

Everything in that first match worked according to plan. After the bell rang and the referee broke the choke, Snuka rallied, and suplexed me down onto the mat and then climbed to the top rope with the flash bulbs sparkling all over the arena and crashed down right over me. It was an eerie feeling laying down there on the mat waiting for a 250-pound man to dive on you, and knowing that even the smallest, adrenaline-fueled miscalculation could lead to a legitimate and catastrophic injury to one or both of us. As it was, Snuka barely touched me, but he made it look great. The fans were shocked as I lay motionless inside the ring getting checked out by Arnold and the doctors, and then eventually got loaded onto the stretcher and carried out of the Garden.

A Beautiful Thing

You know, for Bobby to do that for me — to put me over like — was a really beautiful thing, brother. You know, he didn't have to do that.

But Bobby was a wonderful person and a great athlete and a great champion, and he knew that we could really do something together, you know?

— "Superfly" Jimmy Snuka

What Jimmy did to me in the Garden that night triggered fan interest in our feud the likes of which had not been seen in the federation since Stan Hansen broke Bruno's neck in 1976. The magazines covered it, and the stretcher job in the Garden even got some coverage in the mainstream New York City media. Everywhere I went after that, people expressed concerns for my safety and well-being, and were genuinely worried about how, and whether I was going to be able to find a way not to beat Snuka, but perhaps just to *survive* Snuka.

Meanwhile, this firestorm of interest in the Snuka series relegated both Orton and Mulligan to the back burner. On May 1, 1982, I pinned Orton in our first match at the Capital Center, and I did the same in Boston a few nights later. It was very disappointing for Orton to not get the opportunity to really prove himself after working his way up the ladder for so many years down in Florida with Eddie Graham, and the fact is, Orton and I could have done a lot more with that series than we did.

In fact, the gimmick we used with Orton, who was managed by the Grand Wizard, was that I had ducked wrestling Orton in the amateurs, that he had been chasing me ever since, and, he claimed, he was the one wrestler in the world that I knew I couldn't beat.

It was a pretty interesting booking premise that hadn't been used before, but with all the buzz that summer being about Snuka, only Phil

Zacko, who promoted the Philadelphia Spectrum, saw the merit of giving Orton two main-event title matches with me. Everybody else was lining up for multiple months of Backlund-Snuka.

Meanwhile, it must have been especially disappointing for Mulligan, who was, at that time, a fifteen-year veteran of the business, to come into the territory, be here for two weeks, and end up wrestling a mid-card guy in the Garden while Snuka got the main event and stretchered the champion out. Because all three of those guys had come into the territory at roughly the same time, and with the same expected four-month stay, both Orton and Mulligan had to know where all the buzz about Snuka was going to leave them. They knew where the focus was going to go. And, in fact, only a couple of nights after the first Garden card with Snuka, Mulligan was one-and-done, doing the honors for me in Hartford and Boston.

Meanwhile, there were already some telltale signs developing around Snuka after the fans around the territory got to see him a couple of times. Snuka was the hottest heel the territory had seen during my reign as the champion. The fans were frightened by him, intrigued by him, and just wanted to get close enough to get a good look at him. On May 22, 1982, at the Philadelphia Spectrum, on the card where I had my first main event with Orton (where he beat me by countout), Snuka was in the ring with Morales for the Intercontinental Heavyweight Championship and drew a fair number of *cheers* from the fans, while Morales, normally a favorite in Philly, was booed. Philadelphia had always been something of a heel town, so it wasn't *that* surprising to hear Snuka get cheered there, but it was an interesting development that did not pass unnoticed, either in the dressing room, or among the front office guys.

Snuka and I came back to the Garden on June 5, 1982, which had sold out well in advance. People showing up to buy tickets were being told that the only way they could see the match was to buy a ticket for the closed-circuit broadcast in the Felt Forum, and eventually, that too approached capacity. When Vince Sr. brought us together for the pre-match instructions that night, Jimmy and I both knew that we were going three. There was no way that they *couldn't* have booked it that way given the way that the feud was selling around the territory. Everywhere Jimmy and I wrestled, the people were turning out in droves. Even up in Portland, Maine, our title match drew the largest wrestling crowd in the history of the Cumberland County Civic Center. All the promoters wanted a piece of this match.

"Bobby, Jimmy is going over by count-out tonight," Vince Sr. explained to us. You're both going to get color, and Bobby, you're going to be frustrated that you can't seem to find a way to beat Jimmy, and you're going to chase him out of the ring. And Jimmy, you're going to catch Bobby out there and work him over, and then jump back into the ring for the win. We're coming back next month in the cage, so that's what you're setting up."

The point of the second match, of course, was to continue to give Snuka the air of invincibility—for me to become more and more frustrated that I couldn't beat him—and for the fans to begin to wonder even more whether it was *possible* to pin Jimmy Snuka for the three count. In the ring, it felt like the match came off really well, and we had the fans at their peak at about the twenty-minute mark of the match. Meanwhile, on the undercard, Andre faced the unblemished Mulligan and the two battled all over the building to an indecisive finish. As Vince Sr. expected, in the eyes of the fans, Mulligan presented a *legitimate* threat to Andre's career undefeated streak.

In a really hot three-match series, the third match was always some kind of gimmick match—be it a lumberjack match, a chain match, a Texas Death Match, a Bunkhouse match, or, of course, the steel cage match. Which gimmick was chosen for the blowoff was usually a factor of what the fans in that city had seen or not seen recently coupled with what the wrestlers were capable of. The Texas Death Match was a Funk invention—it was basically a free-for-all match with no countouts or disqualifications, no holds barred, and no stoppages by the doctor for excess blood loss. It usually spilled out into the ringside area and involved the use of foreign objects or whatever might have been around and available at ringside. It also usually involved one or both participants getting color. The Texas Death Match (or its ethnic alternatives, like the Greek Death Match, the Caribbean Death Match) was just an alternative to make sure that the promoter did not have to overdose on cage matches every time a blowoff match was needed. In the WWF, typically, we'd choose a Texas Death Match with a guy like Patera, Muraco, Valentine, or Slaughter, who had enough of a repertoire to not need a cage to sell the blowoff. With a roughhouser or a guy with a limited repertoire, you could use the cage to add a new level of story to the match, because in a cage match, the cage, and the attempt to escape it, becomes the story.

On a card that features a steel cage match, the cage is generally what the people have come to see, and as such, the people expect certain things from you. They're going to be looking for color—so you have to give them that. They are going expect both wrestlers to use the cage as part of their offense and defense—so you can't go into a cage match and start throwing hiptosses, because that doesn't fit the storyline. If the storyline was developed properly, the fans would have already seen those things in one or both of the first two matches. The steel cage was the modern-day equivalent of the Roman Coliseum—so there needed to be a furious pace, some real damage inflicted on someone, and a clear winner and a clear loser. In Vince McMahon Sr.'s WWF, the man with the white hat had to win the war decisively to send the people home happy. There were only a couple of examples in all the years I wrestled where that didn't happen.

People sometimes ask why the WWF's cage match had the stipulation that the way to win the match was to escape the cage, rather than to soundly defeat your opponent for a three count by a referee. Not having the cage match end by a pin or submission was a way to keep heat on the loser and to not have to have him lay down for a pin. Remember that many of my heels would go on to wrestle Pedro for the Intercontinental title after their series with me. If I destroyed them, their ability to draw money as a challenger to Pedro in that subsequent match would be weakened. It was a delicate dance—I had to beat them decisively to send the fans home happy, but not so decisively that there wasn't still considerable doubt as to whether that guy could beat Pedro the following month, or at the local arena card where that match might be the headliner being relied upon to draw the house.

So all of that is a lead up to June 28, 1982—the blowoff with Snuka at the Garden in the cage—in what may well have been the most anticipated title defense of my entire career. The match was so hot, Vince Sr. had no misgivings about going back to the Garden three weeks after our last Garden bout instead of the usual five—which, of course, gave them two weeks less time to promote the match and the card. It didn't much matter though, because the cage match with Snuka drew the largest house of my career at the Garden. The Arena and the Felt Forum were both sold out for the event, and there were a *lot* of people turned away that night. I don't know what the precise paid attendance numbers were, and I'm not sure that anyone other than Vince Sr. ever really did, but I do know that my paycheck from that match was higher than anything I had ever seen at the Garden before.

Contrary to rumor, Vince Sr. never planned to change the belt that night. The fact that there were a lot of photographers, particularly from Japan, at ringside that night was simply an indication of how much interest there was internationally in this match. My cage match with Snuka was simply the logical end to a tremendous series of matches—as good as any that I had ever had in my career with anyone.

That night was absolutely one of the most electrifying nights of my career. The people were on edge. It was just one of those nights when everyone coming into the building knew that they were going to see something truly special. Our match was all anyone was talking about.

Making Magic

What Bobby and I went on to do in New York City was to make magic, you know what I'm saying? It was just magical out there. It was a happening. And the people who were there that night will never forget it.

— "Superfly" Jimmy Snuka

The match had a strange extra stipulation, that the only way to win the match was to go *out the door* of the cage, *not* over the top. The changes to the normal cage match rules were actually announced in the Garden that night so everyone would be clear about the rule change. Although it was hyped that this rules change had been slipped into the "contract" for the rematch by my manager Arnold Skaaland, there were actually two real-life reasons for that change. First, the booked finish had Snuka climbing up to the top of the cage, pausing there to look around, diving off, missing me, and crashing into the mat, allowing me to escape. That finish wouldn't have made any sense if Snuka could have simply turned around at the top and climbed out of the cage instead of trying to jump down on me. So we needed the rules change to take care of that. Second, and probably more important, we needed protection against an accident. Snuka was getting a reputation among the boys for frequently being under the influence of marijuana and, thus, sometimes being a little unstable when climbing and balancing on the top rope. Because it was known that Snuka was sometimes messed up when he wrestled, the office was concerned about whether this finish would come off cleanly, both for Jimmy and for the match.

To be fair to Jimmy, this was hardly an easy finish for him to execute. Vince Sr. was asking Jimmy, with all of that adrenaline pumping through his body, to climb to the top rope in the middle of Madison Square Garden, then turn around and climb another three feet of wobbly chain link fence to the unstable top of two intersecting sections of that chain link fence being held together by a steel cable. He was then to perch his

250-pound frame up there while sweating profusely and bleeding from multiple cuts on his face, and time his leap fifteen feet down onto the mat to both avoid me and avoid hurting himself upon landing.

No problem, right? Just another day at the office.

There were just too many variables involved to run that finish without protection. Vince Sr. needed that stipulation to make sure that if Snuka slipped off the top of the cage and accidentally fell to the arena floor, Vince Sr. wouldn't have had to put the belt on him.

Of course, as everyone knows, the match came off perfectly. The night was a little unusual in that the challenger usually came out to the ring first, but on that night, I wanted to be out in the ring so that Snuka could play up his entrance to the fans just a little bit more. When Snuka came out, he carefully identified which corner of the cage seemed to be the most stable to use for his leap, and he kept track of that corner throughout the match. When the time came, he climbed to the top rope and then to the top of the cage without incident, perched up there for a beautiful photo op for the thousands of people who were ready with their cameras, and then, with flash bulbs sparkling all over the arena, timed his leap perfectly and landed it (missing me) without injuring either one of us.

All that was left for me to do at that point was to crawl out the door and get to the arena floor, where Vince McMahon Jr. was waiting to do a post-match interview with the winner. It was a storybook ending to a great feud, the highest high spot (both literally and figuratively) of any finish I was ever part of, and certainly one of the two or three most memorable nights of my nearly forty-year career in this business.

Although Snuka and I were done at the Garden before the end of June 1982, there were bouts between us scheduled all over North America until mid-September. Only the Madison Square Garden got that finish, though. Because that finish was so risky and so brutal on Jimmy's knees, back, and elbows, we could not replicate it in all the major arenas around the territory. In many of the other arenas, we did Texas Death Matches or return matches with special guest referees. Intercontinental

Champion Pedro Morales was the special referee most often called on to maintain order in those bouts.

As the summer wore on, however, an interesting thing was happening. Jimmy started to get more and more *cheers* from the fans, and our matches started to revert to more scientific wrestling matches rather than the fierce brawls we had at the Garden. The fans were turning Jimmy Snuka into a babyface. By the time I had my last title match with Jimmy at the Spectrum in Philadelphia in September 1982, Jimmy's unplanned face turn was nearly complete. In that "return" match, Jimmy *barely* played the heel, I beat him cleanly with an inside cradle in the middle of the ring, and when he popped up, he stared me in the face, and I extended a hand to him, and he shook it. The fans could not believe what they were watching, but they were cheering madly for it. It had been a wild and crazy six-month run, which took Jimmy Snuka from one of the most feared and hated rulebreakers the federation had ever seen to an unplanned babyface turn that more or less evolved naturally before the fans' eyes.

Toward the end of our series of matches, as things were winding down, Vince Sr. pulled me aside at a television taping and talked to me about Snuka. He asked me, straight out, whether I thought Jimmy could be the world champion. I told Vince Sr. that Snuka's timing in the ring was as good as anybody's I had ever worked with in the WWF, and that Jimmy had the look and the ability necessary to be a great champion *in the ring*. I talked to Vince Sr. about Jimmy's versatility in the ring, and how he had the repertoire of moves to work with people of different styles, from amateur-oriented guys like me, to full-out brawlers like Pedro. But then, as it always did with Jimmy, our conversation turned to the extracurricular activities that he was involved in—most particularly his propensity to get stoned, and whether, given that reality, Jimmy could be relied upon to hold down the top spot on the card. The question in Vince Sr.'s mind was whether Jimmy could be relied upon to show up every night, and to show up prepared and ready to wrestle in the main event in every building he appeared in.

I know that after the fans had turned Snuka into a babyface, Vince Sr. was thinking about making Snuka the next champion. We talked about it. Ultimately, however, Vince Sr. decided *not* to give him a run with either the world title or the Intercontinental belt because the front office guys concluded that there were just too many negatives on the personal side to entrust the business to him. It would take a man like Vince McMahon Sr. to make a decision that would value integrity over money—and that's exactly what he did in making the decision not to put a belt on Snuka, who was unquestionably as big a draw as anyone in the federation at that time. Had it not been for his personal demons, I think Snuka would have ended up with the world title sometime in 1982, either by taking it directly from me, or by quickly winning it from a transitional heel champion. What I respected most about that whole episode, though, is that once again, Vince McMahon Sr. came to me directly—he just came right out and asked me, "What would you think of Snuka as a champion?" To me, that indicated the level of trust and respect that I had earned from Vince Sr.—a fact that made me very happy.

Snuka, of course, went on to turn babyface in September 1982. The office, faced with the fact that they couldn't maintain the façade of Jimmy as heel any longer, scrambled to come up with a scenario that would make it official. Ultimately, they did it through the Buddy Rogers Corner television vignette. There, Rogers, who had been the federation's first world champion in 1963, returned to the federation and "exposed" the fact that Captain Lou Albano had been "stealing" all of Snuka's gate money, and that Jimmy was, in fact, broke. Jimmy then "fired" Albano, and asked Buddy Rogers to be his new manager. In reality, Buddy was hired back because he needed the money, and Vince Sr. needed someone to drive Jimmy around and make sure that he got to the arenas on time and in proper shape to wrestle.

Jimmy got attacked and took a piledriver on the concrete floor by Ray Stevens in a memorable television angle, and Jimmy's face turn was complete.

From there, Snuka would go on to have a memorable feud with Ray "The Crippler" Stevens that headlined many buildings in the fall of 1982 and then a sensational feud with Don Muraco over the Intercontinental title in the summer and fall of 1983. By that point, though, Buddy Rogers had quit driving Snuka because, as it was explained to me, he didn't want to be associated with Snuka's continuing drug use and chemical dependence.

Vince Sr. was running more than one show a day on many days, and was using Muraco's Intercontinental title defense as the main event on many of the cards where I did not appear to defend the world title. Given that newfound responsibility that the Intercontinental Champion was shouldering, Jimmy's personal demons kept him from getting a run with that belt as well. Of course, by that time, Jimmy's personal problems extended well beyond chemical dependence after his girlfriend, Nancy Argentino, was found dead in his motel room in Allentown in May 1983 after a television taping, and Jimmy found himself at the center of a major crimes investigation. I had left for home hours before this tragedy occurred because I only recorded promo interviews and did not wrestle that night at the Allentown taping, so my work was done late in the afternoon.

That same night, another young wrestler on the roster, Eddie Gilbert, was involved in a serious car accident.

Needless to say, it was a tough night for the federation. But we're getting ahead of ourselves.

———◆———

At the television tapings in Allentown the week before the steel cage blowoff with Snuka at the Garden, I had picked up my bookings for the upcoming three weeks and saw the following odd notation in Vince's calendar.

Saturday, July 3	Atlanta, GAWTBS studios TV
Sunday, July 4	Atlanta, GAWTBS studios TV
Sunday, July 4	Atlanta, GAOmni

Seeing that I was heading down to the Omni, which had become the Madison Square Garden of the NWA, for a match on July 4, I figured this was going to be something pretty big. Likewise, WTBS out of Atlanta had become one of the first national television superstations that was broadcast all over the country, which had provided the NWA with a nationwide promotional platform. I tracked Vince Sr. down and asked him who I'd be wrestling there. He told me that I would be facing the current NWA World Heavyweight Champion, Ric Flair, in a world title unification match.

The match had been arranged between Vince Sr., Jim Barnett, who at the time was still running Georgia Championship Wrestling, and Jim Crockett, the promoter in charge of the Mid-Atlantic region and the then-president of the NWA.

There were some pretty interesting goings-on between the NWA and the WWF at the time. In June 1982, Vince Sr. and his partners sold their interests in Capitol Wrestling Corporation (the entity that ran the WWF) to Vince's son. Vince Jr. had until mid-1983 to make the required payments to acquire the shares. I think this whole situation created some heartburn among some of the major players in the NWA, because although those guys had enduring relationships and reverence for Vince Sr., they didn't really like or trust Vince Jr. Vince Sr. was still in charge of the booking, however, and had made the arrangements for the match with Jim Barnett, who I knew well from my days wrestling for him in Georgia. I was actually excited to go down there and have a match like this with Flair.

Vince hadn't said anything to me about unifying the titles, so I knew that the booking would be either a Broadway or some sort of inconclusive finish that I would get from Barnett when I got down there. If Vince Sr. had agreed to a title change, even for a short period, I know that he would have sat me down and explained the booking to me before I left for Atlanta — as he had when we did the short switch with Inoki in Japan in 1979.

I went down to Atlanta, wrestled a match in the ring in the WTBS studios, and then, the following day, did a face-to-face interview with

Flair at ringside conducted by Gordon Solie. I had wrestled Flair once a couple of years earlier up in Toronto for Frank Tunney when Flair was the NWA's US Champion, so I knew him to be a great performer in the ring. I had also been around Ric for a time in Florida—so we knew each other well enough. Ric had really come into his own and grown into his character since defeating Harley Race for the NWA World Heavyweight Championship, and had blossomed into an enormous box office draw all over the NWA territory. Flair was being bankrolled by the NWA to live his character, and as such, was legitimately wearing expensive suits, and Rolex watches, and alligator shoes, and being chauffeured around the territory in a limousine. His gimmick had gotten him over as a larger-than-life character with the NWA fans who were turning out in droves to see him wherever he went.

Unlike Harley and I, however, Ric and I did not have a long history together, or a shared level of trust. Ric and I were not close.

I knew that Flair was a good athlete and a great performer, though, so I knew we were going to have a heck of a match. I felt pretty relaxed during the interview with Gordon Solie, and just tried to look into the camera and give the NWA fans a straightforward, credible interview like any professional athlete preparing to compete for a world championship would give. Ric, who was better on the microphone than I was the day he came out of the womb, gave a somewhat toned-down and respectful, but still pretty cocky accounting of himself. That interview was broadcast across the country on Superstation WTBS, and set the stage for our confrontation. It would be a matchup of two world champions with very different styles: Ric, as the rich, flashy, entitled champion—and me, as the amateur-based, hardworking man-of-the-people. Even though the fans in Atlanta hadn't seen me regularly for five years, they got behind me right away as someone who had the credentials to shut Flair up, take his belt, and unify the world championship. I also liked Gordon Solie a lot—he had been very polite and complimentary to me, and the other wrestlers at the studio had greeted me kindly.

That Sunday taping concluded early in the afternoon, and we went right to the Omni from there. When I got to the locker room at the Omni, I got a workout in while they were setting up the ring, but then, as I was getting ready and doing the stuff that I normally do, something didn't feel right. I don't know why, but I just had a sixth-sense that something was wrong.

No one had greeted me at the arena when I arrived, and no one had come around to talk about the finish or what we were going to do. In the several other world title unification matches that I had done with Harley in New York with Vince Sr., in Miami with Eddie Graham, in St. Louis with Sam Muchnick, or in Toronto with Frank Tunney, we had always had a little meeting with the promoter in the dressing room beforehand to talk about how the match was going to go. On each of those occasions, I had spent a few minutes talking with my opponents about what things we each wanted to get into the match and how best to capture the hearts and minds of the people. That night at the Omni, however, there was no sign of either Barnett or Crockett, or Flair.

Something just felt different—and not in a good way.

I called Vince Sr. from a payphone in one of the Omni's hallways, explained to him that although I couldn't put my finger on anything specific, after being in so many different places with the belt wrestling for so many different promoters, there was something fishy going on that I didn't like. Something didn't feel like business as usual.

I was worried that there might have been some sort of double-cross in the works.

I told him that I would do whatever he wanted me to do—and I asked him what that was.

As it turned out, Vince Sr. had been on the phone arguing with Crockett, the president of the NWA, about the finish. I did not know Vince and Crockett to be close, and they traded talent very infrequently, so I was much more on edge about this match than I ever was wrestling in Florida for Eddie, or in St. Louis for Sam, or even over in Japan where "unusual" things were known to happen on occasion and blamed on the language barrier. Vince Sr. told me that several people on the NWA Board had gotten themselves involved in the discussions. He told me not to worry, but to sit tight and stay near the phone, and that he would call me back.

If Vince had called back and told me that he was worried that the Crocketts were up to something, I would have done whatever was necessary to protect the WWF title that night, including shooting on Ric Flair if that's what was necessary. Other than running away and getting counted out of the ring, there is absolutely nothing that Flair would have been able to do about it. That's what made this whole situation so strange. The NWA Board *knew* that when they decided to have Flair beat Dusty for the belt, they had chosen to put the NWA World Heavyweight Championship on a man who was a great worker in the ring, and a great performer on the microphone, but someone who could absolutely *not* protect himself in the ring, and would stand no chance against a guy who decided to shoot on him.

Ordinarily, no one would have had any concerns about me trying to do that to Ric, because I had grown up in the NWA, had a lot of respect for most of those promoters, and had worked with a lot of them. But now, I was in Atlanta representing Vince McMahon Sr. and the rival WWF at a time when tensions between the WWF and the NWA were high, and I was prepared to do anything necessary to protect Vince Sr.'s and the WWF's reputation. Business was business.

The silence, however, coupled with the knowledge that I had just gained from Vince Sr. that there was some "dispute" going on over the finish to our match, was very unnerving. If there wasn't some discussion about one of us going over the other in some fashion, then what could possibly have been serious enough to get so many members of the NWA Board of Directors on the phone on the night of a match? A decision to go Broadway would have been expected, so that wouldn't have raised an eyebrow. A decision to call for a disqualification or countout finish, whether it put Flair over or put me over, wouldn't have hurt either one of us at all, and that wouldn't have merited such a call either. So the finish being discussed must have been something more serious. Put into context of what was going on politically at the time between the WWF and the NWA, it was not at all beyond the realm of possibility that the Crocketts might have been trying to pull some kind of power move on Vince Sr.

Whatever the problem was, Vince apparently solved it by talking to Jim Barnett, who acted as a go-between with the Crocketts. A little while after Vince and I talked, and before Vince even called me back, Barnett approached me and tried to smooth things over. He had the Crocketts in tow, and they all explained to me that the match was going to spill out of the ring and end in a double-countout. I eyed them all suspiciously, and just nodded to acknowledge that I had heard them, but I didn't say much.

No one will ever convince me that a double-countout finish was enough to warrant scrambling so many members of the NWA Board of Directors for a conference call on the day of the event—so you really have to wonder what it was that had started the controversy. I have never been able to find out, but I'd love to know.

Apparently, one of the ways that this disagreement and concerns about a possible rogue finish was resolved was by a mutual agreement between Vince Sr. and the Crocketts *not* to tape the match. That way, if anything funny happened, there would have been no proof of it to put on television. As amazing as it seems in retrospect, this historic match was, in fact, *not* taped. That was a pretty unusual decision for a match of this magnitude and historical significance, especially given the fact that it had received so much national attention on WTBS. It was certainly not a choice that would have been made voluntarily and in the ordinary course of events.

I never got to the bottom of it, but something had *definitely* been up, because by the time Barnett found me and tried to calm me down, word that I was onto it had gotten back to Flair, and now *he* was then worried about what *I* might do to *him* in the ring that night. When Ric found me before the match later that evening, he was acting strangely and was very sheepish toward me. I guess he felt like had to say *something* to me to break the ice and to put my mind at ease and to let me know that the plan, whatever it had been, was off—because the first thing he did when I saw him was to come up to me in a friendly, joking way and say, "Don't hurt me, Bob."

Notwithstanding these strange circumstances, I liked Ric. I wasn't worried that he was inclined to try to do something on his own, nor was I worried about my ability to take care of myself in the ring with him if he did. What I *was* worried about, though, is what *his* boss might have instructed him to do, or that something else might be going on with a referee that might have been made to look like a mistake or an accident after the fact. My lack of familiarity with the players involved definitely made the situation tense and uncertain. Ric was relatively new in his role as the NWA World Champion, and obviously wanted to make himself and the NWA World Title look as powerful as he could. Of course, I wanted to do the same for myself and the WWF. The growing strain between our two organizations, however, was the new variable that hadn't been present in these types of matches in the past—and that was weighing heavily in my mind. Beyond that, I knew that having to wrestle defensively and not being able to completely trust Ric would detract from the overall quality of the match—both for us and for the people watching that night at the Omni.

Our match was the final one that night, and when we got to the ring, everything went well. We did the short-arm scissor, which really got the crowd going, we did the double bridge, and a whole series of holds and reverses and suplexes and speed moves that the average person out there couldn't do. He got me in the figure-four leglock in the middle of the ring, which as the closest we got all night to any kind of false finish. I could tell from the way Ric applied the hold that night that he had no intention whatsoever of getting cute with me, or even leaving open any possibility for any misunderstanding about that. Everything Ric did in the ring that night was feather-soft. I sold the figure-four for him for awhile before I eventually reversed it to escape. Because of all of the pre-match suspicion, however, neither of us permitted any close calls or two counts that night in either direction. I was in their territory, and once the referee calls for the bell and raises someone's hand, what are you going to do? So I wasn't about to allow my shoulders to be down for a two count and leave myself vulnerable to a referee changing his cadence or making a quick count, or some other mistake. Meanwhile, based on the comment that he had made to me, I'm sure Ric was also a little concerned that if he let me get him in a compromising position with his shoulders on the mat, that I might not let go, and the referee would be forced to make the three count against him.

The match came off as well as it could have given our defensiveness stemming from the cloud of suspicion that hung over the match that night. It was not the kind of fluid, easy, enjoyable match like I had had so many times with Harley, or like the match I had had with Nick Bockwinkel up in Toronto—where you could just put yourself in the hands of the other guy, who was as talented as you were, and not have to worry about a thing. The match was stiff and lacking in drama, and given our unwillingness to include any near-falls, in the end, I think the match was a bit of a disappointment.

Back in the dressing room, Ric and I shook hands, and thanked each other, which was customary after a big match, and that was the end of it. Nothing more was ever said about the controversy that surrounded the match, although perhaps not surprisingly, July 4, 1982, was the last time there was ever a unification match between the NWA and the WWF World Champions. The WWF withdrew from the NWA shortly thereafter, and the war was on.

After the match with Flair, I flew back home, then headed down to Wildwood, New Jersey, with Corki and Carrie for a week on the shore, and I enjoyed some much-needed time off.

———◆◆◆———

After the three-match brawl with Snuka, which featured very little in the way of actual *wrestling*, Vince Sr. was looking to shift gears and again give the fans a little something different. Bob Orton Jr. was the guy he called on. As I mentioned before, I knew both Bob Jr. (Randy's father) and *his* father, Bob Orton Sr., from my time in Florida. Eddie Graham had liked Orton enough to make him the Florida Heavyweight Champion, so I anticipated that he would have talked Orton up to Vince Sr. enough so I would get to do at least a couple and maybe three matches with Orton at the Garden.

But it was not to be.

The match hadn't done a great advanced sale at the box office, which probably had more to do with the date, August 2, than with the fans' response to Orton. New Yorkers tended to escape the heat of the city and head for the shore in early August. Vince Sr. decided to feed Orton to me in a one-and-done match at the Garden, and also called for Orton to submit to the Chickenwing Crossface — a new submission move I had recently debuted.

The Chickenwing Crossface was a fun addition to my matches. Up to that point in my career as champion, I had beaten nearly every challenger I faced with some form of pinning combination — either the atomic kneedrop, the rolling reverse, the inside cradle, or the German suplex. Adding a legitimate-looking submission move was something that made sense for someone like me, who tended to use a lot more wrestling moves in my matches. I had also wanted to do it to add psychological interest to my matches. Now I could "soften up" a challenger's arm during the early stages of a match, not simply to try and disable it for the purpose of rendering the challenger's finisher less workable, but to make my own finisher more credible. Applying the Chickenwing Crossface was also pretty dramatic-looking. It was a complicated hold that had never been seen or done before in the history of the WWF — so I was excited to bring that new element to the fans and see how they reacted to it.

Orton and I had a nice match at the Garden full of fast-paced, amateur moves, playing off the television storyline that we had known each other since our high school days in the amateurs (which was not the case). Orton was in shape, and had no problem keeping the pace of the match fast and furious—and we played it up that when I got the upper hand, he got frustrated, which increased my credibility with the fans. He applied his finisher—the "Superplex" (a suplex off the second rope), and then strutted around, cockily jawing at the fans before giving me a lackluster cover in the middle of the ring, which I kicked out of. Eventually, I slipped behind him and applied the Chickenwing Crossface, and the fans reacted to the hold in a way that made it very clear to both Vince Sr. and to me that we had something.

Orton became my first challenger to go down to defeat by submission.

I was very grateful to Orton for putting the hold over like that. I wish we could have extended our series at the Garden, because I really enjoyed wrestling him. He was a perfect match for me, physically, as we were both about the same size and the same shape, and could use just about everything in both of our repertoires. It would have made perfect sense, coming on the heels of three months of brawls with Snuka, to do a Broadway with Orton in our first match—but the timing just didn't allow for it.

The undercard of that match saw Andre wipe out Blackjack Mulligan in a wild Texas Death Match. That's the problem with a glut of great heels like we had in the summer of 1982—eventually, you have to start giving the people some clean outcomes so they don't get frustrated with the booking—and Andre got one here over Mulligan, which really made it impossible for Vince Sr. to then book him into a title match with me the following month. All of this goes back to Snuka, and the fact that, when these three guys were brought into the territory in the early spring of 1982, no one anticipated how "over" Snuka was going to get, which ended up creating a booking logjam that forced Mulligan and Orton into their secondary matches (with Andre and Morales respectively) before either of them got a main-event opportunity with me.

The July 1982 television tapings saw the arrival of "Playboy" Buddy Rose from Don Owen's Pacific Northwest Territory. Rose exemplified the old saying that you should "not judge a book by its cover." He was a bleached blonde playboy character who was, even at that time, pretty overweight and utterly lacking in muscular definition, but a legitimately good athlete who had played baseball and hockey, and who could flat out work. Knowing that the fans would prejudge him on his appearance, Vince Sr. and Don Owen conspired to put some heat on Buddy before he ever set foot in a WWF ring, and to create some buzz and fan interest around his arrival. To accomplish that, they filmed some fun television vignettes to announce Buddy's arrival in the WWF, including shots of him boarding "his" Lear jet, playing hockey with NHL players and baseball with MLB stars, and being followed around everywhere by two female valets who tended to his every need, including taking his robe off when he made his ring entrance.

This led to the natural booking idea of Buddy, having been born with the proverbial silver spoon in his mouth, wrestling me, the handscrabble, poor Midwestern boy from Minnesota. Vince Sr. knew that the largely blue-collar and middle class fans of the WWF's big cities would instantly relate to that storyline, and would relish the opportunity to watch the cod-dled rich guy get his shoulder ripped apart by the Chickenwing Crossface.

Buddy and I had some great matches together. He was a very agile worker with a lot of great moves, and given how athletic he was, we could do just about anything in the ring together, which really allowed us to put together entertaining matches for the fans. He was also willing to do anything for the match and the storyline, including submitting at the end of most of our matches. Many heels were reluctant to do that, because it is such a decisive victory that it steals a lot of a heel's heat. But Buddy didn't care about that. He understood the storyline and knew that it would really get the people amped up to see him forced into that position—and the people responded. All you need to do is listen to the roar of the crowd at Madison Square Garden at the end of our match in August 1982 when Buddy submits to the Chickenwing, and you'll see what I mean. I think Buddy was probably my most "underrated" challenger in terms of the fans' expectations—I doubt there were many people who saw one of our matches who left the arena disappointed.

As was usually the case, September represented a new "season" in the wrestling business. With the kids back in school, parents settled back into their school-year routines, and everybody back around to watch the television shows on weekends, it was time to roll out the next big angle.

The September television taping in Allentown, Pennsylvania, saw the return of "Superstar" Billy Graham—the man I had beaten for the championship now almost five years earlier. But the Billy Graham who returned to the WWF in 1982 was not the same man who defeated "The Living Legend" Bruno Sammartino to become the federation's seventh world champion, and who had thrilled crowds around the territory for most of 1977. I hadn't seen much of Billy since he left the territory in 1978, and frankly, like most of the rest of the locker room, I was shocked by his appearance upon his return. Gone was the hulking physique, the rippling muscles, the deep tan, the tie-dye, and the flowing blonde hair that had made Billy such a sensation with the fans. Gone too was the confident, cocky attitude, and the easy manner on the microphone. What appeared instead was a much thinner and less muscular Billy Graham, with a bald head, karate pants, and a mustache. He was pained and tentative, noticeably less confident, and a shadow of his former self. People were actually wondering whether Billy was seriously ill.

Graham was still managed by the Grand Wizard, but this time with a karate gimmick that didn't make a lot of sense and never really got over with the fans. Meanwhile, at the same time, Vince Sr. had decided that he wanted to get a new, bigger world title belt (the big green one)—which I didn't like at all. I was used to wearing the one that Bruno and I had worn for years. That one fit comfortably between the top of my trunks and the bottom of my ring jacket, which allowed it to be seen when I entered the ring, but didn't make it hard to walk while wearing it. The big green belt wasn't comfortable, and I also didn't think it looked nearly as good as the smaller one that Bruno and I had worn before.

Going to a new belt wasn't my choice, but once Vince decided that was what he was going to do—since we knew that something dramatic had to be done to create heat for Graham anyway—we decided to have Graham come out during a televised match that I was having with Swede Hansen, grab the WWF championship belt, and claim that I had "stolen" the belt from him. Graham would then interfere in my match, "knock me out" with the belt, and then proceed to smash it to pieces on the concrete floor claiming that if he couldn't have the belt, "nobody could."

The angle, which seemed so promising on paper when we discussed it, fell flat when we did it. First, Graham just didn't seem nearly as threatening with his body looking like it had wilted away like an un-watered plant. Billy had battled depression and addiction during the years after he left the WWWF in 1978, which forced him to stop taking steroids. Getting off the juice, of course, was an incredibly positive step in the right direction for his physical health, but it had also hurt his look—and losing his look had a serious effect on his confidence. The loss of his look and his confidence then led to a serious effect on his mental health. It was a very tough downward spiral for Billy, and one that everyone reading this should think about. I know that if Billy Graham was sitting here today, he'd want to warn all the young kids out there not to make the choices he made, and what those choices ultimately did to his health and to the quality of his life.

I respected Billy for trying to get off the steroids, and I encouraged him as much as I could, but Billy and I were never that close. Billy and I didn't have any real heat, but I think he always resented me as the "child" who cut short his run with the title, so there really wasn't much that I could say that would get through to him. Billy's problem was that he had created his own prison. The "Superstar" Billy Graham character had gotten over with the fans *because* of his superhuman appearance—but that superhuman appearance wasn't sustainable. Steroids give you big muscles and the big muscles give you big confidence—but it's all artificial. When I worked out at the gym, the muscles and muscular definition that I got was a direct consequence of my diet and exercise, and nothing more. Billy's muscular definition depended on the supplements he was taking.

Don't get me wrong, Billy Graham worked out *very* hard at the gym, and he took his weight training as seriously as anyone in the business—but the problem was that the results he had gotten were muscles supported by chemicals, and that's what the people had grown accustomed to seeing. When you stop taking the chemicals, you can't lift the same weights, and even if you put in the same *effort*, your muscles don't respond the same way and you don't get the same look—and when *that* happens, the confidence that you once had goes with it. The Billy Graham who returned to the WWF in 1982 wasn't the "Superstar" who had beaten Bruno Sammartino in 1977, and who I'd beaten for the championship in 1978. Graham knew it—and his interviews did not have the power and the confidence that they had back in 1977 and 1978.

Second, Graham's effort to destroy the belt on television actually failed. He repeatedly smashed it against the concrete floor and then unsuccessfully tried to rip the metal plate off the plastic backing. For Graham, a strongman-type character, to be unable to tear a metal piece off of a rubber backing made him look weak, and made the entire angle look ridiculous.

My part in the angle didn't come off very well either. I was supposed to have been battered by both Hansen and Graham, so after Graham "knocked me out" with the belt, I couldn't just jump right up, go out of the ring, and express outrage over what had happened. I needed to appear groggy from the attack I had just sustained—so I crawled out of the ring, collapsed onto the pieces of the belt, and just screamed "Why!?" over and over again. I thought it was okay when I was doing it live, but the way the whole thing came out on tape made me look weak.

I wasn't happy with any of it.

To be honest, though, the bad kickoff angle was the *least* of our problems once Billy and I started wrestling around the horn. The bigger problem was that Billy really couldn't get up and down much anymore because his hips were so badly damaged from the years of steroid abuse, and his limited wind allowed him to go only ten or fifteen minutes before he blew up and became visibly gassed. So all of that had to be managed as we went around the territory.

Graham had been promised three title matches at the Garden. Because Vince Sr. was a man of his word, Vince Sr. honored that promise to Billy. As a consequence, though, all of our matches at the Garden were shorter than necessary to really draw in the crowd, because Billy's physical condition limited both his offensive repertoire, which had never been huge to begin with, and his ability to take bumps in the ring, which had once been his greatest in-ring strength. Despite all of these problems, our Garden matches *still* drew pretty well. The first of these was on October 4, 1982, where, the premise was that I was so angry over what Billy had done to the championship belt that we brawled for twelve minutes before I got disqualified for manhandling the referee and refusing to break a chokehold.

We came back for the return match at the Garden in November 1982 and agreed to just go at it again in an all-out brawl for as long as we could, and then take the match right back into the dressing room with the premise that we were going to blow off with a lumberjack match the following month.

That match lasted ten minutes.

We came back with the lumberjack blowoff match at the Garden in December 1982, which had the added attraction of the first-ever "heel" guest referee—the same Swede Hansen I had been wrestling on television when Graham attacked me to start the feud. That was done to add a little intrigue to the match, and to make the fans wonder if I was somehow going to be robbed of the belt by a heel referee.

Although I didn't have too many of them, I liked lumberjack matches—it was fun to use the guys outside to help develop the match—especially in a match against a guy like Billy who, at that point in his career, needed the help. As a consequence, I spent the majority of the match letting Graham throw me out of every side of the ring and use the lumberjacks outside to work me over, while Graham got to stay inside the ring to work the fans and preserve his wind. I was hoping that by doing that, we could extend the in-ring time of our blowoff match by a few minutes to build it up a little better. Billy was hurting pretty badly that night, though, so we were even more limited than usual in what we could do.

We teased some false finishes with Hansen doing his part in the drama of the match by giving Graham an extremely fast count when he had my shoulders down on the mat, but giving me an eternally slow count when I had Billy down in a winning combination. That little gimmick also helped us to get the crowd going.

When Billy could only hold me up in the "Superstar Bearhug"—his former finisher—for a few seconds, I knew we had to go home, so we went right from there to the finish, with me applying the Chickenwing Crossface at the twelve-minute mark. It was a nice finish that Vince Sr. had chosen—with Hansen having no discretion to count fast or slow, and being left with no choice but to call the match and ring Billy out in what would end up being one of the shortest title defenses of my career.

I knew that Billy was still angry about the switch in 1978, that he legitimately didn't respect me as the champion, and that he didn't want me to be where I was. That was hard for me, given how hard I had worked both to get to be the champion, and after I became champion. I had hoped my hard work would have changed his view of me, but apparently, it hadn't. This was the man whose brief words to me in the YMCA in Fargo, North Dakota, in 1972 had pushed me to become a professional wrestler. I had a lot of respect for Billy's ability to work a crowd and work the microphone, and talk people into the seats. I appreciated the fact that when he had been asked to put me over for the belt at the Garden in 1978, even though he opposed the move with every ounce of his being, he had still done so professionally without underselling my offense or doing anything else to make me look bad, and that he had subsequently worked hard in all our rematches around the territory. Billy had been a man ahead of his time, and a real visionary in the profession that many guys, most notably Jesse Ventura and Hulk Hogan, went on to emulate. I felt bad for what had happened to him—although in some ways, I was happy for him, because at least he wasn't taking the steroids anymore.

What was really alarming, though, is that not being on steroids had changed his look and every aspect of his life. He was a completely different person. There is no doubt that the drugs had propelled Graham to stardom, and had given him all the notoriety, but at what price?

Meanwhile, promoters in other cities around the territory were also reacting negatively to Billy's look and new gimmick. In Boston, on November 6, 1982, the promoters abandoned plans for a first match and put Billy and me right into a cage match blowoff without any initial development of our feud. In Baltimore, after our first match in October, 1982, ended inconclusively when I was disqualified for hitting the referee after about ten minutes, the promoters decided *not* to schedule a return match, but instead, to have a battle royal the following month with the winner to get the world title match with me. In Philadelphia, promoter Phil Zacko skipped Graham entirely—opting to give an extra main event to "Playboy" Buddy Rose, and then passing over Graham and moving right on to the returning "Magnificent" Muraco.

It was a sad end for Billy—who had meant so much to the Federation, and to our sport in general. It was very clear to me that the premise of our feud was a good one—but it was an angle and a feud that should have happened a couple of years earlier when Billy was still in good physical shape and still had his "look." Had this angle been tried in 1980 or 1981, it almost certainly would have been a big hit with the fans.

Meanwhile, the October 1982 television tapings saw the return of the "Magnificent" Muraco and the arrival of Ray "The Crippler" Stevens. Stevens had been Pat Patterson's partner out in Roy Shire's San Francisco territory for a lot of years, and Patterson, who was now doing the color commentary on the WWF's *Championship Wrestling* and *All-Star Wrestling* television programs with Vince McMahon Jr., had been instrumental in convincing Ray to come East for a run in the WWF. Stevens was, at that point, approaching legendary status in the business. He was a terrific in-ring talent who understood how to develop a match, tell a great story, and get over with the fans. Outside the ring, he was also a great storyteller. Stevens came in to much fanfare (assisted, in large part, by his old partner Patterson on television), as the master of a "crippling" piledriver that Stevens claimed had been "banned" in several states and, according to Patterson, had put countless people out of wrestling. In a memorable television interview with a visually disgusted Vince Jr., Stevens, who was managed and accompanied by fellow West Coast legend Freddie Blassie, announced that he "would cripple my own grandmother if there was money in it."

Shortly thereafter, in a segment of Buddy Rogers' Corner televised on *Championship Wrestling*, Rogers interviewed Stevens and Blassie. and Stevens produced a check and challenged Snuka to a match on television. Although seemingly heel versus heel, the purpose of this match was to turn Snuka face, and to ignite a feud with Snuka that would provide another main-event feud that could headline a building when I was elsewhere.

Naturally, Snuka accepted the challenge, and the "match" was scheduled for *Championship Wrestling*. The match, of course, never began because its real purpose was to allow Captain Lou Albano to attack Snuka, who was being restrained by Stevens. Then Stevens threw Snuka out onto the arena floor (which had been pre-treated with some spilled water) and piledrived him twice into the concrete. Snuka, who had already bladed while getting attacked by Albano in the ring, then bled into the spilled water, making the entire spectacle look like a murder scene. Snuka was then stretchered out of the arena.

At the November 22, 1982, Garden card, Stevens put the piledriver on his next victim—Chief Jay Strongbow—and beat the Chief in under a minute, after which the Chief was likewise stretchered out of the Garden to the horror of the fans. Vince Sr. was really pushing Stevens in an attempt to get him over as a monster heel, and I'm sure that Jay thought they were getting Stevens set up for something pretty big if they asked him to put Stevens over that strongly.

Stevens and I had our first main-event title match out in Harrisburg at the Zembo Mosque a couple of days after Thanksgiving, on November 26, 1982, and surprisingly it didn't draw well. It felt very strange to be wrestling Ray Stevens in the WWF because I had grown up watching him in the AWA. He'd been around a long time by then, and although he had slowed down some and didn't have as much fire as he once had, I was truly honored to have the opportunity to be in the ring with such a legendary talent.

Although Ray was one of the best workers in the business, he was short and not particularly well-defined muscularly. The people I'd had the great fortune to work against in the territory over the prior year and a half were a combination of great workers or monsters (or both) so it took a lot for a heel, particularly an unknown heel who had not appeared in the territory before, to measure up in the eyes of the fans. At that point in his career, Ray Stevens, even with his piledriver and his "crippling" of the Superfly, just didn't move the fans in the same way that Stan Hansen or Sergeant Slaughter or Don Muraco had.

Both Vince Sr. and I wanted Stevens to get over so we could do a longer program with him. Shortly after the match in Harrisburg, I wrestled Stevens again at the television tapings in Allentown because Vince wanted to see Stevens in person and understand why our match, which looked so good on paper, wasn't drawing the fans' interest. The same thing happened in Allentown that had happened in Harrisburg—although the match was good from a technical and artistic standpoint, Stevens, with his short stature and pudgy physique just didn't strike fear into the hearts of the fans. Although Stevens had been a huge success all over California, in Minneapolis, and in virtually every other territory he had appeared in, he was passed over for main-event title matches at the Garden, the Spectrum, and many of the territory's other primary buildings, and ended up feuding with Snuka for the remainder of his time in the territory.

Buddy Rose was the primary beneficiary of the problems with both Graham's and Stevens' anticipated title runs, because he had out-performed expectations and, as a consequence, ended up getting more main-event dates with me around the territory. It was ironic that the glut of heel challengers we had faced not six months earlier had vaporized — and now, with a sudden lack of heel challengers, promoters were forced to schedule me into additional matches with Rose, or to hold a battle royal with the winner to receive a world title match. The battle royal gimmick often had the effect of drawing a curiosity crowd, since the people thought they might get the opportunity to see something novel and unexpected.

Meanwhile, at the November television tapings, a new monster heel in the person of the six-foot-ten-inch, 364-pound Big John Studd made his "first" appearance, and started to take the territory by storm. I put "first" in quotes because Big John Studd, whose real name was John Minton, had previously wrestled in the WWWF as the Masked Executioner #2, and had actually been the first man I ever faced and defeated at Madison Square Garden.

As 1982 ended, the booking began to stabilize, and I looked ahead to the new year, and what, as it would turn out, would be a year of recycled challengers, political turmoil, disappointing bookings, and ultimately, the end of my reign as the WWF champion.

22

It Takes Two to Tango (1983)

"Nothing about life is static."

—Napoleon Hill, "The Rhythms of Life"

———•◆•———

Eager to get back into a knowingly profitable series of matches, many of the promoters around the territory looked to recapture old magic by starting the new year booking title matches between me and the newly returned "Magnificent" Muraco.

Since our historic series of matches in 1981, Don had split his time between the mid-Atlantic and Georgia areas, and had also done some tours of Japan, but returned to the territory retaining his rugged look and exceptional ring skills. Needless to say, I was thrilled to see him return to the territory, and we immediately started a series of matches in Boston, Pittsburgh, Hartford, and Landover—places that had passed up long series with Graham and Stevens.

At the Garden, however, on January 22, 1983, I faced the challenge of Big John Studd. Since Vince Sr. had sidestepped booking me into "big man" world title matches with Blackjack Mulligan in 1982 and Hulk Hogan in 1980 to leave those guys unscathed for their matchups with Andre, I had not faced a true "giant" at the Garden since Ernie Ladd in 1978.

Coming into the match, Studd was promising the people on television that he would not just beat me, but to hurt me so badly he would retire me from the world of professional wrestling. Even Vince McMahon Jr., in our pre-match promotional interviews, warned that notwithstanding my many victories over formidable men at the Garden over the past five years, people were calling Studd the "prohibitive favorite" in the bout.

I hope nobody actually took McMahon's advice and laid money on the challenger that night.

Because of Studd's size and girth, there wasn't a whole lot that I could realistically do with him in the ring. It's not like I could throw credible armdrags and hiptosses and dropkicks at a guy who stood six feet ten inches tall. Further, unlike Ernie Ladd, Studd was not particularly agile, and wasn't the kind of big man who could quickly get up and down a lot in our match. When we met with Vince Sr. in the dressing room before the match, Vince Sr. called for me to go over Studd by pinfall with a quick leverage move that would be made to look like a total fluke. That way, Studd would look like he *could* have handled me easily, and as such, would still be strong for his upcoming summer series with Andre.

As John and I had not met in the ring since 1977, we retreated into the bathroom, reminisced a little bit about that night, and then quickly set about to working out a few things that we wanted to do in the ring, including what kind of move would work for the kind of finish that Vince Sr. was looking for. John came up with the idea of catching me in his finishing hold, the over-the-shoulder backbreaker, clamping it on, and making it look like I had no choice but to surrender the title, before he stumbled a little too close to the ropes which would allow me to use the top rope to kick myself off of his shoulder and backdrop him while holding onto his legs into a quick pinning combination that would knock the wind out of him, causing him to roll out a split second too late.

Since John was going to be holding onto me rather than spreading the impact of that move across a wider area of his body when he hit the mat, that was a very big, and largely unprotected bump for a 364-pound guy like Studd to take. It was inevitable that he was going to hit the mat pretty hard on the way down with my 234 pounds on top of him. I had been thinking of some kind of simpler and much less dramatic leverage move down on the mat, so John's willingness to take that big bump for the good of the match and to put me over in that way was very generous of him.

We needed to make sure that my win was both credible *and* flukey— just a quick and clever little leverage move that would allow me to get past Studd, but leave him with all of his heat for his future series with Andre. The plan we hatched in the bathroom was for John to block everything I tried to do to him and to just pound on me and totally dominate the match— because, in reality, how would it be any other way? Studd had me by eight inches in height and more than 130 pounds, so the only way to make this match look legitimate and leave Studd with his heat was to have him totally and completely manhandle me for the whole match prior to the finish. I had to be the underdog with no way to win—except to survive what Studd threw at me and hope he would make one mistake that I could capitalize on and catch him with . . . and that's exactly the way the match came off.

I don't think Studd even came off his feet in the match until the finish.

It was a shocking and sudden ending to the match less than eight minutes in, but I think it made sense both to the storyline of the match, and for the overall quality of the event. In reality, John had been working hard from the opening bell beating on me and pouring on the offense— and at 364 pounds, he wasn't someone who was going to deliver a lot of quality output fifteen minutes into a match, so we were thinking that a high-quality match with a quick and fluky finish, coupled with my quick escape back to the dressing room with the belt while he screamed at the referee, was the way to go.

I think the fans at the Garden bought into it. Studd and I did a few more turns around the territory in Boston, Baltimore, Philadelphia, and in a few of the towns in upstate New York—but a lot of the cities stayed away from this match, opting instead to keep Studd fresh and unscathed before putting him in the ring with Andre.

Meanwhile, on the undercard of my match with Studd at the Garden, for the second time in three years, Don Muraco stripped Pedro

Morales of the Intercontinental Heavyweight Championship. Don had done very well in his previous run with the Intercontinental title, both in the ring and at the box office, when he held the belt for six months in 1981. He still looked tremendous and had a couple of years more experience, so shortly after his return to the territory, Vince Sr. had opted to have him go over Pedro again and reclaim the number-two spot in the federation. Once Muraco had the Intercontinental title, it was a natural thing to declare him the number-one contender and to again set him up for a matchup with me.

Muraco was, by that point, enough of a draw that he could headline smaller to midsize venues by himself against a credible contender for the Intercontinental Championship. The office was starting to do two-a-days much more often, especially in smaller venues during the week, so with Muraco holding the Intercontinental heavyweight championship, they could put Muraco in there against popular babyfaces like Snuka, Rocky Johnson, Tony Atlas, Ivan Putski, or Mil Mascaras at the top of a card in one building, and me and a top heel on the top of the card in another building, and run two successful shows on the same night. You need a reliable guy who can also draw consistently to be able to pull that off, and Muraco fit that bill perfectly.

Many of the promoters around the territory who opted to stay away from a Backlund-Studd main event in their buildings went right to Muraco even before he had taken the Intercontinental Heavyweight Championship back from Pedro. Don and I had drawn so well everywhere we went in the territory back in 1981 that the promoters, some of whom had experienced some raggedness in their booking and softness in their gates since my series with Snuka ended, were anxious to get back to something reliable. Boston, Landover, and Pittsburgh are just three of the towns I remember that launched directly into a series with Muraco even before it had the allure of a champion versus champion encounter.

At the Garden, however, which, of course, was the WWF's marquee arena and where everything was done in a more "orderly" fashion, Muraco and I had our first bout in February 1983, which was champion versus champion. Vince knew that another Backlund-Muraco feud would, as it had in the past, provide box-office gold, so right out of the chutes, it was decided that I would be disqualified in that first match to set up a Texas Death rematch at the Garden for the March 1983 card.

As always, our match generated tremendous interest and crowd reaction. Muraco was one of the most credible heel challengers I faced as WWF champion—and I think it is fair to say that after watching him pin the formerly unbeatable Pedro Morales not once but *twice* in the span of two years—the fans definitely believed that Muraco had the goods to strip me of the WWF World Heavyweight Championship as well. The first match ended when I had the Chickenwing Crossface on Muraco, we got tangled in the ropes, and the referee disqualified me for refusing to break the hold.

The beginning of March brought the first really definitive signs of the coming changes. On March 5 and March 6, we made our first trip out west for full WWF cards based in San Diego and Los Angeles, California. Mike LeBell's Los Angeles–based territory had just folded, and Vince Jr. saw an opportunity—so we flew out there and rented cars and ran a couple of test cards. I wrestled West Coast guys in the main events on each of the cards out there (Ray Stevens at the San Diego Sports Arena and Buddy Rose in Los Angeles) so fans would at least be familiar with the challengers. We also used some of the local talent from out there to fill out the cards—but even with that, and a fair amount of promotion, the buildings were each less than half full. This again pointed to the critical importance of having local television to familiarize the fans with the wrestlers and the angles.

Elsewhere around the territory, the expansion was also underway— except that expansion meant running two or more cards almost every night of the week, and splitting the roster to fulfill those dates. That made Muraco an even more important player, because when he and I were not wrestling each other in the larger arenas, or part of the six-man, eight-man, and even ten-man tag-team matches that the promoters were experimenting with in 1983, we were nearly always split up to headline different cards on the same night. Doing that meant that each venue got a title match, either with me defending the World Heavyweight Championship, or with Muraco defending the Intercontinental Heavyweight Championship. As I have mentioned before—to be a main eventer in the WWF, you needed to be a reliable guy who could be counted on to show up on time, in shape to wrestle, *and* possess the skills to bring the people to the box office. Muraco could check all three of those boxes, so he was the man chosen to carry the other end of the WWF banner with me as we expanded the territory in 1983.

Our series at the Garden culminated in a Texas Death Match in our second bout of the series in a rare Sunday matinee on March 20, 1983. I was a little surprised that Vince Sr. chose to end that series after two bouts, rather than stretching it to the full three match series this time. When we wrestled at the Garden in August and September 1981, the August match was our first sixty-minute Broadway, and the September match was a Texas Death Match—and we then wrestled a whole series of matches all over the territory, from Broadways to cage matches, to Texas Death Matches, banging out buildings for almost the entire time that Don was in the territory. So I was looking forward to the chance to go three with Muraco at the Garden, but it was not to be.

The other thing was that when we got together in the ring, as we had proved in 1981, Don and I actually liked to *wrestle*. We didn't really need the gimmick of the Texas Death Match to get the match over with the fans—we could do it just by virtue of the fact that we were wrestling in a title versus title match and by building the drama of the match through chain wrestling. On top of that, Dick Kroll (the referee that night), normally the fed's top guy, had an off night and forgot that the match was a Texas Death Match. He broke chokes and counted when we were out of the ring—to the point that we had to actually remind him about halfway through the match that it was actually a Texas Death Match and to stop counting.

But the match *was* billed as a Texas Death Match, so we had to give the fans *something* that qualified—so near the end of the match, I threw Don into the ringpost and he bladed a gusher and bled all over the place, and sold the blood loss for the rest of the match as having weakened him severely. From there, we went into a series of false finishes, with me catching him in an over the shoulder backbreaker, Don backflipping out of it and backdropping me into a pinning combination in the middle of the ring, me bridging out of it and putting him in the Chickenwing Crossface, Don kicking off the ropes, and me giving Don a German suplex into a bridge for the pin. That little sequence was something that we had worked on. We had wanted to make it like the end of a fireworks show—emptying the bag with everything we had to throw at each other—where ultimately, Don's blood loss weakened him enough for me to get the three count on a suplex and bridge.

It was a great finish to a great match that I think the fans really enjoyed. I wish we could have gone three at the Garden—especially given the way the rest of that summer's bookings went. We sold out the Garden *and* the Felt Forum for the Texas Death Match that Sunday afternoon, and I remember hearing in the dressing room that there were hundreds of people milling around outside who wanted to buy a ticket but couldn't get in! I think that pretty clearly demonstrated that Muraco and I had again struck a chord with the fans in New York, and could easily have filled that building for a third time.

Tremendous Humility

In 1983, when I came back and carried the Intercontinental Championship again, we often had two crews running different shows on the same night, and Bob had one crew and I had the other. I had a lot of heat on me at the time, so I just tried to read the newspapers and watch TV and try to keep current with pop culture so I could keep my interviews sharp, but the WWF was already expanding then, and there was a lot of talent, so it wasn't really so much just me and him anymore, there were a lot of people we could rely on to draw.

I think the main thing to say about Bob was just how professional he was in everything he did inside the ring and outside, and the way he represented our profession. He always wore a suit and tie when he traveled, he always traveled alone, watched his diet, and he always did the right things. You know, back in those days we were always heavy kayfabe, so we never really had the chance to get real close. He seldom came out after the matches—most of the time, he drove home to be with his family. I got to know Bob best over in Japan. We went on a tour together over there, and so I got to know him better from being in the dressing rooms and on the busses with him, and running around working out and having a few beers with him after the matches over there when he could let his hair down a little bit more.

For the era we were in, Bob was different from everybody else. What you saw was what you got. He was an honest, hardworking, simple guy who had tremendous humility, a big heart, and who always just worked his ass off. I was proud to have had the chance to work with him, and to have had the matches we did. I was proud of the way he represented the business for me, because I wasn't exactly what you would call a role model for others. He was the consummate pro. I just have the utmost respect for the man.

—Don Muraco

I remember that day at the Garden well—because I showered after the match and drove back to Glastonbury—but not to my home. I was doing double-duty that day. After the matinee at the Garden, I was main-eventing a benefit card in my home town at Glastonbury High School that night against Ray "The Crippler" Stevens— marking the first time that I had wrestled in front of my hometown crowd since Mad Dog Vachon back in Princeton at the beginning of my career.

The April 1983 television tapings saw the return of another one of my favorite opponents—Sergeant Slaughter. Knowing that Slaughter would be one of my primary opponents in the territory throughout the summer, we wanted to do something that would generate some real heat between us right away. I came up with the idea of attempting to do the Harvard Step Test—a challenge of strength and endurance where you step up and down on a step—on television for an hour, and having Sarge come out somewhere late in the hour, criticize my performance, and then attack me and whip me with his riding crop while I was in a weakened physical state.

Given that Sarge had *actually* been a drill instructor in the United States Marines Corps, he was the perfect person to do this with. Sarge did a lot of great things in his career, but whipping me like a dog on television was definitely one of those memorable moments that everyone still remembers thirty years later—and was one of those high points that propelled him to superstardom as a heel. Of course, Sarge was straight out of central casting—he looked more like a drill sergeant than an actual drill sergeant did—but more than that, he was a fantastic performer in the ring.

Sarge was also a terrific guy outside of the ring, and he was actually *very* nervous about this angle because he wanted no part of legitimately hitting me with the whip. I that we needed to legitimize our feud in the eyes of the fans so we could set the world on fire across the territory that summer. I reassured him, repeatedly, that I wanted him to hit me as hard as he could with that whip to make sure that it raised welts on my body that the people could instantly see on television—and still see later when we took the match out on the road. Sarge absolutely *hated* the idea of doing that to me, so I pretty much had to tell him that if he didn't hit me hard enough with it to make the angle work, that I would take the thing away from him and do it to him.

Whipping the Champ

I asked Bob if he had ever been whipped by a riding crop, and of course, he said, "No," and I said, "Well, it's going to hurt and leave marks on you," but he was intent on making that attack look as realistic as he could, so he said, "We only have one shot at it, let's make it count!" Well, he was about fifty-seven minutes into the Harvard Step Test and his skin was sweating a lot and just primed for that riding crop. I felt bad every time I hit him with it because he was up on his tiptoes and I knew that it had to hurt, but he was all about making that angle a winner.

—Sergeant Slaughter

As it turned out, unlike the debacle with Graham, this was a hugely successful angle on television—maybe the best one I ever did. Although I had to reassure Sarge right up to the moment that I went out to start the Harvard Step Test, he *did* actually hit me with the whip as hard as he could, and that thing hurt like heck when it bit into my skin again and again. Some of the strikes went deep enough into the skin to draw blood, and I had those marks on me for a couple of weeks or maybe longer. Whenever I took my shirt off in the gym or in the arena, the people could see that the marks were real—and that made the whole thing take off and lent credibility to the angle, although Corki was madder than heck that I agreed to let someone do that to me.

Slaughter's look and his personality, coupled with the fact that his finisher—the Cobra Clutch—had again gotten totally over with the fans, really made the whole thing work. Ours became a really hot feud, and we milked it all over the territory all summer. We needed it, too, because with Vince Jr. taking over the business from his father, the flow of new heels from the NWA territories into the WWF had slowed considerably, and there weren't as many new guys around for me to wrestle.

Meanwhile, at the Garden in April, I faced the challenge of another returning heel—"The Russian Bear" Ivan Koloff. Koloff was another guy with a lot of history in the business, and a lot of miles already logged in WWF rings. He, of course, was the man who beat Bruno at the Garden in 1972 to end Bruno's first and seemingly insurmountable nine-year reign as WWF champion, which, of course, gave Koloff a lot of credibility with the fans. Because Koloff had beaten Bruno, who many thought to be invincible, the fans figured he was capable of beating me too, and that was something that put people in the seats.

Koloff had significantly slimmed down from the 300-pound strongman he was in the 1970s to a 240-pound wrestling machine. Although we were booked as one-and-done in most places during this series in 1983, my matches with Ivan tended to be lengthier than most of my other challengers because Koloff was a master of chain wrestling, we could start slow and build and tell the story that way. Our matches were very credible, and were among the best and most satisfying of my career. They were also a nice diversion from the matches with Slaughter that were happening at the same time—because the series with Slaughter was more of a feud, and as such, featured more brawling than wrestling.

At the Garden, I beat Koloff with the Chickenwing Crossface after about thirty minutes of really solid wrestling in what was one of the best technical matches I ever had in that building. In other arenas around the territory, Ivan and I wrestled for as long as forty-five minutes before calling for the finish. We were having a great time, and in most of the places we wrestled, we had the fans on the edges of their seats simply by featuring old-school mat and chain wrestling. It was great to see that the fans had learned to appreciate that kind of old-school, psychology-driven *wrestling* match.

By contrast, my two matches with the Sarge at the Garden were total brawling affairs almost from bell to bell—which is not to say that the matches were any less compelling to the fans. He was a terrific worker with tremendous agility for a big man. He was also 100 percent about the match, all the time—which made him a real pleasure to work with. In our first match at the Garden in May 1983, I caught Sarge in the Chickenwing, and he grabbed the whip from the Grand Wizard, who was at ringside and started whipping me with it, causing the referee to declare a disqualification.

Ordinarily, a challenger getting disqualified would be a booking tool to get him *out* of a championship series with me without having to get beaten cleanly. It was usually a tool used to keep someone strong for a later series—often with Andre. In this case, however, it was a finish that allowed *me* to demand the rematch, even though technically Sarge was no longer the number-one contender after losing the match by disqualification. On television, much was made of this point, and of the fact that I might be "losing my cool" a little bit by demanding a rematch with such a dangerous challenger—and that the fact that Sarge had gotten under my skin might prove to be my undoing.

The booking worked great—as the Garden was again full for our rematch in June, which had all the makings of a Pier Six brawl. That match was likewise booked to end inconclusively, with me getting counted out after Slaughter clotheslined me off the ring apron with the Slaughter Cannon after I had been distracted by the referee. This time, however, the blowoff Texas Death Match between Slaughter and me was set for the Meadowlands Arena in East Rutherford, New Jersey, which provides you with the answer to the oft-asked trivia question—who was the only one of my challengers I never defeated cleanly at the Garden? Despite *two* series against Sarge in 1980 and 1983, he was the only heel that I faced for the championship that I never defeated. We did, however, completely sell out the Meadowlands for that Texas Death Match, where I finally got that elusive pin over the Sarge.

The middle of 1983 was a time of transition in the office, and it definitely showed in some of the bookings around the territory. Things began to feel less planned and less organized as Vince Sr. started to loosen his grip. Whereas bookings around the territory used to follow a clearly set schedule and matches and challengers followed a more predictable order, now we were traveling to places that we had never been before and running two or sometimes even three cards a day, and as a consequence, the overall quality of the cards started to diminish.

I faced a strange array of challengers to the title in the summer of 1983, from the expected matches against Muraco, Koloff, and Slaughter in the larger arenas, to other, less plausible matches against Afa, Mr. Fuji, and Iron Mike Sharpe in some of the smaller towns. I think the theory was that simply getting the world champion and a world title match would be enough to draw a house—but as I have always said, it takes two to tango, and it didn't make a whole lot of sense to the fans to see Mr. Fuji getting a title match against me when he had lost a mid-card match in the town a month or two before. That is not to take anything away from Mr. Fuji's ability to put on a great match—it's simply a commentary on the fact that the match wouldn't necessarily be a great box office draw in advance of the card.

Around that time same time, a twenty-two year-old kid by the name of Eddie Gilbert, another second-generation wrestler, had just arrived in the territory. Vince Sr. approached me at the television taping where Eddie debuted and asked me if I would mentor him a little bit by taking him under my wing, train with him, and keep my eye on him out on the road. Naturally, because Vince Sr. was asking, I agreed, and set about to show Eddie the right way to live his life and do the things a young wrestler needed to do to work his way up the ladder. I didn't know at the time why Vince Sr. was asking, but as I would soon find out, Eddie had already taken some shortcuts.

I made time for Eddie, worked out with him, and showed him how to diet to keep his body in top form. Then, one night in Salisbury, Maryland, he was scheduled to wrestle in a singles bout and he was so goofed out on drugs that his opponent had to carry him through the entire match. A few minutes in, I went down to the ring, threw Eddie over my shoulder, and carried him back to the dressing room because he was such an embarrassment. I was furious with him—and when I confronted him about it, he wouldn't look me in the eye, and he wouldn't even admit that he was doing drugs.

That's what the wrestling business can do to you—it can eat you alive if you let it.

I didn't enjoy working with Gilbert not only because was he not doing things the right way, but because he didn't even want to acknowledge he had a problem. I think Vince was hoping that my example would rub off on him, but Gilbert was already caught up in the rat race as young as he was in 1983. Once that happened, and once I realized that he wasn't willing to even acknowledge that he had a problem, I didn't care to be around him anymore.

I didn't even have to tell Vince about what had happened—he had already heard about it from Phil Zacko—the promoter that night. Someone from the front office was in charge of every building where we appeared, and would report in to Vince Sr. either at the end of the night or the next morning. Even though Vince Sr. wasn't out on the road other than at the Garden, he knew everything that went on at the matches, from how big the gate was, to who no-showed, to what matches got the best crowd reaction, from the agent on duty. Anything out of the ordinary would be reported.

Shortly after that, Eddie was involved in a horrific car accident after a television taping in May in Allentown, during which he suffered serious neck and chest injuries. That also happened to be the same night that Jimmy Snuka's girlfriend was found dead at the motel where the boys were staying. Needless to say, that was a long and tragic night for a lot of people, and the weeks that followed were a pretty tough time for the business. After the car accident, Eddie had to recuperate for nearly four months, and didn't return to the circuit until the fall.

We made our second collective trip out to California, again for matches in Los Angeles and San Diego on July 2 and 3. We flew commercial—everybody just flew to LAX from wherever they were on the circuit at the time. Since I had wrestled in upstate New York the day before—I had driven home that night and flew out from Hartford the next day and then rented a car to use in California.

Once again, the cards were a mix of people who had wrestled in the promotions out on the West Coast, and our guys. I main-evented the buildings on both nights, against Sarge in Los Angeles, and against Koloff in San Diego. We drew much better crowds this second time around, and it was exciting to be bringing our brand of wrestling to a new audience. When you're wrestling in an unfamiliar place, you don't really do anything any differently—you just develop the storylines the same way and draw the people in.

Back in those days, we didn't need scriptwriters or long televised vignettes. We could get people to love us or hate us just by being a good worker in the ring, and doing things we knew would draw the fans into the match. Given enough time in the ring on a given night, a gifted worker could get the people whether or not the person had any television exposure beforehand. The *people* would tell you what your next move should be, and the direction you should take the match. You can't script or choreograph the next thing you should do in a wrestling match—because you can't plan how the crowd is going to react to a certain move. You have to be able to listen to what the people are telling you, react, and then reflect that back at them without them knowing you are doing it. That's the art of professional wrestling—and I'm afraid that art is passing into history with my generation of wrestlers—the last group of guys who actually know how to do this and are capable of teaching it to the next generation.

During the summer of 1983, as soon as school let out, we had another of the regular biannual visits from George "The Animal" Steele. Just as he had done so many times previously, Steele took about one television taping to get his wild-man gimmick "over" with the fans. At the June Garden card where Sarge had beaten me by countout, Steele had mauled Chief

Jay Strongbow to a bloody pulp, to the point where the match had to be stopped. That was all it took to set up the inevitable main event with me for the following month.

As Gorilla Monsoon used to love to say in response to watching the wrestling fans, "people are basically sadistic," and although many of them were legitimately frightened of "The Animal," they couldn't wait to buy tickets to the July Garden card where the same guy who had just mauled the Chief would get his chance to become the world champion. And wouldn't you know it, we sold out both the Garden and the Felt Forum that night—and turned several hundred people away from the Garden. The match had sold through so well that even though we hadn't really been planning for it, Vince Sr. couldn't help but call for an inconclusive finish. Steele was just so over with the fans that all it took was for him to come running out into the ring, pull off his shirt to expose the jungle of back hair that he had, eat a turnbuckle, and jam me with the tape-wrapped can-opener that he kept hidden in his boot or his tights or his mouth, or wherever the referee wasn't looking for it.

The fans just ate it up. It was a novelty act, and you couldn't go to it too often, but the "fight for your life" gimmick was box office gold all around the territory, and, if you think about it, all around the world. People came out in droves all over the NWA territory and in Japan, the Caribbean, Mexico, and Australia to see Abdullah the Butcher carve people up with a fork night after night, or to see the Sheik conjure up and throw a fireball at someone. In the WWF, no one had mastered the gimmick like George Steele had—and the people just kept coming out to watch the mayhem.

Our first match at the Garden was booked to end in a disqualification after the referee saw *me* hit Steele with the object after I finally got it away from him. It was a passion play intended to make the fans empathize with me for having to get into the ring and wrestle this guy at all, and then to get them to hate the referee for being so stupid. And what red-blooded

American guy doesn't love to rain hatred down on umpires or referees? The matches with Steele were almost all booked this way, because they were a guaranteed hit.

We came back the following month in the rematch, which was booked as a no-holds-barred Texas Death Match in some places, and just as a "return bout" in others—but the plan in nearly all of those rematches was for Steele to not let me into the ring, and for the referee to have no ability to control him to get him to let me into the ring—and to play off of the predicament for five or seven minutes while the fans became increasingly emotional just watching the simple act of me trying to climb into the ring. Finally, I would just take off my ring jacket outside the ring, hand the belt to Arnold, sneak into the ring, make one move, trick George, pin him, and escape further danger before anyone knew what had happened.

It was a booking plan that George and I had worked out together, and it got the fans night after night after night around the territory in 1983. As I have said before, it wasn't my favorite series, because I preferred the old-school method of actually getting to *wrestle* with someone and develop the storyline—but there was no doubting the effectiveness of this series in putting butts in the seats around the territory.

Doing the Honors

In 1983 we had two matches again, and after the first match ended inconclusively, Mr. McMahon asked me, again, for the same finish: to put Bobby over in a very short period of time. He looked at me, as if he suddenly remembered what had happened the last time he asked me that, but I just looked at him and said, "Sure." I think that shocked the hell out of him, because he looked at me and said, "Jim, why is it that you are agreeing this time when you refused last time?" And I explained to him that I agreed with the finish this time because

I thought Bobby, who by that time had been the champion for almost six years, was ready for that, and I was at the point in my career where it was the right thing to do. And the fans loved it.

After I did the honors for Bobby at the Garden in 1983, Mr. McMahon Sr. called me into his office and he had tears in his eyes, and he said, "Jim, you've been really good to us for a lot of years, and I don't want you to just become another one of the hang-arounds in the name of a few extra bucks. I think it is time for your career to end right here in the WWF. I think Mr. McMahon might have sensed that his time was short, because he was very emotional. We put our arms around each other, we hugged, and that was the end of my career . . . I thought.

—George "The Animal" Steele

During the summer of 1983, Vince Sr. was also experimenting with a lot of eight-man and ten-man tag-team matches in main events or sub-main events around the territory. These matches would allow you to tell more of a story than you could in a battle royal, but the point of these matches was to give the people a different visual, and to see whether matches of this size would attract people's interest at the box office. It was also a way of recycling people who had already had big matches with me back into the ring and to mix up the matchups and just generate interest. Generally, these matches were not elimination matches like the Survivor Series matches are now. They were usually scheduled for the best three out of five falls with a two-hour time limit, which allowed for some internal storytelling and generation of some new storylines.

I was in a number of these matches, usually paired with Andre and some combination of the territory's other main babyfaces (Snuka, Morales, Atlas, Johnson, Putski) against the Samoans and two or three heels who were playing out their string in the territory. It was certainly a good photo-op, and an interesting visual to see five men on a side during the introductions to these matches, and then to see four men on each side hanging on to the ropes on the apron of the ring while two guys did battle in the ring. These matches, of course, were more like a night off, since everyone needed to get some things in, and even if the match went thirty or forty minutes, that left only five to eight minutes of actual in-ring time to any one guy.

During the remainder of the summer of 1983, I wrestled Koloff, Slaughter, and Steele in the primary buildings, secondary civic centers, and finally, in many of the high school gyms or ice rinks in the smaller towns in the territory.

The first set of August television tapings on August 2 and 3 in Allentown and Hamburg saw the first appearances of the Masked Superstar— the first masked heel to come into the territory during my tenure as WWF champion. Superstar featured a terrific-looking finishing move called the Swinging Neckbreaker, in which he would catch his opponent in a front facelock and then, holding his opponent's other wrist in his hand, corkscrew around before slamming his opponent neck and back first into the canvas. The hold was put over from the first matches Superstar wrestled on television as one that had been "banned" in several states, and one that had crippled wrestlers across the country. The first two men he wrestled on television were stretchered out after falling to the finishing move in the ring. Vince McMahon Jr. and Pat Patterson sold the move like crazy on the television broadcast.

Superstar was a big and agile man, and most of all, a man of mysterious origin. He was extremely articulate, and served notice, with piercing blue eyes staring through the eyeholes of his wrestling mask, that he would cripple whomever he needed to until he was granted a world title match against me. From the outset, guesses were made at his identity, as on television, announcers Vince Jr. and Pat Patterson fueled speculation that he was a famous athlete who wanted to conceal his identity.

This was actually all a ruse. The Masked Superstar was actually a guy named Bill Eadie, who I did not get to know too well outside the ring, other than that he was a former schoolteacher who was bright, articulate, and very interested in making sure that an angle or a match was as good as he could possibly make it. Prior to coming to the WWF, he had traveled the world, and was well-experienced in telling a compelling story. Obviously, the front office loved his Swinging Neckbreaker and wanted to get that move over with the fans—and this angle accomplished that in spades!

It was clear to anyone watching that a confrontation between us was brewing. Superstar was, without a doubt, the most interesting and awe-inspiring new heel to come to the federation in some time—and he was quickly gathering a head of steam with the fans, which did not evade the ever-present, watchful eye of Vince Sr.

Thus, at the next set of television tapings, on September 13, 1983, Eddie Gilbert returned after recovering from his automobile accident—which had been acknowledged to the fans—and challenged the Masked Superstar to a match on television. Superstar defeated Gilbert easily after punishing him with not one but *two* Swinging Neckbreakers in the ring, and then threw him out of the ring and delivered the Neckbreaker to the still-recovering Gilbert out on the arena's concrete floor. This resulted in Eddie Gilbert not just being stretchered out, but taken immediately into a waiting ambulance. The angle was a slower one—but the idea was that Superstar was going to injure my young protégé first, as a way of serving notice that I would be next.

I always thought it was a liability to have to wear a mask in the ring because you couldn't show your facial expressions, but Eadie was one of the most successful masked men in the wrestling business. It was an interesting gimmick, and I would put his finisher up there with Hansen's Lariat, Slaughter's Cobra Clutch, Snuka's Superfly Splash, and Adonis' Goodnight Irene as one of the three or four most "over" finishers with the people that I had seen during my tenure as champion.

On October 8, 1983, I wrestled my first match against the Masked Superstar at the Boston Garden. The building was sold out on the strength of this match and Muraco's cage match blowoff with Snuka over the Intercontinental title. We were coming back the following month, so I agreed to put Superstar over as strongly as possible by giving him the only other stretcher job I had done in my career. He gave me the Neckbreaker inside the ring, then threw me out of the ring where I got counted out. Arnold Skaaland was at ringside and went over to protect me, but Superstar attacked Arnold and then gave me the Neckbreaker on the floor of the Boston Garden, and then left me laying there to get stretchered out.

On October 23, Superstar did the same thing to me in our first match at the Madison Square Garden, but since I had already done a stretcher job there for Snuka, we didn't want to go back to that well, so I just laid there and got counted out.

Between those two dates, on October 12, 1983, Ernie Roth, the Grand Wizard of Wrestling, died suddenly and unexpectedly of a heart attack in Florida. Everybody loved Ernie, and the news came as quite a shock to all of us. He had been a mainstay in the WWF for a long, long time, and during his tenure, had managed most of the top guys in the business. He was just terrific on the microphone selling his heels and putting butts in the seats with his scholarly promos. He helped Vince Sr. behind the scenes with tickets and a little bit of everything before, in the later years, retreating to his home in Fort Lauderdale and making appearances only at the television tapings, the Garden, and occasionally at the Spectrum, the Boston Garden, or one or two of the other larger arenas.

It was around this time that I decided to cut my hair short and to go back to wearing a singlet. No one told me to do it—I chose to do that myself. Around that time, the WWF was becoming a bit more focused on entertainment, and a little less focused on wrestling. I always liked wearing singlets in high school and college, so I thought that I would make that little change in my appearance as a nod to my amateur background, and as a reminder to people that notwithstanding the recent changes, the name of the game was still *wrestling*.

November 21, 1983, was the date of my much-anticipated rematch with the Masked Superstar at the Garden. As he always had, Vince Sr. brought Bill Eadie and me together in the bathroom and told us what he wanted at the end of the match. He told us that Superstar was to try and put the Neckbreaker on me again, but that this time, I was going to block it and catch him in an inside cradle for the three count.

Vince Sr.'s words didn't seem to affect Eadie one way or another, and he didn't show any kind of disappointment to learn that he would be doing the honors for me in our second match. I'll be honest though, I think I was more surprised than he was because of what we had just done in Boston, and what we had done on television. I thought for sure that they were setting us up for a three-match series at the Garden that would culminate in some kind of final match that would resolve the feud, and permit me to get some kind of punctuated revenge against Superstar for what he had done to me and to Eddie Gilbert.

What I didn't yet know, however, was that the sands running through my hourglass as the WWF World Heavyweight Champion were rapidly running out, and that there wasn't going to be time for a third match at the Garden between me and Superstar.

The winds of change were blowing. I just didn't feel them yet.

That match against the Superstar would prove to be my final success-ful title defense at the Garden.

23

The Night the Lights Went Out on Broadway
(December 26, 1983)

"Defeat should be accepted merely as a test. . . . Defeat is never the same as failure until it has been accepted as such."

—Napoleon Hill, "Learn from Adversity and Defeat"

The television tapings for December 1983 were held in Allentown and Hamburg on December 6 and December 7, 1983. The bad news came on December 6, 1983, in Allentown, the same place where it had all begun for me.

"Bobby, can I speak to you for a moment?"

It was Vince Sr. at my side. It had been nearly seven years since I had first heard him utter those words to me, but this time, I could tell just by looking at him that something was different.

That morning, as we began to cut the promos for the upcoming month, I had looked at Vince Sr.'s calendar book containing the upcoming cards, and collected my bookings. I hadn't noticed anything unusual. I was going to the same places I would usually go, and was scheduled to wrestle Iron Sheik, Sergeant Slaughter, and the Masked Superstar—the expected set of challengers to the WWF title. We had just completed taping the three weeks of promotional interviews for the upcoming towns, and that too, had pretty much been business as usual. I was main-eventing all of those towns, and talking about defending the WWF title against Sheik, Slaughter, or Superstar, with an occasional match against Muraco still thrown in for good measure.

We were standing next to the ring when Vince Sr. turned to me, looked me in the eye, and dropped the bombshell.

"Bobby, we're going to have a change. We're going to put the belt on the Sheik at the Garden in December. What would you suggest for a finish?"

My heart sank.

I had known this day would eventually come—but to be honest, I hadn't seen it coming. The gates all around the territory had been very strong throughout the summer and fall for the matches with Steele and Slaughter and Superstar, and I hadn't sensed any real restlessness from the fans, the office, or the boys in the dressing room. Then again, it *had* been almost six years—although it felt like those years had passed in the blink of an eye.

As I stood there with Vince Sr., this man who had chosen me to be his All-American Boy, and who had given me the wonderful opportunity to be his world champion, I was overcome by a sense of tremendous gratitude, and I wanted to make sure that I did right by him in what he was asking me to do. I started thinking about the different times in the past when titles had changed hands, and how someone would almost always have their foot on the ropes, or under the ropes, or something. There was always a little out so that the champion didn't have to have to lay down completely.

I didn't like that. In my mind, when it is your time, you should put the challenger over the way you would want to be put over yourself.

So standing there by the ring with Vince Sr., I came up with this idea of the Sheik trapping me in his Camel Clutch, and not being able to break the hold, and Arnold being forced to throw in the towel because I had no prospect of escaping the hold, but wouldn't submit, putting myself at risk of permanent injury. It would go down as a submission finish that would put the Sheik over much more strongly than a fluky pin with a foot on the ropes. It was a finish that I knew had never been done before, and a finish that the people would never forget. So that's what I suggested.

Vince Sr. nodded as he listened to me lay out the proposed finish, and then patted me on the backside, almost apologetically, as he left my side.

"I like that. Thanks, Bobby."

The conversation was very short—but it was one that I would replay over and over in my mind for the next many years. In the years that would follow, I often wondered if there was any question that I might have asked, or anything that I might have said that would have changed his mind. I really believe that in Vince Sr.'s heart, he wanted the good guy to win in the end because it was good for society. In his mind, though the battle might be bitter and the war long, ultimately, the guy with the white hat always had to end up standing tall in the end—because that is what gave people hope. In the end, hope was what we were selling with this story of the "All-American Boy." For almost six years, we told that story together, and we had given people hope.

The next night in Hamburg, Vince Sr. told me that they wanted me to do a little angle with The Iron Sheik's Persian Club Challenge that night at the tapings. The Sheik would come out and insult all the American wrestlers, and taunt them for their inability to work out with the Persian Clubs. I was to burst out of the dressing room, taking off my suit coat and shirt as I went, ready to take up the mantle and defend America's honor. In the ring, I would deliberately fail on my first attempt, but then eventually hoist the clubs up and start swinging the clubs just like the Sheik did, prompting him to attack me while I had the clubs up in the air. My job was to make sure that one of the clubs landed on the back of my neck, so that I could sell an injury to my neck and shoulder that would set up the match with the Sheik at the Garden on December 26, and set *me* up for the Sheik's "Camel Clutch" submission hold, which, of course, targeted the neck and shoulders.

Vince Sr. told me that he liked the finish I had suggested, and that he knew that, coupled with this injury angle they were building in, it wasn't going to be bad for me—that his All-American Boy wasn't going to get buried by the finish, even though I would be losing the world title to an Iranian madman on the day after Christmas in Madison Square Garden. I think Vince Sr. thought, at that time, that I was going to be in the wrestling business for a long time after my title loss, and he wanted the finish to keep me strong.

The angle on television went off awkwardly. Although I had worked out with the Sheik's clubs before, they legitimately weighed eighty pounds each and were difficult to swing over your head, and even more difficult to drop carefully on yourself without *actually* injuring yourself while doing it. When the Sheik attacked me, the club mostly missed me on the way down, and I had to almost pull it back on top of me in order to make the injury angle look more compelling. But I sold the injury on television as instructed, and the stage was set for me to pass the torch at the Garden on the twenty-sixth.

At that point, I still didn't have the *real* picture of what was about to happen—only that I would be passing the title to The Iron Sheik at the Garden then. Vince Sr. told me that I would have a main-event rematch against the Sheik at the Garden in January, and Vince Jr. even told me that I'd be getting the belt *back* from the Sheik at that card, but that the details of all of that hadn't been worked out yet. In retrospect, I think Vince Jr. must have just told me that to make sure that I would cooperate with the plan they were hatching.

Not cooperating never even entered my mind.

The next day, when I arrived home from the tapings, I told Corki about my conversation with Vince Sr., and that my days as the world champion were at an end. Corki reminded me of how grateful we should both be for the amazing run that we had—and I felt the same. I was lucky to have the boss I had for so long and to have had the opportunity to please the people for as long as I did.

It was a strange feeling traveling the circuit during the first three weeks of December as a lame duck, knowing that, in each building that I appeared, it would be for the last time as the world champion. My last stop was in Pittsburgh at the Civic Arena on Christmas Day, where I pinned the Masked Superstar. I stayed over in Pittsburgh on Christmas night, alone with my thoughts, and then made the long and lonely drive from there to New York City the next day. Along the way, I thought about the past, about all the things that had happened to me in the wrestling business, about my relationships with the Funks, and Eddie Graham, and Jim Barnett and Sam Muchnick and Harley Race, and most of all with Vince McMahon Sr., and about the fact that a major chapter in my life was coming to an end.

If I had to lose the belt to someone, I was pleased that it was going to be to Khosrow—a real athlete, and someone I had known for so long. I tried to stay positive and make the best of it—but it was definitely not an easy thing. Over the years, there have been a lot of rumors and stories that I refused to drop the belt to Bill Eadie because he did not have a legitimate amateur background, or that I handpicked Khosrow because he did.

Both are false. Vince McMahon Sr. approached me for the first time about changing the title on December 6 at the Allentown tapings. He told me I'd be losing the belt at the Garden to the Sheik on the December 26. The only thing I had any say in was the finish.

When I arrived at the Garden that night, I walked up the ramp and rode the elevator up to the dressing rooms where it was pretty much business as usual. Sheik, who had just been told by Vince Sr. that night that he was going over, was excited to get the rub of a world championship run, so he was ebullient. Khosrow gave me a set of his Persian clubs that I still have at the house to this day, so I knew that he had the utmost respect for me, as I did for him. We liked each other, and had known each other for a long time, going almost all the way back to the beginning of our careers. It just kind of made sense I would be passing the belt to him.

Vince Sr. called us together in the bathroom and gave us the finish—which was the ending I had suggested. I went through the same pre-match preparations that I always did, trying to retreat into my routine. I had always known, in the back of my mind, that this day would come, and I wondered how I would react. Now that the day was upon me, I was bound and determined to do it with honor, as Billy had done for me years earlier. I imagine it was a little bit like dying will be. You know it's going to happen to you sometime, but it still catches you a little bit by surprise when the day actually comes.

Going to the ring, it was hard not to give anything away by the look on my face. Standing there in the ring, with my red white and blue American flag jacket on, and the big green world title belt around my waist, and Arnold Skaaland at my side, and the people still cheering wildly as Howard Finkel announced my name—I wish I could have frozen time. My mind flashed back to February 20, 1978, when I was standing on the other side of this ring, and Billy Graham was over here, thinking the thoughts that I was thinking—and suddenly and finally, I understood what that was like for Billy.

A lot of you are probably reading this and thinking to yourselves, "If the whole thing is predetermined anyway, what's the big deal to simply pass the world title to another guy in the group?" Think of it like playing the lead role in a play or a musical on Broadway that closes. For years, you have the lead role, basking in the cheers of the crowd, living in the spotlight, and of course, enjoying the financial rewards that come with it. Then, all of a sudden and largely without warning, the play closes, the lights go out, and the dream is over. Instead of being an instantly recognizable face all around the country and in many parts of the world, you start to fade back into anonymity. Instead of receiving a bag full of fan mail every three weeks, the volume dwindles, until eventually, the people stop writing.

It had been a great run, and one in which I tried every day to give the very best of myself to the people, to carry the championship with the honor and dignity that it deserved, to serve as a role model for my fans and to do myself and the company proud. In those aspirations, I think I succeeded. All that remained, then, was to do my very best to execute this match, and make the transition a good and memorable one.

The End of an Era

Bob was a great college wrestler, a great athlete, and a good man. And he trained all the time. He was a hard-working man, and I got along very well with him. He impressed me. And we were friends going all the way back to the days in the AWA, you know?

I found out the same night, when Vince Sr. told me that I was going to take the championship. I was very surprised, but very excited and happy that I was going to get the opportunity. Mr. McMahon told me that I was to get Bob in the Camel Clutch and that Mr. Arnold Skaaland was going to throw in the towel and I would be the champion. But I didn't have any idea how long I was going to hold the belt. Nobody told me that.

—**The Iron Sheik**

Sheik and I sold my neck and shoulder injury throughout the match, running off a couple of false finishes where I was unable to complete a move because of the "injury" to my neck and shoulder. On the television broadcast on MSG-Cablevision, Gorilla Monsoon and Pat Patterson punctuated every point. They painted me as a courageous warrior—a champion who could have pulled out of the match entirely, or left the ring to get counted out to save my title once I understood that I was too hurt to continue, but instead, chose to compete and defend the honor of the United States against the hated Sheik.

Then, before I wanted it to, the moment came.

I have played the moment over repeatedly in my mind's eye, too many times to count. I was down on the mat, with the Sheik on my back, pulling back on my chin and putting on only enough pressure to make the hold look convincing. Looking over at Arnold, and watching, almost like it was in slow motion, as he balled up the towel in his hand and threw it into the ring from his position at ringside. I watched the towel come fluttering into the ring and land at the feet of referee Dick Kroll.

Kroll, who was not in on the finish, looked incredulously at Skaaland, who nodded at him and gestured for him to call for the bell.

Kroll motioned to the timekeeper, the bell rang, the Sheik released the hold, I collapsed onto the canvas, and before I could draw a breath, Arnold was on me, massaging my neck and whispering in my ear.

"Well done, Bobby. It's okay. You did good," he said as he leaned over me, still massaging my neck, not realizing that the only pain I felt was on the inside. The emotions rushed through me, as he put my good arm over his shoulder and helped me from the ring and down the runway back to the dressing room.

The people were in shock—and you could see it all over their faces. On the day after Christmas in New York City, an Iranian madman had just beaten the All-American Boy for the World Heavyweight Championship. Freddie Blassie cackled at the ringsiders, as he showed the belt off again and again.

The match had gone off pretty much as expected. After the match, back in the dressing room, Sheik shook my hand and thanked me for doing the honors. I did the obligatory post-match interview, took a shower, got in the car, and went home. Corki and Carrie were both waiting up for me when I got there.

I was most grateful for that.

He Drew Like Gangbusters

You know, for a lot of years, Vince was a part of the NWA and acted as a voting member of the board. After he left, we battled him, and for a short time, Bobby was on the other end of that, because he was working for Vince. Vince Sr. wanted control of the National Wrestling Alliance. He wanted control of the NWA World Heavyweight Championship. And when he got sick in 1983, it was a battle that wasn't over yet. The Alliance was composed of thirty-two promoters from the territories and organizations across the country. And basically, the person who could control those members could control the belt—and that's what it was all about. You had to have the numbers—and if you had the numbers, you could control the alliance and decide the champion, and decide his schedule. See, the belt was very important to every member. If you had the NWA World Champion defending the belt in your territory, you were going to make money. That's why Vince ultimately pulled out of the NWA—because he could not control the Alliance and get the champion when he wanted to and where he wanted to. He had to share him, and Vince Sr. wanted a world champion for his buildings—especially the Garden.

Vince Sr. kept Bobby on top for six years, which was a tremendously long time for someone to stay a champion, even back then. He wouldn't have kept Backlund on top if Bobby wasn't drawing like gangbusters and making lots of money for the company. You don't stay with a dead horse, no matter what promises you might have made to him. On the other hand, if you've got a good horse then you ride him for as long as you can—and believe me, I don't care where you are the champion—six years is a long, long time to be champion in one stint. If you look at that, there are not many champions in the whole long history of professional wrestling in this country that have been able to run with a belt for six years.

As the champion, you're sitting there, and there are very competitive, envious eyes all around—competitive in the ring, competitive performance-wise, and competitive behind the scenes. There are a lot of daggers being thrown, there is a lot of stabbing going on as people try to jockey for position. Even when the top guy is drawing money, people want to tear the top guy down—because that top guy gets to make a lot of money, and everyone wants to be there. But what got Bobby there is everything that Bob Backlund was. Was it luck? Well, luck is always a part of it—but it wasn't luck. His honesty and credibility were huge assets—because the promoters knew that they could count on him to show up, in shape, ready to go every day, to put asses in the seats, and to protect the belt if he ever needed to. He was also very dependable. If he had a torn up knee, or a bad back, or the flu or whatever it might have been—and he had a championship matchup there in the Garden, I'll guarantee you he would have found a way to crawl down that aisle and climb into the ring and not disappoint those people. That was another asset that the promoters knew they could count on.

I'm not talking about being a "yes man"—I'm talking about being a man's man. There's a whole lot of difference between those two things. And Bobby Backlund was no yes man. He was a man's man.

—**Harley Race**

A Great Ambassador for the Business

I met Bob in May of 1985 which was officially my first day in the business when I was asked by the show's promoter, Tommy Dee, to work on the ring crew. So from that point on, I felt like I was officially in. I met my first wrestlers ever that day—and meeting Bob stands out because I had my picture taken with him, which I still have, by the way. I asked Bob if he might sign it for me. For the first and only time in my entire career, a wrestler wrote down his address and said send it to me and I'll sign it for you. I walked out of there that night saying wow, these wrestlers are all so friendly—but I didn't realize then, as I realize now, that Bob was really at the very top of that friendly scale. There is really only one guy in the history of the business who would give a fan, working on the ring crew, his address to get a photo signed.

So that was my first experience with Bob, and frankly, an experience that portrayed wrestlers in about as favorable a light as was possible.

Bob was such a great ambassador for the business. I grew up right after the Bruno era, and Bob Backlund was my champion that I grew up watching at a time when the champions didn't change very much, so you always had that stability and I think Bob as champion meant that you got to see a procession of wild, colorful heels to counteract Bob, who was like the greatest, clean-cut wrestling babyface of all-time. Having him as champion allowed so many great heels to come in and out of the old WWF territory to challenge Bob. And I go back and still love watching Bob's old matches from Madison Square Garden that I used to tape, whether it was the classic with the Superfly, or the series with Sergeant Slaughter. I was there the night Bob dropped the championship to The Iron Sheik, so I saw a little bit of history—but Bob was a great champion and a big part of my younger years.

—Mick Foley

24

The Choice (1984)

"Recognize that the blessings you have are a gift to be used for the common good . . ."

—Napoleon Hill, "Assemble an Attractive Personality"

<hr>

The next day, December 27, 1983, Vince Jr. held a television taping at the Chase Hotel in St. Louis where the St. Louis–based NWA program *Wrestling at the Chase* had always been filmed. I wasn't invited. In fact, despite the fact that I had been the Missouri State Champion and would have been known to the people watching in the building that day, I don't think my name was even mentioned as being part of the promotion.

One person who *was* there, though, was Hulk Hogan. That was beginning to send a message.

I was in Buffalo, wrestling the Masked Superstar without the belt. Sheik was at a spot show somewhere in Pennsylvania *with* the belt. It felt very lonely to be out there in the main events at these places without the championship. People were stunned to learn that I had lost the belt—and I continued to sell the neck and shoulder injury to make sure that the story held together when we finally broke it on the next set of television tapings in January 1984 in Allentown and Hamburg.

Those tapings saw the debuts of a bunch of new talent, including Hogan, Roddy Piper, Paul Orndorff, and "Dr. D" David Schultz, as well as announcer Gene Okerlund, who Vince Jr. had apparently lured away from the AWA at the same time he lured Hogan. I knew Piper from the match I had with him at the Olympic Auditorium in Los Angeles, and I knew Orndorff from Florida. I was pretty close with Roddy, and I visited with him and Orndorff at the Allentown taping just on a social level.

During the first hour of the Allentown taping, I was in a match with one of the Samoans, and the booking plan was to have the other Samoans and Albano at ringside during the match—so I could go back to the dressing room and bring somebody back to second me in my corner. That person, of course, was Hulk Hogan. The point of all of this was for me to introduce Hogan to the fans to put the rub on him and quickly get him over as a babyface. This was important, since only a couple of years earlier, Hogan had been in the territory managed by Freddie Blassie, and had been a vicious heel that had feuded with Andre the Giant. Of course, between those two points, Hogan had starred as "Thunderlips" with Sylvester Stallone in *Rocky III*, and had become something of a sensation in the AWA and in Japan. Vince Jr. saw the potential of Hogan's marketability and jumped all over it.

I had known Hogan from his prior stint in the territory. He was young in the business, and very green back then, but Hogan and I had some pretty good matches in 1980. I didn't really like what Hogan was doing and what he was about behind the scenes, but the McMahons had been very good to me, and I owed them some loyalty in return. The point of the whole thing was to pair us up and have it be more or less a passing of the torch from me to him, and for me to let my fans know it was okay to cheer for Hogan and to trust him and to believe in him.

During the next hour of the television taping, I teamed with Hogan against Mr. Fuji and Tiger Chung Lee, and Hogan got the pin. Again, this was simply about re-orienting the fans and using me to ensure that Hogan was understood to be a babyface. It was an easy transition and the fans readily accepted Hogan—and we reinforced that Hogan had "changed his ways" during a ringside interview.

After that had been laid down to tape about two weeks before the Garden card, Vince Jr. approached me and informed me that notwithstanding the fact that the January 23, 1984, card at Madison Square

Garden had been announced as a Sheik-Backlund rematch for the WWF title, that they had decided to put Hogan into the main event as my replacement. At that point, I knew for certain that Hogan was going to be their next guy.

Other than the television tapings, Hogan did not make any house-show appearances in the WWF before taking the title from the Sheik at the Garden. Sheik and I, however, continued to travel the circuit. Khosrow and I faced each other in a rematch at the Boston Garden, where the fans were behind me even more than usual to try and get the title back, but of course, it was not to be. The Sheik was disqualified in that bout. We also wrestled at a few spot shows on a tour of Pennsylvania, with similar finishes. Elsewhere, I faced Muraco for the Intercontinental Championship a few times in the strange position as the *challenger* to *his* title, finished up rematch commitments with Masked Superstar and Sergeant Slaughter in a few of the bigger buildings in the territory, and wrestled a couple of matches against Paul Orndorff. I wished that Piper and Orndorff had come into the territory six months earlier so I could have had a series with each of them before I dropped the championship. I think the fans would have enjoyed what Roddy and Paul and I could have put together.

The "official" announcement was that I was "too injured" to wrestle at the January 23, 1984, Garden show, and in the promo interviews for the card, Hogan was named as my replacement. Before I learned that I had been taken out of that match, I had promised tickets to some friends who had helped me organize the Bob Backlund kids' wrestling tournaments out on Long Island, so I went to the Garden to make sure that they got their tickets and could get into the matches. Because I was "injured," I was not scheduled to wrestle on the card, so once I knew that my friends and the kids had gotten into the building, I didn't hang around for very long—but I did hear that there was some drama between the Sheik and Hogan and some possible involvement by Hogan's former promoter, AWA boss Verne Gagne.

According to what I heard in the dressing room, Gagne was very unhappy about Vince Jr. luring Hogan away from the AWA, and had offered a legitimate bounty to the Sheik to severely injure Hogan so he would not be able to wrestle again. Rumors of this bounty were rippling around the dressing room, and were apparently causing some real heartburn in the office, because Khrosrow was a shooter and would have had no problem breaking Hogan's leg before anyone knew what was happening. And no one really knew what Khosrow was going to do.

Vince Jr. had a real issue on his hands. If the threat was legitimate and Vince Jr. sent Hogan out to the ring, his new superstar might be permanently injured before Hulkamania could even begin. Should they pull Hogan from the main event until the rumor could be sorted out? Doing so would, of course, disrupt the main event and likely cause the Garden crowd to riot. Or should they just proceed with the main event as scheduled and assume that it would all work out?

Was the threat a real one, or just a spurned promoter venting to one of his trainees?

I had already been cast aside as "too injured" to wrestle, so it was no longer an option to use me in a rematch with the Sheik while the office sorted this out. So the only thing everyone could do was wait and watch what happened.

Break His Leg

True story. We were in Pittsburgh at a motel out at the airport and I had just started doing some pushup blocks when there was a knock at the door, and it was The Iron Sheik, and he said, "Sergeant, I need to talk to you," and I asked him why, and he said, "Coach called me and wants me to break Hogan's leg and bring the title back to the AWA, and he will pay me a lot of money," and he started telling me all about it and explained to me that he didn't know what to do. So I told him, there is only one thing to do, and that is to uphold your obligation to Mr. McMahon, your boss, he is the one that is paying you, and I don't think it would be a very smart idea to do that because you'd have a bad reputation and people wouldn't ever trust you again.

When we went to the Garden, I was hoping that he would take my advice, but people in the back were certainly on the edge of their seats wondering what was going to happen that night. But he did the right thing, and did the favor for Hogan, and did it quite well, and thank God he did.

Bob Backlund was Vince McMahon Sr.'s guy. He just loved Bob. Bob was always very well respected because Bob was a shooter. If someone wanted to take him on, he was a guy who could defend himself. He just had a lot of respect from the boys and the promoters. He was always very reliable, stayed in great shape, and you never had to worry about him. He was just a wonderful guy to go in the ring with for me because we had fun. He was always open to suggestions and wanted things to be the best that they could for the people.

—Sergeant Slaughter

. . . Or Not

I saw Hulk Hogan for the first time at the Allentown, Pennsylvania, television taping when he came in and talked to Mr. McMahon when I was the champion. I didn't know that I was dropping the championship to Hogan until the night we got to the Garden when Mr. McMahon Sr. came to me and told me that he wanted me to drop the championship to Hogan.

Verne Gagne had called me and he said Khosrow, I need a favor. Mr. McMahon took Hogan from me. Now, don't drop the belt to him. Break his back, break his leg, come to Minnesota, and I will take care of you . . . we'll all take care of you. I told him, let me think about it for twenty-four hours. I talked to Sgt. Slaughter and my wife, and after that, I decided to just go into the ring and have a good match, because the hand that feeds me, I cannot bite that hand. So I didn't do that—I didn't double-cross the WWF for Mr. Gagne.

—The Iron Sheik

I didn't stay at the Garden enough to find out what happened. My friends told me later that Hogan had squashed the Sheik in five minutes and that the crowd was into it big time.

Immediately after winning the title, Hogan left with the belt on a two-week tour for New Japan, and I finished up my remaining, which roughly coincided with the time that Hogan was in Japan. Once Hogan returned from Japan with the belt, however, Vince Jr. put me in mothballs. I was not invited to the next set of television tapings, and was given no bookings for the next three-week period. I was supposed to have wrestled a Texas Death Match against the Khosrow in Boston, but they replaced me with Hogan and made that a title match where Hogan again squashed Khosrow. If you aren't booked on a card, you can't just show up at the building, so I was adrift. I wasn't getting any new bookings, so I figured that they had probably gotten what they wanted from me, and that I was done.

I had no idea what was going on, and I assumed they had decided to move on and hope the fans would forget all about Bob Backlund.

As it turned out, I think they just wanted to give Hogan a month out on the road to establish himself with the people as the champion, and as the territory's new number-one babyface. That is a lot easier to do when the former champion isn't in the same buildings competing for the same role.

I was invited to return at the March 6 Allentown television taping—and I did so. Although I didn't wrestle, I held an amateur wrestling demonstration with a couple of winners from the Bob Backlund Youth Wrestling Tournament up in Connecticut. I also did a ringside interview with Gene Okerlund, where I announced that I was healthy again, and ready to get back into wrestling full time. It was at that television taping that Vince McMahon Jr. pulled me aside and asked me if I would be willing to participate in an angle where I became jealous of the fact that the fans had adopted Hogan as their new hero and "forgotten" about me, turn heel, and work against Hogan.

I told Vince in no uncertain terms that I didn't want to do it. I pointed to the fact that my daughter was six years old and wouldn't understand why suddenly everyone hated her father. I was also working with kids and sponsoring youth wrestling tournaments all over the territory, and I was worried about how I could continue to do those things that were so important to me, personally, while playing the heel role. I didn't think that the people, and especially those kids, would understand how their hero could just throw over everything that he stood for just to make a few bucks. Vince Jr. told me to think about it—and shortly thereafter, gave me a very lucrative contract for a lot of money to become a heel and chase Hogan.

I still have that contract.

Fortunately, I followed my heart and opted not to make that heel turn. If I had, chances are that I would never have had this opportunity to tell my life story, because my co-author, then a twelve-year-old fan of mine, agrees that he would have "felt totally betrayed" by the man he considered his childhood hero.

I went back out on the road on March 25, 1984, where I headlined the Garden against Greg "The Hammer" Valentine and the match sold out both the Garden and the Felt Forum—prompting Vince Jr. to ask for a rematch the following month. This was the first Garden card in recent memory to *not* feature a defense of the WWF World Heavyweight Championship. It was very evident that they were trying to keep Hogan and me apart. I don't think there were more than a handful of times in the six months that I continued to wrestle in the WWF where Hogan and I appeared in the same building.

March 31, 1984, however, *was* one of those times. That night, despite my clear and plain refusal to consider it, they teased my heel turn in a match I had with the Sheik in the main event at the Spectrum in Philadelphia. In that match, Sheik loaded up his boot and tried to kick me with it, prompting Hogan to run into the ring swinging a cowboy boot to "make the save," which ended up getting me disqualified for outside interference. Hogan then started posing in the middle of the ring and "grandstanding," prompting me to walk out on him and leave him there. It wouldn't have taken much more to execute a complete heel turn off of that scenario—but the fact is, *I just didn't want to do it.*

They also booked me, against my will, into matches with Salvatore Bellomo, Brian Blair, and eventually, even against the newly crowned Intercontinental Champion Tito Santana to see if the crowd would push me into the heel role—but my fans never abandoned me, and these matches all came off as straight babyface matches.

Vince McMahon Sr. died of pancreatic cancer in North Miami, Florida, on May 24, 1984, at the age of sixty-nine. I went to the funeral in Fort Lauderdale. Eddie Graham was there, Arnold Skaaland was there, Vince Jr. was there, and I was there. It was an incredibly sad day for me.

Once Vince Sr. was gone, I just lost my heart for the business entirely. My friend, who had been like a father to me, was gone . . . and gone with him was the honest, straightforward way that he did business with everyone. I wrestled only sporadically after that, taking whatever bookings Vince Jr. gave me, but it was clear that we were at an impasse. I was continuing to refuse to sell out and become a heel, and Vince Jr. did not want me around as a babyface with Hogan on top.

By this point in my career—I had really started to live my character because in my mind, I meant too much to too many people. It hurt me in the business, but it didn't hurt me in life. That's probably why I didn't go anywhere in the business after I lost the title. I give speeches to kids about working hard, and playing fair, and following the rules. How could I do that during the day, then turn my back on all of that and become a heel, and cheat and lie and break the rules at night? Just to prolong my career in the business? Just for a few more big paydays? It just wasn't something

I was willing to do. To a lot of people in the business, the business was a joke—but to me, the business had given me another life—one that was just as important to me as the business was. People often talk about Hulk Hogan being the biggest "hero" the wrestling business ever saw—but what kind of hero was Hulk Hogan? That was all just for show. What I was doing with kids in my life away from the ring was real—and I wasn't about to trade that away for anything.

My match against Salvatore Bellomo at the Philadelphia Spectrum on August 4, 1984, would be my last match in the WWF for nearly eight years. After I pinned him, I grabbed the microphone and reminded the fans that I was ready to be their champion again anytime, and ironically, because Philly had never been my best town, the fans cheered for me one last time.

Some people over the years have asked me whether I would have rather been wrestling after 1984 because of all the money and the exposure and pay per view and all of that. My consistent answer is "no," because I got to work for one of the most honorable men I had ever met—and someone who was like a father to me. I wouldn't have traded that time for all the money in the world.

It Was All About Hogan

I wasn't around at the time of the transition in 1983, but I know a lot about it. At the time, a lot of us were very loyal to Mr. McMahon and to the business, maybe to a fault. Because after the switch from Bobby to the Sheik and then to Hogan, a lot of our loyalties, including Bobby's, were swept under the table. Once Hogan had the belt, it was Hogan's show and screw everybody else. Junior had a vision for where he wanted the thing to go, and it was all about Hogan. So our old-school wrestling business blossomed into a totally different business—what I call the "cartoon era." But to be honest, the way the business was, with kayfabe and untelevised finishes and all of that, would not have been able to continue the way it was in the world of social media and the Internet. The finishes and the prerecorded television saved for three weeks wouldn't have worked, they would have been instantly all over the place. The old-school way of doing business would have eventually become impossible, so the change probably saved the business from Vince McMahon Jr.'s point of view.

I never expected Junior to call and invite me back after that. In hindsight, doing the cartoon character that I ended up doing was very good for my retirement, but not real good for the lasting image of my character or for wrestling, but after Bobby's run, once Hogan took over, wrestling became a cartoon business selling lunch boxes. Unfortunately, I think doing that tainted everything that I had done before with Bruno and Pedro and Bobby that had been so real and good and strong. But it fit in great with Hulk.

Bobby was a real gentleman and I'm really glad that he had the run that he had, because he was very deserving and he was a great champion. We had a lot of fun together over the years, particularly over in Japan, and it was a pleasure to work with him.

–George "The Animal" Steele

It Became About Show Business

Late 1983 and 1984 was a time of transition. It was a time where the promoters wanted more show business—and they didn't realize that the marquee said wrestling. So it became a time that the great pure wrestlers were starting to get pushed aside for people who were more flamboyant. Because all of a sudden there was Hollywood, and there was MTV, and they were going all over the world. With professional wrestling, one reason that it was so popular all over the world is that you didn't need to know anything about it—you didn't need to speak the language—you just needed to turn the TV on and if the psychology was being handled right, you could tell what was going on. It was universal.

When Hogan came along—he was a completely different piece of work than Bobby Backlund. Vinnie was pushing entertainment—from more of a high-paced, show business, entertainment, Liberace and the Rockettes kind of place. And he was surrounding the wrestling talent with that kind of entertainment to help it appeal to a larger audience outside of wrestling. Vinnie was trying to take wrestling into the entertainment mainstream. So the great technical wrestlers kind of got poo-poo'ed. They wanted Hogan, who was a movie star having just completed *Rocky III* with Stallone, to take his vitamins and say his prayers. They would rather set things up for Hogan to hulk up and flex his muscles—and in the blink of an eye, relatively speaking, the business changed, and the great technicians, the guys who knew how to use psychology to get the people and who were formerly the cornerstones of the business became dinosaurs.

The shame of that is that the business now is suffering because no one realized how great the art that those men had mastered was, and what they brought to the table in terms of the art of telling a story in the ring through psychology. Now, the psychology is not known. As I was coming in, Bobby was on his way out, because the promotion had decided to go with entertainment instead of wrestling.

There was a lot of talk about trying to turn Bobby heel after they took the belt off him. I was around for those discussions. They didn't want anybody around on the babyface side that could go in there and show up Hogan. They wanted to cotton ball Hogan. Hell, I'd do an interview with Hogan where he'd say something about my kilt and I'd say something about his bald head, and they'd yell, "Cut, cut! You can't say that about Hulk—he's on the Wheaties box!" This was pro wrestling we're talking about—but even there, the definition was changing. They had started to redefine everything. It had just become a gigantic marketing machine with a little wrestling on the side, and they wouldn't let anyone get close to dinging up Hogan in any way.

So Vinnie put a great technical wrestler like Bobby in mothballs in favor of what he thought was a more entertaining kind of match, animated by characters that they created and could market. But now, we look back on it and see that the wrestlers of this new generation don't have the training in the psychology of how to tell a story in the ring like Bobby Backlund did—so they have to do all kinds of song and dance to try to keep the thing going instead of just having one man who knew the art, like Bobby Backlund did, come into an arena cold and draw tons of money simply because of his ability to tell a story in the ring, and leave with everybody looking great. That's what a real champion does—and that's a guy who can stay over with the people all by himself, just by his own storytelling in the ring with one other man—as opposed to putting someone in a fucking clown outfit and hoping he can sell you a few T-shirts and ice cream bars.

— "Rowdy" Roddy Piper

25

Killing Mr. Kirkley (1985–1992)

"Sunflowers don't grow from turnip seeds."

—Napeolon Hill, "Use Cosmic Habitforce"

———◆◆———

After I left the WWF, I dabbled around for a little while in a few different promotions. The Pro Wrestling USA promotion, which was comprised of an unstable alliance between the NWA and the AWA, had offered me steady work, but there was too much infighting between the promoters to allow it to be successful. Although some jointly promoted cards did get off the ground, the problem was that the promotion was comprised of two different competing groups (the NWA and the AWA), and neither one was going to permit its champion to be overshadowed by the other's. There was no clear leadership in the group—and as a consequence, although the promotion showed promise, and could have been successful if an effective leadership team had been established, that never happened. I don't think anyone realized at the time that their collective future depended on it.

I also spent some time wrestling in the AWA, but there, Verne Gagne had already invested in Rick Martel, another scientific babyface champion. I also did some independent tours of Japan, wrestled a little bit for the Savoldis in the IWCCW territory up in Maine, and even did a little bit of independent promoting of my own in the Springfield, Massachusetts, area. I know I could have continued in the business had I wanted to, by just soldiering on in any one of those promotions and helping make any one of them succeed—but my heart really wasn't in it. I missed Vince Sr., and I missed my role as the world champion. I missed the fans, the arenas, and the routine.

It just wasn't the same anymore.

Meanwhile, Vince Jr.'s national expansion was in full swing, and his gamble on Hulk Hogan, and the rock and wrestling connection, and Wrestlemania, had paid huge dividends. Vince Jr. was parlaying those victories by buying up television slots across the territories, cutting off blood supply to the NWA's regional promotions, and eventually acquiring their top talent until the entire NWA territory system had become unstable. Even though the NWA had an existing board of directors, and a leadership team that could have and should have been able to stave off Vince Jr.'s challenge, the local promoters were more concerned about their own survival and self-interest than they were about the survival of the alliance as a whole, even though they knew, in their heart of hearts, that the survival of the alliance was the only way they would be able to survive individually. The NWA's inability to come together was ultimately what permitted Vince to win the war for the airwaves and territorial supremacy.

So after these few forays in 1984 and 1985, I retreated from the spotlight, and returned to Glastonbury to help raise Carrie and be with my family and my community. Eventually, even though Corki was working full time as a teacher and gymnastics instructor, I needed to find something to do, so I worked construction, spent some time as a bail bondsman, ran for Congress, and coached amateur wrestling at the high school level at a couple of places in Connecticut.

I also became very depressed, and experienced some of the darkest days of my life during these days away from the business. It is hard to explain the impact on your life when the lights go out, the people go home, and you are forced, once again, to become an ordinary person with an ordinary life. That was something I struggled mightily with during the second half of the 1980s and the beginning of the '90s until the lure of the spotlight finally called me home.

The People Let Him Do It

The territories all had their own TV stations, and some of them were quite large. But the WWF was located in the right vicinity—right in the heart of the country's media centers. The three biggest ones were Los Angeles, Atlanta, and New York. So when the war began, those were the three territories that should have been the survivors because they were the ones that controlled the media—and the local media centers are what fueled wrestling in the territories. But it was a fruitless war—and I realized that at a very early stage in the Amarillo area because no matter what we did and what our TV did, we just couldn't keep up.

The best way to understand what happened to the wrestling business is to compare it to something else that happened around the same time. We used to have a five and dime store in Canyon, Texas. And that five and dime store was run by a guy named Mr. Kirkley. And by golly, when you went into that store, Mr. Kirkley would call out a greeting to you by name as soon as you walked in there. And Mr. Kirkley would ask you about your children and your parents, and anything that might be going on in your life and your job, and then, once you had picked out the things you wanted or needed and paid for them at the register, Mr. Kirkley would help you carry your bags out to your car. Everyone just loved Mr. Kirkley, and going into his store and buying what you needed just made you feel good, you know?

But then along came Wal-Mart, with its bright lights and easy parking, and lower prices, and more variety and what not—and people just up and forgot about Mr. Kirkley even though they loved him. And that's the way it was in the wrestling business. When Vince Jr. decided to go national, he just started buying up the local television rights and cutting off the oxygen to all of the territories. And the people let him do it, because even though they used to love the local product, they were the ones who lined up to buy the tickets. They were the ones who made it possible to kill Mr. Kirkley.

—Terry Funk

26

Being Bad by Being Good:
The Birth of "Mr. Backlund" (1993–94)

"If your life isn't already what you want it to be, it is because
you have drifted into your present circumstances. . . . You can
change that!"

—Napoleon Hill, "Use Cosmic Habitforce"

———◆———

George Foreman had just staged an incredible comeback in the world
of boxing, and had become the world champion again at an advanced
age. As it so often does, wrestling imitates life. I was about as old as
George was, so in 1992, with business in the WWF worse than I had
ever seen it, and in the wake of the steroid scandals that had rocked the
company, I was invited to make a comeback nine years after I lost the
title.

I met with Vince McMahon at his office in Stamford, and we
sketched out a plan for how this was going to work. By that time, Carrie
was a teenager, and I wanted to be back in the business. So I broke out my
old "All-American Boy" ring jacket and set about to prove I could make it
back to the top of the business.

We tested it out a little bit in a few arenas near home in the summer
of 1992, and things felt good, so the WWF put some money into a series
of promotional videos to be aired on the WWF broadcasts touting my
return to the ring after a nine-year absence from the sport. Those videos
ran in the early fall of 1992, and I went out on the road again on a full-
time basis in October of 1992.

It didn't take too long to realize, however, that professional wrestling, and the expectations of the wrestling fans had changed a lot in the nine years I had been away. My clean-cut, return to the All-American Boy gimmick wasn't really getting over with the majority of the fans, because by that point, even the babyfaces in the business were lying and cheating and swearing. The lines between babyfaces and heels, and between good and evil, had become so blurred that there was no way that a pure babyface like me, especially an older one, was going to get over in that environment. Being a pure babyface made me an anachronism—a strange and goofy throwback to an earlier era that nobody seemed to understand anymore.

To their credit, Vince Jr. and the guys in the office did everything they could do to help to make the angle work. They had all kinds of people put me over in an effort to make the people love me again in the way that they once had, but the sad truth was that it just wasn't catching fire the way we had all hoped it would.

Then, one night, I was riding down the road flipping around the radio, and I came upon the Rush Limbaugh show. Rush was listening with an increasing level of impatience to a caller who was complaining about how bad her life was. Finally, when he couldn't take it anymore, Rush started yelling at her for the long series of bad choices she had made in her life that she was refusing to take responsibility for.

There, in that moment, it all crystallized for me.

I realized that there were now a lot of people out there who didn't want to *hear* about working hard, and being responsible, and having goals and making the right choices. There were too many people looking for the quick and easy path, or needing immediate gratification. In the years I had been gone, we had become much more of a "me" culture, where people were putting themselves first, not thinking about other people, and not caring about our country or our world. I realized that the fan base that had once cheered the "All-American Boy" was gone.

And then it hit me.

I couldn't get Vince on the phone fast enough. I asked him for a meeting at the next possible opportunity.

When we got together, I looked Vince in the eye and I told him that I wanted to turn heel. He looked shocked, given that this had been the issue that had caused the major rift between us nine years before, when he wanted me to turn heel and chase Hogan for the title. Understandably, Vince asked me why I wanted to turn heel now, after all this time, and I explained to him that my "All-American Boy" routine had become an anachronism, but that reality had presented me with the very real opportunity to be bad by being good.

A moment passed as Vince Jr. thought that through, and then he started nodding.

In that moment, "Mr. Backlund" was born.

Turning heel gave me an incredible burst of energy, because it allowed me to pour out all of my own anger and frustration at what the business had become, at what so many of the fans had become, and at how much our society had weakened since the days when I grew up. I was, in reality, disgusted at what I was seeing, and found myself longing for the days when people still had morals and values, and when people still raised their children the right way. I meant every word of what was coming out of Mr. Backlund's mouth. It was coming straight from the heart.

So Mr. Backlund became the moral echo—the unspoken and forgotten conscience of our society in the '90s. I know Vince McMahon was snickering inside, because I don't think he thought I'd be able to pull it off. He was probably thinking, "Bob Backlund can't shoot a promo to save his life, so how in the world is he going to come back and pull this off?" In fact, I think he was nearly certain that I would fall on my face and make a fool out of myself.

We decided to launch the new character at a *Monday Night Raw* where the old Bob Backlund faced the current WWF World Champion Bret Hart for the belt. This was to have been the culmination of all of the work we had done with the old character—where, if Bob Backlund had gotten over, he would have won the title at forty-two years old and overcome those incredible odds. But we had all agreed that the babyface Bob Backlund wasn't over enough with the people to have a successful reign as the WWF champion. The people didn't want to see it, and so we needed to respond in kind.

I proposed to Vince that we have forty-two-year-old babyface Bob Backlund character *lose* to Bret Hart in that match after he *thought* he won, and then, when that reality hit him, to have Bob Backlund "snap" on television, turn heel, and become Mr. Backlund.

So that's the way the match was booked.

Bret Hart, who was the son of legendary wrestler and wrestling trainer Stu Hart, was a terrific babyface *wrestler*—which enabled Bret and me to have a great babyface match for about twenty minutes on *Monday Night Raw*. We traded holds and counterholds, and the fans, who were no longer accustomed to longer, wrestling-based matches, liked it a lot. It was an old-school match all the way to the end when I got him in a cradle and I thought I heard the ref slap the mat three times, released the hold, and threw my hands in the air and began to celebrate. In reality, the ref had only counted to two, and pushed my hands down. I turned around, and Bret surprised me with his own small package and the referee counted to three and the match went to Bret—ending my winning streak, and the dream of a being a champion once again.

According to plan, Vince was on television talking about how my comeback effort had fallen just short, but what a wonderful story it all was, but in the ring, the story was just beginning, as the real angle was about to bloom. Bret extended a hand to me in a token of sportsmanship, and whereas the old Bob Backlund would have shaken it and held his arm up in a token of victory—the newly emerging Mr. Backlund stared him down for a long beat, and then slapped him across the face, put him in the Chickenwing Crossface, and refused to release the hold.

The fans turned on me in a heartbeat, and I grimaced and scowled and bugged my eyes out, and acted like I had gone insane—refusing to release the hold until a bunch of other wrestlers jumped into the ring and intervened. I then did that little gesture where I turned my palms up and looked down at my hands, as if I wasn't even sure what I had done—and that little gesture became my new calling card.

To this day, fans still do that when they see me.

From there, I set about building up a "voluminous vocabulary" so I could "agitate the plebeians." I donned the red suspenders and bow tie, and set about to become everyone's moral conscience.

And suddenly, the people hated me with a fury hotter than lava.

Over the next several weeks on *Monday Night Raw*, we cemented that hatred through a couple of additional in-ring angles. First, they had Arnold Skaaland intervene and try and talk some sense into me—but I refused to shake his hand and blamed him for throwing the towel in the ring back at the end of 1983 and ending my six-year reign as WWF champion. He apologized and insisted he did it to save my career, and I snapped again and put the Chickenwing on *him*, and refused to release it until he was injured.

Then I slapped it on WWF writer Louis Gianfredo, and I almost killed him.

All of this not only brought the fury of the people upon me, but it also cemented the Chickenwing Crossface as a fearsome finishing hold. Unfortunately, half of the new guys weren't even flexible enough for me to apply the hold properly by bending their arm back behind them far enough for me to apply the Crossface and clasp my hands—which is one of the reasons why the Chickenwing Crossface that I used in 1982 and 1983 looked better than the one I used in 1993 and 1994. It wasn't that I was being sloppy with it—it was that many of the guys I was putting it on in this chemically enhanced generation had such ridiculously big and inflexible arms that you couldn't bend their arm behind their back without breaking them.

All of this activity, of course, led to a rematch with Bret Hart for the WWF title, where Bret's Sharpshooter submission hold was pitted against my Chickenwing Crossface. It was a submission match, and appropriately for the storyline, the only way to lose the match was to have your corner man throw the towel in on your behalf. Owen Hart (Bret's brother) was my second, and British Bulldog Daveyboy Smith (Bret's real-life brother-in-law) was his second. Bret's mother Helen and father Stu were both in the crowd. Bret and I had another great scientific match trading holds and counters until eventually, I got him in the Chickenwing and had him in the hold for eight minutes—until my fingers literally went numb from holding it on him for so long. The announcers played it up that Bret was going to suffer permanent injury to his shoulder and Owen pleaded with his mother to convince Daveyboy to throw in the towel, which he had thus far been refusing to do. Finally, Bret's mother couldn't take it anymore, grabbed the towel from Daveyboy, and threw it into the ring signaling Bret's submission.

And with that, I was the world champion once again.

The crowd jeered venomously at me, which was everything we had hoped for. I played it up in my post-match promo—holding the belt up and looking into the camera with an insane look in my eyes and exclaimed, "I feel like God!"

Of course, that brought their hatred down even more strongly.

Before the match, Vince and I had talked. Seeing the way the fans were reacting to me, he told me that he was going to let me run with the title as a heel for about a year and then ask me to return the honors by dropping it back to Bret. I was excited for the opportunity to run with the title as a heel, and really irritate and antagonize the people. I had a couple of scheduled title defenses over the weekend against Daveyboy, and then went to Madison Square Garden as the champion where I was scheduled to face Diesel.

In the interim, "Macho Man" Randy Savage, who had been one of the company's biggest babyfaces, had unexpectedly jumped to WCW.

We were losing the Monday Night Wars to Ted Turner and WCW, and WCW had started raiding our talent. That night, when I got the Garden, Vince pulled me aside and explained to me that they needed someone to replace Savage and they had decided to try and get Diesel over in that role, but they needed to give him the belt. The plans had changed. Vince asked me to drop the belt to Diesel that night, and to do it as convincingly as possible.

Needless to say, I wasn't crazy about putting Diesel over because I had been told I was going to run with the belt for a year, and now, my run was ending after only three days. But I also understood that business was business, and if that is what Vince needed me to do, that is what I was going to do for the benefit of the company as a whole. So we agreed that the bell would ring and that I would stick my hand out to shake Diesel's hand, and that he would kick me in the gut, pick me up, and Powerbomb me in the middle of the ring and get the three count right then and there. I figured that would put him over as strongly as I could possibly put him over—and that to top it off, I would sell his Powerbomb by laying in the middle of the ring for a while and then crawling out of the ring and all the way back to the dressing room.

So that's what I did.

The problem was, Diesel was a little too excited about the match, and probably a little nervous also—and he slammed me down on my hips instead of flat on my back where I could have cushioned the blow. That's the problem with the Powerbomb—there really isn't any way for the person *getting* Powerbombed to participate in the hold or to do anything about it. You are totally in the hands of the person applying the hold—and if he doesn't drop you correctly, there is virtually nothing you can do to defend yourself. I felt that blow rattle up my spine, and it hurt a lot.

To Diesel's credit, despite the fact that he had a lot to celebrate, he checked on me in the locker room immediately after the match to make sure I was okay, and to thank me for putting him over so strongly. I know that was a big deal to him, and he knew that I didn't *have* to sell the loss as much as I did—but knew that it was my job to put the hold over as strongly as I could for him. That was what was right for the business, no matter how I might have felt about it. One last time, the tide that had flowed in and given to me, was now flowing out and seeking a return. It didn't matter to me that Diesel wasn't a wrestler—what mattered to me was giving him the best possible start as champion that I could give him.

After the loss to Diesel, Vince didn't really know what to do with the Mr. Backlund character. That was the only problem with it—it had a limited shelf life in that you could only milk it for so long. Vince more or less just stopped booking me, and the character just died off. But it was a great run while it lasted. For a time, the Mr. Backlund character was as over as any heel in the company had been for a very long time. In fact, Mr. Backlund was so hot that I was getting death threats at home, and I could give an interview by simply standing at the microphone and look-ing into the camera and not saying a word. All I needed to do was bring the microphone to my mouth, and the closer I brought that microphone to my lips, the louder the cascade of boos became. I never needed to say a word because the people didn't want to hear anything. I think I was the first person in the history of the WWF to go into an arena to do a five-minute interview at a house show and to never actually have to do anything but come out and look into the camera—the fans hated me that much. What took thirty minutes for the babyface Bob Backlund to do—to bring the crowd to its emotional peak—Mr. Backlund could do in thirty seconds.

That is what it meant to get over. Making the people have an emo-tional reaction to you.

Going back to the WWF in 1992 was good for me. It was something that helped get me going in the right direction again. For nearly all of my life, I lived as the All-American Boy, quiet and shy, with lots of confidence in the ring, but not much confidence outside the ring. When I became Mr. Backlund, it helped pull me out of my shell, and I was very motivated to try to do the same things as a bad guy that I had done as a good guy.

When I became a heel, the hatred I felt from the fans everywhere I went in the '90s was even stronger than the love and adulation I got from the fans when I was the champion in the '70s and '80s. It made me wonder whether the raw emotion of hate is stronger than love.

I was glad I had the chance to heel once in my career—but I'm glad I waited to do it until it made sense in my life. And I think we made a memorable time of it!

27

Looking Forward, Not Behind

"Put ideas and your definiteness of purpose to work."

—Napoleon Hill, "Develop Definiteness of Purpose"

———◆———

And thus, we come to the present of my story.

I say the "present" and not the "end," because I don't believe the best years of my life are yet behind me, and I certainly don't believe that we are at an "end" of anything. We are merely at a place where we have stopped for a time to acknowledge and reflect on what has come before. Five years ago, I could have never imagined that I was about to receive a letter from an old fan that would set into motion this book about my life, a reconciliation and renewed relationship with Vince McMahon Jr. and the WWE, and an induction into the WWE Hall of Fame. Before Rob reached out to me, I had pretty much given up hope on the idea that I would ever get to tell the story of my life—or even that there was anyone left out there who cared to hear it. Over the years since I first lost the belt in 1983, a number of sportswriters had contacted me asking me to do a book with them, but none of them fully understood me, what I was about, and why I made the choices I did. Rob says, in his introduction to the book, that he reached out to me at a time in his life when he needed his hero again. Well, the same can be said for me. Rob reached out to me at a time when I needed to *be* a hero to someone again—to be remembered. So this project has been a remarkable re-awakening for both of us.

I have much to be grateful for in my life. I owe much to *my* two greatest role models, Vince McMahon Sr., who was like a father to me and the most honorable man I ever met in the wrestling business; and to my wife Corki, who has provided the stability and support for our family for all of these years. But I also recognize that the remarkable experiences I have had, and the many things I have been taught and lessons that I have learned over the past fifty years or so have left some clues that I hope others might follow. So before I close this chapter of my life, I thought it might be valuable to sum up the major lessons I have learned on this remarkable roller-coaster ride that has taken me from the farm fields of Princeton, Minnesota, to the top of the world, and then all the way back again with a safe landing.

I think of these as my Eighteen Principles of Healthy Living. I hope some of these might resonate with you as well.

1. In each and every interaction you have with people, treat them the way you would want to be treated. Be kind to each other. The fact is, if everyone in the world just did that, most of the world's problems would be solved. I have tried my best to do this every day—both inside and outside the wrestling business—and it has served me well.

2. Find a way to get your kids involved in athletics from a young age. Doing so will teach them discipline, responsibility, and how to be part of a team. It will give them strength and balance and build their concentration and their self-esteem. As this story has shown, although I did not get involved in athletics until I was ten years old, once I did, athletics saved my life.

3. Eat to fuel your body, not for emotional support. Quality going in means quality coming out. People have always asked me what I ate to maintain such a healthy body for so many years. For breakfast, I have either an emulsification of raw spinach, raw sweet potato, banana, yogurt, a scoop of low-sugar protein powder, and strawberries or blueberries or cantaloupe; or oatmeal with peanuts, raisins, and pumpkin seeds. I also take one multivitamin and a shot of

Braggs Apple Cider vinegar, which I am convinced eliminated the rheumatism in my joints. Lunch is lots of veggies and some lean protein—I don't eat bread anymore, and I never put man-made sugar into my body. Dinner is a wrap, or a salad with chicken or turkey on it, or we make homemade soup. Basically, the more green you eat and the less meat you eat the better off you are. Doing those things has helped me maintain a strong body, overcome a bout with Lyme Disease, and battle the aches and pains that invariably come from forty years of bodyslams and suplexes.

4. Get enough sleep. Getting enough rest at night is how your body heals itself and how your immune system gets restored. I go to bed at 9:30 or 10 p.m. every night and get up at 6:30 a.m. If you are ever short on sleep, lie down on the floor, put your hands by your side, get in a relaxed state, and try to lower your heart rate as much as you can and get into a meditative state for fifteen to thirty minutes. After that time, your body will be revived and you will be able to finish the day with energy and enthusiam, but not affect your sleep at night.

5. Maintain a positive mental attitude (PMA) no matter what happens to you. Search tirelessly for the silver lining that will allow you to turn a negative into a positive—as there is almost always a way through the toughest of times. If you ever find yourself feeling hopeless, just remind yourself that—before I became a world champion—I was homeless, starving, and living in the trunk of my car. Imagine how different my life would have been if I had abandoned my PMA and given up.

6. Apply mental focus. I have been physically and nutritionally fit for most of my life. But in 1984, when I got out of the wrestling business, I realized how important the intellectual part of life was, how lacking I was in that area, and how hard it was to change something that you had been ignoring for thirty-five

years. When I got my mind set the right way, I realized that it was probably going to take me until the end of my life to get my mind where I want it. And I'm willing to accept that challenge. Remember that both the mind and the body have to be exercised, and that both will get better with age and use as long as you continue to use them. You can augment your intelligence at any age—it's when you quit using it and get lazy that your mind deteriorates. There are two books I read that helped me get my mind in the right place after wrestling—Napoleon Hill's *Think and Grow Rich,* and his *Seventeen Principles of Success.* I recommend them both to you for your thought and reflection.

7. Cultivate a healthy self-esteem. Find little ways that you can "win" every day, whether that is simply by pushing hard through a daily workout or practice, solving a tough problem, or just by eating right all day. By accumulating these little victories, your self-esteem will grow from a seedling into an oak tree.

8. Resist peer pressure, and set the example you know is right for others to follow. After my experience at the Kitten Club in eighth grade, I learned never to do things because other people wanted me to, to make other people happy, or to try and make friends. Instead, I tried to be a role model for others to follow. It was not always easy.

9. Be respectful. Be more concerned about giving respect where it is deserved than getting respect, because the fact is, when you give respect, you get respect. Teach your children to respect themselves, their teachers, and their elders. It is an increasingly rare sentiment in the world that instantly makes the world a better place.

10. Be reliable. Be on time, trustworthy, and accountable. When you say, do, and when you promise, deliver. That is the stuff that champions are made of.

11. Be self-reliant. Be hard-working and industrious and take control of the things that matter in your own life. If you depend on yourself, you should never be disappointed.

12. Save money on a daily basis. Save to educate your children, and teach them, also, to put a little bit away every day. Pay yourself first with the money you make so that there is always something in the kitty. My wife and I play a little game each day where we each try to find the most money that other people have dropped or left lying around. It helps to keep us focused on the importance of every dime, and to remember the days when we didn't have enough.

13. Don't live above your means. Financial struggle is one of the biggest strains on marriages and families. Someone who doesn't have the income to support it shouldn't have three big-screen TVs and a Cadillac. For a long time, I was one of those people. I've eaten a lot of tuna fish out of a can, and Corki and I bought our first house with cash, not a mortgage. Try to have at least a year's worth of money saved up so if things take a turn for the worse, or you are confronted with an unusual opportunity, you won't be caught short. Remember that when Vince Sr. asked me if I had the $80,000 deposit for the world title, I had the money to give to him, even though he never actually made me produce it. Imagine how I would have felt if I hadn't saved enough for the deposit, and had been passed over because of that?

14. Find something to do that you love doing, and then keep doing it. I know a lot of people who are over eighty, didn't retire, are still active physically and mentally and spiritually, and are still going strong. I started an oil business when I was fifty-nine years old, sold it when I was sixty-five, and am now moving on to the next exciting phase of my life as an author and a motivational speaker.

15. Make your work life fun. You can find some way to do this no matter what your career is as long as you can get your mind focused on the right thing. When I was delivering oil to someone's house, I focused on how I was keeping other people's children warm, and that's what got me up at 3:30 on a snowy and cold morning to deliver that oil.

16. If you are a parent—take the responsibility to raise your own children. Don't leave that most important work for others to do. Set rules and guidelines with your children so that they understand their purpose, and then require your children to live by them. When our daughter Carrie was growing up and went out with her friends, the rule was that Carrie had to come home and give my wife a kiss when she got home. It was a simple rule, but it was one she agreed to. We didn't have a lot of rules at our house, but that was one of them. My wife stayed home while Carrie was young until she went to school. They spent a lot of time together when I was away, and our daughter is a mature, responsible citizen of the world because of it.

17. There is joy to be found in every day. Seek it.

18. Look forward, not backward. The past is gone. Learn what you can from it, cherish your memories, and move on. Stay focused on the many great things that are going to happen for you in your future. After I lost the world title, I thought that my best days were behind me, and that there would be no way to recapture that kind of happiness again. I was wrong.

Although the outcomes of my professional matches may have been predetermined, the story of my life, and the relentless pursuit of my dreams, is real. My American Dream was to use my athletic gifts to become professional wrestling's world champion, and to then use that stature make a difference in people's lives. The first part of that dream—the wrestling part—may now be in my past, but the second part—the making a difference part—is still very much a part of my present.

Rob's American Dream is to use his substantial gifts as a writer to tell stories that inspire people, to be a great husband and father, and to be a positive influence and a force for good in his community and his world. He found me—his childhood hero, and believed in me enough to want to work for five years to bring my story to life in a way that no one else in the world could have. His story and mine will now be forever intertwined, and while I was once his hero from afar, we are now close friends, and I am very grateful for that. Having met his family and friends, and having become a part of their lives and their community over the past few years, it looks like he's well on his way to realizing the rest of his American Dream as well.

So now it's your turn.

First, to all of you who have ever shaken my hand, given me a high five, or cheered for me from a seat in an arena or a seat in your living room, thank you.

Thanks for believing in me, and what I stood for.

Thanks for remembering the times that we shared together.

And thanks for caring enough about that part of your past to buy this book, and to want to remember those days.

But now, my challenge to each of you is the same one I now face—to look ahead, not behind.

This part of my story is now told. By the time you read this, I will already be working on what the rest of this story is going to be. And I hope that each of you will join me in that journey as well.

Realizing the American Dream is possible for each one of us. All you have to do is get focused on what your dream is, and stay relentlessly committed to it. It is what our country was built on, it is what has carried us through in the darkest of times, and it is precisely what each of us needs to do, right now, to help our country become strong again.

We can do it together, each and every one of us.

So let's get busy.

When times get tough, you can recall the stories in your own mind of our days together when we were both younger, battling the forces of evil in a wrestling ring, and you can draw strength from those happy memories. Or, if you prefer, you can recall the story you now know, about how, before I was champion, I was homeless, eating tuna out of a can, and sleeping in the trunk of my car in Louisiana.

If I could make it, you can too.

PMA. Always and forever.

See you out on the road!

ACKNOWLEDGMENTS

Bob Backlund

I want to start by giving a big thank you to Rob for reaching out and sending me the letter that got this whole project started. Many other people reached out to me in the past, but I had been waiting for the right person to come along—and the words that Rob put in his letter convinced me that he was that person to write the book about my life. When we met in Glastonbury, Connecticut, the first time, I was amazed, because I thought that meeting would never take place and that I would have to leave this earth without having had the opportunity to tell my story. When we met, I was also very concerned that Rob would be disappointed in me, because I would not live up to my billing as his childhood hero—I was just me. But after we met, it reconfirmed for me that Rob was indeed *the* guy. He wanted to know the truth about my life, to tell the real story, and to learn about who I was not just as a wrestler, but as a person. I wasn't into the politics of wrestling, so I knew very little about what was going on behind the scenes and was amazed to learn, through this project, about some of the things that were going on in the wrestling business. The sheer amount of research that was done and the conversations that Rob had with a variety of my peers has really helped to flesh out my history in the wrestling business and to make this a far more interesting book than it otherwise might have been.

When I received Rob's letter, I owned an oil company, and was a long way away from the wrestling business. This project brought me back to life and has given me the opportunity to do the things I've always dreamed of doing: to get back into the limelight a little bit with an eye on motivating young people and being a positive role model again. The project has opened doors for me all over the world, with the WWE, with youth groups, and others that remember me and want to hear from me again, and for all of that I am truly grateful. I can't wait to get back out on the road and meet all of you again and talk to you about your lives and mine and what we've all been up to for the past thirty years.

Of course, I want to thank my wife, Corki, with whom I just celebrated my fortieth wedding anniversary, and my daughter Carrie for supporting me during my wrestling career, and for supporting everything else I have done in my life. I know it hasn't always been easy for them, moving from territory to territory and place to place, but they have both always been very patient and supportive through all of the havoc of the business. I know they're both very proud and excited about this book and what it represents.

I would like to thank Mr. Barry Trievel for allowing us to use some of his interviews and content about me that he collected years ago. Barry was an old teammate of mine from the North Dakota State University football team, so we go way back and share a lot of history. Thank you, Barry, for all you have done and contributed to this story.

Big thanks also to Mike Gratchner, for his willingness to let us use so many photos from his personal collection in this book.

I would also like to gratefully thank the many people who took time out of their busy and hectic schedules to make time for us, including "Rowdy" Roddy Piper for his gracious foreword, Bruno Sammartino for the generosity of his time and thoughts on my career, and to both Harley Race and Terry Funk for their contributions to understanding the history of my career in this business, but also for having faith in me in the early years to push me along my path.

To Vince McMahon Jr. and Triple H for opening the door and allowing me to come home to the WWE, inducting me into the Hall of Fame, and entrusting me with the responsibility to talk to children and adults about the choices I made in my life and why I made them. To Scott Amann for helping to make it possible for wrestling fans the world over to find and enjoy this book and meet me out on the road with the WWE. And to Sue Aitchison from WWE Talent Relations, who handles my scheduling with the WWE with such grace.

To Jake Elwell, our literary agent at Harold Ober Associates, who believed in this project from the beginning, helped us find the right publisher for it, and for his many bits of great advice along the way.

To Tony Lyons and Jason Katzman at Skyhorse Publishing for their faith in the project despite the many delays that it took to make it the way we wanted it, and for their great work in taking the book from a large pile of paper to what you now hold in your hands.

And finally to Vince McMahon Sr., no doubt riffling a stack of quarters in a back hallway up in Heaven, for trusting me to be his "All-American Boy" and giving me the chance of a lifetime.

Rob Miller

First and foremost, to Bob, for trusting me to voice the project that he had been waiting twenty-five years to write, and for his generosity, honor, and steadfastness of character. Few people in this world get to meet their childhood hero. Far fewer find that person more worthy of that status than your imagination had allowed.

To Jake Elwell, my literary agent at Harold Ober, who for five books and fifteen years has provided me with his wisdom, ideas, and good counsel.

To Tony Lyons and Jason Katzman at Skyhorse Publishing for their entrepreneurial spirit and undying faith in this project, and to Tom McCarthy for his editorial notes and assistance.

To Napoleon Hill, for all of the inspiration that has fed Bob and me for the long years in the making.

And finally, to Carolyn, Nick, and Lucas, for putting up with all of the stories and time away that was necessary to make this project possible. I love you guys.